The Eighteenth Century in Russia

**GARRARD, J. C., ed. The eighteenth century in Russia. Oxford,
1973. 356p il. 21.00. ISBN 0-19-815638-3**
The title of the book is a misnomer. It is really devoted to the Enlightenment in 18th-century Russia. It is a history of letters primarily and to a lesser extent of the arts. It is, of course, pervaded by
the theme of Westernization and of Russia's dependence on Europeans
and European models in her quest for culture, and it provides excellent
comment on that important subject. Anthologies or collections of articles are rarely of first-rate importance, but this one is an exception for
two reasons: first, because of the high quality of its contents; second,
because good English literature on 18th-century Russia is not nearly so
abundant as it is on 19th-century Russia. There are chapters on classicism in Russian literature, the educational reforms of Peter I, Feofan
Prokopovich, Russian journalism (Novikov), Diderot in Russia, the
Russian Rosicrucians, the British in Russia, painting and architecture,
Russian music, and urban planning under Catherine II. Suitable for
both graduate and undergraduate reading. Forty-one illustrations;
index.

The Eighteenth Century in Russia

Edited by
J. G. GARRARD

OXFORD
AT THE CLARENDON PRESS
1973

Oxford University Press, Ely House, London W. 1

GLASGOW NEW YORK TORONTO MELBOURNE WELLINGTON
CAPE TOWN IBADAN NAIROBI DAR ES SALAAM LUSAKA ADDIS ABABA
DELHI BOMBAY CALCUTTA MADRAS KARACHI LAHORE DACCA
KUALA LUMPUR SINGAPORE HONG KONG TOKYO

© *Oxford University Press 1973*

*Printed in Great Britain
at the University Press, Oxford
by Vivian Ridler
Printer to the University*

Preface

IT has been argued, with justice, that the roots of a great deal that has happened in modern Russian history can be traced back to the fact that the Russians were denied a Renaissance. Harder to accept is the claim of some historians that the Russians did not have an 'eighteenth century' either. Rather one should view the eighteenth century as the period when the Russians first made a major concerted effort to recover from the lack of a Renaissance and to regain a prominent place in the cultural and political life of Europe. This is what the 'modernization' or the 'Europeanization' of Russia means: a conscious and deliberate decision, at first in the mind of one man alone, that Russia's place was with Europe, with the West and not the Orient.

As historians from Cassirer and Paul Hazard to Peter Gay and Franco Venturi have demonstrated, the eighteenth century marks the true beginning of the modern age. It is no denigration of de Tocqueville's insight to note that by 1835 there was already a good deal of evidence to suggest that America and Russia were indeed destined to become the two super-powers of the world. On the wings of Europe these two nations partook tangentially but significantly of the cultural and intellectual life of the time. Much has been made of the imitative nature of Russian (and American) life during the eighteenth century, but the dominant national cultures of the period were clearly those of England and France, and the Enlightenment itself, *pace* Cassirer, appears at times to have been a private intellectual ping-pong game between the two countries, watched by either enthusiastic or apprehensive bystanders. The Russians, like other nations, received more than they contributed, but they were part and parcel of the century, which cannot be fully understood without taking their participation into account.

In his sane and crisply written book, *In Search of Humanity*

(London, 1960), Alfred Cobban traced the modern world's debt to the eighteenth century—to the rise of science, of scepticism, toleration, political liberalism, and the rule of law. Essentially what happened was, for Cobban, an 'ethical revolution'. The eighteenth century was all this and more. Recent historians have been probing the darker side of the Enlightened century and there has been renewed interest in such ambivalent figures as Johnson, Rousseau, and Diderot. Herbert Dieckmann has written of 'a deep polarity, a dialectical movement of disbelief and belief' in this period, and Sir Isaiah Berlin has devoted a series of stimulating essays to Vico, Herder, and Hamann (as a founding father of the Romantic movement)—men who stood to one side of or in opposition to the Enlightenment.

What then is an 'eighteenth century'—if we agree that the Russians had one? The time is past when all that is significant and fresh in the century can be subsumed under such portmanteau words as the Enlightenment, which naturally enough come under attack as shorthand descriptions of whole generations in the cultural life of nations or even groups of nations. The use of the term 'eighteenth century' may seem innocuous enough (one envies French scholars their neat self-description as *dix-huitiémistes*), but appears to do little more than side-step the problem of definition. It does, however, indicate a healthy awareness of the complexity of the century as a whole and can still helpfully serve as an acceptable term to cover what most would agree is an identifiable nexus of ideas and attitudes having their beginnings in England and France and spreading later to Germany and the remainder of Europe, and across the Atlantic to North America.

The eighteenth century had a rich harvest to offer the Russians: the discoveries and hypotheses of Newton and Locke, popularized in France and elsewhere by Voltaire; the works of Voltaire himself; an unsolved and insoluble debate on morality and the nature of man, begun by Shaftesbury and Mandeville; Pope's *Essay on Man*; alarming and exciting new ways of looking at man in his relationship to God and in his social and political roles (Montesquieu, Hume, Rousseau); the extension of Lockean psychology to the materialism of La Mettrie, Condillac, Helvétius, and

D'Holbach; the discovery of national culture and folklore (the collections of Percy and Herder), a reappraisal of aesthetic values and hierarchies; the rise of the novel, the *drame bourgeois*, and the *comédie larmoyante*; Ossianism and Sensibility; the investigations and experiments of Diderot; and much else besides.

From this rich and heady variety the Russians made a selection conditioned by their own cultural background and particular needs. Their 'eighteenth century' was thus not the same as that of England or of France, nor should we expect it to be. The eighteenth century in Russia has many elements that are reassuringly similar to those in the countries of Western Europe, but some that are not. It is the aim of the present volume of essays to point to at least some of these elements, both familiar and peculiar.

The contributors are not concerned with the increasingly important role of Russia as a major political and military force during the eighteenth century—this is assumed. Instead they have devoted their attention to intellectual and cultural history, to the nature and results of Russian contacts with the art and thought of Europe. In each case the aim has been to go beyond the simple assertion and proof of borrowing or adaptation by Russian thinkers, writers, painters, and composers, and to come to grips with more complex and fruitful questions: what did the Russians choose to borrow, and why; and further, what was the result of the amalgam of Western borrowings and the survival of native Russian attitudes, together with the pressures of Russia's own intellectual and socio-political growth? The Introduction sketches in the background of Russia's 'eighteenth century' and attempts to exemplify, with special reference to literature, the types of changes that took place, and to illustrate the paradoxes and dynamics of the period.

This is not a collaborative history of eighteenth-century Russia, it is not designed to 'cover' the period in any systematic way. However, it is hoped that the contributors have addressed themselves to most, if not all, of the significant problems that were faced in the cultural development of Russia from Peter the Great to Alexander I. Among these were the formation of the standard literary language, the creation of new forms and modes in art and music, the acquisition of a secular culture (both that of Classical

Antiquity and of contemporary Europe), and initial Russian efforts
to define national identity and purpose.

The eighteenth century contains more than a record of the
Russian acquisition of various aspects of European civilization.
During this period the Russians were beginning to grapple with
the central problem of their existence as a nation: how to assume
their rightful place in the European cultural community, but at
the same time to retain their integrity as a viable cultural unit; how
to be good Europeans and good Russians at one and the same time.

My first debt of gratitude as editor of this volume is of course
to the scholars on both sides of the Atlantic who have contributed
essays to it; whatever merit the book has is due to their knowledge
and willingness to participate in such a joint enterprise. I am
particularly grateful to Marc Raeff for his generous support and
assistance.

Secondly, on behalf of all the contributors as well as myself, I
wish to thank the American Council of Learned Societies for supporting an initial meeting of contributors held in Hanover, N.H.,
at which we were able to discuss and agree upon the general
format and aims of the volume.

J. G. G.

Contents

List of Plates

(*between pp. 266 and 267*)

JOHN G. GARRARD

Introduction: The Emergence of Modern Russian Literature and Thought

IT is unlikely that any major country has been so radically transformed in such a brief period of time as was Russia during the
eighteenth century. One has only to think of Russian life in the
reign of Tsar Aleksey Mikhaylovich and contrast it with that of
Catherine II to grasp the magnitude of the Russian achievement.

A quick measure of the changes that took place in Russia's
relations with Europe on a political and military level can be taken
by comparing two visits to Paris by Russian tsars, the first by
Peter the Great in 1717 and the second by Alexander I in 1814 (the
Grand Duke Paul and his wife paid a successful social visit to
Paris in 1782). Peter travelled to seek French aid in his prolonged
struggle against Sweden and also to test the ground for a possible
marriage between his daughter Elizabeth and the Dauphin. In
striking contrast Alexander entered Paris in triumph at the head
of a coalition that had fought Napoleon to a standstill all across
Europe. It is true that Peter's victory at Poltava in 1709 had given
notice to the rest of Europe that Russia was a new power that
would have to be reckoned with, but the Russian triumphs under
Alexander seemed of a different order of magnitude. Alexander
stood out as the leading light of the Holy Alliance, which rearranged the map of Europe.

The contrasts between these two visits are not, however, limited
to those of military power and political prestige. Peter failed to
gain an alliance, either military or marital, with the French because of political considerations, but the unfavourable impression
he and his suite made on the French court cannot have helped his
cause. Almost everyone was fascinated by Peter's natural ability
and boundless energy, but for the most part his rough exterior

B

and the constant drinking bouts he engaged in with his companions did not sit well with Versailles and the salons.

Peter does not appear to have changed much in the twenty years between his visit to Paris and his earlier, more extended stay in Western Europe. In his *Diary* John Evelyn, whose house at Sayes Court Peter and his party used as their headquarters while in England in 1698, wrote with evident distaste about the outlandish manners of his royal guest: 'I went to Deptford to view how miserably the Tzar of Muscovy had left my house after three moneths making it his court, having gotten Sir Cr: Wren his Majesties Surveyor & Mr. London his Gardener to go down & make an estimat of the repairs, for which they allowed 150 pounds in their Report to the L: of the Treasury.' Evelyn had earlier received an ominous note from one of his servants informing him that Sayes Court was 'a house full of people, and right nasty. . .'.[1]

Although they came as conquerors, it is doubtful that Alexander and his staff were ever regarded by any cultivated Frenchman as 'right nasty'. Even Russian junior officers were well-read, well-behaved, and sophisticated European gentlemen, such as hardly existed one hundred years previously. Chateaubriand was quite taken by the Russians he met, as was Mme de Staël, who visited Russia in the autumn of 1812 shortly before Napoleon's invasion.[2]

But the changes that had taken place amounted to a great deal more than the fact that Alexander did not follow Peter's habit of riding through carefully cropped hedges in a wheelbarrow, or that he and his staff knew how to make polite conversation and how to hold a wineglass correctly.

By the beginning of the eighteenth century many Russians had a deeper understanding of the essence of Western culture and thought, of what constituted its superiority over their own. At the same time, they were conscious of their own Russianness and eager to use their knowledge and position to improve the lot of their

---

[1] *The Diary of John Evelyn*, ed. E. S. de Beer, v (Oxford, 1955), 290 and 284.
[2] However, in her memoirs *Dix années d'exil* Mme de Staël comments: 'Toute la bonne compagnie a des manières parfaites, mais il n'y a ni assez d'instruction parmi les nobles, ni assez de confiance entre des personnes qui vivent sans cesse sous l'influence d'une cour et d'un gouvernement despotique, pour que l'on puisse connaître les charmes de l'intimité.'

less fortunate brethren. They had acquired the European spirit, not only the external appurtenances of Western life.

Of course the appurtenances, and together with them the military might, were adopted first. This is what attracted the attention of those foreigners who gave any thought to Russia in the eighteenth century. Frenchmen were little concerned with Russians as a separate people with their own national culture. This was a cosmopolitan age, but one can justifiably speak of a 'mirage russe' in France.[3] Several of the *philosophes* were very much taken with Russia as the land of promise and opportunity, where Catherine was putting into practice their ideas, but Frenchmen were not well informed about Russian reality. If Russians did not imitate Western manners, they were regarded as barbarians; if they did, they were regarded as 'singes': the greatest compliment a Frenchman could pay a Russian was to say that he behaved indistinguishably from a Frenchman. In the second half of the eighteenth century, and later, there were Russians who would have felt flattered, but not the leading intellectual figures and writers who were shaping Russian life and culture.

If the eighteenth century marks the beginning of the modern age, it does so for Russia no less than for any other nation. The rise of modern Russia may be considered one of the most significant long-term developments of the century, equivalent in its impact to the Russian Revolution in the present century. Scholars and ideologues will continue to grapple with the precise ratio of continuity to change in Russian history, but it seems fair to say that if we turn back to the past in search of the roots and sources of the great super-power that Russia has become today, then we shall find ourselves stopping not so much at the year 1917 as two hundred years earlier during the period of the great reforms of Peter the Great.

Historians since Solovlëv's time have cautioned against placing too much emphasis on the revolutionary aspects of the Petrine reforms, pointing out correctly that certain developments during his reign represented a continuation of trends that had their beginning well before his appearance. It was of course natural that both

---

[3] Albert Lortholary, *Le Mirage russe en France au XVIIIe siècle* (Paris, 1951).

supporters and opponents of Peter's rule should have stressed the novelty of his reforms and the complete break they represented with what had gone before. And yet it would be hard to exaggerate the range and rapidity of the changes he effected in almost every area of human activity.

It is in the military area that Peter may be seen most obviously as completing trends begun earlier. In effect, his break-through to the Baltic, which helped to establish once and for all Russian pre-eminence in north-eastern Europe, solved a fundamental problem that had confronted the Russian state since as far back as the thirteenth century. In a sense, then, the eighteenth century marks the culmination of much that had gone before in Russian political history and international relations. It was to be expected that the rulers of the Muscovite state should have sought to expand their territory westward to regain lands that had formerly belonged to the eastern Slavs, and also to gain access to the Baltic and the Black Sea. Ivan the Terrible's unsuccessful attempts to leap-frog Catholic Poland and establish amicable relations with Elizabethan England and his efforts to push Russian frontiers to the Baltic look forward to Peter the Great, as does the growth of the so-called Foreign Quarter (*nemetskaya sloboda*), with the difference that Peter ended the isolation of the Quarter and the obscurantist suspicion of foreign machinations: he created a whole city that was a Foreign Quarter and made it the national capital. It was in his reign and the reign of Empress Catherine II that Russia's major foreign-policy objectives were attained.

This accomplishment was, however, the result of a conscious and deliberate effort on the part of Peter and his successors during the eighteenth century to ignore and overcome many traditional Russian attitudes and the effects of historical circumstances. First among these, both chronologically and in importance, was the fact that Kievan Russia had accepted Christianity from Byzantium. Relations between the Roman and Eastern churches were strained before the formal break in the middle of the eleventh century. With the passion of converts the Russians throughout the medieval period, but particularly in Muscovite times, gradually developed a deep-seated attitude of hostility and suspicion toward the 'Latin heresy' of Western Europe, which was reinforced by ideological Messianism and the cult of the Third Rome in the sixteenth century. It is possible that doctrinal differences might have been set aside sooner and some acceptable accommodation reached with the heretical West, had it not been for the Mongol invasion, which crushed a Kievan state already weakened by internecine princely rivalries. The Tartar yoke, which lasted for well over two hundred years, robbed the Russians of whatever chance they might have had for such an accommodation.

These facts are well known and there is no need to rehearse them at any great length. However, it is essential to bear in mind the full impact they have had. The Russians withstood the Mongol onslaught and protected the rest of Europe. The results of religious differences, topography, military and political pressures were such that the Russians were denied direct contact with the rest of Europe at precisely that period when the nation-states of England, France, and Spain were being formed. The Muscovite state was coming into existence at about the same time, but without the benefit of the cultural and scientific ideas of the Renaissance. By the sixteenth century the rulers of Muscovy found themselves hemmed in to the west and south-west by powerful neighbours, who were not only hostile but also possessed of superior technological and military expertise. Subsequent Russian history is much involved, admittedly at varying levels of consciousness and intensity, with the efforts to come to grips with the West's self-evident scientific and material superiority and its alleged inferiority in spiritual or human terms. This is a point I shall return to later.

According to Klyuchevsky, the poet Kheraskov once said that Peter gave the Russians bodies and Catherine II gave them souls. This is an acceptable generalization, which reflects the practical nature of Peter's reforms as opposed to the more cultural and intellectual concerns of Catherine, although one might recall that the Empress was sufficiently hard-headed to achieve two major foreign-policy objectives by partitioning Poland and extending the Russian Empire to the shores of the Black Sea. Kheraskov's remark is not entirely fair to Peter, although flattering to Catherine—a thought that no doubt crossed the poet's mind.

The range of Peter's interests and activities was quite extraordinary. He had his agents purchase paintings in Europe, including several Dutch interiors and other masterpieces that now grace the walls of the Hermitage; he was directly involved in the design and layout of buildings for his new capital; and he persuaded the French architect Leblond to build him a Russian Versailles at Peterhof. However, on the whole Peter was not artistically or philosophically inclined—not even his most ardent admirer could claim that. Moreover, Peter was at war throughout most of his reign and his reforms had the prime objective of helping him win it. The first order of business was to establish medical, engineering, and artillery schools—institutions that would turn out men with the skills needed for his prolonged struggle against Sweden. Peter had little time for art or even pure science. Although he had been in correspondence with Leibniz (who liked to call himself the Solon of Muscovy), it was only at the very end of Peter's reign and after the Peace of Nystadt that the Russian Academy of Sciences was founded.

While Peter may have been little concerned with the souls of his subjects (he certainly appears to have given no thought to his own), his reforms obviously had a profound effect on their minds. No doubt it must have appeared to many that Peter was wasting time trying to make silk purses out of sows' ears, but as he forced Russians of the upper classes to adopt Western dress, fined them, or worse, for not wearing wigs and for not cutting off their beards, dragooned them into attending formal occasions at which they were obliged to stumble as best they could through dances in the Western manner, imported foreigners to teach them or sent them abroad to study, Peter was willy-nilly changing their outlook on life, their attitude toward God and toward their fellow man.

It is something of a paradox that a practical man of action like Peter should have exercised so profound an influence on the arts and thought of his country. In his own person he provided a subject for both literature and intellectual debate for at least two hundred years. There is surely a great deal of substance to John Maynard's assertion that Peter's reforms 'are always a touchstone of Russian

opinion'. At the same time, through his reforms Peter also supplied the tools and concepts by means of which the debate about
their utility and effects was conducted. Peter essentially brought
into focus the fundamental question of Russian national identity
and purpose.

One might perhaps argue that the Petrine period marks, or
better, presages, a sharper break artistically and intellectually with
what had gone before it than it did in political and military history.
Ultimately Peter was responsible for the appearance of a modern,
secular culture in Russia. His own generation, however, continued
to live off the out-of-date products and tastes of the previous age:
the Baroque poetry of Simeon Polotsky and the sub-literature of
manuscript tales (chapbooks), translations and adaptations of late
versions of original Western European works that dated from
medieval times. The first quarter of the century produced little or
nothing that was new in literature. It has been demonstrated by
recent research that the so-called Petrine tales, for example, all
date from after 1725.

During Peter's reign the hustle and bustle of events was too
compelling, people were swept along with little time to think or
write. Peter himself certainly had neither the time nor the inclination to appreciate *belles-lettres*. His spasmodic interest in the theatre,
which led to an abortive effort to have a foreign troupe establish
a company in Russia, and his somewhat more successful attempt
to revise the Cyrillic alphabet so as to create a civil type (the
grazhdanka) in 1708, were both motivated by the desire to assist
and accelerate the propagation of his programmes. The same is
true of his interest in the Russian language. In his customary
energetic and peremptory way he set translators to work to make
available to his subjects many essential (and some quite worthless)
books on every conceivable topic. The wretched translators often
did not understand the original works and even when they did,
could find no equivalent term for an object or concept that simply
did not exist in Russia. Peter was constantly reviewing translations, making corrections, scribbling notes urging his translators
to choose more comprehensible equivalents taken from the spoken
language of the time.

Kievan Russia, in accepting Christianity from Byzantium, was permitted to use the Slavonic liturgy which had evolved from that introduced into Greater Moravia a century before by Cyril and Methodius. This was a rare privilege, but a mixed blessing as it turned out, since the Russian vernacular and Church Slavonic (the liturgical language) gradually drifted further and further apart, and yet Church Slavonic remained the only accepted written language. Thus at the beginning of the eighteenth century the Russians found themselves without any standard literary language. They used an unbelievable jumble of lexical elements taken from Church Slavonic itself, from the vernacular, and foreign words borrowed, usually by imprint, from half a dozen languages. To compound the problem, the churchmen could not agree among themselves on what the true form of Church Slavonic should be.

The creation of a standard literary language was one of the major cultural achievements of the eighteenth century. It was finally arrived at by blending certain elements from Church Slavonic with the Russian vernacular and a considerable number of words from foreign languages. The precise nature of the blend and the process by which it came about remain subjects of debate among historical linguists. One thing is clear, however, and that is that modern Russian has been enriched lexically by Church Slavonic in much the same way as our own language has gained from a healthy admixture of Latin and Greek words.

The Russians never had prolonged contact with either Latin or Greek. Shakhmatov may have been correct in claiming that we have a lop-sided and incomplete picture of Kievan literature because of the enormous loss of manuscripts through fire, neglect, and war. Possibly it was a great deal less theologically oriented than now appears from the manuscripts that have survived. However, it is generally acknowledged that native Slavic priests were not obliged to know Greek, and the Kievan state and its Muscovite successor did not have direct access to the full range of Greek culture, either pagan or Christian. Lacking a knowledge of Greek and particularly of Latin, the lingua franca of cultivated Europe, and not being part of any other major civilization, the Russians were at a distinct cultural disadvantage. It is significant that the beginning of their cultural revival in the late seventeenth century was in fact aided by the importation of Greek scholars and clerics, and most importantly of Ukrainians. Many of the leading figures of seventeenth-century Muscovy, if not Ukrainians themselves, were trained at the Kievan Academy or had been taught by its graduates.

Peter naturally sought out these men, mostly clerics, for assistance in areas which required a knowledge of Russian and Church Slavonic, such as civil service, translation, educational projects, and, of course, church reform. Stefan Yavorsky, who later turned against Peter, and Feofan Prokopovich, the outstanding intellectual figure of his age in Russia, were both Ukrainians and had taught at the Kievan Academy. Peter could hardly fail to realize the superiority of the educational backgrounds of such men. To his credit he saw the value of formal instruction in Classical languages and philosophy as taught in the Kievan Academy, far and away the best institution of higher learning in Russia. Although it was not a project that occupied much of his attention, Peter did encourage the revival and reorganization of the Moscow Academy (*Slavyano-Greko-Latinskaya Akademiya*), which had been a church school, as a Classical academy on the model of Jesuit institutions established in Europe during the Counter-Reformation.

In the latter part of his reign this initiative began to bear fruit as Kantemir and Trediakovsky attended the Moscow Academy in the early 1720s and attained a fairly good grounding in Latin and the literature of Classical Antiquity. A decade later Mikhail Lomonosov was also a student there and received a sufficiently good background to enable him to pursue his studies at the Academy of Sciences in St. Petersburg and later at Marburg and Freiburg.

In a political or economic history of Russia one would doubtless want to begin a discussion of the modern period in the late seventeenth century, certainly with the accession of Peter. But in a literary or cultural history the periodization would be somewhat different. Traditionally the end of the Old Russian period is placed at about the year 1700 (a neat round figure), although Istrin and others have argued that it should be placed earlier, at least in 1654, when Khmelnitsky allied himself with Tsar Aleksey Mikhaylovich and thus brought Muscovy into direct contact with the Left Bank Ukraine. It is true that the church's hegemony over the written word was suffering a decline during the course of the seventeenth century. This is shown by the popularity of imported romances and satirical tales (some anticlerical) that were becoming available in chapbooks. Furthermore, the Schism certainly inflicted a damaging blow upon the authority of the church. The general drift toward a secular culture can be discerned here, but it is only a prelude to the full emancipation of Russian culture from the church, which came about in the following century, after the Petrine reforms.

It seems best to regard the reign of Peter as a transitional period, however pallid the description may appear in connection with such a dynamic figure. Cultural pursuits tended to fade into the background, with the notable exception of architecture: modernization could not, after all, be carried out at the same pace and at the same level in all fields of human activity. Institutions of higher learning devoted to liberal education as opposed to scientific or technical training were not founded until after the death of Peter. Most notably, the Cadet School (*Sukhoputny shlyakhetny kadetsky korpus*)—the equivalent of what might be called today a liberal arts college—opened its doors in 1731. Moscow University, with its two gymnasia (one for members of the nobility and one for *raznochintsy*), was not established until 1755, and then only as a result of the strenuous efforts of Lomonosov and the enlightened patronage of Count Ivan Shuvalov.

Therefore one feels justified in placing the beginning of the modern period, certainly in literature, at about the year 1730, when Trediakovsky returned from five years abroad in Paris and Holland. Trediakovsky himself, and also Kantemir and Lomonosov, were very conscious of the fact that Russian literature was in fact beginning with them; they regarded the past as a cultural waste-land. This is particularly noticeable in a poem by Trediakovsky, where in typically gauche but touching manner he assumes the *persona* of Russian Poetry and expresses heartfelt thanks to Apollo for deigning to visit Russia at long last and assures the god that he will not regret the decision. In the thirties and forties of the eighteenth century there was in fact a strong echo of what has been called the eleventh-hour mentality of the early Kievan period. Just as Russian churchmen expressed their gratitude to providence and Grand Duke Vladimir for enabling them to partake of God's grace and join the Christian fold at the last moment, so in similar fashion Russian writers celebrated Peter for leading Russia into the European concert of nations. The comparison between Vladimir and Peter and their respective civilizing roles seems not to have escaped the attention of Feofan Prokopovich, whose funeral oration on the death of Peter contains conscious stylistic echoes of Hilarion's 'Sermon on the Law and the Grace', although Feofan naturally at no time makes the comparison explicit.

The first Russian writers of the modern period were isolated figures, but that they appeared when they did was no accident. They were the products of the Petrine reforms in the sense that these had provided, or were providing, the necessary underbrush of elementary Western education, a certain level of material civilization, an ambience of European manners. Trediakovsky and Lomonosov are obviously direct products of the Petrine period. Both were of non-noble origin, but managed to make their way to Moscow and take advantage of the new educational and career opportunities available; both travelled abroad, although Trediakovsky's stay involved no formal education. Lomonosov was always a strong advocate of Petrine reforms; indeed one feels he had been born too late—he would have been in his element in Peter's reign and the tsar would have made him his right-hand man.

Kantemir is less directly a product of the Petrine reforms. His father was Moldavian and he was brought up in an environment in which Greek and Italian were spoken, not Russian; he would have become a cultivated European gentleman no doubt, whether Peter had lived or not. However, he as well as Trediakovsky and Lomonosov were enthusiastic supporters of Peter, albeit after the fact, and all three were influenced by direct contacts with contemporary Europe.

The enthusiasm and optimism of the early poets faithfully reflected the atmosphere of their time, at least in St. Petersburg. It should be remembered that in discussing the Europeanization of Russia we are dealing with only a small minority of the population. The nobility or *dvoryanstvo*, brought to prominence by Peter with his promulgation of the Table of Ranks (*Tabel o rangakh*) in 1772, at no time in the eighteenth century numbered more than 1 per cent of the total population. However small their numbers, for the supporters of the Petrine reforms (and very soon after his death these numbered most members of the nobility and numerous others aspiring to join its ranks) attractive new horizons were opened up. They were excited by their own prospects and the future glory that beckoned. They were proud of their country's new power and prestige, and particularly rejoiced at Russian triumphs on the battlefield. But more than this they became aware of the possibility of creating a new society, of enabling men to develop to their full potentials.

This early excitement and optimism were given theoretical underpinning by the pervasive ideas of rationalism and Natural Law philosophy, which began to trickle into Russia during the second third of the century.[4] The universalism of these ideas had the same appeal to the Russians as had the universalism of Christianity seven centuries previously. Men were equal everywhere and deserved the same rights and opportunities: hence the Russians, though late on the scene, could afford to hold their heads high in any company. The belief in human progress and inevitable betterment naturally had great attraction for the Russians. The educational theories of Locke reinforced the conviction that men could be shown their faults and that with the proper instruction they would correct the error of their ways. The great eighteenth-century search for human happiness—the 'Grail of the modern world', as Paul Hazard called it—was as much a part of Russian thought and endeavour at this time as in the rest of Europe.

⁴ Marc Raeff, *Origins of the Russian Intelligentsia. The Eighteenth-Century Nobility* (New York, 1966), particularly Chapter V, 'The Impact of Western Ideas'.

The result of such ideas in literature was a preponderance of didacticism and political moralizing. The panegyric, occasional odes of Lomonosov and the tragedies of Sumarokov were designed as 'lessons to kings', guides to behaviour, and reminders of the lofty responsibility to continue the work begun by Peter. Sumarokov's plays in particular also aimed at encouraging the nobility to take heed of its privileges and social duty. His tragedies provide models of behaviour, while his satires and comedies ridicule vulgarity and foppishness and, like all satire, have the serious purpose of seeking an improvement in manners.

From all appearances, then, Russian rulers and the Russian nobility were marching hand in hand toward a brighter future. In sharp contrast to the situation in France, for example, where intellectuals and writers were for the most part opposed to the *ancien régime* and all its works, in Russia the government seemed to have the writers' enthusiastic support. And yet one hundred years after the death of Peter came the Decembrist Revolt, a revolution not by a suppressed class or minority, but by the most privileged class in the country, this same nobility (or better, its élite echelons) which had earlier given its support to the government. What had happened to spoil the relationship after such a promising start?

Two features of the modernization of Russia during the eighteenth century must be borne in mind if we are to understand both the process itself and later developments. The first is that modernization along European lines was a policy directed from above and imposed on the people—a latter-day repetition, as we have implied, of the enforced Christianization of Kievan Russia at the end of the tenth century. The purpose of the *Aufklärung* was to aid the state to catch up with the West. The second feature is that modernization was not only forced, it was of necessity compressed and often haphazard. Peter's reforms were linked to the war effort; this was obviously not the time for carefully considered plans. Although pursued with far less urgency and under less immediate pressure, some of the administrative and cultural measures decreed by later sovereigns also have an air of capriciousness. Furthermore, as has been pointed out, modernization and the new ideas affected only a minuscule proportion of the population. The result was a period of 'dual faith' or *dvoeverie*, similar to that of the first centuries after the Christianization of Kievan Russia.

Small wonder that Western visitors were struck by many great incongruities, that Europeanization seemed at best a hothouse growth in an inhospitable climate. Government by decree, at the whim and caprice of the sovereign, led to a series of contrasts between theory and practice, grandiose plans and spasmodic or incomplete implementation, between an increasingly lavish Europeanized court and abysmal poverty and medieval backwardness in the rest of the country, in general between the thin European veneer and the essentially pre-Petrine society consisting almost exclusively of peasants, which lay beneath. Such contrasts and incongruities not only struck visitors, but soon began to impinge upon the consciousness of leading Russian intellectuals and writers.

The hundred years from the death of Peter to the Decembrist Revolt witness a growing sophistication and a surprisingly rapid acquisition of Western culture on the part of the Russians, the closing of the 'cultural gap' about which Aleksey Veselovsky wrote with such wit and sensitivity.[5] But they also saw the evolution among the Russian nobility of three interrelated trends: disaffection from the government, an uneasiness about the value of the Petrine reforms, and an ambivalence toward the West combined with a malaise about their own position.

The nobility's disaffection from the government was probably inevitable, particularly after 1762 when Peter III abolished all service obligations, one of his few acts before being garrotted by one of his wife's favourites. 'To leave a nobility without occupation is to render it *frondeuse*', said Georges Sorel. This was as true in Russia as it had been earlier in France, but for rather different reasons. There is irony in the fact that the Russian government was sowing the seeds of its own destruction by educating young members of the nobility and sending them abroad at its own expense to continue their studies. Even men who had not studied abroad must have been deeply disturbed by the marked difference between

---

[5] Aleksey Veselovsky, *Zapadnoe vliyanie v novoy russkoy literature*, 5th ed. rev. (St. Petersburg, 1916).

the Enlightenment ideas and programmes on the one hand and the brutal facts of Russian reality on the other. The chief of these was serfdom, which offended the sensibilities of men like Novikov equally as much as those like Radishchev, who studied in the late sixties at the University of Leipzig. Radishchev's indignation at serfdom, at the insult to the rights and self-respect of his fellow man, cries out from every page of his *Journey from St. Petersburg to Moscow* (1790).[6]

As Marc Raeff has shown, the Russians' humanitarian motives were given added momentum by the influence of the Pietists in Halle.[7] The Russian branch of Freemasonry, as headed by Novikov, also placed great store by philanthropy. A further point is that in the intellectual waste-land that Russia had been, new ideas tended to be swallowed whole; they loomed much larger than they would have done on a much more cluttered horizon. Unlike Western writers, who tended to engage in a discussion of ideas as a sort of intellectual exercise, the Russians approached new concepts with a naïve passion and total commitment: if these ideas were true, then they should be put into action at once. This attitude has been particularly noted among Russian intellectuals in the nineteenth century, for example Belinsky, but one can detect it in earlier generations. It would of course be impertinent, as well as incorrect, to deny that other intellectuals in the West have not embraced ideas fully or attempted to live them and put them into practice, or to pretend that the Russians have a monopoly of humanitarianism, but in comparison with many Russian intellectuals, their Western counterparts do seem very much like 'raisonneurs de cabinet'.

The results of this growing disaffection in literature were a decline in didactic poetry designed to correct manners, a switch from the satire of manners to social satire, particularly in the early journals of Novikov; panegyric odes gradually recede into the background (at least those of the Lomonosov variety), and in

---

[6] On Radishchev (in English) see Allen McConnell, *A Russian Philosophe Alexander Radishchev 1749–1802* (The Hague, 1964).

[7] Marc Raeff, 'Les Slaves, les Allemands et les "Lumières"', *Canadian Slavic Studies*, i (Winter 1967), 521–51. Raeff draws upon the research of a group of scholars in East Germany, headed by Eduard Winter.

general public verse is replaced by more personal lyrical poetry, and later by the prose tales of Karamzin with their cult of sensibility. Former liberals, losing hope of government action, and profoundly shaken by the Pugachev Rebellion, either joined court circles or withdrew from literature proper, for example Bogdanovich and Vladimir Lukin. Naturally, the organic development of Russian literature during the eighteenth century resulted significantly from its own internal laws and through contacts with Western movements, for example, pre-Romanticism, yet even at this early stage the intimate links between Russian literature and the social and political background are quite evident. They were to become more compelling in later times.

Doubts about the Petrine reforms and their possible validity and effects, fears that they may have robbed later generations of part of their heritage, occur fairly soon, for example in Sumarokov, but are best known in the works of Shcherbatov and later of Karamzin. This is the beginning of the great debate that raged in the middle of the nineteenth century between the Slavophiles and the Westernizers over the essential nature of the national character and Russia's destiny.

As the enduring symbol of Peter, his reforms, the new era in eighteenth-century Russia, stood the city he founded. Once again Trediakovsky can claim pre-eminence, at least chronologically, in celebrating St. Petersburg in verse: he judges the city superior to all others, even London and Paris.[8] He was followed by many others. The Empress Catherine II, who lost no opportunity to link her name with that of Peter and sought to portray herself as his lineal descendant in beautifying the city and continuing his reforms, made an early decision to raise a statue to his memory. The result was Falconet's magnificent equestrian statue of Peter in the Senate Square. It bears the legend: 'Petro Primo—Catharina Secunda'. The ubiquitous William Coxe was in the city as preparations were being made to unveil the statue and offers an eye-witness account.[9]

---

[8] 'Pokhvala Izherskoy zemle i tsarstvuyushchemu gradu Sanktpeterburgu.'
[9] William Coxe, *Travels in Poland, Russia, Sweden, and Denmark,* ii (London, 1784).

Falconet's statue and the city of St. Petersburg were both much admired, but they were to become ambiguous symbols in Russian literature of the nineteenth century, reflecting a growing disenchantment with Europeanization and the conflicts it had aroused, between Russian intellectuals and their government and also the vast majority of the Russian people. Pushkin's *The Bronze Horsemen* is probably the most famous work about Peter and demonstrates with great poetic force his ambivalent attitude toward the tsar, his reforms, and the autocracy. The theme of St. Petersburg continues to provide a rich source for writers well into the present century. Very early on in the last century, we find the young Gogol writing to his mother in 1829 shortly after arriving to seek his fame and fortune in the new capital and describing its inhabitants as a curious breed: they are neither foreigners nor Russians, but an indefinable and not very attractive amalgam.[10] Gogol himself, and also Dostoevsky, used the city as a brooding and malevolent background to their works: Dostoevsky wrote of St. Petersburg as 'the most contrived city in the world'.

Even in the eighteenth century one finds many Russian writers and other members of the nobility losing their initial excitement and wonder at the marvels of Peter's city. From a practical point of view, first of all, the city was a very expensive place to live, far from the ancestral estates of most members of the nobility or landed gentry. It was a civil-service town and life revolved around the court. In addition it was full of ambitious and ingratiating sycophants, both foreign and domestic.

Particularly in the reign of Catherine II the city became associated with 'Voltaireanism', superficial anticlericalism, and a rather distasteful flippancy, which did not sit well with the serious social and humanitarian concerns of the leading intellectuals. Many preferred to live in Moscow, since it was nearer their estates, but also because it became a symbol of Russianness as opposed to the foreign and even alien capital. Significantly Sumarokov moved from St. Petersburg to Moscow in 1769 after

---

10 '. . . inostrantsy, kotorye poselilis syuda, obzhilis i vovse ne pokhozhi na inostrantsev, a russkie, v svoyu ochered, obynostranilis i sdelalis, ni tem ni drugim.' In *Sobranie sochineniy*, vii (Moscow, 1967), 62.

falling out with Catherine. A decade later Novikov made a similar move to rent the two presses of the University of Moscow at the invitation of Kheraskov, the Rector. In fact the University became a focal point of intellectual life, especially during the period of ten years in which Novikov rented the presses. Through his influence also the city became the centre of the vitally important Masonic movement in Russia.

Although regarded as seditious from at least the mid eighties by Catherine, the Masons did not in fact present a serious political threat. Novikov was not a radical; rather he was apolitical. As Bogolyubov has pointed out, Novikov and his friends decided to reject Voltaireanism and reason as a means of achieving the ideal of the virtuous, enlightened man: they chose instead the path of inner, moral regeneration.[11] For such men, and many of the leading cultural figures of the time were Masons, Freemasonry offered a way out of the impasse of superficiality and autocratic rule by urging re-education of the individual as a preliminary to the re-structuring of society. Society would improve if each of its members were virtuous; the precise form or nature of institutions was of little importance.

Russian reaction to the more extreme forms of Westernization of their country is not hard to find quite early on in the eighteenth century. One thinks of the countless satires against Francomania and the *petits-maîtres* from Kantemir to Fonzivin. However, it is in Moscow during the reign of Catherine that one finds a move away from a purely negative satire to a more positive response, a more considered reaction to the pressures being brought to bear by the rapid and apparently wholesale Europeanization of Russian life and manners. Russians began to search for something in their own culture, in their own past, which they could match up against foreign imports.

It seems clear that well before the end of the century many of the more thoughtful members of the nobility were uneasy about their privileged position and more importantly about the fact that they appeared to be living in a cultural and social vacuum. Of course, large numbers of the nobility never gave such problems a

---

[11] V. Bogolyubov, *N. I. Novikov i ego vremya* (Moscow, 1916), pp. 139–42.

moment's thought and were content to enjoy life's bounties to the hilt. No doubt we should take care not to present an anachronistic picture of eighteenth-century Russia as 'un monde kafkaien dans lequel le noble russe évoluait sans le comprendre, et où il était voué à se nourrir de l'ombre des choses, de l'apparence des relations sociales et du masque des hommes'.[12] There can be no denying that many of the leading intellectual figures of the period (all nobles) were becoming slowly aware that the Petrine reforms had served to provide them with a European culture, and yet they were living in an environment which seemed to have little direct connection with it. On the one hand the government was a denial of Enlightenment ideas and ideals, on the other hand the vast majority of the people belonged to an age left behind by Peter the Great.

Novikov and Fonvizin, and later Karamzin, exemplify the ambiguous position in which such intellectuals and writers found themselves. Novikov and Fonvizin both wrote satires against Francomania. Novikov, however, soon became disillusioned by his research into Russia's pre-Petrine past and in addition he was perfectly well aware of the value and necessity of Western culture. Warning against an indiscriminate borrowing of foreign ideas and customs, he set about making available to his compatriots the best that the West had to offer in translations published by his Typographical Company in Moscow.

Fonvizin was far more belligerent than Novikov. The letters he wrote while abroad, especially those on his second trip, are designed to cut France down to size, to show his countrymen that the French are really rather silly and hardly worth respecting, let alone imitating. He strikes a note that was to resonate often enough in later Russian debates when he argues that, although the French have an active political life and institutions, even elections, they are in fact not truly free as are the Russians. He also echoes Herder in arguing that the Russians may have come on the scene late, but they will go further than Western nations, whose history has now

[12] Michael Confino, 'Histoire et psychologie: A propos de la noblesse russe au xviiie siècle', *Annales: Économies, Sociétés, Civilisations*, xxvi, no. 6 (Nov.–Dec. 1967), 1175.

almost run its course. Fonvizin also looks forward to another common argument when he says that the Western Europeans may have more material wealth, but the Russians are somehow spiritually superior (*my — bolshe lyudi*).[13]

The example of Karamzin serves as a warning that anxiety about the Petrine reforms need not be linked with political opposition. In many ways the position that he adopted in his later years looks forward to that of the Slavophiles. Karamzin started out as a great admirer of Western culture, making a Grand Tour of Europe just after the French Revolution and annoying many of his acquaintances on his return both by his liberal views and by his exaggerated Western manner and dress, but he soon afterwards became aware of the superficiality of such behaviour and sought consistently and consciously to introduce more Russian features into his works. He urged the development of Russian literature and criticism, and then devoted the last twenty-two years of his life to a massive history of Russia from the earliest times, which remained unfinished at his death.

Karamzin's became the best-known and most influential history of Russia throughout much of the nineteenth century, but it was not the first. There had already developed an interest in Russia's past among many writers and intellectuals in the reign of Catherine II. The search for a respectable national culture also found an outlet in the great curiosity about Russian folksongs. Mikhail Chulkov's collection of 1770–4 went through four editions and was widely imitated; this development is an interesting echo of Ossianism and the collections of Percy and Herder. It has also been noted that the very popular comic operas of the time contain much ideological content. The special interest in these works is that the ridicule of Francomania, for example in Knyazhnin's *Misfortune from a Coach* (*Neschaste ot karety*) is linked with the idealization of the Russian peasant. Here, then, we have opposition to foreign mannerisms, together with the portrayal of the peasant as the epitome of native Russian common sense and wisdom, and also

---

[13] For a good discussion of these matters see Hans Rogger, *National Consciousness in Eighteenth-Century Russia* (Cambridge, Mass., 1960), pp. 75–84. However, I think he has not quite got the sense of *My — bolshe lyudi* with his translation 'We are bigger people'.

of course veiled social satire against the system of serfdom. It was this potent combination that was to provide many members of the nobility, and later members of the intelligentsia in the nineteenth century, with a means of incorporating both Western ideals of human dignity and equality, and also themselves, into Russian social reality.

By the reign of Alexander I the upper echelons of the nobility had become truly enlightened and Europeans in more than name only: they were beginning to leave their rulers behind. The way was open not only for the increasing estrangement of certain elements of the nobility (and their successors, the Russian intelligentsia) from the government of the country, but also for Russian literature to assume its special ethical and social role. Before too long the Russians would begin to demonstrate their peculiar talent for taking over ideas, themes, modes of writing from the West, then reworking them and exporting them back again in new and dazzling combinations.

The Russians came late on to the European scene and their eighteenth century was an abbreviated one, but it existed, as I hope the essays in this volume demonstrate. In order to accommodate Russia in an over-all view of the eighteenth century we can perhaps adopt Goethe's concept of the fugue: each nation performs its part in the total design by playing the melodic theme allotted to it at the appropriate moment. The fugue fails if the contrapuntal pattern is not maintained, if there is no interweaving of voices and melodies. In the Enlightenment and in the century as a whole the two major parts were taken by England and France. Russia's part was minor and she came in late and a little out of tune, but the fugue is not complete without her presence.

Part One
History of Ideas

MARC RAEFF

The Enlightenment in Russia and Russian Thought in the Enlightenment

WITH the reign of Peter the Great Russia entered the eighteenth century, but in his reign, too, 'Europe' moved into Muscovy. Whether Peter's decision to put Russia into apprenticeship with 'Europe' was revolutionary or not, the fact remains that it did not occur without the country's being prepared for it in some measure. For almost three-quarters of a century before the accession of the great reformer, Moscow had received foreign travellers and residents from countries lying west of Poland.[1] The Foreign Quarter (*nemetskaya sloboda*) was of great importance in the formation of young Peter's outlook. It was here that he spent much of his time, that he was introduced to the pleasures of love and social intercourse, and that he became acquainted with Western technical and scientific expertise.

A few words about the nature of the foreign culture available through the *nemetskaya sloboda* at the end of the seventeenth century may be in order at this point. For all its importance in East European military and diplomatic affairs, Muscovy was still very much on the periphery of Western European consciousness; at best it was a frontier outpost, at worst the beginning of Asia. Only the most adventurous, those unable to find a suitable role for themslves in their homeland or in other Western countries, enrolled in the service of the tsars. Many of them were remarkable characters, but none belonged to what may be called the creative leadership of contemporary European culture. To the Russians they had little to offer beyond practical competence in a relatively narrow speciality. Their general knowledge of contemporary

[1] Not to mention the powerful influence that came by way of the Ukraine, especially through the mediation of the Kievan Graeco-Latin-Slavonic Academy. But it was mainly felt in ecclesiastical circles.

scientific, philosophic, and artistic culture was superficial and limited to what they would have picked up in their youth, i.e. about half a generation earlier. They transmitted slightly outdated factual, theoretical, and artistic knowledge, the kind of knowledge that was the common possession of Western society at large, not the most recent knowledge acquired by its creative and pioneering élite. Or to put it in slightly different terms—Muscovy was exposed to the widely accepted and vulgarized achievements of Western European culture, not to its *avant-garde* discoveries and speculations. There was nothing unusual about this situation: we can observe it in many places in our own days.

Another aspect of cultural contacts at the time of Peter's accession should be kept in mind. With a few relatively unimportant exceptions, the foreigners who contributed their skills and services to Muscovy came from Protestant lands: Holland, England and Scotland, German states. There were perfectly good reasons for this. In the first place the Russians viewed with the greatest suspicion all Catholics; this eliminated the neighbouring Poles and the Latin peoples. Secondly, the ravages of the Thirty Years War, as well as the political and confessional rivalries between the German principalities, limited greatly the opportunities available to the learned and skilled Germans; to a more limited extent this also applied to England and Scotland, which had both gone through long periods of civil and religious strife. Thirdly, Dutchmen and Englishmen had established and retained lively trade contacts with Russia since the sixteenth century, so that the ground was better prepared to attract craftsmen, traders, and technicians from Holland and Britain. In addition, we may also mention that Peter's military victories made available the knowledge and skills of Swedish prisoners of war; and here again we have Protestants whose cultural affiliations were with the Germanies and England. In short, only one group of European nations and men played an active role in first transmitting Western culture to Russia. This situation was to have a lasting effect, as we shall see.

Quite naturally, when Peter the Great adopted policies requiring the expansion of cultural and technical contacts with Western Europe, he addressed himself to the foreigners on the spot to help him contact and recruit newcomers. His own first travels abroad also took him primarily to Germany, Holland, and England, where he personally recruited technicians. Not that other parts of Europe remained completely outside the purview of Peter and his government. For example, a few young noblemen were sent to study in Spain and Venice; but for a variety of reasons their experience had less of an impact than that of students sent to north-western Europe. Primarily it was a matter of numbers, for many more were sent to Holland and England than to Venice and Spain; but surely the less receptive atmosphere that prevailed in Russia for the Catholic and Mediterranean worlds played a role too.

We are, therefore, not dealing with a single 'Europe' or 'Western culture' which interested the Russians. They did not learn about the 'high' culture of the West European artistic and scientific élites, but they absorbed the applied technology and the 'consumer-oriented' popular culture. Furthermore, not all areas of 'Europe' were equally involved in influencing Russia directly. To be sure, some aspects were shared by all European countries at the time, e.g. the arts; but this was precisely an area of culture in which Russia did not become actively engaged until much later. The fact of several Europes from which one could draw inspiration did not escape the notice of Peter's countrymen. It found expression, for instance, in the opening sentences of a well-known tale of the time, *Povest o rossiyskom matrose Vasilii Koriotskom*, with a reference to Europes (Evropii).[2]

As we survey the process by which Russia entered the eighteenth century, became part of 'Europe', we must keep in mind this basic fact of the existence of several Europes—in both the geographic and the cultural sense. The question then arises which of the 'Europes' had an impact and which ones did not, and why this should be so. A related question is that of the chronology of such impacts.

[2] The phrase occurs, it is true, in a context identifying the European part of Russia, but the use of the plural—be it only to indicate an opposition between Russia and Europe—is significant enough. 'Povest o rossiyskom matrose Vasilii Koriotskom', in G. N. Moiseeva, ed., *Russkie povesti pervoy treti XVIII veka* (Moscow and Leningrad, 1965), 191–210.

Conscious assimilation of European culture dates from the reign of Peter the Great in the sense that from this time on the Russian élites endeavoured to reshape Russia in the image of the West, rather than merely to use foreign inventions without transforming the traditional Muscovite pattern, as had been the case in the seventeenth century. As is well known, Peter's main interest, which he imparted to his collaborators, was in the domain of technology. He recruited engineers, shipwrights, architects, naval officers—and instructors in these fields. Concerned also with the development of the economic potential of Russia, especially its manufactures, Peter invited not only foreign industrialists and merchants, but also technicians and craftsmen in various fields such as metallurgy, textiles, glass, mining. Whatever contemporary theoretical, scientific, and philosophic knowledge did penetrate into Russia did so through the mediation of these specialists and had a distinctly subordinate role. The first schools established by Peter did not offer much beyond the pragmatic aspects of the major technical disciplines (mathematics, navigation, artillery). Even such a significant step as the establishment of the Academy of Sciences, although suggested by the great speculative thinker Leibniz, was taken with only immediate practical aims in view.

But philosophy and theoretical science did come to Russia along with technology, for in the early eighteenth century the scientific revolution had progressed so far that even for limited practical applications a knowledge of the theoretical framework was required. We must, however, remember that the practitioners usually were somewhat behind the frontiers of speculation and experimentation, and whenever they gave expression to theoretical or philosophical considerations they were those of their mentors a generation earlier. For the history of Russia's cultural development it is also important to note that Leibniz and Christian Wolff were the most imfluential advisers on scholarly and academic matters in the first third of the eighteenth century. They helped recruit mainly German technicians, scientists, and professors who naturally were often their own followers and pupils. From the very beginning, therefore, in spite of the presence of a few pragmatic Englishmen, the scientific and philosophic orientation of those who came to work in Russia was that of Cartesian rationalism, rather than that of the empiricism of Bacon and Locke. Towards the end of his life, Peter also became more interested in introducing the arts and social graces to his new capital St. Petersburg. He hired architects and artists to build up Petersburg and the suburban palaces and to organize lavish festivities at which proper etiquette was rigidly enforced. Although the model for the former was naturally Versailles, the chief artists were Italians or Germans trained in Italy.[3] This facet of the process of Europeanization needs further investigation, however. No satisfactory explanation has yet been given why so many Italian architects (e.g. Rastrelli, Quarenghi) and artists should have come to and settled in Russia. Some preliminary considerations may be offered: the French artistic guild had enough to do in Versailles and elsewhere, even during the difficult last years of Louis XIV—and the building boom resumed under the Regency (and kept up until the Revolution). If they left France at all, French artists went for shorter periods to less remote places, to Germany and Austria, for example. For their part, the Italians had influential schools and academies, a great tradition and reputation; but they could not easily find scope for their talents at home.

Thus from the very beginning of the eighteenth century, Russia took in several 'Europes'—the German scientific and philosophic, the Anglo-Dutch technical, and the Italian artistic. More significant than the diversity of geographic origins, however, were the implications that this selection had for the basic intellectual orientation of the early European influences.

The dominant conceptual framework of those foreigners who came to work and teach in Russia was provided by Cartesian rationalism and the philosophies of natural law as expounded and popularized by Pufendorf, Leibniz, and especially Christian

[3] Although Dutch models (and presumably architects) were used in planning the residential sections and quarters of St. Petersburg. Cf. E. Beletskaya, N. Krasheninnikova, L. Chernozubova, I. Ern, '*Obraztsovye' proekty v zhiloy zastroyke russkikh gorodov XVIII–XIX vv.* (Moscow, 1961), ch. 1. On artistic life see, among others, the interesting memoirs of the future President of the Academy of Fine Arts, Karl Stählin, *Aus den Papieren Jacob von Stählins, Ein biographischer Beitrag zur deutsch-russischen Kulturgeschichte des 18. Jahrhunderts* (Königsberg i. Pr. und Berlin, 1926).

Wolff.[4] This intellectual background suggests one reason why the Russians proved more receptive to Cartesian rationalism than to Newton's cosmology and Locke's epistemology. But it could not be the only reason, for after all the Russians were also in close contact with England, and many English or Scottish engineers and teachers (such as Farquharson and Bruce) worked and even settled in Russia in the reign of Peter the Great, as well as subsequently. A further factor in this easy receptivity may lie in the form in which it was presented by the German scholars of the day: Cartesianism seemed to conflict less with traditional Christian dogma and its cosmology. The duality of mind and matter appeared to preserve better traditional cosmological and ontological beliefs than the more radical effort at overcoming this duality by the English empiricists.[5] Another less obvious and even unconscious reason may stem from the fact that empiricism implies a respect for observable reality as the basis of both knowledge and action. Yet it was exactly the reality of Russia that Peter aimed at transforming, and in this aim both his Russian and foreign collaborators concurred. The rationalistic, perhaps abstract, but neat and comprehensive approach of Descartes and German natural-law philosophy could serve as basis for the construction of a new socio-political institutional system without as much regard for an empirical reality that was to be discarded.[6]

The role played by German universities in providing and training scholars and professionals for service in Russia served to anchor this intellectual tradition firmly and preserve its ascendancy in Russian academic and scientific life during the eighteenth century. It was quite natural that it should be so. The German scholars who came to Russia recommended that promising students be sent to those universities where they themselves had studied or taught,

4 We find this influence also in Feofan Prokopovich (especially in his *Pravda voli monarshey*). It remained a vital element in the curricula of the ecclesiastical schools throughout the eighteenth century and in this way affected also the clergy, and sons of clergy who went into government service and scholarship and literature.

5 See the suggestive observations of Robert Lenoble, *Esquisse d'une histoire de l'idée de Nature* (Paris, 1969), 2ᵉ partie, ch. 4.

6 This is not to deny Peter the Great's pragmatism. But he did frequently act as if he conceived himself in the role of a secular creator giving the well-known 'chiquenaude' to put the new social and institutional machine in motion.

and quite naturally too they recommended their own friends and former colleagues for positions in Russia. Thus Peter's physician, Blumentrost, as President of the Academy, appealed to his Alma Mater (Halle) and his contacts there to find suitable candidates for posts at the Academy. While Leibniz himself did not come to Russia he recommended Christian Wolff who played a most active role in suggesting professors, members of the academy, and other professionals to the Russian government. This function was carried on by the scholars who were hired, as is amply demonstrated by their published correspondence with German academies, universities, and individual scholars.[7]

The best-known names—e.g. Mueller, Euler, Schloezer, Pallas, Stählin—were those of individuals connected with the major institution of learning and scholarship in eighteenth-century Russia: the Academy of Sciences. In spite of all efforts made by pre- and post-1917 scholarship to show the rapid Russification of the Academy, the fact remains that until almost the end of the century it was dominated, if not actually run, by German and German-trained scientists and scholars. Of course, in many instances—which grew more frequent as time wore on—a number of these German scholars settled in Russia for good and became partly Russified. Their children, too, followed often in their footsteps, but born and raised in Russia they were in fact bilingual and bicultural, so that in spite of their German names they may be counted among the Russian scholars. Yet even these Russo-German scientists usually received their advanced training in German universities (not until the middle of the nineteenth century was the entire academic training completed in Russia, although even then it was usually followed by a travelling fellowship to a German academy or university). In gauging the intellectual influence exercised by these scholars it should be kept in mind that the Academy's role extended beyond the narrow confines of its purely scientific work. For long periods in the eighteenth century its publications were the most important vehicle for the wide dissemination of

7 For example, A. Juškevič and E. Winter, *Die Berliner und die Petersburger Akademie der Wissenschaften im Briefwechsel Leonhard Eulers*, 2 vols. (Berlin, 1959–61); E. Winter, ed., *August Ludwig v. Schlözer und Russland* (Berlin, 1961).

general knowledge and cultural interests. Its members were called upon to work for the government (and to assist individual dignitaries) in planning and implementing in a variety of areas concerning all facets of the country's public life. Individual members of the Academy were also active in various educational and scientific institutions in the capital, for example the Corps of Cadets, the Imperial Free Economic Society, and the like. They thus had many opportunities to make an impact on Russian educated society in general, to popularize and maintain throughout the eighteenth century the basic philosophic conceptions and intellectual orientations which had taken shape in Germany in the late seventeenth century.

Of the many German universities that could provide well-trained scholars, scientists, and technicians and also serve to educate selected Russian students, only a few in fact did play this role to any significant degree. These were the universities of Halle, Marburg, Leipzig,[8] and at the very end of the century Göttingen.[9] Why these universities, particularly Halle, Marburg, and Leipzig? Professor E. Winter and his study group in Berlin have pointed out the main factor: Pietism.[10] The philosophical light of Pietism, Christian Wolff, whose role in staffing Russia with academicians we have noted earlier, was the major influence in Halle and later in Marburg. Leipzig, too, remained under strong pietist influence throughout the century.

We have also to consider what may at first glance appear as a paradox. In modern estimation, the most significant intellectual achievements in Russia in the first half of the eighteenth century were the works of 'loners' whose importance and influence were recognized by their fellow-countrymen only very much later. The earliest

---

[8] Connections with Russia seem also to have been maintained by the universities of Greifswald and Königsberg—these are in the process of being studied by East German and Russian scholars.

[9] Göttingen, founded in the middle of the eighteenth century, did not play a very influential role until the end of the century when Schlözer received the chair of statistics and political economy after leaving Russia. The heyday of Göttingen's role in the education of young Russians was in the first decade of the nineteenth century when it helped popularize a liberal cameralism in Russian economic thought.

[10] M. Raeff, 'Les Slaves, les Allemands et les "Lumières"', *Canadian Slavic Studies*, i, no. 4 (1967), 521–51 and the literature cited therein.

modern Russian poet, Prince Antiokh Kantemir, something of a Renaissance man, was much influenced not only by French poetics (Boileau in particular), but also by the cosmology of Newton and the epistemological ideas of Locke.[11] Kantemir's contemporary, V. N. Tatishchev, too, displayed a strong empirical bent in his scholarly and scientific interests. A 'fledgling of Peter's nest', a pragmatic administrator, he tended to view all scientific and scholarly problems in terms of their usefulness for better administration and more effective economic development. His philosophical writings were, it is true, couched in fashionable German mould, but his research was carried on in the positivistic and empirical tradition of a Francis Bacon. Neither Kantemir's nor Tatishchev's philosophical ideas and scientific work made an immediate impact on Russian intellectual development. Kantemir's advocacy of Newton and Locke was ignored, while Tatishchev's manifold contributions to the study of geography, geology, history, climatology, etc. remained buried in his papers. Aside from the facts that Kantemir spent a large part of his adult life abroad (he died in Paris after a six-year assignment as ambassador in London) and that Tatishchev's cantankerous character limited his personal contacts with colleagues, their lack of influence in their own time may be explained by the fact that they did not share the prevailing intellectual orientation based on Cartesian rationalism and the natural-law philosophies taught by the Germans.[12]

An even more interesting illustration is provided by the career and reputation of the universal scientific and literary genius, M. V. Lomonosov. He himself was a product of German pietist schools (Marburg, Freiburg), in both science and literature. At first he followed in the footsteps of his mentors; for example, he translated the most popular and influential Wolffian textbook of physics into Russian. In the realm of literature he never went beyond this German influence, which may explain why this side of his genius

[11] Kantemir's cosmopolitan education was quite exceptional for a Russian in his time. See the interesting unpublished doctoral dissertation of V. Boss, 'Newton's influence in Eighteenth Century Russia' (Harvard University, 1962).
[12] Of course national rivalries of the level of academic politics and influence played a role too, but their effects should not be exaggerated.

found immediate resonance and recognition abroad as well as at home, and supported his reputation for a long time to come. But in his scientific work, especially chemistry, he freed himself from his teachers. In many ways his intuitions and inklings were of a very advanced nature and put in question many *idées reçues* of his time, especially Cartesian physics and Wolffian cosmology. This fact alone, apart from his bad personal relations with the German scholars at the Academy of Sciences, largely explains the neglect with which his contributions were treated until the late nineteenth and early twentieth centuries. In opposition to the orientation prevailing at the Academy of Sciences, Lomonosov was instrumental in organizing another institution of higher learning, the University of Moscow; but it did not come into its own until more than half a century after his death.[13]

What is the explanation for the profound influence exercised by the German academic—i.e. scholarly and scientific—orientation that lasted throughout the eighteenth century and even beyond? Some factors come to mind immediately. The late seventeenth and early eighteenth centuries witnessed a German intellectual and scholarly 'imperialistic drive' under the aegis of the pietist circles of Halle. For the sake of the reconstitution of Christian unity and the bringing together of Asia and Europe culturally as well as economically, the Pietists endeavoured to develop contacts and gain influence in Eastern European countries. As a little-explored and potentially valuable and powerful land, Russia was an obvious target. The Pietists' programme happened to dovetail with Peter's own plans for the modernization and economic development of Russia. He thus was happy to receive the merchants, technicians, and scholars trained at Halle who were recommended to him by Leibniz, Chr. Wolff, and his own physician Blumentrost, a graduate of Halle. On the other hand, the religious, political, and economic fragmentation of the German states drove many scholars and scientists to look for better opportunities in the unknown and promising empire of the tsars. Those who went

---

[13] G. Mühlpfordt, 'Lomonosov und die Mitteldeutsche Aufklärung', *Studien zur Geschichte der russischen Literatur des 18. Jahrhunderts*, ii (Berlin, 1968), 135–231, and the same author's 'Leipzig als Brennpunkt der internationalen Wirkung Lomonosovs', ibid. iii (1968), 271–416.

first to Russia used their personal connections to draw in others and to help send Russians to Germany for study and training. Naturally, there was also the factor of proximity, for France and Italy were further away (and less penetrable to Protestant proselytism). As for the English and the Dutch, they had enough outlets for their energy in their own land or empire without seeking fortune elsewhere.

But on a deeper level, we must try to identify the reasons why the orientation of Halle, as represented by the philosophy of Chr. Wolff and his pupils, was particularly congenial to the government and educated classes of Russia. In the first place was their sincere and complete acceptance of Christian doctrine and the injunction to obey constituted authorities, an attitude most welcome to a monarch jealous of his absolute power. No less significant a factor was the Wolffian interpretation of natural law. It stressed the conceptions of obligation and duty as the prerequisite of individual rights, in contrast to the 'possessive individualism' of the Hobbesian and Lockean tradition. It also gave priority to the community and to social institutions over and against the claims of the autonomous individual, as emphasized by the English and French notions of natural rights. Such an orientation, buttressed by a strong belief in a neo-stoicism which assigned a major role to human will and activity within the framework of generally valid universal moral laws, appealed to a service-oriented society dedicated to total change of traditional circumstances. The doctrines taught by Wolff and his followers gave moral and philosophic sanction to the goal-directed, wilful, active state administration that Peter the Great had rooted in Russia.[14]

Wolff's original teaching at Halle and Marburg was carried on and further developed in Leipzig. This city served both Russia and 'Europe' as the main clearing-house of information pertaining to all fields of learning. In addition, its university remained a major centre of natural-law jurisprudence in the eighteenth century and was selected by the Russian government for advanced training of

[14] Another aspect of this orientation was the church settlement on the Protestant model imposed by Peter and Feofan Prokopovich. Cf. also my book, *Origins of the Russian Intelligentsia* (New York, 1966), ch. 3.

prospective officials. Its most famous Russian graduate was to be Alexander Radishchev, who drew much inspiration from the natural-law doctrines of Leipzig jurists, and took good advantage of the opportunity it offered for becoming acquainted with pietist spiritualism, as well as with the most recent European philosophical literature. But Leipzig not only had a university, it was a publishing centre as well and its major periodical publication, *Neue Zeitungen von gelehrten Sachen*, was a principal source of information for both Russians and Germans on what was going on in their respective countries. In Leipzig, too, the moralistic and sentimental literary circle around Gottsched maintained contacts with Russia. It played a significant role in preparing Russian literary taste for an easy acceptance of the *Sturm und Drang* and of English sentimentalism.[15] This continuing role of contacts with pietistically oriented universities and cultural centres should be kept in mind in any description of the gradual Westernization of Russian intellectual life.

From the social and economic points of view, Russia was closer to most German states than to the more advanced trading and manufacturing Holland and England or the immensely wealthy France. From the time of Peter I the Russian government was acutely aware of the necessity for developing the empire's potential resources. This had to be accomplished within an antiquated and unwieldy socio-institutional framework (e.g. lack of an entrepreneurial class) compelling reliance on state leadership and rational planning. Thus Russia seemed most suitable for the application of the precepts and practices of *Kameral- und Polizeiwissenschaften* which had been developed in response to similar circumstances in German lands. German-trained jurists, therefore, like Strube de Piermont, proved most influential in developing Russian legal and social doctrines; Justi and Bielefeldt influenced Catherine's political and economic outlook, while the Austrian enlightened cameralist Sonnenfels and the pedagogue Jankevich de Mirievo provided her with practical models for institutional reforms.

---

[15] G. Mühlpfordt, 'Leipzig als Brennpunkt der internationalen Wirkung Lomonosovs', *Studien zur Geschichte der russischen Literatur des 18. Jahrhunderts*, iii (Berlin, 1968).

durable bridge between the poetry of the so-called Russian classicism and that of the second half of the century. Before Russian literature had finished transplanting the high classicism of the West, it had already begun to absorb the newer literary impulses antithetical to classicism; this is apparent in Sumarokov's poetry from the mid 1750s. To speak, therefore, of a Russian classicism in any Western sense is hazardous; the movement shaped the character of certain genres, such as the ode and tragedy, rather than the greater or complete *œuvre* of any of the writers who came to the fore in the first half of the eighteenth century. It yoked disparate trends as a consequence of the need for literary telescoping and the shift away from classicism in the West precisely at a time when the Russians began transplanting what they regarded as the Western classicist tradition. Moreover, as we can see in the case of Lomonosov, the indebtedness was by no means exclusively to France.

II

This brings us now to the matter of Classical Antiquity in eighteenth- and early nineteenth-century Russian literary development. The general assumption is that until the assimilation of Western classicism in the first half of the century, the 'experience' of the classical Graeco-Roman past was of little significance for Russian culture. With the absorption of Western classicism, however—so the traditional interpretation reads—this state of affairs changed and the treasures of ancient Greece and Rome at last lay open to the Russians.

The assumption is partially correct. Until the efforts to transplant French classicism from the 1720s—Russia's first extensive contact with Western literature—Classical Antiquity played virtually no role in the development of Russian culture. The causes are rooted, of course, in the absence of the Renaissance in Russia and the self-imposed isolation of Muscovy in the sixteenth and seventeenth centuries. However, when classicism was being Russianized in the first half of the eighteenth century, the assimilation of Classical Antiquity hardly kept pace. Russian writers studied the classical languages and, to be sure, translations of the

E

classics were undertaken and original works with classical motifs began to appear. But until after the middle of the century, it is difficult to speak of a solidly based Russian 'classical' culture. Why was this so? There are several reasons:

1. Despite their acquired reverence for Classical Antiquity, the Russian writers engaged in the assimilation of Western classicism in the first half of the century—Kantemir, Trediakovsky, Lomonosov, Sumarokov—took (French) classicist works as their models, by and large, and rarely sought out the Greek or Latin prototypes; their prime goal, of course, was the transplantation of Western classicism, not Classical Antiquity, although by assimilating Western classicism they doubtless believed that the assimilation of classical culture was also taking place. As a satirist first and foremost, Kantemir was certainly familiar with Juvenal, but modelled himself primarily on Boileau whom he translated together with Fontenelle and Voltaire; Trediakovsky's contribution to the epic was neither Homeric nor Virgilian, but in the form of adaptations of Tallemant's *Voyage à l'isle d'amour* and Fénelon's *Télémaque*, and when he chose to essay the Pindaric ode, to *pindarizovat*, as he called it, in his ode on the capture of Danzig in 1734, he simply followed Boileau's classicist Pindaric adaptation, *Sur la prise de Namur*, without exhibiting any real interest in or familiarity with the original Pindaric style; the master, above all, of the solemn state panegyric ode, Lomonosov derived much less from Pindar or Horace and the other Latin poets he translated than from the classicist (later) Malherbe in France or the late German Baroque poet Johann Christian Günther; except for lip-service to Classical Antiquity (notably in his verse epistles on language and literature in the 1740s) and a few small imitations of Horace, Sappho, and Anacreon, Sumarokov, who by training and inclination had less reason to be interested in Classical Antiquity than Kantemir, Trediakovsky, or Lomonosov, seldom strayed from French classicist models and when he translated, like Kantemir and Trediakovsky, his choices were almost exclusively from among the works of seventeenth- and early eighteenth-century French classicist writers.

2. The Russians shared with Western classicism the greater

Western familiarity with and regard for Roman culture as opposed to the Greek, the legacy certainly of the Renaissance and of the former universality of Latin in Western, Central, and parts of Eastern Europe (e.g. Poland, Hungary). Until the Hellenism of the later eighteenth and early nineteenth centuries, Greek authors were known but were less frequently turned to as sources than Roman. Virgil *not* Homer was the model for the classicist epic (with the possible exception of Fénelon's quasi-epic *Télémaque*); not Theocritus, but Virgil again, was assumed to be the greatest eclogic poet of Classical Antiquity and hence the principal source of inspiration for classicist enthusiasts of the genre; the classical comic dramatist held in highest esteem was Terence and, to a lesser extent, because he was coarser, Plautus, not Aristophanes or Menander; Seneca not Aeschylus or Euripides was deemed the flower of classical tragedy; Juvenal was to be consulted on satire, Martial on the epigram, Tibullus on the elegy, and, until the attribution of some profound political wisdom to Anacreon later in the century, Horace dominated the lyric.[1]

The pattern of Russian literary translation in the first half of the eighteenth century points up this distribution of interest. Kantemir translated poems of Anacreon, but these are far outweighed by his French translations and the influence on his work of Horace and Juvenal; Trediakovsky translated a chorus from a Senecan tragedy and several fables of Aesop mainly as exercises in iambic and trochaic hexameters, but as regards Classical Antiquity seems to have been most interested in making Rome and its culture more familiar to his fellow Russians than Greece, a fact handsomely demonstrated by the years devoted to translating the many volumes of the Roman histories of the French scholars Rollin and Crevier; apart from a few anacreontics published only much later, the bulk of Lomonosov's translations were from Latin—Virgil, Ovid, Lucretius, Martial, and Juvenal; they appeared for the most part as citations in his book on rhetoric, *Ritorika*; and finally Sumarokov, as we have seen, limited his translations almost exclusively to French classicism.

[1] For a general survey of Horace in Russia, see: Wolfgang Busch, *Horaz in Russland* (München, 1964).

General assumptions about the dissemination of classical culture in eighteenth-century Russia also have to be qualified in the light of the relatively late appearance of translations and original works with classical subjects. Virtually all the translations by Russian authors from the Greek and Latin in the first half of the century were printed only after 1750: Trediakovsky's translations of Seneca and Aesop, for example, appeared for the first time in the volume of his original compositions and translations published in 1752, while Lomonosov's *Rhetoric*, containing his classical translations, came out in 1759. On the basis of the published translations then, classical literature, particularly that of Greece, was still a relatively uncommon cultural experience in Russia in the first half of the eighteenth century.

Very much the same situation prevailed with respect to original Russian compositions in the first half of the eighteenth century making use of classical settings, characters, motifs, and so on. Until about mid century there is little real use of Classical Antiquity. Perhaps the first works that come to mind after Trediakovsky's *Tilemakhida*, which is primarily a translation and was published in 1766, are the tragedies of Trediakovsky and Lomonosov: the *Deidamiya* of the former and the latter's *Demofont*. But *Deidamiya* was written late in 1750 and published in 1755; *Demofont* was also written toward the end of 1750 and published in 1752. Lomonosov's 'classical' idyll *Polidor*, which is really a panegyric using Greek motifs to celebrate the elevation of Kirila Razumovsky to the hetmanship of the Ukraine, also belongs to the mid century; it was written and published in 1750. The programmatic *Razgovor s Anakreonom* (*A Conversation with Anacreon*), also by Lomonosov, which relates to the surfacing of the tradition of the *poésie légère* in Sumarokov's writing, was composed even later, sometime between 1756 and 1761, and published only in 1771. In one sense, though, it is an earlier work. The anacreontic songs in it, to which Lomonosov offers polemical replies on the matter of lofty as opposed to light poetry, were translated earlier in the poet's career. Sumarokov's 'classical' works, which are more interesting than those of Trediakovsky or Lomonosov, also belong to the second half of the century. They consist of

Anacreontic, Sapphic, and Horatian poems, written between 1755 and 1758 and notable primarily for Sumarokov's attempts to use classical Greek metres in response probably to the examples of these given by Trediakovsky in his revised treatise on versification of 1752, and eclogues and idylls in conventional alexandrines composed in 1768.

About the time Sumarokov started experimenting with classical Greek lyric metres in 1755, becoming thereby the first Russian poet to do so in something other than a treatise on prosody, one of the most far-reaching developments in the Western rediscovery of the classical world occurred. That was the publication in 1755 of the German art historian Johann Joachim Winckelmann's now famous treatise *Gedanken über die Nachahmung der griechischen Werken in der Malerei und Bildkunst*. To Winckelmann, the essential attributes of classical Greek art were 'eine edle Einfalt und eine stille Grösse' (a noble simplicity and a calm grandeur), a view developed further in his history of ancient art, *Geschichte der Kunst des Altertums* (1764).

If Winckelmann's rapturous pronouncements about classical Greek art, coming not long after the excavations at Herculaneum (1738) and Pompeii (1748), did not actually motivate, they gave considerable stimulus to contemporary artists to seek inspiration directly among the splendours of the ancient world and not through the medium of often distorted Renaissance and classicist interpretations and transmissions. As the second half of the century progressed, classical Rome, which heretofore had been the focus of the classicist interest in Antiquity, receded in importance (until the Roman revival in Napoleonic France) and interest began to centre on Greece. Roman culture was now seen as essentially derivative and hence less valuable, a matter of no small importance at a time when the concept of original composition was being widely disseminated with the advent of pre-romanticism. Winckelmann's formulaic 'edle Einfalt' and 'stille Grösse' became universally accepted as the hallmark of classical Greek art as the new cult of Antiquity with its Hellenistic focus began to crystallize.

For European literature in the second half of the eighteenth and the early years of the nineteenth centuries the results of the new enthusiasm for Classical Antiquity were formidable. The pace of

artistically noteworthy translation quickened, classical scholarship
made great strides, and writers sought to capture in their original
works the qualities they now attributed to classical Greece—the
noble simplicity and calm grandeur Winckelmann spoke of and
the harmonious balance of life's forces they saw as the ideal of
Greek art at its best. More and more Greek motifs were introduced
and a distinct literary Hellenism came into being. In the epic,
Homer not Virgil now became the model,[2] the *Aeneid* descending
to the butt of the travesty of the mock epic genre (the precedent
having already been established by Paul Scarron's seventeenth-
century French parody, *Virgile travesti*); the light, frivolous writings of Anacreon were put almost on a par with the *Odes* of
Horace and the Greek poet newly esteemed as a philosopher
whose thought, taken as a complement to Horace's, could come
to supplant Christianity as a source of spiritual guidance. The
comparison of Christianity and the gods of the ancients in Schiller's
Die Götter Griechenlands (1788), for example, works to the clear
disadvantage of the former, just as Gibbon's *Decline and Fall of the
Roman Empire* is permeated with anti-Christian sentiment.

Greek art, it was believed, represented the most perfect creation
of the human spirit. 'In the history of mankind', wrote Herder,
himself an ardent Hellenophile, in his *Auch eine Philosophie der
Geschichte zur Bildung der Menschheit* (1774), 'Greece will remain
the place where mankind experienced its fairest youth and bridal
beauty . . . noble youth with fair anointed limbs, favourite of all
the Graces, beloved of all the Muses, victor in Olympia and all
the other games, spirit and body together in one single flower in
bloom.'[3] And, in another place, still more rapturously: 'Greece,
type and exemplar of all beauty, grace, and simplicity! Youthful

    [2] For an exhaustive study of Russian translations of Homer in the eighteenth
and nineteenth centuries, see: A. N. Egunov, *Gomer v russkikh perevodakh XVIII—
XIXvv* (Moscow and Leningrad, 1964).
    [3] '. . . in der Geschichte der Menschheit wird Griechenland ewig der Platz blei-
ben, wo sie ihre schönste Jugend und Brautblüte verlebt hat . . . edler Jüngling
mit schönen gesalbten Gliedern, Liebling aller Grazien und Liebhaber aller Musen,
Sieger in Olympia und all' anderm Spiele, Geist und Körper zusammen nur eine
blühende Blume!' Johann Gottfried Herder, *Werke*, ed. Karl-Gustav Gerold, ii
(München, 1953), 23. Quoted in English, source unidentified, in Hugh Honour,
Neo-Classicism (Harmondsworth, 1968), pp. 61–2.

blossoming of the human race—Oh would that it could have lasted forever!'[4] To the Swiss scientist J. K. Lavater, the excellence of classical Greek sculpture reflected the superiority of the ancient Greek physique, a view he presented in his *Physiognomische Fragmente* (1775–8). Out of a desire to enjoy a more perfect knowledge of the beauties of Greek literature, not only were older, more classicist translations, particularly of the Homeric epic, updated and 'authenticized' (such as the English poet Cowper's ambition to improve on Pope's version of the *Iliad* to the extent of wanting to translate it into the English of Chaucer's time—he finally settled for Miltonic blank verse), but new translations far more faithful to the spirit and letter of the originals were undertaken such as those of both the *Iliad* (1781) and the *Odyssey* (1793) by the German poet J. H. Voss (1751–1826). New appreciations of Homer also came off the presses such as Robert Wood's *Essay on the Original Genius and Writings of Homer* (1769), which was translated into German in 1771 and into French some four years later.

For several reasons, analysis of which would extend far beyond the scope of this study, the European Hellenism of the second half of the eighteenth and the early nineteenth centuries had its greatest impact on German writing and thought. A list of major works in the Hellenistic vein by German classicist and *Sturm und Drang* writers surely would encompass nearly every major figure of the period. Apart from the better-known poems and dramas of Goethe and Schiller, we have to consider such representative contributions as Wieland's *Agathon* (1766–7), *Musarion* (1768), *Idris und Zenide* (1768), *Die Geschichte der Abderiten* (1773–81), *Sokrates Mainomenos oder die Dialogen des Diogenes von Sinope* (1770), *Agathodämon* (1799), and *Aristipp und einige seiner Zeitgenossen* (1801), and Hölderlin's *Hyperion oder der Eremit in Griechenland* (1797–9), *Der Tod des Empedokles* (1797–9), and a series of poems in Greek alcaic metre. The same passion for the classical Greek past informed German scholarship as well.

---

[4] 'Griechenland! Urbild und Vorbild aller Schöne, Grazie und Einfalt! Jugendblüte des menschlichen Geschlechts — o hätte sie ewig dauern können!' Herder, op. cit., p. 25.

Winckelmann's studies in classical Greek art, followed by those of Lessing (*Laokoon oder über die Grenzen der Malerei und Poesie,* 1766), and Hölderlin (*Geschichte der schönen Künste unter den Griechen bis zu Ende des Perikleischen Zeitalters,* 1790), were augmented by the highly influential literary studies of Friedrich Schlegel from the end of the century: *Über das Studium der griechischen Poesie* (1797) and the *Geschichte der Poesie der Griechen und Römer* (1798).

The very special appeal of classical Greece for Germany in the later eighteenth and early nineteenth centuries was really a unique development only in the sense of degree. All European culture fell under the sway of Greek Antiquity during this period—the first truly meaningful exposure of European civilization to the classical Greek—but none so massively, so overwhelmingly as the German.

If the English produced no outstanding Greek-oriented scholarship to rival Gibbon's *Decline and Fall of the Roman Empire* or the Latin skills of a Samuel Johnson and a Walter Savage Landor, literary Hellenism was handsomely represented somewhat later by such Romantic works as Keats's *Endymion* (1818), Shelley's *Prometheus Unbound* (1820), and Thomas Moore's *The Epicurean* (1827).

The harvest of the new Hellenism in France was also impressive in its own way. One of the earliest notable works was the *Voyage du jeune Anacharsis en Grèce* (1788) by the abbé Jean-Jacques Barthélemy. It was followed soon by the *Hermès, Bucoliques,* and other poems of André Chénier, the foremost Hellenist of late eighteenth-century France, the prose poems *Antigone* (1814) and *Orphée* (1827) of Pierre Simon-Ballanche, and the *Poèmes antiques et modernes* (1826) of Alfred de Vigny.

Against this background, what of Russian Hellenism? Although certain parallels suggest themselves in the pattern of literary evolution in both Germany and Russia in the eighteenth century, Classical Antiquity and Hellenism, above all, never took hold of the Russian consciousness in the way it did the German. The absence of the Renaissance in Russia doubtless must be considered the deciding factor. Nevertheless, Russian literature in the later eighteenth and early nineteenth centuries also responded to the new European enthusiasm for the classical past and generated an interesting Hellenism of its own.

The anacreontic, which had already caught the attention of Russian poets in the first half of the eighteenth century, was cultivated still more extensively in the second half, notably by Sumarokov in the 1750s, Kheraskov in the 1760s,[5] Muravëv, Lvov,[6] Derzhavin, and Karamzin in the last three decades of the century, and bore more original fruit in the poetry of the pre-romantic Yury Neledinsky-Meletsky (1752–1828), whom the poet Konstantin Nikalaevich Batyushkov (1787–1855) characterized as the 'Anacreon of our time'.[7]

The *Greek Anthology*, which attracted many European poets in the later eighteenth century, was first known in Russia in a *French* translation by the Russian writer S. S. Uvarov. Batyushkov, who knew no Greek, translated several of the Uvarov versions into Russian and with Uvarov's assistance prepared an article on the *Anthology*.[8] The translations, which are free and in some respects meritorious as original poetry, were published as a separate booklet in 1820. Batyushkov followed this the next year with a cycle of poems based on classical Greek models entitled *Podrazhaniya drevnim* (*Imitations of the Ancients*).

Prior to the Uvarov translations and the 'classical' poetry that followed soon after, Batyushkov had already demonstrated a profound admiration for Classical Antiquity. In the prose piece *Progulka v Akademiyu Khudozhestv* (*A Stroll to the Academy of Arts*, 1814), for example, he praised in classical art the 'echo of the deep

---

[5] Although titled *Anacreontics* and adhering to one of the traditional anacreontic meters, Kheraskov's poems in this vein actually exceed the limits of the genre by becoming a programmatic espousal of the cause of the poetry of feeling.

[6] Lvov's translations from Anacreon, published in 1794, were not done from the originals but from literal translations supplied him by a Greek ecclesiastic living in Russia named Evgeny Bulgaris (1715–1806).

[7] K. N. Batyushkov, *Polnoe sobranie stikhotvoreniy*, ed. N. V. Fridman (Moscow and Leningrad, 1964), p. 15.

[8] Ibid., p. 315. A detailed analysis of Batyushkov's works in a classical vein, as well as those of the poets Delvig and Gnedich, can be found in Mara Kažoknies's *Studien zur Rezeption der Antike bei Russischen Dichtern zu Beginn des XIX. Jahrhunderts* (München, 1968). My thanks are due to Professor Roberta Reeder of Tulane University for bringing this work to my attention.

knowledge of nature, the emotions and the human heart' ('otgo-
losok glubokikh poznaniy prirody, strastey i chelovecheskogo
serdsta'),[9] while in his better-known lecture *Rech o vliyanii lëgkoy
poezii na yazyk* (*The Influence of Light Poetry on Language*, July
1816), he was unreserved in his enthusiasm especially for Anacreon, Sappho, Catullus, and Tibullus, among the ancients.

Two of Batyushkov's early original poems inspired by classical
Greece won the immediate admiration of his contemporaries:
Vakkhanka (*Bacchante*, 1815), a short vivacious poem in trochaic
trimeters about the pursuit of a young nymph at a bacchanalia,
which Belinsky called the 'apotheosis of sensual passion',[10] and
Gesiod i Omer — soperniki (*Hesiod and Homer—Rivals*, end of 1816–
January 1817), a rather free translation of Milveux's *Combat
d'Homère et d'Hésiode*,[11] but with some original accents.

The confluence of rococo taste and the cult of Antiquity in the
works of the much-admired eighteenth-century German poet
Wieland produced one of the masterpieces of German Hellenism
and rococo literature, the miniature verse epic *Musarion oder die
Philosophie der Grazien* (1768). Similar circumstances led to the
appearance of an outstanding and long-appealing work of eighteenth-century Russian poetry, Ippolit Bogdanovich's *Dushenka*
(1778–83). Although usually characterized as a mock epic, which
it is in a certain sense, *Dushenka* is something else as well that sets
it poles apart from that other famous mock epic of eighteenth-
century Russian literature, Vasily Maykov's *Elisey*. Like Wieland's
Musarion, it is a splendid specimen of a rococo poem inspired by
classical Greece. Indebted to La Fontaine's *Les Amours de Psyché et
de Cupidon* and derived ultimately from an episode in Apuleius'
Golden Ass, *Dushenka* aspires to the same idea of grace and
moderation embodied in the 'philosophy of the Graces' as Wieland's *Musarion*.

The new Hellenism also had an impact on Russian prosody.
To all intents and purposes, the problem of Russian metric reform had been resolved by 1752. The work most notably of

---

9 K. N. Batyushkov, *Sochineniya*, ed. D. D. Blagoy (Moscow and Leningrad, 1934), p. 329.
10 K. N. Batyushkov, *Polnoe sobranie stikhotvoreniy*, p. 47.
11 Ibid., pp. 307–8.

Trediakovsky and Lomonosov had guaranteed the primacy of the syllabo-tonic system and by the time Trediakovsky's revised treatise on versification appeared in 1752, there was no question of the course Russian metrics would follow. Binary metre was used far more often than ternary and the iambus held sway over the trochee. Classical Greek and Latin metres were known and described in the major treatises on prosody, but Russian poets did not make any real attempt to use them until the second half of the century. Trediakovsky's preference for the hexameter instead of the French-derived alexandrine in his translation of Fénelon's *Télémaque* is probably the first example that comes to mind. The translation was first brought out in 1766, however. Before then, doubtless under the influence of the two examples Trediakovsky gives in his treatise of 1752, Sumarokov used the Greek sapphic metre in his *Gimn Venere* (*Hymn to Venus*) and *Oda saficheskaya* (*Sapphic Ode*), and the Horatian or alcaic metre in his *Oda goriatsianskaya*. However, in all three instances Sumarokov parted company with his classical models by introducing rhyme. Trediakovsky's version of *Télémaque* when it appeared in 1766 was the first significant use of classical metrics in eighteenth-century Russian poetry. Translators of classical literature as a rule employed Russian metres instead of Greek or Latin; thus the translations of parts of the *Iliad* or *Odyssey* that were made from time to time throughout the eighteenth century used the Russian equivalent of the French alexandrine.

Although not as well known as he should be, the interesting sentimentalist poet Mikhail Nikita Muravëv (1757–1807), who translated from the works of Homer, Sappho, Anacreon, Horace, Virgil, Livy, and Petronius, among classical authors, made the first attempt by an eighteenth-century Russian writer to translate verses from the *Iliad* in classical hexameters. This was in 1778. Little else of particular interest in the field of Russian metrics occurred until the late 1780s.

Doubtless in response to the new Hellenism and the then fashionable cult of Antiquity in European literature, which he could have become acquainted with not only through literary events in Russia but through his familiarity as well with contemporary German letters, the most important prose writer of eighteenth-century Russia, Nikolay Karamzin, experimented with a variety of metres between 1787 and 1793:[12] iambic hexameters (*Iz pisma k I. I. Dmitrievu*, 1787, and *Gimn*, 1789, from Thomson's *Seasons*), trochaic tetrameter ('Chasto zdes v yudoli mrachnoy . . .', 1787, 'Schaste istinno khranitsya . . .', 1787, *Graf Gvarinos*, 1789), iambic tetrameter (*Gospodinu D[mitrievu] na bolezn ego*, 1788, *Vesennyaya pesn malankholika*, 1788, *Voyennaya pesn*, 1788), iambic trimeter (*Anakreonticheskie stikhi*, 1788, *Mishenke*, 1790, *Fillise*, 1790), dactylic-trochaic trimeter (*Osen*, 1789, *Vyzdorovlenie*, 1789), and dactylic-trochaic tetrameter (*K D[mitrievu]*, 1788). Particularly noteworthy in Karamzin's metric experimentation is his preference for *unrhymed* verse, a feature of classical poetry which only on rare occasions had attracted the previous interest of Russian poets. In fact, the only important use of unrhymed verse before Karamzin was in Trediakovsky's *Tilemakhida*.

Karamzin's experiments were anything but unique and should be thought of more as a response to the literary climate of the time with its marked classical leanings. Karamzin's prominent contemporary, Alexander Radishchev, though not associated primarily with poetry, not only wrote several quite interesting poetical works (later in his career, unlike Karamzin with whom the poetry comes instead at the beginning) but dealt at some length with problems of Russian poetry and prosody in his *Journey from St. Petersburg to Moscow* (1790) and was no less interested in metric experimentation than Karamzin.

The thrust of Radishchev's remarks on poetry in the *Journey* can be summed up in just a few words: Russian poetry has been too long under the tyranny of rhyme and the iambus and it was high time for poets to start cultivating alternatives. As in the case of Karamzin, the inspiration was attributable, above all, to the impact of contemporary German literature with its strong Hellenistic character—like Karamzin, Radishchev knew Germany at

---

[12] On Karamzin's early poetry, see especially: Anthony Cross, 'Problems of Form and Literary Influence in the Poetry of Karamzin', *Slavic Review*, xxvii, no. 1 (Mar. 1968), 39–48.

first hand and was familiar with the poetry, metric innovations, and literary views of such figures as Klopstock, Wieland, and Herder.

Radishchev's espousal of prosodic variety and his desire especially to rehabilitate the trochee resulted in several interesting works: the *Pamyatnik daktilokhoreicheskomu vityazyu* (*Monument to a Dactylo-Trochaic Champion*, 1801), an enthusiastic defence of the much-berated Trediakovsky; *Saficheskie strofy* (*Sapphic Stanzas*, 1801), in which he brings Sumarokov's earlier use of the sapphic form into conformity with classical practice by abandoning rhyme; the long poems *Bova* (1799–1801, first published 1807) and *Pesn istoricheskaya* (*Historical Song*, first published 1807), in which he uses the by then familiar unrhymed trochaic tetrameter; *Pesni, petye na sostyazaniyakh v chest drevnim slavyanskim bozhestvam* (*Songs Sung at Contests in Honour of the Ancient Slavic Deities*, first published 1807), where Radishchev not only forsakes rhyme but enriches the rhythm by varying line length and metre within the same work; and the philosophical and historical *Osmnadtsatoe stoletie* (*The Eighteenth Century*, written 1801, first published 1807), by which Radishchev became the first Russian poet to make extensive use of the classical Greek elegaic couplet.

The same year in which the first collected edition of Radishchev's works, containing his metric experiments, appeared—1807 —Russian Hellenism truly came of age. It was in this year that the writings of Russia's foremost Hellenist, Nikolay Ivanovich Gnedich (1784–1833), first came to the attention of the reading public.[13] Gnedich's greatest contribution to Russian literature was, of course, his translation of the *Iliad*, the first complete translation of the Greek epic into Russian. Gnedich's version, which was made from the original, unlike the later translation of the *Odyssey* by the poet Zhukovsky, was done over a period of about sixteen years, from 1812 to 1828. The entire translation was published for the first time in 1828. Prior to Gnedich, the closest anyone came to a complete translation of the *Iliad* was the poet Kostrov's version of the first six books in alexandrines, published in 1787. In 1807,

[13] For a valuable general introduction to Gnedich, see: N. I. Gnedich, *Stikhotvoreniya*, ed. I. N. Medvedeva (Leningrad, 1956), pp. 5–55.

Gnedich began what he envisaged as no more than a continuation of Kostrov employing the same metric pattern. But he grew enamoured of the project and probably in 1811 decided on an entirely independent version, one for which he chose to abandon the alexandrine of French classicism in favour of the classical Greek hexameter. The matter of the choice of metre became a subject of debate at the time, with Napoleon's invasion of Russia deciding definitively against the continued use of the French-derived alexandrine and the issue then boiling down to arguments involving Gnedich, Uvarov, and the poet and dramatist Kapnist concerning the respective merits of the classical hexameter and the metre of the Russian folk epos, the *bylina*. Rejecting the classical dactylic-spondaic hexameter as virtually impossible in Russian and expressing dissatisfaction even with Gnedich's dactylic-trochaic hexameter, Kapnist advocated the metric pattern of the *bylina*; Karamzin's *bylina*-inspired poem *Ilya Muromets* (1794) was held up as something of an example worthy of emulation. Gnedich settled, however, on the hexameter; to achieve a richer rhythmic pattern he occasionally interspersed trochees among the dactyls and, following Trediakovsky, permitted some lines to begin with pyrrhics.

Gnedich's skilful handling of metre and his admirable resolution of stylistic problems contributed to the great success of the translation, despite some carping about archaisms from a few critics. To the contemporary Russian reader, the work was not only a brilliant translation of Homer's poem but, given the subject of the *Iliad*, an epic of contemporary relevance in view of Napoleon's recent invasion and the great campaign by the Russians to rid their country of the French.

Gnedich's copious research into the Homeric poems and classical Greek civilization in general, reflected in the very extensive commentary to his translation of the *Iliad*, led also to translations of the Homeric Hymns: *Gomerov gimn Minerve* (*Homer's Hymn to Minerva*, 1807?), *Gomerov gimn Diane* (*Homer's Hymn to Diane*, 1807?), *Gomerov gimn Venere* (*Homer's Hymn to Venus*, 1807?). Involvement in Homeric scholarship inevitably led as well to his consideration of the problem of the creation of the Homeric epics, which he deals with in the poems *Setovanie Fetidy na grobe Akhillesa* (*The Lament of Thetis Over the Grave of Achilles*, 1815) and the lengthy *Rozhdenie Gomera* (*The Birth of Homer*, 1816). Another classical genre to which Gnedich addressed himself and which the classicists of the seventeenth and eighteenth centuries had carried quite far from the Greek and Roman sources was the idyll. Gnedich's major effort at giving the Russian reader a better idea of what the classical Greek idyll of Theocritus was like was *Sirakuzyanki, ili Prazdnik Adonisa* (*The Girls of Syracuse, or The Holiday of Adonis*, 1820–1), a translation of a work by Theocritus. The novelty of Gnedich's version was his avoidance of classicist stylization in favour of a natural style appropriate to that of the Greek original. Reflecting the crystallizing nationalism and folk-loristic proclivities of the romantic movement, Gnedich apparently also held the conviction that once contemporary authors could appreciate the values of the classical idyll of Theocritus, which he hoped his version of *The Girls of Syracuse* conveyed, it would be possible to develop a Russian national idyllic genre appropriate, above all, for treating of folk subjects. The prose introduction to *The Girls of Syracuse* makes this ambition abundantly clear. Gnedich went beyond theory, however, and within a year of the Theocritus translation produced an original idyll entitled *Rybaki* (*Fishermen*, 1821, published as a separate work in 1822). In order to envelop his simple Russian fishermen with a Homeric aura, to lend them moreover a certain dignity as literary subjects in his readers' eyes, Gnedich approached the matter of style more conservatively than in his Theocritus translation. The result was a certain archaic quality and bookishness; nevertheless, *Fishermen* still met with a favourable reception, particularly among the poets of Decembrist leanings to whom such a heroic idealization of simple people had a strong appeal.

Of the poets influenced by Gnedich's idylls the most important was Anton Antonovich Delvig (1798—1831), the editor after 1825 of the yearly miscellany, *Northern Flowers*. Delvig's interest in the genre dates back to his days at the Lyceum at Tsarskoe Selo where he and Pushkin were close friends: between 1814 and 1817 he wrote his first idyll—*Tsefiz*—a translation actually of the German

Zefis by the poet Ewald Christian Kleist (1715–59). But more serious cultivation of the genre had to wait until 1821, precisely the year when Gnedich undertook his most important work in the form. Delvig not only knew Gnedich, but was an admirer of his. Not unnaturally, when the older poet probed the possibilities of the classical idyll for future Russian poetic development Delvig renewed his earlier interest and set out on the same path. Between 1821 and 1829 he produced several idylls, among them: *Damon* (1821), *Kupalnitsy* (*The Bathing Women*, 1824), which Prince Mirsky incidentally speaks of in his history of Russian literature as 'unquestionably the highest achievement in Russian poetry in the more purely sensuous vision of classical antiquity',[14] *Druzya* (*Friends*, 1826), *Konets zolotogo veka* (*The End of the Golden Age*, 1828), with an ending similar to Shakespeare's description of the death of Ophelia (as Delvig himself points out in a note), *Otstavnoy soldat* (*The Retired Soldier*, 1829), a 'Russianized' idyll composed of a dialogue between a soldier and a shepherd and inspired, in part, by Gnedich's *Fisherman*, and *Izobretenie Vayaniya* (*The Invention of Sculpture*, 1829), a poetic account of the origins of the sculptor's art.

Accompanying Gnedich's major and most influential Hellenistic works were others in a minor key. These include the *Podrazhanie Goratsiyu* (*Imitation of Horace*, 1812), a free translation of Horace, *Odes* i. 16, a 'light' poem *K Morfeyu* (*To Morpheus*, 1816), a translation of a poem by Anacreon (*Ode XLIII*, 1822) of which earlier versions had been done by Lvov in 1794 and Derzhavin in 1804, excerpts from the eleventh book of the *Odyssey* (1827), and others. Apart from the use of unrhymed verse in both the classical translations and original compositions, which was no longer a novelty by Gnedich's time, and his 'renovation' of the hexameter, Gnedich experimented also with unrhymed anapaestic, amphibrachic, and dactylic lines and chose as the metre for *Fishermen*, which he regarded as the best of his original poems, the then rarely encountered unrhymed five-foot amphibrachic line with feminine ending, a prosodic form known to Classical Antiquity.

Gnedich's important contribution to Russian Hellenism had a

---

[14] *A History of Russian Literature* (New York, 1958), p. 81.

contemporary as well as classical dimension. The Greek independence movement of the 1820s aroused the enthusiasm of the political liberals and romantics throughout Europe, and when Byron made the cause his own, the appeal of the Greek struggle became irresistible. The events in the Balkans were followed closely in Russia, above all, by the Decembrists whose own abortive revolt was modelled in part on the Greek liberation movement. Counting several of the Decembrist poets among his closest acquaintances, Gnedich also took an interest in the world of contemporary Greece. To his translations of classical Greek poetry and original compositions based on classical models, he added a cycle of translations of the *Popular Songs of the Greeks of Our Own Day* (*Prostonarodnye pesni nyneshnikh grekov*, published in book form in early February 1825), based on the French collection by the romantic revolutionary poet Claude Fauriel (1772–1844), *Les Chants populaires de la Grèce moderne* (vol. i, 1824; vol. ii, 1825).[15] Gnedich prefaced his translations, which are notable especially for their metric variety, with a two-part prose foreword in which he repeats factual information contained in Fauriel's work and then, more originally, considers the links between Greek popular poetry and Russian, going back to Greco-Slavic relations in Antiquity. The reception of the translations was at once favourable and writers and critics from Pushkin to Belinsky were lavish in their praise.

Gnedich's interest in the contemporary Greeks and the liberation struggle went back at least to 1821 when he published in *Vestnik Evropy* (*The Messenger of Europe*) a reasonably close translation of a Greek revolutionary hymn by the Greek poet and revolutionary Constantine Rigas (1754–98), which Gnedich titled *Voenny gimn grekov* (*Military Hymn of the Greeks*). Rigas's original collection of hymns was published in Jassy only in 1814, but circulated widely in manuscript during the poet's lifetime.[16] In the course of his trip to Greece in 1811, Byron transcribed them and then made his own translations, doubtless contributing most to their general European popularity. Gnedich's translation of

---

[15] Gnedich, *Stikhotvoreniya*, pp. 817–20.
[16] Ibid., pp. 805–6.

Rigas, followed a few years later by his translations of Greek popular songs and the attempt by the tsar's censors to exclude the version of the Rigas poem from the 1832 collected edition of Gnedich's works, left no doubt of the poet's liberal inclinations among the revolutionary enthusiasts of the day, a fact confirmed by the number of poems addressed to him by poets associated with or sympathetic to the Decembrist conspiracy.

The popularity of the Greek cause among the romantics resulted in a proliferation of poems with contemporary Greek subjects. Encouraged by Gnedich's example, Russian poets, particularly those on the political left, were quick to add their own voices, so that by the late 1820s Russia had an ample poetry on modern Greek themes. There was Vilgelm Karlovich Kyukhelbeker's *Grecheskaya pesn* (*Greek Song*, 1821), Orest Mikhaylovich Somov's *Gretsiya* (*Greece*, 1821–2), Ivan Ivanovich Kozlov's *Plenny grek v temnitse* (*Captive Greek in Prison*, 1821–2), Vasily Vasilevich Kapnist's *Vozzvanie na pomoshch Gretsii* (*An Appeal to Aid the Greeks*) and *K vosstavshemu grecheskomy narodu* (*To the Insurgent Greek Nation*), both written in 1822, Vasily Ivanovich Tumansky's *Grecheskaya oda*, *Pesn grecheskogo voina* (*Greek Ode, Song of a Greek Warrior*, 1823), three sonnets entitled *Gretsiya* (*Greece*, 1825), and *Grechanke* (*To a Greek Woman*, 1827), Vasily Nikiforovich Grigorev's *Grechanka* (*A Greek Woman*, 1824), and Dmitry Vladimirovich Venevitinov's unfinished *Smert Bayrona* (*Death of Byron*, 1825) containing a dialogue between Byron and a Greek leader, and *Pesn greka* (*Song of a Greek*, 1825).

By 1825 and the suppression of the Decembrist revolt, literary Hellenism had fully come of age in Russia. In its classical aspect it had succeeded in establishing the influence of Greece and Rome in Russian culture, while in its contemporary aspect it had brought Russian literature into the mainstream of European literary and political romanticism. Hellenism in Russia never produced the kind of aesthetic and literary theoretical scholarship that it did in Germany, but the German situation was virtually unique and Russian Hellenism in this respect was not radically different from the French or English. The impact of Hellenism on Russian literature was considerable and resulted in several interesting and important developments, which this study has tried to characterize. If no splendid romantic works in the classical Hellenistic vein were produced in Russia to rival those of Keats or Shelley in England, it is probably because Russian romanticism developed in a truly significant way only after 1825 by which time Hellenism had already lost its grip on the European literary consciousness. But here a parallel with France suggests itself, for the romantic movement came late to France also with no brilliant flowering of a romantic classical Hellenism as an outstanding attribute of it.

Part Two
Aspects of Petrine Russia

JAMES CRACRAFT

3 *Feofan Prokopovich*

PROKOPOVICH (1681–1736) lived at a time of profound cultural crisis not only in Russia, but in Europe generally, and in his career and writings can be discerned the uncertainties, the ambiguities, the frequent paradoxes of that difficult age as well as the method of their eventual solution—the ultimate direction, in Snow's phrase, of time's arrow. His was, I have suggested elsewhere,[1] the first authentic voice in Russia of the early Enlightenment, and a more appropriate figure to consider in a book of essays devoted to Russian culture in the eighteenth century is unimaginable.

For Prokopovich was both a friend of piety and an implacable foe of superstition, both a preacher-polemicist and a government propagandist, unashamedly the outstanding champion of the new learning and a man, we must suppose, who regularly prayed. He was the close collaborator of Peter the Great in the later and decisive years of a reign that is still rightly regarded as marking Russia's great lurch into modern times. He was the chief ideologist of the revolutionary Petrine state whose doctrines no doubt helped to sustain the awakening minds and troubled consciences of the ruling classes of his own and succeeding generations. He was the author, in the literal sense of the word, of Peter's church reform, the most radical, that is the most clean in its break with the past, of all the Petrine reforms. And it is my tentative conclusion that he invented not only the Holy Synod, both the name and the thing (this can be fairly well documented),[2] but the titles 'All-Russian Empire' and 'All-Russian Emperor', which like the Synod itself would for two hundred years remain signs of that most absolute of modern European states.

---

[1] *The Church Reform of Peter the Great* (London and Stanford, Cal., 1971), p. 54.
[2] See ibid., esp. pp. 153–7, 178 and n. 4.

Moreover, a versifier himself of transitional importance, he was the esteemed patron of Antiokh Kantemir, the first poet of the Russian language, of Tatishchev, the first Russian historian, and of Lomonosov, the polymath for whom is claimed a place in the pantheon of the Enlightenment proper. Yet he was, too, the author of learned treatises *De Deo Uno*, *De Deo Trino*, *De Processione Spiritus Sancti*, which first as lectures and then in print provided theological students throughout the eighteenth century with a measure of relief from the recondite nonsense of contemporary Russian scholasticism. Indeed, as well as countless tomes by Roman Catholic and Reformed divines whose present obscurity seems wholly deserved, there is evidence that Prokopovich had read, or was well aware of, the works of Erasmus and Luther, of Buddeus and Bellarmine, of Descartes; of Galileo, Kepler, Bacon, Machiavelli, Grotius, and Pufendorf; of Guicciardini, Hobbes, and Locke. And in his argumentation he was at once passionate, subjective, even irrational—and abstract, consensus-seeking, scientific: relentlessly logical and highly rhetorical: naïve in a monkish way and coldly realistic; and would appeal equally to nature and to authority, to reason and to revelation. Prokopovich steadfastly believed in the reformative power of education—so long as it was grounded in the 'fear of God' and controlled by the Church. He was a Greek-Russian Orthodox of pronounced Protestant leanings, a 'Latinizer' who hated the Roman Church, a humanist corrupted by the politics of monarchical absolutism, a man of religion who contributed mightily to the secularization of Russian culture and society. An essay in English describing his life, however briefly, and attempting to suggest the nature and scope of his achievement, is long overdue.[3]

[3] The principal studies of Prokopovich are in pre-Revolutionary Russian: I. Chistovich, *Feofan Prokopovich i ego vremya* (St. Petersburg, 1868)—a major work of some 700 pages; P. Morozov, *Feofan Prokopovich kak pisatel* (St. Petersburg, 1880); and B. Titlinov, 'Feofan Prokopovich', *Russky biografichesky slovar*, xxv (St. Petersburg, 1913), 399–448, with complete bibliography. The foremost authority on the church reform of Peter the Great, P. V. Verkhovskoy, should also be consulted: *Uchrezhdenie Dukhovnoy Kollegii i Dukhovny Reglament* (Rostov-on-Don, 1916), i. 116–41: also ii, *passim*, for critical editions of some of Prokopovich's works; and Yurii Samarin's 1843 dissertation on Prokopovich as a churchman and rival of Stefan Yavorsky is still useful: *Sochineniya Samarina*, v (Moscow, 1880). Perhaps daunted by these achievements, post-Revolutionary

I

At first glance Prokopovich's background seems not significantly different from that of the mass of those Ukrainian-born, Kiev-educated, Jesuit-inspired clerics who dominated the Russian Church, and hence to some extent Russian culture, from late in the seventeenth century until about the middle of the eighteenth.[4] Yet it is a fact that in his maturity he was constantly at odds with these people, his compatriots and colleagues, who periodically attacked him in public and bitterly resented his influence. And unless we are to accept their charges as true (Prokopovich treated them with contempt), unless we are prepared simply to judge him a wicked opportunist, a hypocrite, a kind of traitor (as some have done), we must search more carefully the meagre record of his early life for clues to his later development. For childhood, Proko-povich himself has written, 'is as it were the root whence both

Russian scholarship has added little more to the literature than a (usually negative) reinterpretation in a general study (e.g. the 'zhutky chelovek' of G. Florovsky's *Puti russkago bogosloviya* (Paris, 1937), pp. 89 ff.) and an Academy edn. of some of his works: I. P. Eremin (ed.), *Feofan Prokopovich: Sochineniya* (Moscow and Lenin-grad, 1961)—a collection which though representative does not replace the earlier *Slova i rechi*, in 4 Parts (St. Petersburg, 1760–74), or the editions of both major and lesser of his works by, for instance, Verkhovskoy (as cited above), or the various eighteenth-century editions of his purely theological works (e.g. M. Sokolov [trans. from the Latin], *Feofana Prokopovicha . . . Chetyre sochineniya* (Moscow, 1773), or indeed his *Epistolae . . . variis temporibus et ad varios amicos* (Moscow, 1776)).

Recent Western studies include, principally, R. Stupperich's patient explora-tions of 'Feofan Prokopovič in Rom', *Zeitschrift für Osteuropäische Geschichte*, v (1931), 327–39; 'F. Prokopovič und Johann F. Buddeus', ibid. ix (1935), 341–62; 'F. Prokopovičs theologische Bestrebungen', *Kyrios*, iv (1936), 350–62; 'F. Proko-povič und seine akademische Wirksamkeit in Kiev', *Zeitschrift für Slavische Philo-logie*, xvii (1941), 70–101; and Franco Venturi's brilliant 'Feofan Prokopovič', *Annali della facoltà di lettere e filosofia e di magistero dell'Università di Cagliari*, xxi, pt. 1 (1953). See also J. Tetzner, 'Theophan Prokopovič und die russische Frühauf-klärung', *Zeitschrift für Slawistik*, iii (1958), 351–63; and, much less useful, J. Šerech (Shevelev), 'On Theofan Prokopovič as Writer and Preacher in his Kiev Period', *Harvard Slavic Studies*, ii (1954), 211–23. G. Kowalyk, *Ecclesiologia Theophanis Prokopovycz: Influxus protestantismi* (Rome, 1947), is rightly dismissed by Venturi (op. cit., p. 21, n. 2) as a revival of contemporary theological disputes written from a Roman Catholic point of view.

Preparation of this essay, the bare bones of a projected biography, was facili-tated by grants from the American Philosophical Society and the Graduate College of the University of Illinois at Chicago, which I gratefully acknowledge.

[4] A story which is told in great detail by K. V. Kharlampovich, *Malorossiyskoe vliyanie na velikorusskuyu tserkovnuyu zhizn* (Kazan, 1914).

good and evil grow throughout the whole of life . . .: as the boy is, so the man shall be'.[5]

Our sources in this respect, as just indicated, are not plentiful.[6] But from them it seems certain that he was born in Kiev on 9 June 1681 of parents who were citizens of that city; that he was a robust, contentious, highly intelligent child;[7] that within the first few years of his life his parents had died and he was adopted by his uncle Feofan, a learned monk and rector of the Kiev academy who taught the boy his Latin and Russian letters and entered him in that school; that in 1692 the uncle also died; and that through the benevolence of Metropolitan Varlaam Yasinsky of Kiev and the generosity of an anonymous lay patron Prokopovich was able to stay at the academy and to complete, about the age of seventeen, its curriculum of Latin, language arts, and the rudiments of scholastic philosophy and theology. And from these few facts of his early life we can fairly infer the source of some of the traits of the mature man: his obvious ambition, for instance; his taste for good living, perhaps; the detachment with which he was able to view the ecclesiastical vocation; his belief in the power of education. For Prokopovich, it must be stressed, was an orphan, bereft of independent means, by origin vaguely middle class, urban, and from an early age bound without choice to a career in the Church, on which he was wholly dependent not only for his schooling but for his very sustenance. It was a distinctly less favourable background than that, for example, of Stefan Yavorsky, the offspring

---

[5] From the Preface to his *Primer*, which is discussed below.

[6] Though they are not so scanty as a reading of the authorities listed above, p. 76, n. 3, would suggest. For example, none of them has used the biography written about four years after his death by his friend and protégé Antiokh Kantemir as a note to the third of his, Kantemir's, satires (Z. I. Gershkovich (ed.), *Antiokh Kantemir: Sobranie stikhotvoreniy*, with Introduction by F. Ya. Pryma (Leningrad, 1956), pp. 100–1: the satire, 'On the Variety of the Human Passions', is dedicated to Prokopovich). Given Kantemir's intelligence, sophistication, and closeness, for a time, to the subject, his biographical note might have been taken to establish conclusively such facts as the exact date of Prokopovich's birth.

[7] 'Vividis oculis, temperamento sanguineo, cholericus', in the words of another contemporary, the anonymous author of the 'Vita Theophanis Procopowitsch', in Scherer (ed.). *Nordische Nebenstudien*, i (Frankfurt and Leipzig, 1776), 251. Venturi (op. cit., p. 7) identifies the author, quite reasonably, as G. S. Bayer, a young German classicist and orientalist who was one of the first members of the St. Petersburg Academy of Sciences.

of Polonized Ukrainian gentry who was successively professor of theology at the Kiev academy, temporary head of the Russian Church, and Prokopovich's adversary.[8]

Nor was this the only significant difference between him and many of his future colleagues, whether at the Kiev academy or in the Russian hierarchy. In 1698 Prokopovich, like Yavorsky and other exceptional students before him, like Metropolitan Yasinsky himself, was sent to pursue his studies at various of the Jesuit colleges in Polish territory. He was at the school in Vladimir, in Volyniya, it seems certain; and perhaps also at those in Vitebsk, Lvov, and/or Cracow. And to do so he had to become, as had Yavorsky and all the others before him, a Uniate: he took Catholic orders and for the duration of his stay abroad was a dependant, now, of the Roman Church. He did well. As another compatriot and future opponent would have to admit, 'for his zeal the Uniate bishop [of Vladimir] made him a prefect in the local school and a deacon; and then the Uniates sent him, to complete his education, to the Pope in Rome, where he lived as a student for a good while and studied much'.[9] Indeed, our most recent investigator of Prokopovich's Roman *stage* has identified him in the records of the so-called Greek College of St. Athanasius, according to which he studied philosophy for two years, was of 'optimum intelligence', made 'maximum progress', and publicly defended 'the whole of philosophy *cum laude*'.[10] According to this source, Prokopovich left the College on 28 October 1701, after almost exactly three years in residence, 'without any reason and with great scandal (no clue was ever discovered)', though the College later learned that he had on his return to Kiev succumbed once more to 'madness'.

The words 'scandal' and 'madness' in the records of the College, which was the Vatican's training centre for its Counter-Reformation offensive in Eastern Europe, ought not to bother us, meaning in the context no more than that Prokopovich had had enough,

[8] For Yavorsky's background, see the details and references in Cracraft, op. cit., pp. 122 ff.

[9] Markell Radyshevsky, in his 1730 deposition against Prokopovich to the Supreme Privy Council, as printed in 'Delo o Feofane Prokopoviche', *Chteniya v imperatorskom obshchestve istorii i drevnostey rossiyskikh pri Moskovskom universitete*, i (1862), 1.

[10] Stupperich, 'Prokopovič in Rom', pp. 333–4.

that his Jesuit masters had been sorry to see him go, and that on arriving home he had renounced his Uniate vows and promptly reverted to Orthodoxy. The more interesting question to ask is how, after completing the philosophy course in two years, Prokopovich had spent his third year at the College. Various suggestions have been made by contemporary friends: that he had studied— 'day and night'—scholastic theology and, bored with that, the classics, the Church Fathers, Italian, or the works of the humanists. One of his teachers is said to have taken a deep personal interest in the young scholar from Kiev, to have specially tutored him, and to have got him into libraries which were ordinarily closed. And indeed in the light of later evidence, especially that of his own writings, it does seem likely that Prokopovich had spent not only his last year in Rome, but all three years, overcoming his dislike of scholasticism by reading the Fathers, by conceiving a lasting admiration of classical literature, and by absorbing humanism (with its rationalistic, anti-papal critique of Roman Catholicism). Then he had laid the foundations, it would seem, of that broad culture which so distinguished him in later life.

Moreover, it appears that in Rome Prokopovich had kept his eyes and ears open, witnessing, among other ceremonies, a papal coronation (Clement XI's), hearing papal bulls ineffectively anathematizing heretics and schismatics publicly proclaimed, and avidly examining the city and its churches, relics, and monuments. Prokopovich had beheld Rome in all its classical ruin and melancholy Baroque splendour—and was troubled by it. He was later to remark that nowhere was the truth of Christianity so much in doubt as in Italy. One patent effect of this close contact with the Roman Church was to instil in the young Prokopovich a permanent dislike of the papacy and all that it seemed to him to stand for, a sentiment which would have been reinforced by the works of the Reformation he quite possibly read that winter of 1701–2 on his way from Rome back to Kiev. And this attitude, which would only intensify in the years that followed, marks another great difference between him and most of his later colleagues, those devotees of the 'Latin learning [*Latinskoe uchenie*]' who, if they did not positively admire the Roman Church, tended to use uncritically its language, its art, its philosophy and theology, and its militantly anti-Protestant, anti-modernist propaganda.

In other words, at first glance Prokopovich belonged by birth and upbringing to that proud, East Slavonic, 'Renaissance' civilization which was centred in Kiev and in its academy, was formed of Polish-Latin and native Russian elements, and though Greek Orthodox in religion (until the 1680s the diocese of Kiev was under the jurisdiction of Constantinople) was heavily influenced by Roman Catholicism. This civilization had flourished throughout the seventeenth century among the upper classes of the territories under Polish sovereignty, and, after Kiev and the Ukraine east of the Dnieper were incorporated in the tsardom of Moscow (1667), had begun to infiltrate Muscovite society, thus initiating the process of Westernization in the Russian heartland.[11] But now it would seem that, owing partly, perhaps, to an element of insecurity and of social inferiority in his background, and partly no doubt to his aversion from the Roman Church, Prokopovich was less than impregnated with this upper-class culture of his native land. He perhaps saw it less as a way of life and a thing to be treasured, than as a thing primarily of literature, a thing of the mind, and therefore mutable, if not dispensable. At the age of twenty-one, when he had returned to Kiev from Rome, Prokopovich, I am suggesting, was not fully satisfied with his cultural heritage. And these early differences between him and most of the members of his cultural community, as well as the fact of his robust brilliance (which would have aroused the envy of those to whom he was unkind), must be borne in mind when we come to consider his later career.

II

Prokopovich's intense, capable, restless mind was remarkably open, as we have seen, to new ideas. About 1720, in an indirect

[11] H. Birnbaum, 'Some Aspects of the Slavonic Renaissance', *Slavonic and East European Review*, xlvii (Jan. 1969), 37–56; L. R. Lewitter, 'Poland, Ukraine, and Russia in the Seventeenth Century', ibid. xxvii (May 1949), 414–29; R. Stupperich, 'Kiev — das zweite Jerusalem. Ein Beitrag zur Geschichte des ukrainisch-russischen Nationalbewusstseins', *Zeitschrift für Slavische Philologie*, (1935), 322–54; and Kharlampovich, op. cit., pp. 149 ff.

reference to the 'Latinizers', to those votaries of the dominant scholasticism of the Kiev and (after 1700) Moscow academies, he himself wrote that 'an educated man, despite his regular education, is never satisfied with what he has learned, and will never desist from studying though he live for as long as Methuselah'; that 'among the wise, this adage has been affirmed: it is a property of the wise man to change his opinions'.[12] True to his word, when within a year or two of his return to Kiev and reversion to Orthodoxy Metropolitan Yasinsky appointed him to the academy, where he first taught poetics, then rhetoric, and beginning in 1707 the course in philosophy, it was always with a difference. His lectures in Latin on the theory of literature, which have survived in the form of two treatises, manifest an attempt to purify the discipline, on the basis of classical models, of medieval and Baroque accretions.[13] In his philosophy classes he would encourage the students (we are assured by his critics) in effect to reject, indeed to ridicule, the sterile syllogisms of the Jesuit schoolmen: to accept nothing, in short, on the 'magister dixit' principle which their own reason could not accept. As early as 1707 he attempted to introduce arithmetic, geometry, and modern physics into the academy's curriculum by teaching the subjects in his own classes. A contemporary Danish traveller, who much admired the depth and breadth of his knowledge, noted in his journal that Prokopovich exhibited an 'indescribable love' of mathematics.[14] And at this time the young academic (he was still in his twenties) expressed in a major literary effort both a secularist disdain for clerics and a national consciousness that was tinged, inevitably, with politics. In the Jesuit tradition of academic drama he wrote a five-act tragicomedy in verse on the theme of the Christianization, indeed enlightenment, of the 'Slavonic-Russian lands' under the tenth-century prince of Kiev, St. Vladimir. It was performed at the Kiev academy on 3 July 1705 in the presence of Ivan Mazepa, hetman

[12] From Verkhovskoy's critical edition of Prokopovich's *Dukhovny Reglament* (*Ecclesiastical Regulation*), op. cit. ii. 53.

[13] 'De arte poetica', first published Mogilev 1786, reprinted, with Russian translation, in Eremin, op. cit., pp. 229–458; the 'De arte rhetorica', dating from a course of lectures given 1706–7, has never been published (see ibid., p. 4, n. 18).

[14] Quoted in Chistovich, op. cit., pp. 627–8.

(prince) of the Ukraine, a patron of the academy, and an ally (or rather satellite) of Peter I. It concluded with the chorus chanting these words:

> . . . Grant might and strength,
> Grant length of days and to every undertaking
> A happy conclusion; and in war, always victory!
> Grant health, power, peace, security!
> Grant this to Tsar Peter, crowned by Thee,
> And to his most loyal chieftain, Ivan![15]

In the summer of 1706 Peter himself came to Kiev to inspect the fortifications of the Monastery of the Caves and on 5 July attended services in the Sofiysky cathedral, where he heard Prokopovich, now a prefect of the academy, preach. No doubt the latter had already begun to perfect the distinctively terse, dramatic, unbaroque style which characterizes his later sermons and has earned for him the status of founder of a school of preaching.[16] But there is no evidence that on this occasion the tsar did anything more than make a mental note of Prokopovich's existence. In 1708, however, unlike most of the higher clergy of the Ukraine, he swiftly took Peter's side when Hetman Mazepa, in league with Charles XII of Sweden, betrayed him. It was a critical moment in Peter's long war with the Swedes, in the history (we now know) of his reign, in that of Russia, indeed of Europe; and when Peter, who was determined to retain control of the Ukraine, inquired of his governor in Kiev, Prince D. M. Golitsyn, concerning the loyalty of the local clergy, he was told that 'all the monks avoid us: in all of Kiev I have found only one man, namely the prefect of the [academy], who is well disposed towards us'.[17]

---

[15] The critical edition of 'Vladimir' is printed in Eremin, op. cit., pp. 149–206. For a lengthy analysis of the play, see N. S. Tikhonravov, *Sochineniya*, ii (Moscow, 1898), 120–53. It was Tikhonravov who first suggested that when Prokopovich describes, in the play, the gluttonous, drunken, hypocritical, credulous, superstitious priests of pagan Russia, he was really referring to the clergy of his own day: cf. Verkhovskoy, op. cit. i. 131, quoting Morozov quoting Tikhonravov.

[16] Chistovich, op. cit., pp. 603–6; D. Čiževskij, *History of Russian Literature from the Eleventh Century to the End of the Baroque* (The Hague, 1960), p. 363; also Cracraft, op. cit., p. 268, quoting the rules for preachers laid down in the *Ecclesiastical Regulation*.

[17] Quoted in Kharlampovich, op. cit., p. 463. In 1726, when Prokopovich's loyalty was challenged, he would rejoin, 'as early as 1708 and 1709, when Mazepa's

And then in 1709, following the great Russian victory at Pol-tava, Peter came again to Kiev, and again was formally welcomed in the Sofiysky cathedral by Prokopovich, who now addressed to 'His Most Sacred Majesty the All-Russian Tsar' a magnificent panegyric that cannot have failed to please him. His victory was celebrated both in the panegyric and in Prokopovich's contemporary 'Epinikion' or 'triumphal canto', as a victory not only over the external enemies of the All-Russian realm, but over treasonous internal forces as well; and both the panegyric and the canto are suffused with a sense of Russia's grandeur, and of Peter's heroic struggle to promote it. The panegyric is mentioned in the official history of Peter's reign, which was composed under his personal direction in the last years of his life.[18] It was immediately published in Kiev in Polish and Latin as well as Slavonic so that the 'whole of Europe should know of this triumph'.[19]

Aleksandr Menshikov was the long-standing favourite of Peter the Great, a general of his army, and governor of the Baltic region. In December 1709 he too was greeted in Kiev by the academy's leading scholar and within months was recommending him to the influential Metropolitan Job of Novgorod, the wealthiest see in Russia. As Job understood it from Menshikov by way of the senior official (*landrat*) of Novgorod, Prokopovich was a 'most learned man of fine estate, a speaker of many languages, and an excellent teacher' who, for 'his great talents and sound Orthodox profession', was to be appointed head of a local monastery.[20] But before any such action could be completed Peter himself intervened. In June 1711 he summoned Prokopovich to military headquarters in Moldavia, where on the second anniversary of the

treachery revealed him to be an enemy of the fatherland, I was then for the sovereign and the state, as his excellency Prince D. M. Golitsyn can testify' (quoted Chistovich, op. cit., pp. 14, n. 3, and 220).

[18] M. M. Shcherbatov (ed.), *Zhurnal ili podennaya zapiska . . . Gosudarya imperatora Petra Velikago, s 1698 goda dazhe do zaklyucheniya neyshtatskago mira (1721)*, i (St. Petersburg, 1770), 224.

[19] A copy of the Latin version of Prokopovich's *Panegyricus Petro Primo . . .* (Kiev, 1709) is preserved in the British Museum (cat. no. 590. i. 23, doc. 2). For the text of the Slavonic version, see Eremin, op. cit., pp. 23–38, and his notes, pp. 459–63; for that of the 'Epinikion', ibid., pp. 209–14.

[20] Job's letter of 23 Feb. 1710 to the *landrat* thus describing Prokopovich is quoted in Chistovich, op. cit., p. 15.

Poltava victory he preached a rousing sermon. He remained to witness the Russian defeat by the Turks at the battle on the Pruth (in July), and recorded the event in a poem where he urged that an enlightened Christendom would yet be liberated from the 'power of paganism'.[21] His efforts continued to please the Tsar. Later that year, only a few months after his thirtieth birthday, and no doubt to his immense delight (for it represented the summit of achievement in the world in which he had grown up), he was appointed igumen (abbot) of the Kiev Brotherhood monastery, rector of the Kiev academy, and professor of theology there. And in view of his age, of the independence of his attitudes, of the intensity of the opposition to him which would subsequently emerge, it must be supposed that Peter's influence had played an important role in these appointments.

Indeed the key role politics played in Prokopovich's career from as early as 1705 (the production of 'Vladimir'), and certainly from 1708 to 1709, must be emphasized. For in a few years, after he had gone for good to St. Petersburg, politics would determine his life entirely, would make of his writings (it has been rightly observed) 'œuvres de circonstance', if not *a posteriori* justifications for the tsar's decisions':[22] in a word, would so preoccupy his mind, and dominate his activity, that it would corrupt him. For politics, we know, 'is a second-rate form of human activity, neither an art nor a science, at once corrupting to the soul and fatiguing to the mind, the activity either of those who cannot live without the illusion of affairs or [of] those so fearful of being ruled by others that they will pay away their lives to prevent it'[23]—the *boutade* (though it is a little more than that) applying with special force to the man of learning, of sensibility, and contemplation, who abandons himself to public affairs. In Prokopovich's case, apart from the fact that he would be *commanded* by the most imperious of monarchs to join him in his capital, it was probably for a combination of the reasons suggested above that he succumbed. Though meaning in

[21] The poem is printed in ibid., p. 16, and in Eremin, op. cit., pp. 214–15.
[22] Simone Blanc, 'L'Église russe à l'aube du "Siècle des Lumières" ', *Annales Économies Sociétés Civilisations*, xx (May–June 1965), 460.
[23] Michael Oakeshott, in his Introduction to Hobbes's *Leviathan* (Oxford, 1957), p. lxiv.

no way to denigrate his achievements as a politician and government propagandist, and as a patron, at least, of learning, we may
regret the poetry that was therefore never written, the philosophy
that was never thought out, above all the greater contribution he
would undoubtedly have made, had he had the time, to the formation of modern Russian: to making the Russian language, that
much sooner, a natural instrument of abstract thought.

III

But to be fair to Prokopovich, when late in 1715 he received
Peter's summons to St. Petersburg, he left Kiev with some misgivings. This and his ambivalent reaction to the prospect of a
bishopric, which he believed was being held out to him, are reflected in a letter to his friend Markovich of 9 August 1716:

> You have perhaps heard that I am being called to the episcopate.
> This honour both attracts and repels me, as if they had decided to fling
> me to the wild beasts. I envy good men their mitres, copes, crosiers,
> and other paraphernalia; add to this still bigger and tastier fish. But if
> I am attracted to them, if I should desire them, may God punish me in
> some even worse way. I like episcopal affairs and would like to be a
> bishop, were it not that to be a bishop one must indulge in histrionics;
> for that is a most corrupt profession if it is not guided by divine wisdom.
> For my part, I will make every effort to avoid this honour and to return
> to you, which I pray God will be soon. I have not yet finished my
> theological lectures . . .[24]

He left Kiev in the autumn of 1716 and never, in fact, returned.
But it is true that from the time of his appointments in 1711 until
his departure he was pleasurably absorbed by the administration
of the academy and especially by his theological lectures. Years
later he would recall nostalgically the efforts of the energetic
young abbot-rector to put the academy's economy on a sounder
footing; and the long passage in the *Ecclesiastical Regulation* of 1721
devoted to the schools, a passage replete with detailed advice on

---

[24] Letter printed in Chistovich, op. cit., pp. 24–5; this portion both in Russian
and in its original Latin (from the *Epistolae* . . . no. 5), in Verkhovskoy, op. cit. i.
130 and n. 3.

curriculum, methods of teaching, and academic discipline,[25] is written with the confidence of a successful educator. It is clearly a product of Prokopovich's happy tenure at the Kiev academy.

As for the admittedly unfinished course of lectures in theology, those which were posthumously published have been studied *qua* theology, after a period of neglect by the Russian ecclesiastical establishment,[26] by several more recent authorities, all of whom have discovered with a greater or lesser degree of alarm Prokopovich's debt to Protestant, rather than Roman Catholic, divines.[27] But as a system of thought (if it can be called a system), we may note that it has been aptly described as critical-historical, in the sense that he consistently argued that the exposition of dogma must be based on a critical reading of Scripture, of the works of the Fathers, and of church history, especially early church history, which as it happened had been written almost entirely by Western Europeans and so was to be used with special care. And

---

[25] See Verkhovskoy, op. cit. ii. 51–65, and the discussion in Cracraft, op. cit., pp. 262 ff.

[26] Thus the skimpy references to Prokopovich in Metropolitan Makary (Macaire), *Théologie dogmatique orthodoxe*, trans. anon. (Paris, 1859), i, and in Archbishop Filaret, *Pravoslavnoe dogmaticheskoe bogoslovie* (Chernigov, 1864), i, where the reader at one point is referred to the same author's *Obzor russkoy dukhovnoy literatury* (Kharkov, 1859–61), ii. 3–12, for notes on this theologically unimportant writer of 'ecclesiastical literature'. So by the middle of the nineteenth century official Orthodoxy had been sufficiently well defined, with respect to the challenge of Western theology, to exclude Prokopovich from serious consideration—a procedure which may be theologically respectable, but will not deceive historians. Cf. the judgement of a recent Orthodox student of Orthodox history: 'Looking back on [the seventeenth and early eighteenth centuries] . . . one is struck by the limitations of [Orthodox] theology in this period: one does not find the Orthodox tradition in its *fullness*' (T. Ware, *The Orthodox Church* (London, 1963), p. 109). Or as Father Florovsky says, 'the historical fate of Russian theology in the eighteenth century was to be decided in the course of a struggle between the epigoni of post-Reformation Roman and Protestant [*sic*] scholasticism' (op. cit., p. 97). In such a situation Prokopovich the theologian can in consistency and fairness no more be called a 'Protestant' (as he was and is) than Stefan Yavorsky can be called a 'Roman Catholic' (as he was and is)—a point which Samarin in the 1840s implicitly accepted when he in effect denounced them both for attempting to force what he called Orthodoxy into one form or another of Western, 'rationalist' straightjacket (op. cit., pp. 11–163).

[27] See Samarin's dissertation, which was only published in 1880 (op. cit.); F. Tikhomirov, *Traktaty Feofana Prokopovicha o Boge edinom po sushchestvu i troichnom v Litsakh* (St. Petersburg, 1884); Florovsky, op. cit., pp. 89–97; Stupperich, 'Theologische Bestrebungen' and 'Akademische Wirksamkeit in Kiev'; and Kowalyk, op. cit.

Prokopovich preached what he practised. In the *Ecclesiastical Regulation*, where he literally lay down the law to the Russian clergy, he declared that

he who would teach theology must be learned in holy Scripture and able to expound correctly its true essence and to corroborate all the dogmas with scriptural evidence. And for help in this matter he should diligently study the writings of the holy Fathers, especially those of the Fathers who studiously wrote on dogma out of a need to combat the heresies that had arisen in the Church. . . . Similarly, the acts and deliberations of the ecumenical and local councils are most useful. . . . And while a teacher of theology may seek assistance from modern authors of other faiths, he must not imitate them and give credence to their expositions, but only accept their guidance in the arguments they employ from Scripture and the Fathers, particularly as regards those dogmas wherein other faiths agree with us. However their arguments are not to be credited lightly, but rather examined to see whether such and such a quotation is to be found in Scripture or in the writings of the Fathers, and whether it has there the sense in which they use it. . . . Thus a teacher of theology must not teach according to foreign expositions, but according to his own understanding.[28]

As in his philosophy classes, Prokopovich was encouraging his theology students to think, within the limits of their basic religious faith, for themselves. Whether for this reason, or simply because he was a good teacher, his lectures proved a great success with them.

At the same time, Prokopovich's theological lectures inevitably excited the hostility of many—if not most—of his colleagues, some of whom, inspired partly no doubt by malice, would both then and later repeatedly accuse him of heterodoxy, of Protestantism (either the Lutheran or Calvinist variety: it did not seem to matter), of free-thinking, of blasphemy, of heresy, of being in the end a 'son of Satan'.[29] And to them Prokopovich's approach and

[28] Verkhovskoy, op. cit., ii. 55.
[29] e.g. Markell Radyshevsky, op. cit. See also the account (in Cracraft, op. cit., pp. 134 f.) of the attempt by Metropolitan Stefan Yavorsky in May 1718 to use such grounds to block Prokopovich's consecration to the see of Pskov. Yavorsky was backed in this by the teachers Theophylact Lopatinsky and Gideon Vishnevsky of the Moscow academy, both of whom were also Latinizers and products of the Kiev academy, where they had been Prokopovich's (critical) colleagues.

method and whole style must indeed have seemed radical, as a comparison of his lectures with the finest flower of Russian scholasticism, Stefan Yavorsky's *Rock of the Faith*, which was written about 1713, will confirm.[30] Indeed, one of our authorities has remarked that Prokopovich's theological lectures have a philosophical character comparable to the musings on God of Bacon, Descartes, Spinoza, or Leibnitz, most of whom he had in fact read.[31] In his theological lectures, as he had in his courses on literary theory and on philosophy, Prokopovich was attempting perhaps to reconcile his heritage with what he had found, and continued to find, in the wider world of post-Renaissance, post-Reformation, early Enlightenment Europe: in essence to reconcile, though he may not have realized it, the Bible, or Revelation, with the demands of reason and nature. It is surely not too much to say that Prokopovich was attempting, in the intellectually barren field of Russian Orthodoxy, to adumbrate in his theological disquisitions an appropriate response to the challenge not just of Western theology, but of radical Western theology, and even of secular thought.[32]

In Prokopovich's model school,[33] two years of theology—the study of the 'principal dogmas of our faith, and God's law [or Christian morality]'—would still dominate the curriculum, but they would be preceded by six years of '1. Grammar, together with geography and history; 2. Arithmetic and geometry; 3. Logic or dialectics . . .; 4. Rhetoric and poetics; 5. Physics, supplemented by a brief course in metaphysics; [and] 6. the short Politics of Pufendorf'—that is Pufendorf's *Politia brevis*, which is a condensed version of his work *On the Duties of Man and the Citizen According to Natural Law*, which in turn is an epitome of his magisterial *On the Law of Nature and Nations*, which 'became standard fare in the educational curriculums of the eighteenth century' and a seminal book of the Enlightenment.[34] For

[30] See I. Morev (ed.), *'Kamen Very' Mitropolita Stefana Yavorskago* (St. Petersburg, 1904).   [31] Tikhomirov, op. cit., p. 65.

[32] Thus his *Discourse on Atheism . . . (Razsuzhdenie o bezbozhii . . .*), published Moscow, 1774, esp. pp. 15–18 (against Spinoza).

[33] As projected in the *Ecclesiastical Regulation* (see Verkhovskoy, op. cit. ii. 57).

[34] L. Krieger, *The Politics of Discretion: Pufendorf and the Acceptance of Natural Law* Chicago and London, 1965), pp. 256 ff. Prokopovich's large library contained

Prokopovich knew, as he declared in a striking sentence of the *Ecclesiastical Regulation*, that 'When the light of learning is lacking, it is impossible that the Church should be well run, that it should not be disorderly and subject to numerous ridiculous superstitions, as well as dissensions and the most absurd heresies'.[35] And that was what mattered: that the Church should be well run: that the Russian Church, both the official Church and the dissenting 'Old Believers', should leave the slavish imitation and sordid secrecy of medieval Muscovy and join the brighter, tidier modern world.

And it was during these prosperous years in Kiev that Prokopovich would retire to the house of Prince Golitsyn, the governor, or to that of his aristocratic former pupil and close friend, Ya. A. Markovich, where in a comfortable and wholly secular atmosphere they passed long evenings discussing the ancients and moderns with local and itinerant intellectuals. Perhaps it was there that he conceived an interest in the natural-law theories and political philosophies of Grotius, Pufendorf, Locke, and especially (to judge from his later work) Hobbes. With some of his students he helped Golitsyn to organize a series of Russian translations of the principal works of these vital thinkers of the Protestant West. The translations never amounted to anything more than fragments of the great treatises, and were never published.[36] But for Prokopovich such speculative exercises were to prove of practical value when politics took over his life.

IV

He arrived in St. Petersburg in October of 1716, and at the Tsar's order immediately set to work. He wrote a popular catechism

copies of several of Pufendorf's works (see Verkhovskoy, op. cit. i. 124; also the contemporary catalogue of the library printed in ibid. ii, sect. V, pp. 23, 27, 28, 31, 39, 40, 42, 43). An epitome of the work in question was published in a Russian translation by Prokopovich's friend and Synodal colleague Gabriel Buzhinsky in St. Petersburg in 1726 (*O Dolzhnostyakh cheloveka i grazhdanina po zakonu estestvennomu* . . .).

[35] Verkhovskoy, op. cit. ii. 51.

[36] I owe this information to A. S. Lappo-Danilevsky, 'L'idée de l'état et son évolution en Russie depuis les troubles du XVIIe siècle jusqu'aux réformes du XVIIIe', in P. Vinogradoff (ed.), *Essays in Legal History* (London, 1913), pp. 356–83.

which was not published because, as he says in a note attached to his manuscript, it had not fulfilled Peter's requirements for 'brief and simple instruction, suitable for study and memorization by youths'.[37] But that winter he also compiled a regal table of the Russian grand princes and tsars, from Vladimir to Peter (supposedly a continuous line), which was published.[38] Moreover, he began to preach on important state occasions, usurping in this respect the position of Stefan Yavorsky, the nominal head of the Church whose declining fortunes (it was partly Prokopovich's fault) have been retailed elsewhere.[39] In June 1717 he preached at the customary commemoration of the Poltava victory in the Trinity Cathedral of St. Petersburg; in October he publicly welcomed Peter home from abroad on behalf, as he said, of the Russian people; in November, again in the Trinity Cathedral, he orated in honour of Peter's wife.[40] The sermon to Peter on his return from more than a year in Western Europe (he had been, this time, in Denmark, North Germany, Holland, and Paris) is notable for Prokopovich's bold affirmation of the value of foreign travel—of travel, that is, in the more civilized parts of Europe—which

is the best, the living, the true school of politics. I refer not to maps, but to the real thing; not to hearsay, but to personal knowledge of the customs and ways of nations. . . . There [abroad] the sensible man sees oft-changing fortune at play, and learns humility; sees the causes of happiness, and learns the lesson; perceives the key to eloquence, and learns how to be vigorous and to defend himself; sees also in foreign nations, as in a mirror, himself and his own people, both their good points and their bad . . .

The impressive public expression of such sentiments, which closely corresponded to Peter's own, can only have raised him in the Tsar's estimation. Indeed they soon became, it seems, as close as a subject and his monarch, an intellectual and a practical man of affairs, a learned Kievan and a gross Muscovite, a cleric and Peter, could have become. Prokopovich would be allowed to entertain

[37] The note is printed in Verkhovskoy, op. cit. i. 389 f.
[38] *Rodoslovnaya rospis velikikh knyazey i tsarey rossiyskikh do gosudarya Petra I* (St. Petersburg, 1717).
[39] Cracraft, op. cit., esp. pp. 135 ff.
[40] All three sermons are printed in Eremin, op. cit., pp. 48-59, 60-7, 68-76.

the Tsar and to visit him at his various retreats; and apart from high ecclesiastical office and important royal commissions, his efforts would be rewarded more tangibly: with a gift of books, a pleasure boat, a house by the sea, additional estates, or hard cash. These were tributes to the purity and steadfastness of his loyalty, to be sure; but also to the power of his intellect, the breadth of his culture, to the energy with which he executed the Tsar's plans and defended his policies, to his cosmopolitanism, his tolerance. In his *magnum opus* Tatishchev, one of Peter the Great's 'new men' —soldier, engineer, civil servant, historian—often thanks for his help 'our archbishop Prokopovich, who was so learned in the new philosophy and in theology that hitherto in Russia there was none to equal him'.[41] And Herr Vockerodt, secretary to the long-standing (1717–28) Prussian ambassador to St. Petersburg, Marde-feld, found in him, apart from wide learning, 'qualities such as one rarely meets in the clergy, namely unusual restraint, complete disinterestedness, and an ardent concern for the good of the country, even at the expense of the clergy's interests'.[42]

On Palm Sunday (6 April) 1718 Prokopovich preached a remarkable sermon on the 'power and glory of the Tsar'. It was a time of unrest in Russia. Successive interrogations of Peter's hapless son, Tsarevich Aleksey, had revealed a loosely organized but widespread conspiracy against the Tsar and his innovations, and in his sermon Prokopovich deftly combined condemnations of the conspirators and of all 'oppositionists' with lamentations on the general state of ignorance and salutary warnings against the snares of false religion. 'Do we not see here [in the story of Christ's triumphal entry into Jerusalem] what honour is paid to the King? Does this not require us to speak out about the duty of subjects to esteem the supreme authority [or sovereign], and about the great resistance to this duty that has been exposed in our country at the present time?' For we see, declared the preacher, 'that not a small part of the people abide in such ignorance that

[41] V. N. Tatishchev, *Istoriya rossiyskaya*, i (Moscow and Leningrad, 1962), 315 and *passim*.
[42] 'Rossiya pri Petre Velikom (Zapiski Fokeroda)', *Russky arkhiv*, ii (1873), col. 1372.

they do not know the Christian doctrine concerning the secular authorities. Nay more, they do not know that the supreme authority is established and armed with the sword by God, and that to oppose it is a sin against God himself, a sin to be punished by death not temporal but eternal'. And after disposing of the 'abominable words' of the 'enemies of true doctrine', of those 'babblers' who ignorantly deduced from Scripture that 'wisdom, power, glory, and all human authority are abominable in the sight of God', Prokopovich proceeded to explain what 'nature herself and the word of God teach us concerning human authority'.

The student of the new philosophy—of the works especially of Grotius, Hobbes, and Pufendorf—pointed out to his Russian audience that 'laws like these are written in the heart of every man: to love and fear God, to preserve one's own life, to wish for the never-declining prosperity of the human race, not to do to others what one does not wish for oneself, and to honour one's father and mother. . . . And might there not also be among these natural laws this one: that there must be an authority holding supreme power in every nation? There is indeed! This is the supreme law.'

For because the ill-will of a depraved race does not hesitate to break the law to love one another and not to do to others what we do not wish for ourselves, always and everywhere a guardian has been desirable, a protector and a strong upholder of the law. And this is the authority of the state.

Therefore 'we hold it certain that the supreme authority receives its beginning and cause from nature herself'. But 'if from nature, then from God himself, the creator of nature . . . we cannot help but call God the cause of the authority of the state'. And Prokopovich assured his audience, with numerous quotations from Scripture, that the 'written word of God . . . seals the establishment of governments with His blessing and commands that they be obeyed'.

And he dealt briskly with 'one doubt that remains like a thorn in the conscience', namely the belief that the clergy were exempt from the duties of service and loyalty to the sovereign. 'This thorn

—or better say sting, for this is the sting of the serpent—is the papist spirit.' For just as there was

one task for the army, another for civil administrators, another for doctors, another for the various artisans, so also pastors and teachers and all those concerned with ecclesiastical affairs have their particular task; and they, too, are subject to the authority of the state, in order that they should remain steadfast in their vocation . . . and fulfil the obligations they have in common with the rest of the people. . . . The clergy is another order or rank of the people, and not a separate state.

Nor did Prokopovich neglect fulsomely and feelingly to praise Tsar Peter,

the Orthodox monarch who has so benefited Russia that from the beginning of the All-Russian state historians cannot point to one equal to him. . . . He has given Russia a new birth. But what is his reward from us? Terrible to his enemies, forced to fear his own subjects! Glorious among foreigners, dishonoured among his own people! . . . Let us beware that this saying does not arise about us: the sovereign is worthy of such a country, but the people are not worthy of such a sovereign.

If Peter had need of any further proof that Prokopovich was willing and able to assist him in the radical reform of the Church (on which the Tsar had about made up his mind), this sermon surely provided it. And Prokopovich's sermon of Palm Sunday 1718[43] marked his public début as the chief ideologist of the Petrine state and the original propagator of the Petrine legend. It was a role for which he was prepared, one which suited his disposition and abilities, and one which he was to play with distinction in the remaining years of his life. For in his sermons, orations, and poems Prokopovich did not overlook any opportunity to extol Peter's genius or to praise his achievements, however mundane.[44] He helped to prepare the official history of

[43] 'Slovo o vlasti i chesti tsarskoy . . .', printed in Eremin, op. cit., pp. 76–93. The sermon was published in St. Petersburg that August (see T. A. Bykova and M. M. Gurevich, *Opisanie izdaniy napechatannykh kirillitsey (1689–1725)* (Moscow and Leningrad, 1958), no. 117).

[44] See Eremin, op. cit., pp. 103–12 and 219–20 for, respectively, a sermon 'In Praise of the Russian Fleet' and a poem 'On the Ladoga Canal'.

Peter's reign and by himself wrote an account of the years up to the Poltava victory.[45] In 1722 he published a treatise on the 'right of the monarch's will' in which he justified, on the basis of natural law and historical precedent, Peter's assumption of the right to name his own successor, explaining that his acts were 'independent of any superior power, in that they cannot be annulled by any other human will'.[46] He also published an essay expressing the view that since Constantine's time the Christian emperors had exercised the powers of a bishop, 'in the sense that they ruled the clergy'. It was a justification of Peter's assumption of complete control of the government of the Church; for a 'Christian sovereign', Prokopovich concluded in a celebrated definition of the term, can rightly be called not only a bishop, 'but the bishop of bishops, because the Sovereign is the supreme authority, the perfect, ultimate, and authentic supervisor; that is, he holds supreme judicial and executive power over all the ranks and authorities subject to him, whether ecclesiastical or secular'.[47] 'Patriarchalism'—the belief that a patriarch should continue to rule the autocephalous Russian Orthodox Church—Prokopovich equated with 'papalism', and dismissed it accordingly.

V

But such works were for the few who cared about politics and could be reached by logic and learning. In accordance with Peter's directive and with a provision of the *Ecclesiastical Regulation*, Prokopovich produced, in 1720, a *Primer* which remained the

[45] *Istoriya imp. Petra Velikago, ot rozhdeniya ego do Poltavskoy batalii*, ed. M. M. Shcherbatov (St. Petersburg, 1773). I follow Chistovich (op. cit., p. 122) in attributing this work to Prokopovich, though there is some doubt.

[46] *Pravda voli monarshey vo opredelenii naslednika derzhavy svoey* (Moscow, 1722). The treatise was also published in Latin at Leipzig, 1723, and in German at Berlin, 1724. In Russia it was regarded as an official document and appended to the succession law (*Polnoe sobranie zakonov rossiyskoy imperii s 1649 goda*, 1st ser. (St. Petersburg, 1830), vii, no. 4870); and either independently or together with the law it was frequently reprinted. The *Pravda* is analysed, from a narrowly juridical point of view, by G. Gurvich, '*Pravda Voli monarshey*' *Feofana Prokopovicha i eya zapadnoevropeyskie istochniki* (Iurev, 1915).

[47] See his essay 'Rozysk istorichesky o pontifikse . . .', printed in Verkhovskoy, op. cit. ii, sect. III, pp. 5–20.

basic textbook of moral and religious instruction in Russia for the next hundred years.[48] Thousands upon thousands of copies were printed: it was required reading for all clergy and in all the church schools: it was recommended to 'pious parents, teachers, guardians, masters, and all others who exercise parental authority over children'; and in recognition of the widespread popular illiteracy, the Synod in 1723 ordered that extracts from it be read out loud in all the churches of Russia. Tatishchev in 1736 recommended that it be used in the elementary state schools which he was planning for the Ural region;[49] and Prince Shcherbatov, that learned misanthrope of the age of Catherine II, recalled being required to learn its lessons at an early age.[50]

Prokopovich's *Primer*, to quote the author's preface, was 'a little book clearly explaining the law of God [the Ten Commandments], the [Nicene] Creed, the Lord's Prayer, and the nine Beatitudes', to which were added simple literal and syllabic exercises. The essay on the Beatitudes, which comes at the end of the book, is a pious exhortation to lead a Christian life of true humility, submissiveness, simplicity, and purity; it was highly commended to the Synod by Peter himself and was also separately printed to aid the faithful in their devotions and so to promote religious reform. The brief explanations of each article of the Nicene creed seem, so far as they go, not incompatible with Orthodox teaching as it was embodied in, say, the nearly contemporary *Confession* of Peter Mogila,[51] although in the political-ideological conflicts of the years after Peter's death Prokopovich's

---

[48] *Pervoe uchenie otrokom. V nemzhe bukvy i slogi. Takzhe: Kratkoe tolkovanie zakonnago desyatosloviya, Molitvy Gospodni, Simvola very, i devyati blazhenstv* (St. Petersburg, 1720). I am grateful to the Lenin Library for supplying me with a microfilm of the 12th impression (Nov. 1724) of this work. For further details of the *Primer*'s history, and a discussion of its contents, see Cracraft, op. cit., pp. 276–90.

[49] See N. F. Demidova (ed.), 'Instruktsiya V. N. Tatishcheva o poryadke prepodavaniya v shkolakh pri Uralskikh kazennykh zavodakh', *Istorichesky arkhiv*, v (1950), 170.

[50] A. Lentin (ed. and trans.), *M. M. Shcherbatov's 'On the Corruption of Morals in Russia'* (Cambridge, 1969), p. 17.

[51] A. Malvy and M. Viller (eds.), 'La confession orthodoxe de Pierre Moghila: texte Latin inédit', *Orientalia Christiana*, x (1927). See also the Moscow 1709 edn., a copy of which is deposited in the British Museum (cat. no. 3505. df. 25); and for further details, Cracraft, op. cit., pp. 278–9.

enemies would charge that they, as well as other parts of the *Primer*, contained 'foreign' or 'heretical' or 'Protestant' elements. As for the phrase-by-phrase devotional commentary on the Lord's Prayer, the following passage is worth noting:

Give us this day our daily bread. Give us, merciful Father, all that is necessary to support our life: wholesome air, an abundance of the fruits of the earth, and thy blessing on our labours. Bless the government. Grant health and long life to our Most Blessed Sovereign Peter the Great, Emperor and All-Russian Autocrat, and to all his Court and army. Grant that the chief lords [*bolyare*] may be utterly loyal. Preserve all the higher and lower officials in love and harmony . . .

And the tendency to subordinate piety to the interests of the state is even more clearly evident in the detailed, practical, highly didactic exposition of the Ten Commandments which forms by far the longest and most remarkable section of the *Primer*. For example:

Question: Are soldiers and judges to be considered transgressors of the commandment 'Thou shalt not kill' when they put a man to death?

Answer: No; for judges only execute the power entrusted to them by God. Nor do soldiers transgress this commandment when they slay the enemy; for they are only doing their duty when, in defence of their country and in obedience to their Sovereign, they kill. It is the duty of kings to see that war is undertaken for just causes.

Or again:

Question: What is ordained by God in the fifth commandment ['Honour thy father and thy mother']?

Answer: To honour all those who are as fathers and mothers to us. But it is not only parents who are referred to here, but others who exercise paternal authority over us.

Question: Who are such persons?

Answer: The first order of such persons are the supreme authorities instituted by God to rule the people, of whom the highest authority is the Tsar. It is the duty of kings to protect their subjects and to seek what is best for them, whether in religious matters or in the things of this world; and therefore they must watch over all the ecclesiastical, military, and civil authorities subject to them and conscientiously see that they discharge their respective duties. This is, under God, the highest paternal dignity; and subjects, like good sons, must honour the Tsar.

The second order of persons enjoying paternal authority, the *Primer* explained, are the 'supreme rulers of the people who are subordinate to the Tsar, namely: the ecclesiastical pastors, the senators, the judges, and the other civil and military authorities'. The ecclesiastical authorities were to 'guide the people along the path to salvation; the civil, to dispense justice; the military, to teach sound military doctrine, to lead skilfully, and to incite valiant deeds'. The remaining orders of persons vested with paternal authority included parents—'though first in the natural order, the first two orders [mentioned above] have responsibility for the common good and therefore greater dignity'—other relations, teachers, lords, and masters, to all of whom children or students or servants or the people generally owe love, honour, obedience, and loyal service. And the *Primer* provided certain maxims to guide the faithful in the performance of these duties. 'Aged persons enjoy paternal authority, though civil authority takes precedence over age; for a young king is a father to his elderly subjects.' Or:

Question: What is to be done when one paternal authority commands one thing, and another forbids it?

Answer: When neither of them has authority over the other, you must look not to the persons who command, but to what is commanded. For instance: if your master requires you to do something with regard to the service you owe him, and your father forbids it, obey your master and not your father. But if one authority is superior to the other, obey the superior: thus if your master or father commands you to do something that is forbidden by the civil authorities, obey neither your father nor your master. And if the civil authorities order you to do anything that the Tsar forbids, obey the Tsar.

Thus in the *Primer* of Prokopovich, which was intended to

educate children in the 'will of God' and to promote a 'Christian reform', the idea of the absolute state is merged with the more traditional doctrine of paternal authority, a solution that had been advanced by Prokopovich, only much more elaborately, in his sermon of Palm Sunday 1718. In the *Primer*, a hierarchy of power is erected which culminates, 'under God', in the Tsar, to whom the ecclesiastical, civil, and military authorities of the state were subject and to whom all the lesser 'orders of paternal authority', and their subjects, owed ultimate obedience. To be sure, the *Primer* also attempted to enlighten the people and to improve their religious and moral standards: superstition, defined as the attributing of a 'power to do good or evil to persons or things which in truth have no such power', and rebaptism (which was practised by some Russian schismatics and traditionally demanded by the official Church of Western European converts) were explicitly condemned. So too were bribery, simony, the promotion of unqualified persons to positions of authority ('as a result of which the people suffer'), dishonest business practices, all forms of slandering and backbiting, and the rendering of 'true worship', instead of appropriate forms of 'respect', to icons. Over-scrupulous Orthodox Russians were assured that it was permissible to have sexual relations with their wives. But it is difficult to avoid the conclusion that the chief pedagogical purpose of the *Primer* was to instil a respect for all forms of authority, especially that of the Tsar (or state). The things of God, the people were being taught by Prokopovich, were the things of Caesar, and vice versa: the two could not be distinguished.

And in this respect the *Primer* stands in striking contrast to the more classically clerical, Byzantine, even papal complexion of the *Orthodox Confession* of Peter Mogila, the founder of the Kiev academy, whose authoritative work would not be replaced in Russia until the nineteenth century. In his commentary on the Lord's Prayer, for example, Mogila confines himself to a prayer for spiritual and physical foods, with no mention of the government. Furthermore, in his explanation of the commandment to honour father and mother, Mogila *first* discusses the duties of children towards their parents, which 'even natural reason would teach us', and then shows that the words father and mother embrace all those 'from whom we receive any benefit, as our spiritual fathers [i.e. the clergy], our teachers, masters, relations, kings and officials, and the like'. Not only is the order of Mogila's hierarchy noteworthy, but equally his final exhortation: 'we must be careful that nothing be done contrary to the glory of God or his most holy commandments, always remembering that we must obey God rather than our parents, as Christ says (Matthew 10: 37): "He that loveth father and mother more than me is not worthy of me." And the same is to be understood of all our superiors.'[52] It is no wonder that Mogila's *Confession* was slighted, in a passage of the *Ecclesiastical Regulation*, by Prokopovich: its doctrine that the things of God (or of his clergy) sometimes take precedence over the obedience owed to 'all our superiors' was obviously incompatible with the doctrine of the absolute state.

Indeed, a comparison of Prokopovich's efficient little *Primer* with Mogila's complex, weighty catechism suggests another cause of friction between the former and his numerous clerical opponents, in this case both learned Latinizers and Muscovite traditionalists: his attitude towards the Tsar and his state. The comparison suggests that it was not only the character of Prokopovich's theology (and of his attitude towards them) that moved his opponents to denounce him as a heretic, but also what they dimly perceived to be his Protestant, secularist, rationalist political theory. For Prokopovich, in his sermons and political writings (and after he came to St. Petersburg there was little that was not political), consistently implied that the Christianity of a 'Christian king' was only an accidental, not an essential attribute of his office; that it was only one of his many characteristics, not the distinguishing one; that it gave him the right to rule the Church, not his right to rule at all. Prokopovich had all but embraced Hobbes's 'mortal god'. And in this his theory was profoundly unlike either the Byzantine-Muscovite or papal theories of his critics, not to mention the more or less eschatological teachings of the Russian schismatics. Proko-

---

[52] I quote from J. J. Overbeck's *The Orthodox Confession . . . of Peter Mogila* (London, 1898), which is a modernized version of the eighteenth-century English translation by P. Lodvill.

povich was the crucial figure in the transition in Russia from a concept of the state that was essentially religious to one that was essentially secular, from what we have learned to call a characteristically medieval idea to one that we could call modern.[53]

But the existence of Prokopovich's *Primer* reminds us of why he wished to see all power concentrated in the hands of the monarch and his government, which in the broadest sense should include the leaders of the Church. He wished to *reform* Church and society, to bring them closer to a condition which from his travels and studies and conversation with enlightened minds he had perceived was best. In his sermon at the official opening (in February 1721) of the Holy Synod, Prokopovich in effect challenged anyone to deny that in Russia 'the misery and poverty of a Christian people deprived of ecclesiastical instruction and discipline is seen', and that 'seeing this, we see how necessary is the [Synod]'.[54] He was a born reformer, and his wishes in this respect fully accorded with Peter's aims.

VI

The *Ecclesiastical Regulation*, which he was commissioned by the Tsar to write in the latter part of 1718 and which was promulgated in January 1721, is Prokopovich's greatest literary achievement. The legislative embodiment of the church reform of Peter the Great, it provided, above all, for the abolition of the Russian patriarchate and for the establishment, in its place, of an 'Ecclesiastical College'. Yet despite its official character—and it was officially reprinted, for the last time, as late as 1904—it retains the lineaments of an academic treatise and the personal stamp of its extraordinary author. It is not accidental, for instance, that the necessity of education is an insistent theme of the *Regulation*, and that fully a fifth of its text is devoted to a discussion of the projected church schools. Similarly, to students of Prokopovich's earlier career, the *Regulation*'s denunciations of half-educated sophists and florid preachers and boorish schismatics have a

---

[53] Cf. Lappo-Danilevsky, op. cit.
[54] Sermon quoted in Chistovich, op. cit., pp. 72–3.

familiar ring. We are not surprised to find in the document, knowing its author, a defence of 'secular learning' or a provision recommending that the 'ancient and modern philosophers, astronomers, rhetoricians, historians, etc.', as well as the Church Fathers, be read by seminarists. Only Prokopovich, among contemporary Russian churchmen, would have adduced specific examples of the 'nonsense' practised in Italy with respect to relics as a guide to the reformers of the Russian Church.

The numerous provisions of this revolutionary document, by which the Ecclesiastical College was empowered both to rule and to reform the Church, cannot be dealt with in this essay.[55] It may be observed, however, that Part I of the *Regulation* contains Prokopovich's lengthy justification of Peter's decision to found the College and therefore to abolish the patriarchate. All but one of the nine 'weighty reasons' adduced therein proceed from purely practical grounds, arguing, that is, that the institution of the College would promote more honest and efficient administration of the Church, arguments similar to those advanced by Peter when creating, at about the same time, the colleges of war, justice, foreign affairs, etc. But the central administrative organ of the Church, the patriarchate, which the Ecclesiastical College was meant to replace, had not been just another department of the Tsar's government, as had the predecessors of the other colleges; and some concession to this fact was logically demanded. Such was the task of point 7 of Part I of the *Ecclesiastical Regulation*, which is by far the longest of the reasons set forth to prove that an Ecclesiastical College was the 'most perfect' form of church government, 'better than one-man rule' and particularly suited to a 'Monarchical State, such as our Russia'. No single passage of the *Regulation* is more suggestive of the nature and flavour of Peter's church reform, and none shows more clearly how in this great enterprise Prokopovich deployed his wit, his tact, and his learning.

The fatherland [he wrote] need not fear from an administrative council [the Ecclesiastical College] the sedition and disorders that proceed from the personal rule of a single church ruler. For the common

[55] But see Cracraft, op. cit., esp. chapters 4, 5, 6 *passim*.

folk do not perceive how different is the ecclesiastical power to that of the Autocrat, but dazzled by the great honour and glory of the Supreme Pastor [the patriarch], they think him a kind of second Sovereign, equal to or even greater than the Autocrat himself, and imagine that the ecclesiastical order is another and better state.

The passage continues:

Thus the people are accustomed to reason among themselves, a situation in which the tares of the seditious talk of ambitious clerics multiply and act as sparks which set dry twigs ablaze. Simple hearts are perverted by these ideas, so that in some matters they look not so much to their Autocrat as to the Supreme Pastor. And when they hear of a dispute between the two, they blindly and stupidly take sides with the ecclesiastical ruler, rather than with the secular ruler, and dare to conspire and rebel against the latter. The accursed ones deceive themselves into thinking that they are fighting for God himself, that they do not defile but hallow their hands even when they resort to bloodshed. Criminal and dishonest persons are pleased to discover such ideas among the people: when they learn of a quarrel between their Sovereign and the Pastor, because of their animosity towards the former they seize on the chance to make good their malice, and under pretence of religious zeal do not hesitate to take up arms against the Lord's Anointed; and to this iniquity they incite the common folk as if to the work of God. And what if the Pastor himself, inflated by such lofty opinions of his office, will not keep quiet? It is difficult to relate how great are the calamities that thereby ensue.

Prokopovich explains:

These are not our inventions: would to God that they were. But in fact this has more than once occurred in many states. Let us investigate the history of Constantinople since Justinian's time, and we shall discover much of this. Indeed the pope by this very means achieved so great a pre-eminence, and not only completely disrupted the Roman Empire, while usurping a great part of it for himself, but more than once has profoundly shaken other states and almost completely destroyed them. Let us not recall similar threats which have occurred among us.—

A reference, perhaps, to the activities of the usurpatious Patriarch Nikon (1652–66), from which had issued the great Russian schism as well as his own deposition; and perhaps also to the very recent revelations of the Tsarevich Aleksey conspiracy, which had implicated several of the leading members of the Russian hierarchy, including Stefan Yavorsky himself, still (since 1700) the temporary head of the Church. Thus behind the author's characteristic reference to papal pretensions plainly lay Peter's apprehension that a new patriarch should become a focus of wrong-headed opposition to his regime; indeed, that the continued existence of the patriarchal office itself was inconsistent with the good of his state. Prokopovich concludes the argument, most pragmatically, with the assurance that

in an ecclesiastical administrative council [the Ecclesiastical College] there is not room for such mischief. For there the president himself enjoys neither the great glory which amazes the people, nor excessive lustre; there can be no lofty opinions of him; nor can flatterers exalt him with inordinate praises, because what is done well by such an administrative council cannot possibly be ascribed to the president alone. . . . Moreover, when the people see that this administrative council has been established by decree of the Monarch with the con-currence of the Senate, they will remain meek, and put away any hope of receiving aid in their rebellions from the ecclesiastical order.[56]

At its official opening (at which Prokopovich gave the sermon) the Ecclesiastical College (of which despite his junior position in the hierarchy he was appointed second vice-president) was re-named by Peter (probably at Prokopovich's suggestion) the 'Most Holy All-Ruling Synod', a distinctive and more dignified title which could not conceal the fact that the supreme administration of the Russian Church had become an agency of the Tsar's will. And it was Prokopovich who inserted into the draft of the Synodal oath of office, which was based on the oath taken by all senior officials of Peter's reorganized government, a sentence which reads: 'I acknowledge on oath that the Supreme Judge of this [Synod] is the Monarch of All Russia himself, our Most Gracious Sovereign.'[57] It would be difficult to exaggerate the importance of the *Ecclesiastical Regulation* and related documents in the creation

---

[56] See Verkhovskoy, op. cit. ii. 31–2, for the whole passage.
[57] Ibid. ii. 1ᵛ .п. 23, and i. 189.

and maintenance of the characteristically absolute Russian state of modern times and in the consequent secularization of Russian society. They embodied the fundamental principles according to which the Church was governed until 1918.

Prokopovich survived Peter the Great by about ten years, during which time he acted as a chief custodian of the first emperor's political legacy, propagated his myth, and mourned him in verse. He also remained, in the comparatively lazy, sometimes friendly, sometimes reactionary reigns of Peter's immediate successors, an extremely active churchman. Surviving at least two attempts to have him condemned for heresy, he became archbishop of Novgorod, the leading see of Great Russia, and the unchallenged leader of the Synod. In the midst of the political infighting he found time to befriend or patronize, as mentioned, the poet Antiokh Kantemir, Tatishchev the historian, and Lomonosov, with the first two of whom he formed their self-conscious 'Learned Guard', a term that he had invented.[58] And he resolutely resisted at least two attempts to restore the patriarchate—to undo, as though it were possible, Peter's church reform. Whatever else may be said of him, he was devoted to Peter and to his memory, and until his death in 1736 remained a champion of what came to be called enlightened absolutism.

Kantemir wrote a fitting epitaph: 'Feofan Prokopovich was loved and honoured by four successive sovereigns: Peter the Great, Empress Catherine, Peter II, Empress Anna. And among churchmen none was so learned and none so respected by the people'[59]— respected, probably feared, often hated, and scarcely remembered.

[58] P. P. Epifanov, ' "Uchenaya druzhina" i prosvetitelstvo XVIII veka', *Voprosy istorii* (Mar. 1963), pp. 37–53.
[59] Gershkovich, op. cit., p. 100.

4

MAX J. OKENFUSS

The Jesuit Origins of Petrine Education[1]

THE reader who finds the title of this article either heretical or obscure may be relieved to learn at the outset that it is primarily metaphorical. In 1700, the word *Jesuit* denoted a respectable Christian institution, well-organized and endowed, of official ecclesiastical stature, and world-wide in scope. While the Jesuits were attacked long before the *philosophes* made it fashionable to do so, while *Jesuit* was already a synonym for casuist, in the early eighteenth century the word had not yet attained the post-Enlightenment aura of intrigue or prevarication which it possessed when Coleridge denounced 'the low cunning and *Jesuitical* trick with which she deludes her husband'.

In the context of early eighteenth-century education, the Jesuits were universally associated with that kind of good schooling which was derived from Renaissance models, that 'severe training in Logic, Philosophy, the Latin and Greek Classics, and Latin Composition', that unified education in Christianity, grammar, and the classics which was the common heritage of Corneille, Molière, and Fontenelle in the seventeenth century, and of Montesquieu and Voltaire in the eighteenth.[2] It was that old grammatical, rhetorical, and humanistic learning which now

[1] The author expresses his gratitude to the Foreign Area Fellowship Program, and to the Russian Research Center at Harvard University, for support of research leading to this article, an earlier version of which was prepared for delivery at the Northeastern Conference of the American Association for the Advancement of Slavic Studies, at Montreal, Quebec, Canada, 4–8 May 1971.

[2] On Jesuit schooling and its similarity to other seventeenth-century instruction see, for example, Allan P. Farrell, *The Jesuit Code of Liberal Education* (Milwaukee, Wis., 1938), pp. 342–57 and *passim*; Philippe Ariès, *Centuries of Childhood* (New York, 1962), pp. 142 ff. and *passim*; W. A. L. Vincent, *The Grammar Schools. Their Continuing Tradition 1660–1714* (London, 1969), pp. 75–100 and *passim*; and Samuel Eliot Morison, *The Founding of Harvard College* (Cambridge, Mass., 1935), pp. 247–51 and *passim*.

underlies Peter Gay's interpretation of the *philosophes* as a classics-fed family of pagans.[3] Jesuit schools were church schools, ecclesiastical institutions, which were dedicated to that classical education which was the common heritage of doctor, lawyer, poet, scientist, governor, or, finally, cleric.

It is our threefold purpose here to redefine certain Petrine educational institutions as 'Jesuit' schools, that is, to suggest that Peter the Great endowed Russia with schools similar in structure and purpose to the famous Jesuit college at La Flèche, the Society's academies in Poland, and such schools as Harvard College; secondly, to challenge the shibboleth that Petrine schooling was 'technological and utilitarian',[4] a view common to all authors concerned with eighteenth-century Russia; and finally, to suggest some social implications of this kind of schooling in Russia.

Our principal topic, therefore, is not the activities of the Jesuits in Russia, although they were there.[5] While Peter was basically hostile toward Catholicism, he was also pragmatic, and between 1699 and 1705 Czech Jesuits were teaching Russian youths in Moscow with his full knowledge and approval. They were successful in attracting about thirty well-born students, and the Jesuits entertained the hope that Peter might formally recognize their school as a royally chartered academy. The Jesuits, however, were soon competing with the Lutheran school associated with its founder, Pastor Glück, and with another school in Moscow, the one which is the primary concern of this paper: the famous or, shall we say, the notorious Moscow Slavo-Greco-Latin Academy.

The Moscow Academy has not fared very well among historians. Recently Paul Dukes, for example, saw it as the symbol of how desperately Petrine Russia required modern schools. Patrick Alston characterized it as 'the sole source of civic training', but found that 'its circumscribed spirit precluded it from introducing secular learning'. A widely used textbook declares that 'church

[3] Peter Gay, *The Enlightenment: An Interpretation. The Rise of Modern Paganism* (New York, 1966).

[4] Marc Raeff, *Imperial Russia 1682–1825* (New York, 1971), p. 136.

[5] On the Jesuits in Russia, see the *Pisma i doneseniya iezuitov o Rossii kontsa XVII i nachala XVIII veka* (St. Petersburg, 1904), and A. V. Florovsky, 'Latinskie shkoly v Rossii v epokhu Petra I', *XVIII vek. Sbornik pyaty* (Moscow and Leningrad, 1962), pp. 316–35.

schools served church needs, i.e. the training of the clergy, and stood apart from the main course of education in Russia'. Even more indicative of its low repute is the fact that it has not been the subject of a major monograph since 1855.[6]

Peter's own association with the Moscow Academy dated from a 'conversation' with Patriarch Adrian in 1700, in which he talked about transforming the school. Historians of Russian education have cited his words on that occasion more frequently than anything else he ever said or wrote concerning education: '[After the school is transformed,] those who have studied well in this school should be put to various uses: Church and civil service, military occupations, architecture, and healing medicine.'[7] This passage has been variously used to 'prove' that Peter meant to subjugate the Church and its schools to civil control, that he intended to create a modern polytechnicum, that he was wholly concerned with 'professional training', that he sought to banish philosophy and philology from his realm, and even that he

... wanted the Church to give its blessing to scientific thought. *As the first step* [*sic*], he wanted the students of the theological academies to know not only the gospel, but also such practical matters as how to conduct military operations, how to erect public buildings, bridges, and how to cure the sick.[8]

[6] Paul Dukes, *Catherine the Great and the Russian Nobility* (Cambridge, 1967), p. 25; Patrick L. Alston, *Education and the State in Tsarist Russia* (Stanford, Cal., 1969), p. 4; Nicholas V. Riasanovsky, *A History of Russia* (New York, 1963), p. 319; Sergey Smirnov, *Istoriya Moskovskoy Slavyano-Greko-Latinskoy Akademii* (Moscow, 1855).

[7] 'I iz shkoly vo vsyakiya potreby lyudi blagorazumno uchasya proiskhodili, v tserkovnuyu sluzhbu, i v grazhdanskuyu, voinstvovati, znati stroenie i doktorskoy vrachevskoe iskustvo.' The 'Conversation' is undated, and has been variously assigned to 1698, 1699, or 1700; an unreliable English translation is provided in Georges Bissonnette, 'Peter the Great and the Church as an Educational Institution', *Essays in Russian and Soviet History*, ed. John S. Curtiss (New York, 1963), pp. 5–6; Bissonnette believed that the 'transcript' had first been published only by N. A. Voskresensky, *Zakonodatelnye akty Petra I* (Moscow and Leningrad, 1945), i. 33–4; this is the established text; however, it appeared in both Slavonic and a Russian translation in N. Ustraylov, *Istoriya tsarstvovaniya Petra Velikago* (St. Petersburg, 1858), iii. 511–12, 355–7. The translation here follows that of Marc Raeff, *Peter the Great* (Boston, Mass., 1966), p. 58. The formal Slavonic language of the 'Conversation' suggests careful editing, and probably does not represent Peter's actual speech.

[8] The views are those of Bissonnette, Pekarsky, Vladimirsky-Budanov, Ustraylov, and Alexander Vukinich respectively. For a fuller discussion of these and

It is difficult to imagine Peter as naïve as this latter view suggests. Too frequently historians have overlooked the fact that in the 'conversation' with Adrian, Peter specifically mentioned the school which was to be the model for the transformation of the Moscow Slavo-Greco-Latin school: it was the academy at Kiev. Indeed, within a year, dozens of teachers and students had arrived from Kiev, and opened their books. What kind of remarkable school was this Kievan academy which, according to the 'conversation', had convinced Peter that it would lead both to an educated clergy, and to the production of skilled technicians and of doctors?

The school at Kiev was one of scores founded between 1580 and 1650, strangely enough, as part of the general Counter-Reformation in Eastern Europe. The most famous and most successful of these schools were those opened by the Jesuits. Poland's great anti-Lutheran Prince-Bishop of Ermland, Hosius, invited the Jesuits to found a college at Braunsberg (Braniewo) in 1564. Under Stephan Batory (1575–86) and Sigismund III (1587–1632), the Society opened schools at Yaroslav, Lvov, Ostrog, Kiev, Lutsk, and Pułtusk (Płock diocese), Vilna, Poznan, and elsewhere, while their Protestant antagonists claimed institutions in Vilna, Lublin, Mogilev, Turov, Brest, Minsk, Vitebsk, and other cities.[9] This competition between Catholics and Protestants stirred the large Orthodox community of Belorussia and the Ukraine. Quickly it too opened schools, the first being founded by Prince Konstantin of Ostrog in 1580. Konstantin and other Orthodox patrons had the Slavonic Bible published, and circulated Scripture and liturgical books in Slavonic. Melety Smotritsky compiled the first printed Slavonic grammar. Konstantin's was the first Orthodox Greco-Latin school for teaching the 'liberated or free sciences (liberal arts)'.[10]

Although the Orthodox brotherhood schools (*bratskie shkoly*)

---

other interpretations, all of them questionable in my view, see my unpublished doctoral dissertation, 'Education in Russia in the First Half of the Eighteenth Century' (Harvard, 1970), pp. 255–61.

[9] B. N. Mityurov, *Razvitie pedagogicheskoy mysli na Ukraine v XVI–XVII vekakh* (Kiev, 1968), pp. 33–41.

[10] K. Kharlampovich, *Zapadnorusskiya pravoslavnyya shkoly XVI i nachala XVII veka* (Kazan, 1898), pp. 237–76.

are discussed in histories of Russian education, it must be remembered that at their founding and during their most active period, they were not in Russia, but in Poland. Even after the Armistice of Andrusovo (1667) most of them remained in Poland, including the famous one at Lutsk, whose two statutes constitute the most important source for studying these schools. Their location was significant, since it meant that the Orthodox brotherhood schools emerged and developed in an area where the power and interests of the Orthodox state of Muscovy did not and could not determine their regulations, teachers, or curriculum. Largely ignored by the Polish government, they were subject to varying control by the Patriarch of Constantinople, the Metropolitan of Kiev, and the hetmanate, but in their formative period, they were not subject to the defensive and xenophobic policies of Moscow. Free of this direct state–church power, these Orthodox schools competed with the Jesuits' institutions by using the most obvious, the most powerful, the most effective tool at their disposal: *imitation*.

Although Soviet historians admit no similarity between the Jesuit colleges of Eastern Europe and the Orthodox schools such as the one at Kiev,[11] long ago it was shown that the statutes of the Kiev brotherhood college were modelled on those of the Jesuit schools, and in places word-for-word borrowing was involved.[12] Furthermore, it has been shown that in all important respects— curriculum, administrative procedures, and rules for students and teachers—Jesuit and Orthodox schools in the Ukraine were virtually identical.

Indeed the Kiev school resembled other contemporary institutions as well. Compare, for example, these two curricula:

1. *Analog* or *Fara*. Reading and
   writing. Elementary compre-

---

[11] See, for example, the works of E. N. Medynsky, *Bratskie shkoly Ukrainy i Belorussii v XVI i XVII vv. i ikh rol v vossoedinenii Ukrainy c Rossiey* (Moscow, 1954), and *Istoriya russkoy pedagogiki do Velikoy Oktyabrskoy Sotsialisticheskoy Revolyutsii*, 2nd ed. (Moscow, 1938), and their influence on authors such as M. V. Sokolov, *Ocherki istorii psikhologicheskikh vozzrenii v Rossii v XI–XVIII vekakh* (Moscow, 1963), p. 250.

[12] N. I. Petrov, *Kievskaya Akademiya v vtoroy polovine XVII veka* (Kiev, 1895), pp. 110–11, and K. Kharlampovich, op. cit., pp. 356–63, especially p. 359.

hension of Latin; Slavonic or
Polish.

2. *Infima*. Introductory grammar
class; Latin etymology using
the *Institution* of Alvarez; catechism.

First Form. Introduction to Latin
grammar; declensions, verbs,
vocabulary.

3. *Grammatica*. Continuation of
Alvarez as far as 'syntaxis
ornata'. Cicero, Ovid. (Intro.
to Greek grammar.)

Second. Latin grammar, genders
of nouns, verb tenses, Cato,
Erasmus's *Colloquies*.

4. *Syntaxis*. Completion of the
grammar; Cicero, Catullus,
Virgil, Aesop. (Greek, the
'eight parts of speech'.)

Third. Completion of grammar.
Cicero, Terence.

5. *Poetica*. Caesar, Sallust, Livy,
Curtius, Virgil, Horace.

Fourth. Verses. Terence, Cicero,
Ovid.

6. *Rhetorica*. Cicero, the *Poetics* of
Aristotle.

Fifth. Orations: Sallust, Livy,
Tacitus, Curtius, Caesar, Virgil.

Sixth. Horace, Juvenal, Lucian,
Seneca, etc.

The curriculum on the left represents a composite form of the
subjects taught at the Kiev school in the seventeenth century, and
is virtually identical to that of Jesuit schools in Poland.[13] The one
on the right is the general curriculum of English grammar schools
in the second half of the century;[14] other examples could be shown
in Germany, in France, and in colonial America. Both consist of
three forms of Latin grammar, followed by two or more forms in
the humanities, poetics and rhetoric, that is, literature and elocu-
tion. One inescapable conclusion suggests itself: the seventeenth
century saw the introduction into Eastern Europe by Catholic and
Orthodox communities of the European classical grammar schools.

The Latin grammar schools were the dominant educational
institutions throughout Europe in the sixteenth and seventeenth
century. Everywhere they produced clergymen and were carefully supervised by the local ecclesiastical establishment, but they

---

[13] Petrov, op. cit., pp. 6–13, 74–86 and *passim*.
[14] Vincent, op. cit., pp. 75–7.

were never closed theological seminaries. Their narrow grammatical base was increasingly attacked by leading educational theorists, and they were challenged by demands for instruction in the vernacular tongues, but they survived almost unchanged well into the eighteenth century.[15] In some places, such as England, they were independent public schools, whose alumni were able to continue at the university. Elsewhere, in France and in central Europe, they were called 'colleges' or 'academies', indicating that the higher arts course, philosophy and theology, was taught in the same institution. The struggle against the Lutherans in the late sixteenth and early seventeenth centuries signalled the spread of this latter type of institution into the East Slavic world, where they were quickly imitated by the Orthodox community.

That the Orthodox schools, and especially the one at Kiev, were founded on the European-wide Jesuit notion of education, can be shown by the subjects taught, and by the textbooks used. All the records of the Kiev school in the seventeenth century refer to one single Latin grammar, that of *Alvar*. This was none other than *De Institutione Grammatica Libri Tres*, by Emmanuel Alvarez (1526–82), a Portuguese Jesuit, and a teacher of grammar at St. Ignatius's first college in Lisbon. First published in 1572, Alvarez's *Institutiones* by 1591 had become the official grammar of the Jesuits everywhere except in France.[16] Used by the Society's schools in Poland, it was the exclusive text for the Kievan Orthodox school as well.

Soviet scholarship, anxious to deny any Jesuit influence which would lessen the Russianness of schools in the Ukraine, has emphasized that the Orthodox schools taught Slavonic, while the Jesuit schools taught Polish. The Kiev school did use Smotritsky's Slavonic grammar, first published in Vilna in 1619. In the religious competition with the Jesuits, the Orthodox churchmen who founded the brotherhood schools were anxious to circulate Scriptures in the Slavonic tongue, and it is not surprising that they also taught Slavonic in their schools, and that the liturgical language remained a school subject beyond the introductory *analog* form.

[15] See, for example, Vincent, op. cit., pp. 98–101.
[16] The adoption of Alvarez is described in Farrell, op. cit., pp. 441–54.

Latin, however, remained the keynote of the Kiev school and its principal language of instruction. The students of the lower forms constituted *sodales Minoris Congregationis*, and those of the higher *sodales Majoris Congregationis*. The school was directed by a *rector* and a *prefect*; each class had student disciplinarians called *seniores*, and a *censor* oversaw religious observance. Latin was the language of the disputations, the orations and declamations, and of the readings for the various forms.[17] Latin, of course, played an identical role in the Jesuit schools.

It is common to call the Kiev school an *academy*, but the term is inaccurate until the 1690s. In its most illustrious period under Bishop Peter Mogila, the highest form at Kiev was philosophy, taught by Innokenty Gizel. In his course in 1645–7, he dealt with theological issues as well as Aristotelian physics and metaphysics, but a formal theology form was not taught.[18] By contrast, the Jesuits were able to add both academic forms quite easily, and their college at Vilna was raised 'to the rank of an academy with a philosophical and theological faculty' as early as 1579.[19] In Kiev this did not occur until 1691–3, when Ioasaf Krokovsky offered a formal course in theology for the first time. The completion of the course in 1693 was a significant occasion, and was marked by a request, addressed to the Tsar, that the school be officially recognized by the state as one 'for the study of the philosophical and theological sciences'. The request was granted in a patent dated 11 January 1694. The school was commissioned to accept 'children of the Russian people of all ranks and from other countries', who were 'defenders of the holy Greco-Russian faith'. Instruction was to be provided in 'not only Poetics and Rhetoric, but also Philosophy and Theology'. With the injunction to guard against heresy, the rector and teachers of the school were granted their salaries by Moscow. *De jure* recognition of the new status of the Kiev school finally came on 12 September 1701, when Peter formally elevated it to the rank of academy. The author of the Privilege, possibly the acting-Patriarch Stepan Yavorsky (named

[17] V. I. Askochinsky, *Kiev s drevneyshim ego uchilishchem Akademieyu* (Kiev, 1856), i. 127, 142–52.   [18] Petrov, op. cit., pp. 77, 84–6.
[19] *The Cambridge History of Poland. From the origins to Sobieski* (Cambridge, 1950), pp. 406–7, 409, 563.

to that post on 16 December 1700, after the death of Adrian), was aware that such a formal elevation was 'customary for other academies, in all foreign countries'.[20]

This then was the school which Peter selected as the model for restructuring the one in Moscow, which had languished since the expulsion of the Greek Lichud brothers in 1694. The Kiev academy was a classical school of the European-wide Jesuit type, a Latin school founded on a vertical curriculum of grammar and the humanities. Controlled by the Church, with an exclusively ecclesiastical faculty, it was both a school of general education, and a training-ground for future clerics, as were most Western colleges.

The Moscow school sorely needed rejuvenation.[21] In the 1680s, advised by resident Ukrainian intellectuals and by the patriarchs of the Eastern Church, the Muscovite Patriarchate decided to open an academy (*Akademii ustroiti*) for the teaching of the liberal arts (*svobodnye mudrosti; mudrosti, po grammaticheskoy khitrosti, i prochikh nauk svobodnykh*), which its charter defined as including grammar, poetics, rhetoric, philosophy (specifying dialectics, logic, natural philosophy, and ethics), and theology; it also added 'the study of justice, clerical and secular [canon and civil?] law, and the other Liberal Arts'. The author of the charter was obviously acquainted with the universal academic curriculum. There was, however, one striking difference between the Moscow school and Western colleges. The 'Greek' party of the clergy, temporarily victorious over the 'Latins' in the post-*raskol* theological debates, was able to stipulate Greek as the official language of instruction. Accordingly, the first teachers were Ioannicius (1663–1716) and Sofronius (1652–1730) Lichud, born on Cephalonia, and recommended to Moscow by Patriarch Dionisius of Constantinople. They arrived in Moscow on 6 March 1685, and in four years had

[20] See N. Mukhin, *Kievo-bratsky uchilishchny monastyr* (Kiev, 1893), pp. 113 ff.; Petrov, op. cit., pp. 47–52; and the texts of the patents in Medynsky, *Bratskie shkoly*, pp. 165–72.

[21] For this brief history of the pre-Petrine Moscow school, see the charter in *Drevnyaya rossiyskaya vivliofika*, 2nd ed. (Moscow, 1788), vi. 390–420; Smirnov, op. cit., pp. 1–81; on the Lichuds, M. Smentsovsky, *Bratya Likhudy* (St. Petersburg, 1899); and the full discussion and sources in Okenfuss, op. cit., pp. 133–52; see also James Cracraft, *The Church Reform of Peter the Great* (Stanford, Cal., 1971). pp. 92–3 and *passim*.

over 150 students, enrolled in an elementary class of Slavonic and Greek, in three forms of Greek grammar, and in rhetoric. In March 1690 Sofronius began to read a course in philosophy, beginning with logic, and continuing with physics. In the early 1690s the Lichuds began to teach Latin, and Ioannicius compiled his first lectures in theology, a course in Latin, *De anima*, which was explicitly based on the *doctor angelicus*, Thomas Aquinas. This was too much for the conservative faction of the hierarchy. On 9 August 1693 Patriarch Dositheus of Jerusalem denounced the Lichuds, and within a few months they were purged and confined to a monastery. Between 1693 and 1701 the Moscow school was operated by two of their students, Fedor Polikarpov and Nikolay Semenov, who were allowed to teach only the lower forms, and exclusively in Greek. Latin, philosophy, and theology were struck off the curriculum, and the school languished.

This shell of an academy was all that remained when shortly before his death, Patriarch Adrian appointed Pallady Rogovsky to the school. He was a Muscovite who had studied briefly with the Lichuds, and had finished his education in Jesuit schools in Poland, receiving his doctorate in a Uniate college in Rome. Returning to Russia in June 1699, he was received back into Orthodoxy by Patriarch Adrian, and assigned to teach Latin at the Moscow school. His appointment may have resulted from the 'conversation'.

With the death of Adrian (October 1700) and Yavorsky's assumption of patriarchal duties, the Moscow school underwent a major transformation. Already on 11 January 1701 the Jesuits in Moscow reported rumours of the Ukrainians' imminent arrival. On 16 February they reported that 'several Kievan monks have arrived and have begun to teach in the schools'. Two weeks later, they could note that

. . . at the present time twenty more monks have arrived here from Kiev; they teach the humanities [*humaniora*], philosophy, and theology, because the most serene Tsar has founded an academy and a dormitory for those of its students who desire to become church servitors. All sons of priests are enjoined to study Latin . . .[22]

[22] *Pisma i doneseniya iezuitov*, pp. 60–1, 66, 258–60, 263–4.

There seems to have been no immediate effort to enrol anyone except the sons of the clerical estate. The Jesuits had some thirty pupils of Latin, most of them apparently of the Russian nobility. Patriarch Adrian had warned of the potential harm in allowing Orthodox youth to attend this heretical school, but the Jesuits numbered a Prince Golitsyn, two Naryshkins, Apraksins, Dolgorukys, and Golovkins among their students. The Jesuits reported that none of their pupils wished to transfer to Yavorsky's classes. During the spring and summer of 1701, the two schools coexisted, and even in September the Jesuits still felt their relations with the Kievans to be tolerable. In the autumn, however, Yavorsky charged the Jesuits with heresy on the issue of Transubstantiation, and in 1702 he demanded that the *Posolsky Prikaz* cease assigning students to the Jesuit school. Vainly the Jesuits requested from their superiors in Prague someone knowledgeable enough to win the forthcoming theological debates with the Orthodox clergy; vainly they asked for someone to stage a school theatrical (a standard part of the rhetorical exercises), since the Kievans had produced one which was well received; in vain they hoped a new teacher, incognito in lay dress, might permit their school to remain open. Peter temporized, arguing that 'what is well begun is not to be permitted to be ended', but by 1703 the Jesuit school was all but closed, beaten by Yavorsky and the Kievans, and by the new Lutheran language school opened by Pastor Glück.[23]

Yavorsky's Latinizing impact on the Moscow school was swift and decisive. Within only three years the philosophy form could be introduced, because advanced students as well as teachers were imported from Kiev. The first philosophy class in 1704 numbered only three students with great Russian names, while thirty-one others had Ukrainian, Belorussian, or Polish names. Likewise in 1709, only five of twenty-one students were Great Russians.[24]

Yavorsky created in Moscow a duplicate of the Latin Academy in Kiev. The curriculum was identical. There were six lower forms

[23] For the above, *Pisma i doneseniya iezuitov*, pp. 57–61, 69–76, 183–5, 256–60, 266–72, 359–61; Florovsky, op. cit., pp. 321–4.
[24] Smirnov, op. cit., p. 81; A. I. Rogov, 'Novye dannye o sostave uchenikov Slavyano-greko-latinskoy Akademii', *Istoriya SSSR*, 1959, no. 3, pp. 142–3.

of grammar and humanities, followed by the arts course of philosophy and theology. At no time was instruction given in the conduct of the Divine Service or in other areas needed solely by the clergy. The teaching staff was almost exclusively Kievan, including all of the teachers of philosophy and theology. Moscow borrowed the Kievan principle of the 'rotating regency', a form of school organization which dated from the medieval University of Paris, in which one teacher brought a group of students through the higher academic forms, assuming administrative posts which corresponded to his current teaching. The principle of the 'rotating regency' was in operation at Harvard for over a century. At Moscow, the prefect taught philosophy, as did Feofilakt Lopatinsky in 1704–6, and subsequently theology, as rector of the school. The career of Feofan Prokopovich at Kiev followed the same pattern: he read poetics in 1705, rhetoric in 1706, philosophy (as prefect of the academy) between 1707 and 1711, and finally theology (as rector) between 1711 and 1716.[25]

We have several European accounts of the reformed Moscow Academy which are distinguished by their matter-of-fact reporting of its curriculum and administration. One was the Danish ambassador in Moscow, Just Juels, himself no lover of the Russians. In 1709 he noted that he had

. . . collected some evidence on the construction and position of the great Moscow patriarchal school or gymnasium [*sic*]. This school is located near a monastery, in which are allowed only Orthodox monks of Polish [*sic*] origins [as teachers]. The Archimandrite or Superior of this monastery, Feofilakt Lopatinsky, is at the same time rector of the school. His class consists of 17 students; he teaches them theology. He receives a stipend of 300 roubles annually from the Tsar.

Juels then lists the other forms at the school, giving them by their usual Latin names:

professor philosophiae	16 students	
„ rhetorices	15	„
„ poeseos	10	„
„ sintaxeos	21	„

[25] Smirnov, op. cit., pp. 193–8; on Kiev, D. Vishnevsky, *Kievskaya Akademiya v pervoy polovine XVIII stoletiya* (Kiev, 1903), pp. 17–44; on the rotating regency, see Morison, op. cit., pp. 137–8.

magister grammatices   20 students
   ,,   infimae grammatices anologiae et linguae
          germanicae   84   ,,

He also noted that one of the Lichud brothers, 'originally from the island of Cephalonia', was teaching the Greek language, and that all teachers received their salary from the Tsar.[26]

The Hannoverian resident in Moscow, Weber, also described the Moscow Academy, calling it a *college*. He saw the school in 1716, when it was staffed by

> several learned Russian Monks, who studied in Poland, Ukraina and Prussia. In the [Academy] are between two and three hundred Scholars, Polanders, Ukrainians, and Russians, divided in different Forms, where they are taught the Principles of Literature by Monks, who are able Men, and of good Sense. They have showed me their Buildings and Churches, and gave me an Account of their Method of Teaching; and afterwards a Student of the first Form, who was a young Knees [*Knyaz* —Prince] made a handsome Speech in Latin, for which he had prepared himself, and which consisted of Compliments . . .[27]

The Jesuits, Juels, and Weber could discuss the Moscow Academy without criticism, without explanations of its structure as alien or exotic, and without amazement. Everything suggests that what they saw there was familiar and comprehensible. And well they might, since the grammatical and humanistic forms were a European-wide phenomenon, the official definition of *education* every-where, now spread to Moscow by scholars who were educated in similar schools throughout Eastern and Central Europe.

Neither at Kiev nor at Moscow were significant changes in the vertical curriculum introduced in the first half of the eighteenth century. In both schools six Latin forms, *fara* or *analogiya*, *infima*, *grammatika*, *sintaksima*, *piitika*, *retorika*, were followed by philo-sophy and theology. In Russia, as in the West, teachers expected entering students to be conversant in Latin, and were frequently

---

[26] Yust Yul, 'Zapiski Yusta Yulya, datskago poslannika pri russkoy dvore (1709–1711)', *Russky Arkhiv*, 1892, no. 3, pp. 142–3; compare the identical list of classes in Vishnevsky, op. cit., pp. 92–3.

[27] F. C. Weber, *The Present State of Russia* (London, 1723), i. 128–9.

disappointed. As in the West, Kiev and Moscow had to introduce a preparatory class: in Kiev, Polish was usually taught, while in Moscow it was called the *Slavyansko-russkaya shkola*, teaching basic literacy in Slavonic, and the Latin alphabet. The first form was *fara*, better described as its alternative name, *analogiya*, since it consisted of learning the necessary Latin vocabulary by the use of multi-lingual phrase books. The three grammar classes, *infima classis*, *media classis grammatices*, and *suprema classis* (syntax) meant progressing through the *Institutiones* of Emmanuel Álvarez. No other text is mentioned. Erasmus's *Colloquia* supplemented the Jesuit's grammar, and other manuals of grammar exercises were also used. Classical Latin history and geography texts were used for translation exercises, but there was no formal change in the outward appearance of the curriculum. A great deal of stress was placed on translation, Polish and Latin at Kiev, Slavonic and Latin in Moscow.[28]

The two 'humanities', poetics and rhetoric, were taught according to texts compiled by the teacher himself. The most famous of these is Prokopovich's *De arte poetica*,[29] which he read at Kiev in 1705–6. For the period from 1690 to 1750, twenty-six poetics teachers at Kiev are known, and the texts of seventeen have survived. For the same period, twenty-three rhetoric teachers are known; Feofan's *De arte rhetorica*, read 1706–7, bore the common title. The higher academic forms, philosophy (logic, physics, metaphysics) and theology, showed little innovation until the middle of the eighteenth century: Aristotle and Aquinas respectively were the recognized guides.[30] Occasionally, at the discretion of the teacher, arithmetic and geometry were taught, usually in the philosophy form as, for example, was done by Prokopovich in 1707. This also corresponded to contemporary practice in Europe.[31]

[28] Vishnevsky, op. cit., pp. 89–176; Smirnov, op. cit., pp. 108–15, 136–76.

[29] The Latin text and a Russian translation of this course are given in Feofan Prokopovich, *Sochineniya* (Moscow and Leningrad, 1961), pp. 227–456; the best study of the humanities forms, poetics, and rhetoric, is N. Petrov, 'O slovesnykh naukakh i literaturnykh zanyatiyakh v Kievskoy Akademii ot nachala ee do preobrazovaniya v 1819 godu', *Trudy Kievskoy dukhovnoy akademii*, 1866, no. 7, pp. 305–30; no. 11, pp. 343–88; no. 12, pp. 552–69; 1867, no. 1, pp. 82–118; 1868, no. 3, 464–525.

[30] See Smirnov, op. cit., pp. 136–70; Vishnevsky, op. cit., pp. 175–268.

[31] See, for example, the provisions for the inclusion of mathematics in the

As in the West, there were no set time periods for the completion of any portion of the curriculum. Until the middle of the century, scheduled examinations were not part of the process of moving from one class to the next; a student moved to the next higher form by mastering the subject as certified by the teacher, and this could happen at any time in the year. Expulsion from the school for academic reasons was virtually unknown. Even a twenty-four-year-old youth, who was graded as 'hopeless' (*beznadezhny*) in the third form, grammar, was not dismissed.[32] There were, in accord with the phenomenon described by Philippe Ariès,[33] no age limits for admission or graduation, and actual ages varied a great deal. The *infima* class at Kiev ranged from eleven to twenty-two, with most students spending their mid- to upper-teens and early-twenties in the school. These practices were unchanged at Kiev and Moscow throughout the first half of the century.

This classical education was not a total novelty in Russia. Chernigov in the Ukraine boasted such a school. Dmitry Tuptalo, Metropolitan of Tobolsk, born and educated at Kiev, briefly directed a classical school, which used Alvarez's text, at Rostov. Between 1705 and 1716 Metropolitan Job of Novgorod operated a school, in which he utilized the services of the ageing Lichud brothers, who again taught a Greek curriculum. But the systematic spread of this kind of schooling throughout Russia began with Feofan Prokopovich and his *Ecclesiastical Regulation* (1721).

Feofan himself was committed to the type of education current in the two schools, although he was more innovative than most of his Ukrainian or Russian contemporaries. His course in rhetoric at Kiev had included an exceptionally large amount of classical historical literature. His philosophy course added ethics, arithmetic, and geometry to the customary Aristotelian logic, physics, and metaphysics. He did not tamper with external forms of the curriculum, but introduced new subject-matter within them, in the manner

statutes of William and Mary in 1727: R. Hofstadter and W. Smith (eds.), *American Higher Education* (Chicago, Ill., 1968), i. 44.

[32] Vishnevsky, op. cit., pp. 95, 311.

[33] Ariès, op. cit., pp. 189–240.

which was gradually becoming commonplace in the slow rejuvenation of Western colleges. His sections on schools in the
Regulation opened the way for such innovations at an increased
rate, and called for the establishment of such schools in all the
Russian dioceses.[34]

Three interrelated developments characterized the ten-year
period after the promulgation of the *Ecclesiastical Regulation*.[35]
First, there was a concerted effort on the part of some Muscovite
bishops to subvert the Latin-humanistic curriculum, and to
establish simpler, more traditional, and less 'heretical' schools of
elementary Slavonic literacy. This deception was revealed in
Synodal surveys of the late 1720s, and was effectively countered
only when Feofan reached the height of his influence after Anna
came to power in 1730. Secondly, a conflict developed between
the Holy Synod and the Admiralty in various towns over the
control of schooling. Beginning in 1716 the Admiralty had forced
many dioceses to open 'ciphering' schools of elementary mathematics. The diocese was expected to enrol sons of the clergy as
well as other *raznochintsy*, and to assume the full cost of the arithmetic school. Instructed in 1721 to open diocesan schools, local
bishops argued, usually successfully, that they should not bear the
cost of a ciphering school as well. The conflict with the Admiralty
produced much bitterness, and thereafter many local bishops
were openly hostile to accepting any but sons of the clergy in their
schools, and defensive about their exclusive right to educate
youths under Synodal jurisdiction. Both of these difficulties
were overcome and the Latin curriculum was introduced because
of a third development: Ukrainian clergymen became the
bishops throughout Russia. Of 127 bishops appointed between
1700 and 1762, 70 were Ukrainians or Belorussians, 47 were Great

[34] The Ecclesiastical Regulation is discussed in James Cracraft, *The Church Reform
of Peter the Great* (Stanford, Cal., 1971); for a full analysis of its provisions for
education, see Okenfuss, op. cit., Chapter 4.

[35] The first two of these developments are fully described only in Okenfuss, op.
cit., pp. 293–323; see also I. Chistovich, *Istoriya pervykh meditsinskikh shkol v Rossii*
(St. Petersburg, 1883), pp. xxvii–xliii; P. Pekarsky, *Vvedenie v istoriyu prosveshcheniya v Rossii* (St. Petersburg, 1862), pp. 107–21; P. Znamensky, *Dukhov-
nyya shkoly v Rossii do reformy 1808 goda* (Kazan, 1881); and Cracraft, op. cit.,
pp. 270–1 and *passim*.

Russians, and the remaining 10 were Greeks, Rumanians, Serbs, or Georgians.[36] Dioceses in the Ukraine led the way educationally: full Latin courses appeared first at Kharkov, Belgorod, and Smolensk. Elsewhere in Great Russia, the introduction of the Latin curriculum was usually preceded by the appointment of a Kievan-trained bishop. Through his efforts the Muscovite diocese acquired its Latin college.

The pattern of Kazan was fairly typical.[37] A school opened in 1723 with 52 students. Almost immediately 9 were sent home because they were too poor, 11 as too young, 14 fled, 2 were dismissed for stupidity, and 6 died. All in all, only 5 of the original contingent remained after one year. Additional students were recruited and by April 1724 the teacher could report that 26 students had memorized the Slavonic primer and were studying Slavonic Grammar, 'orthography, etymology, orthographic prosody and the eight parts of grammar', that is, the contents of Smotritsky's book. Ten students were reading the Breviary and Psalter. An additional 13 recently baptized Tatars and Cheremiss were learning Russian. The grammarians had also learned the Latin alphabet. A report of 1726 indicated that elementary arithmetic had been added, as well as ethics, probably using the recommended text by Pufendorf.

In April 1732 a new bishop was sent to Kazan. Ilarion Rogalevsky, born in Lithuania, arrived and immediately called upon Kiev for teachers. The former teacher of Slavonic was retained to instruct beginners in the Primer and Psalter, but three Kievans quickly added the traditional six Latin forms *do retoriki*. The transition to a Latin academy was not smooth and painless. In 1735 a new bishop, 'raised in the old spirit and hostile to the Petrine reforms', reduced the size of the school from 120 to 50, and dismissed the Kievans. But a Synodal investigation revealed what had happened, and another new bishop (1739) reintroduced

[36] K. Kharlampovich, *Malorossiyskoe vliyanie na velikorusskuyu tserkovnuyu zhizn* (Kazan, 1914), pp. 459, 633.

[37] P. Znamensky, 'Kazanskaya seminariya v pervoe vremya eya sushchestvovaniya', *Pravoslavny sobesednik* (Aug. 1868), 271–91, 299, 311; see also A. Artemev, *Kazanskiya gimnazii v XVIII stoletii* (St. Petersburg, 1874), pp. 3–8; Znamensky's book, cited in footnote 35 above, is the best guide to the transformation of other schools during the period.

the Latin curriculum and the school flourished. In the thirties it became a *seminarium*, a word introduced by Feofan in the *Regulation* to designate a college with boarding facilities. Kazan was not, in the first half of the century, a 'clerical seminary' in the modern sense of the term; its curriculum and regulations were those of grammar schools everywhere.

At Kiev the curriculum remained unchanged after the *Ecclesiastical Regulation* except for the temporary addition of elective courses in Greek, German, and Hebrew in 1738. In the first half of the eighteenth century the Kiev Academy was not even primarily for the sons of the clergy or for those intending to become clergymen. In the 1730s and 1740s the sons of the clergy comprised only about one-third of the total enrolment. The vast majority of students enrolling did not continue through the philosophy and theology forms; most completed the humanities, and then freely left the school. Roughly one out of five or six of the students went on to philosophy, and only one-half of the philosophy class entered theology. In the Russian schools founded after the *Dukhovny reglament*, the ratio was somewhat higher. One out of three students at Pskov entered the higher forms. Sons of the clerical estate were proportionately more numerous in the schools in Russia than they were in the Ukraine, but non-clerics regularly attended at Moscow. Under Anna, in spite of other provisions for the education of the gentry, the Moscow Academy was ordered to enrol 158 gentry scholars, including Obolenskys, Golitsyns, Dolgorukys, and Meshcherskys, where they attended classes with the sons of priests, clerks, and common soldiers. In the 1730s only one-third of the students at the Moscow Academy were the sons of clerics.[38]

By the end of the reign of Anna, owing to the efforts of the

[38] A. Knyazev, 'Ocherk istorii Pskovskoy seminarii ot nachala po preobrazovaniya eya po proektu ustava 1814 goda', *Chteniya v Obshchestve istorii i drevnostey rossiyskikh*, 1866, no. 1, sect. V. pp. 27–9; Vishnevsky, op. cit., pp. 293–4; N. I. Petrov, 'Spiski studentov i professorov Kievskoy Akademii 1736–1737 po 1757–1758 god', *Trudy Kievskoy dukhovnoy akademii*, lv, no. 5 (1914), 115; Smirnov, op. cit., pp. 107, 179–80; for Moscow, see also B. V. Titlinov, *Pravitelstvo imperatritsy Anny Ioannovny v ego otnosheniyakh k delam pravoslavnoy tserkvi* (Vilna, 1905), pp. 389–90; and M. V. Sychev-Mikhaylov, *Iz istorii russkoy shkoly i pedagogiki XVIII veka* (Moscow, 1960), pp. 48–9.

ageing Feofan Prokopovich (d. 1736), most of the diocesan schools were becoming Latin 'seminaries', that is, boarding academies. By 1738 they had an enrolment of 2,500. By 1750 there were twenty-six such colleges, seven having the theology form, and four others going as far as philosophy. All the rest ended with rhetoric. By 1764 the twenty-six diocesan academies numbered some 6,000 students. Civil legislation until mid century continued to insist that the sons of non-clerics be accepted, and that they produce men of use to both the religious and civil professions.[39]

At mid century, therefore, Russia possessed a sizeable and growing network of colleges modelled on the Kiev Academy. Everywhere they were staffed primarily by Kievans and by the Kievan-trained. Their curricula were probably slower to accept innovations than were the reawakening colleges of Western Europe, but the potential of solid classical studies was there. Due to the struggle with the Admiralty in the early years of the *Dukhovny reglament*, they were over-defensive in terms of accepting non-clerics into their classes, but they were absorbing them, and producing scores of educated men for every one who finished the theological form and joined the clergy.

The system of Russian diocesan schools, ultimately modelled on the seventeenth-century Kiev Academy and its West European prototypes, testifies against any characterization of Petrine education as narrowly technical or utilitarian. Peter's Russia abounded in specialized training centres, for navigation, artillery, medicine, and engineering. In the diocesan schools it also boasted the origins of a system of general education, directed, operated, and maintained by the ecclesiastical establishment, as was the case throughout Europe.

These diocesan schools were not narrowly religious or exclusively theological academies. In the first half of the eighteenth century, it is more accurate and meaningful to describe these schools as 'Jesuit'. A detailed study of their curriculum, classroom procedure, textbooks (or lack of them), and administrative regu-

[39] Znamensky, op. cit., pp. 140–55, 175–7, and *passim*; Kharlampovich, *Malorossiyskoe vliyanie*, p. 636.

lations—and we have given only the bare outlines here—shows them to be identical to the dominant form of education in Europe. They would change, in Europe and in Russia. In England, the dissenting academies would pioneer a new secondary education; in France, Rousseau and Condorcet would outline a new world of both elementary and secondary education; in Germany, Fröbel would introduce the Kindergarten; in Switzerland, Pestalozzi would give a new emphasis to child development; and everywhere in the late eighteenth and early nineteenth centuries governments and private churches and societies would call for universal popular education, which meant the slow abandonment of the classical Latin curriculum. To some extent Russia too would participate in this general educational revolution. But neither the rise of popular education nor the reform of the colleges can properly be dated before 1760.[40] In the pre-Enlightenment world of Peter the Great the old classical schools still constituted the very definition of *education*, and the Petrine diocesan schools were grounded in it. In Russia, as everywhere in Europe, the faculty and staff were clergymen or monks, and the schools were administered by the ecclesiastical establishment, but this did not make them 'theological seminaries', institutions exclusively for the training of ministers of the Gospel.

To redefine the Kiev and Moscow Academies as classical colleges, to remove the misconceptions engendered by calling them religious schools, constitutes only a footnote to the history of education in Russia, unless that redefinition leads to a reinterpretation of other aspects of eighteenth-century Russian culture. What are the implications of calling these institutions Western colleges?

In the first place, a number of our favourite jokes about the Petrine reforms suddenly lose their humour. At one time or another all of us have laughed at the first professors at the gymnasium of the Russian Academy of Sciences trying to lecture in Latin. If, on the other hand, Peter and Prokopovich had instituted

[40] See, for example, Hugh M. Pollard, *Pioneers of Popular Education 1760–1850* (Cambridge, Mass., 1957); and Harold Silver, *The Concept of Popular Education* (London, 1965).

a network of colleges in which a youth had to be conversant in Latin before being admitted to the first grade (first grammar form), then Latin lectures were quite reasonable. The first students of the academic gymnasium were the sons of foreigners and Baltic Germans, and Russian students taken from the Moscow Academy. By recruiting advanced students in this manner, the new gymnasium was able to open immediately in 1727 with four forms, three of grammar and one in the humanities. The structure of the gymnasium's curriculum was, incidentally, identical to that of the diocesan academies until 1747. Instruction in both was in Latin, and there is no direct evidence that it created any problems. The complaints about the early academic gymnasium were either those of gentry families protesting against obligatory education in general, or those of the Synod which argued for jurisdiction over its own youth, thus continuing their earlier identical quarrels with the Admiralty. I know of no first-hand accounts which state that the unpopularity of the gymnasium was due to the inability of its students to understand the Latin lectures of its imported faculty.[41]

Regarding the Moscow, Kiev, and other academies as Western colleges in the first half of the eighteenth century makes the biographies of several individual Russians more intelligible. In the long run, it makes Speransky's clerical origins compatible with his civil career. It explains why Lomonosov might dishonestly claim to be gentry rather than clergy in origin when he enrolled in the Moscow Academy and why he was prepared to study later at Marburg. It helps us to understand how the Moscow Academy could produce three academicians, six professors for Moscow University, the Court portrait-painter Levitsky, the publisher Bantysh-Kamensky, and numerous other secular figures from Russian cultural history in the eighteenth century. The Russian medical profession was almost totally comprised of graduates of the diocesan colleges.[42]

[41] The best study of instruction in the early academic gymnasium is E. S. Kulyabko, *M. V. Lomonosov i uchebnaya deyatelnost Peterburgskoy Akademii Nauk* (Moscow and Leningrad, 1962), especially pp. 33–4 and *passim*; see also the 'Spisok uchenikam akademicheskoy gimnazii s 1726 po 1731 god', *Ucheniya zapiski Imperatorskoy Akademii Nauk po pervomu i tretemu otdeleniyam*, iii, no. 4 (1855), 545–66.
[42] A. Morozov, *Mikhail Vasilevich Lomonosov*, 2nd ed. (Leningrad, 1952), pp. 127, 128; on the careers of Moscow graduates, see Smirnov, op. cit., pp. 225–45;

Indeed, only by considering the so-called 'church schools' as European classical colleges do the biographies of many outstanding Russians make any sense at all. Why, for example, would a well-educated cosmopolitan like Dmitry Kantemir permit his son, Antiokh, to study at the Moscow Academy? Surely not for the priesthood. The famous mathematics professor at Kharkov University, T. F. Osipovsky (b. 1765), received his education at the provincial 'seminary' at Vladimir, one of the score created after the *Ecclesiastical Regulation*. Ya. P. Kozelsky (b. 1728), teacher and 'enlightened' philosopher, was educated at the Kiev Academy where he 'attained the fundamentals of Latin' and 'completed the course in rhetoric'. The physician, anatomist, and academician A. P. Protasov (b. 1724) was educated in the 'seminary' created by Feofan Prokopovich as the model for other schools to be opened by the Holy Synod. The famous medical doctor K. I. Shchepkin (b. 1728) was educated in the Latin college at Vyatka and read philosophy at Kiev, before studying medicine at Padua and Bologna.[43] The biographies of all these men, the sons of priests, soldiers, and peasants, are incomprehensible if their early education is seen as narrowly 'clerical'.

In 1965 M. M. Shtrange published his *Demokraticheskaya intelligentsiya Rossii v XVIII veke*.[44] It argued that between 1750 and 1780 an important intelligentsia of *raznochintsy* emerged in Russia, that it developed a progressive ideology which distinguished it from the gentry, and that Catherine the Great consciously and deliberately checked its growth. Although Shtrange referred to the diocesan colleges as 'clerical seminaries' in the traditional manner, they produced the great majority of the seventy-four 'progressive thinkers' who comprised his 'democratic intelligentsia'.

the best study of the careers of all graduates of Kievan-modelled schools is E. M. Prilezhaev, 'Dukhovnaya shkola i seminaristy v istorii russkoy nauki i obrazovaniya', *Khristianskoe chtenie*, 1879, no. 7–8, pp. 161–87 and *passim*.

[43] For these individuals, see the following: M. I. Radovsky, *Antiokh Kantemir i Peterburgskaya Akademiya Nauk* (Moscow and Leningrad, 1959); I. N. Kravets, *T. F. Osipovsky — vydayushchysya russky ucheny i myslitel* (Moscow, 1955); Yu. Ya. Kogan, *Prosvetitel XVIII veka Ya. P. Kozelsky* (Moscow, 1958); T. A. Lukina, *A. P. Protasov — russky akademik XVIII veka* (Moscow and Leningrad, 1962); and V. V. Kupriyanov, *K. I. Shchepkin — doktor meditsiny XVIII veka* (Moscow, 1953).

[44] (Moscow, 1965); see my review in *Kritika*, iii, no. 1 (1966), 13–22.

The study of social change in eighteenth-century Russia is still in its infancy, but one point is absolutely clear: the 'Shtrange thesis' is tenable *only* if one admits that the schools under Synodal control were colleges of general education, and not 'seminaries' devoted wholly to the improvement of the clergy.

Finally, the history of book publishing in the first half of the century is more understandable if one regards the schools as Western colleges. No textbooks were published for these schools, and none were necessary. The sole Latin grammar in use was Alvarez, and it was never issued in Russia. No textbooks for philosophy or the humanities were issued, since in Russia, as in the West, a 'course' consisted of the manual written by the teacher on the basis of his own education in a similar school. This is how the Lichuds taught in the 1680s, how Feofan taught at Kiev and in Moscow, and how classical schoolmasters taught throughout Europe. Strictly speaking, the content of the instruction was more a tradition than a curriculum, since it was the result of the teacher's previous mastery of the form he was teaching. In the first half of the eighteenth century in Europe, textbooks were appearing for new types of schooling, technical training, for example, but they were unnecessary for the colleges.

Technical manuals are rightfully seen as the dominant publications of the Petrine age. Only by regarding the Petrine Synodal schools as Western colleges, however, can one understand the appearance of a smaller but still important group of books. These include translations of the classics, and of Renaissance standards, reading materials of interest to those educated in the grammar schools, and humanities forms. They included Bernhard Varenius's *Geographia generalis*, described by its translator, a Kievan teacher at the Moscow Academy, as belonging to men of the 'Republic of Letters' (that is, to the academies). To the same category belong the translations of the *Atheniensis Bibliotheces* of Apollodorius of Athens, the famous biography of Alexander the Great by Quintus Curtius Rufus, Polidoro Vergilio's famous book of inventions, *De rerum inventoribus*, Aesop's *Fables*, and many others. In each case the translator was associated with the Latin college in Moscow.[45]

45 On these books see the relevant descriptions in T. A. Bykova and M. M.

These Petrine 'religious' schools deserve serious attention. They have too long been the exclusive concern of church historians, and too long slighted by students of Russian secular, 'modern' culture. In the first place, they were a major feature of the Petrine reforms. Peter rejected the 'Greek compromise' of the Lichud period of the Moscow Academy as too narrowly ecclesiastical, too little 'Western'. The first wave of Ukrainians brought Russia into the mainstream of contemporary Western education, a fact clearly recognized by Peter when he signed the charters of the Kiev and Moscow Academies, as is done 'in all foreign states'. When spread throughout the dioceses, they created a system of general education, which paralleled the Moscow School of Mathematics and Navigation, the St. Petersburg Naval Academy, the ciphering, wharf, and garrison schools which provided technical training to Petrine Russia. In their early phases none of these schools was organized on the *soslovie* principle, that is, none was exclusively for the education of one class. The ambiguity of Petrine legislation toward the *sosloviya*, hostility between the Synod and other bodies, and the social composition of Russia eventually led most of them to become associated with a certain part of the population, but the diocesan schools were not founded on the basis of the clerical classes.

Educationally the diocesan schools were institutions of general education. At the date of their introduction into Russia, they were 'advanced' in that they corresponded to the official schooling of the West. Petrine educators could not have foreseen how short-lived they were to be in Europe. Founded only in the early eighteenth century, jealously guarded by the Church, faced with new class-oriented genteel education for the nobility in Anna's reign, they were less open to innovation than Western colleges. With changes in the West, with the class-oriented educational views of Catherine the Great and her advisors, it is difficult to see how their continued evolution could have paralleled similar schools in Europe.

Gurevich, *Opisanie izdanniy grazhdanskoy pechati 1708—yanvar 1725 g.* (Moscow and Leningrad, 1955), and *Opisanie izdaniy napechatannykh kirillitsey 1689—yanvar 1725 g.* (Moscow and Leningrad, 1958); a fuller discussion of these and other books and their translators and cultural significance is in Okenfuss, op. cit., pp. 152–9, 306–8, 323–5 and *passim*.

In the short run, however, in the first half of the century, they had a major impact on the cultural development of Russia. Students of the Lichud brothers controlled publishing in Russia until they were replaced by the pupils of Prokopovich and the Kievans. Throughout the century they provided Russians with the language skills which made advanced study in European universities possible. Their strong Latin basis was the key to the development of Russian medicine. Their links to the sons of church servitors, of soldiers, and of other *raznochintsy* provided the manpower for the Russian bureaucracy in the eighteenth century. They reproduced their own teaching staff, and provided the instructors for the Academy of Sciences, for Moscow University, for the Gentry Cadet Corps, and eventually for Catherine's district schools. Finally, they provided education for the clergy. In short, they became permanent and important institutions for the education of Russians, affecting the intellectual life and the social mobility of many, including some of the gentry and the peasantry.

It is difficult to judge how much of this Peter foresaw when he instructed Patriarch Adrian to transform the Moscow school along the lines of the Kiev Academy. With Feofan and the spread of these schools to the Russian provinces, we are on surer ground. In the *Ecclesiastical Regulation* he predicted that the students of these colleges, 'after they are perfected in school-learning . . . are capable of being recommended to his Imperial Majesty, and according to his Majesty's order, of being put into different employs'. What more could Peter ask?

MAX J. OKENFUSS

5 Russian Students in Europe in the Age of Peter the Great[1]

PETER THE GREAT's sending of Russian students to Western Europe has been regarded as one of the more humorous educational episodes of the early eighteenth century. Events in the early years of Peter's reign suggest that he was so naïve as to believe that the Muscovites could be enlightened in Europe, without founding schools in Russia. As early as 1737 Johann Vockerodt, the secretary to the Prussian Embassy in St. Petersburg, expressed this view. After Peter returned from his tour to Europe in 1696–7, Vockerodt reported, he dispatched a significant number of 'very coarse and ignorant young people [to the West], but when they had returned with only slightly more ability than they had taken with them, then the need for schools and academies at home became clear to Peter'.[2]

Historians have generally accepted Vockerodt's interpretation. The more generous have viewed the sending of Russians abroad as a temporary 'stopgap' measure prior to the development of schools in Russia. Others have argued that it was a foolish and futile 'attempt to create a scholarly class out of a whole cloth', that is, a project to transform a sizeable segment of the Russian population through direct European contacts.[3] The more moderate of these positions has been clearly stated by Paul Dukes:

Peter's modernization of a navy and of new industrial enterprises,

[1] The author wishes to express his appreciation to the Russian Research Center at Harvard University and to the Foreign Area Fellowship Program for assistance in preparing this article.

[2] Ioann Gottgilf Fokkerodt, 'Rossiya pri Petre Velikom', *Chteniya v imperatorskom Obshchestve istorii i drevnostey rossiyskikh*, 1874, no. 2, p. 100.

[3] For the two views see respectively, S. R. Tompkins, *The Russian Mind* (Norman, Okla., 1953), p. 34; and A. Vucinich, *Science in Russian Culture* (Stanford, Cal., 1963), p. 49.

demanded men of a type that Russia desperately lacked. To bridge this gap, many young Russians were sent abroad, and many foreign experts were invited to come to Russia. The results obtained by these methods did not always justify the considerable financial outlay necessary. In any case, the long-term solution of Russia's educational problems would obviously depend on her ability to build up an adequate indigenous school system.[4]

Implicit in Dukes's careful formulation ,and more explicit in other recent studies, is the notion that the sending of Russians abroad was broadly educational in purpose, and that it was a genuine, if foolhardy, attempt to enlighten Russia.

Even the moderate view implies that the sending of Russians abroad was a failure. Some contemporaries believed likewise. The anonymous English author of a 1724 description of the Russian navy observed that the students in Europe,[5]

... having credit at large, launched out into all manner of effeminate and extravagant living, frequenting the play-houses, gaming tables, etc., according to the prevailing gust of the nation they conversed in, not caring how little they went to sea; and upon their recall, undergoing a strict examination, were found instead of attaining the rudiments of a seaman, to have acquired only the insignificant accomplishments of fine gentlemen. And the Tsar, incensed thereat, gave directions to reduce 'em to common seamen, and employed them constantly in the most servile part of their work. In a word, this great expense was to very little purpose.

This view was not, however, universally held. Alexander Gordon of Achintoul, a major-general in Russian service, had a high regard for the nobles who studied abroad. Most of them, he observed, remained in Europe 'seven years (until they were perfect)', and upon return were employed 'to their capacities, either in the land or sea-service; and those who had no inclination for either, were employed in the police [i.e. civil service]'. In short, 'most of them became well-bred gentlemen, speaking most languages'.[6] Peter

---

[4] Paul Dukes, *Catherine the Great and the Russian Nobility* (Cambridge, 1967), p. 25.

[5] C. A. P. Bridge (ed.), *History of the Russian Fleet during the reign of Peter the Great by a contemporary Englishman (1724)* (London, 1899), pp. 102–3.

[6] A. Gordon, *The History of Peter the Great* (Aberdeen, 1755), i. 141.

himself agreed with Gordon, and boasted that '. . . seamen sprung up from *Russian* blood, . . . from foreign Countries, [were] return[ing] home able Men', and this was why 'the remotest Potentates [were] expressing for us the greatest esteem'.[7] Whatever their evaluation of the practice, contemporaries usually mentioned seamanship together with the sending of Russians abroad. It is our purpose here to re-examine the evidence concerning Russian study in Europe in the Petrine period: why students were sent, who they were, how they fared in Europe, and briefly, what they did upon their return.

The most celebrated group of Russians sent to Europe was the first, a contingent of fifty chamberlains (*komnatny stolnik*: cf. *Kammer Junker*) of the Tsar's household. In early 1697 Peter dispatched them to Venetia, Holland, and England. The Venetian group, which studied on the Yugoslav coast, is best known to us, for its adventures were ably recorded by Petr A. Tolstoy and Boris I. Kurakin.[8] In their commission, which Tolstoy included in his memoirs, they were not ordered to become educated men, scholars, or even generally enlightened individuals. Rather, their instructions were simple and direct: to learn the maps, instruments, and other guides to seafaring, to handle a ship and to know her rigging, equipment, and structure, and if possible, to participate in naval combat and, upon their return, to convey to others the specific naval skills acquired in Europe.[9] A portrait of several of the *stolniki* hangs today in the Naval Museum in Perast on the Bay of Kotor in Yugoslavia; it shows the young Russians with Marko Martinović, whom an inscription identifies as their teacher

---

[7] Peter's comments appear in the preface to his widely reported speech on the 'Transmigration of the Sciences'; the text follows that in [Daniel Defoe], *A True, Authentick, and Impartial History of the Life and Glorious Actions of the Czar of Muscovy* (London, [1725], pp. 420–1; it is reported as a first-hand account in the *Memoirs of Peter Henry Bruce, A Military Officer, in the Service of Prussia, Russia and Great Britain* (London, 1732), pp. 132–3).

[8] P. Tolstoy, 'Putevoy Dnevnik P. A. Tolstago', *Russky Arkhiv* (1888), i. 161– 204, 321–68, 505–52, ii. 5–62, 113–56, 225–64, 369–400; B. Kurakin, 'Zhizn Borisa Ivanovicha Kurakina, im opisannaya, 1676 iyulya 20-go—1709 gg.', *Arkhiv Knyazya F. A. Kurakina*, i. 241–87.

[9] Tolstoy, op. cit. i. 167–8; see also G. V. Plekhanov, *History of Russian Social Thought* (New York, 1967), p. 7.

K

of 'naval sciences'. On a desk are an astrolabe, a compass, and a naval chart.[10]

Specific orders to study seamanship raise the question of how the naval arts were commonly taught in contemporary Europe. By and large in 1700, one did not learn the nautical sciences in a school, but through a naval apprenticeship with the military fleet or the merchant marine. Further, although schools of mathematics and navigation were beginning to appear, they were recent, and few in number; Russians generally did not attend them, nor were they expected to. The bulk of skilled European seamen learned their art through practical training, and not in a classroom. The new schools—the British Royal Mathematical School at Christ's Hospital and John Colson's school at Wapping, Louis XIV's naval schools at Toulon, Brest, and Rochefort, the Mathematical School at Halle, and, it should be added, the Moscow School of Mathematics and Navigation—were designed to prepare young mariners for their practical apprenticeship at sea. Even in the second half of the eighteenth century such schools continued to be regarded as auxiliary to a practical apprenticeship on board ship. As late as 1765, a French report said, 'It's not in a classroom that a man learns seamanship. Some geometry and the general theories of navigation may be taught in school, but seamanship is learned only on the sea.'[11]

The experience of the Russian *stolniki* in Venetia illustrates how this apprenticeship system worked. Venice had no public perm anent institutions for teaching naval science. Instead a knowledgeable ship's captain was periodically given a group of students, a training vessel, and often a master-shipbuilder as an assistant who could explain the structure and rigging of the ship. The person and home of the captain became, in effect, a temporary private school

[10] For assistance in tracing Peter's students in Yugoslavia, I would like to thank Professor Aleksandar Lalošević of the Naval Museum at Perast, and his colleagues at the Naval Museum at Kotor.

[11] F. B. Artz, *The Development of Technical Education in France, 1500–1850* (Cambridge, Mass., 1966), p. 107, also pp. 1–2, 45–55, 102–9. See also N. Hans, 'The Moscow School of Mathematics and Navigation (1701)', *Slavonic Review*, xxix, no. 73, 532–6; N. Hans, *New Trends in Education in the Eighteenth Century* (London, 1951), pp. 213–19; and A. Milošević, 'Pomorska škola u Perastu', *Godišnjak Pomorskog muzeja u Kotoru*, ii (1953), 45.

which functioned until it had trained its assigned contingent. Marko Martinović, a wealthy shipowner long in Venetian service, was such a captain. When Venice decided to accept Russian students as part of a broader anti-Turkish diplomatic manœuvre, he was selected as their teacher. His 'school' included some class-room lessons, but two practice cruises around the Adriatic and Mediterranean were the essential part of his curriculum. The personal apprentice-type teaching was indicated by the fact that the land instruction took place not in Venice but in Martinović's home port on the Boka Kotorska. Even more revealing is the fact that the students were released as soon as they had demonstrated proficiency, and not at the end of any predetermined period of study. They were set ashore at Civitavecchia near Rome and were permitted to return overland to Venice where Martinović awarded their certificates before a Venetian naval board.[12] The captain's apprenticeship 'school' was a common phenomenon, operating in the same manner for Russians and Venetians.

Concerning the content of Martinović's instruction, we have several sources of information. One is a set of notes of unknown authorship, but found in the papers of Petr Tolstoy. Dated 1706, it tells of what was 'learned and remembered' from 'Marko Martinović of Perast'. It contains a totally practical and utilitarian description of the various types of ships, an explanation of the compass, and a listing of the various winds and currents of the Levant.[13] Secondly there are the certificates awarded to the Russians by their Venetian naval board and signed by Martinović. They repeated the naval skills listed in the group's original com-mission, and added 'the theoretical and practical mathematical sciences, without which no one can master the naval sciences'.[14] Kurakin recorded the extent of the mathematics taught by Mar-tinović. He itemized 'arithmetic, the theory of geometry, the five books of Euclid, practical geometry, and trigonometry', in

---

[12] Niko Luković, 'Marko Martinović, matematičar i nautičar', *Godišnjak Pomor-skog muzeja u Kotoru*, ii (1953), 35–44. See also A. V. Solovev, *Russkie navigatory XVII sredi yuzhnykh slavyan* (Belgrade, 1937), pp. 291–301.
[13] 'Russkaya morskaya biblioteka. I. Tsarstvovanie Petra Velikago', *Zapiski gidrograficheskago departamenta morskago ministerstva*, x (1852), 519–25.
[14] Tolstoy, op. cit. ii. 387–8.

addition to celestial navigation, mechanics, and fortifications. He also noted that he learned to converse, read, and write Italian fairly well.[15] In intent and actual performance, therefore, the dispatch of the *stolniki* of 1697 was not an attempt to enlighten Russia, but an early attempt to integrate Russia into the international system of naval apprenticeship.

The *stolniki* did not become Russia's first admirals. Perhaps they were unprepared for their studies, perhaps their training was too brief, or maybe they were too old to make good students. Petr Tolstoy was already fifty-two when sent abroad, and he subsequently became an able Petrine ambassador to the Turks. Yury Yurevich Trubetskoy and Dmitry Mikhaylovich Golitsyn were twenty-nine and thirty-two respectively, and upon return they continued their careers in the civil service and eventually became Senators. Mikhail Afanasevich Matyushkin was twenty-one, and became a general in the army. There is no evidence that any of the original *stolniki* became regular teachers of navigation upon their return to Russia.[16]

Shortly after their arrival in Venetia, the *stolniki* recruited two Dalmatian seamen into Russian service. In March 1698 one of them, Matvej Melanković, was given ten Russian youths for naval training. His brief instruction at Azov can be regarded as the forerunner to the Moscow School of Mathematics and Navigation.[17] This famous school, founded in 1701 on the model of the one at Christ's Hospital,[18] was directed by Henry Farquharson, formerly

[15] Kurakin, op. cit., p. 255.

[16] Biographical data here and elsewhere were taken from the standard *Russky biografichesky slovar* or the Brokgauz and Efron, *Entsiklopedichesky slovar*; see also V. Berkh, *Zhizneopisanie pervykh rossiyskikh admiralov*, 4 vols. (St. Petersburg, 1831–6).

[17] A. E. Suknovalov, 'Pervaya v Rossii voenno-morskaya shkola', *Istoricheskie zapiski*, xlii (1953), 301–6.

[18] On the origins of this school, see Hans, op. cit.; see also, for the influence of the school at Wapping, V. Boss, 'Newton's Influence in Eighteenth-Century Russia' (unpub. Ph.D. diss., Harvard, 1961), pp. 45–9. Basic to all authors are the works of F. F. Veselago, *Ocherk istorii morskago kadetskago korpusa* (St. Petersburg, 1852), pp. 5–34, and his *Ocherk russkoy morskoy istorii* (St. Petersburg, 1875), i. 590–8. The fullest account of the school is now in Chapter II of my unpublished dissertation, 'Education in Russia in the First Half of the Eighteenth Century' (Harvard, 1970). The following paragraphs and the discussion of the St. Petersburg Naval Academy below contain some of my evidence and conclusions.

Liddel Mathematical Tutor at Marischal College, Aberdeen, two
English assistants, and Leonty Magnitsky, author of the massive
Arifmetika (1703), the principal textbook of the school. Situated
in the famous Sukharev Tower, the Moscow School provided a
formal classroom introduction to mathematics for approximately
1,200 students between 1701 and 1715.

The curriculum at the Moscow School was a vertical hierarchy
of mathematical and navigational subjects. In the list of its classes
for 1711–12, the subject-matter was divided as follows:

Arithmetic Geometry Trigonometry Plane navigation	Magnitsky
Mercatorian navigation [The use of] Diurnals (a kind of astrolabe) Spherics Astronomy (celestial navigation) Geography (naval cartography) Great Circle navigation	Farquharson and assistant

These subjects did not represent a range of choice for the student,
but rather a rigid sequence of 'sciences' to be mastered in succession. Students enrolled at the school might be permitted to complete the entire curriculum, or they might be removed at any
moment to fill vacancies in the services, or to be assigned to other
types of training. A typical Petrine order for removal read:[19]

His Majesty orders that those students who have completed navigation
[i.e. the entire curriculum] be sent to the fleet at St. Petersburg for
[practical] training, and from among those students who have completed arithmetic and geometry, twenty be sent to St. Petersburg and
another twenty to Osered for training in artillery.

The Moscow School provided the second group of Russians
who were sent to Europe. Between the school's opening in 1701
and 1705, a sizeable group of students were brought through its
vertical curriculum. Unlike the *stolniki*, they were of diverse

19 *Materialy dlya istorii russkago flota* (St. Petersburg, 1866), iii. 321.

social origins. There were many clerics' sons and soldiers' sons, but gentry, the urban classes (*posadskie*), and the various administrative ranks (*podyacheskie, prikaznye*) were also included. In age they ranged from sixteen to twenty-eight, with most of them in their early twenties.[20]

In 1705, just as the school's register referred to this group of students as 'those who have completed the study of navigation' (the highest class at the Moscow School), Peter contacted the British ambassador, Whitworth. He asked that the students be allowed to serve their apprenticeship on British ships calling at Russian Baltic ports. Without awaiting specific permission from London, Whitworth accepted the idea. He reported to London that they had already learned the theory of seafaring, 'but now wanted to see the practical side of navigation'. He saw no danger in having them on merchant ships, and merely queried his government about permitting them on naval (military) vessels. In his report, Whitworth noted that accepting such naval apprentices was a common international practice of the day: 'It is very usual to have Danish, Swedish, and other foreign volunteers aboard the fleet.'[21] Thus, in routine fashion, Peter brought Russia into the general European naval apprenticeship system. In a follow-up report a year later, Whitworth described the Muscovites in the British fleet as 'thirty in number, lusty young men, and few or none under twenty years old',[22] and objected only that the seamen were inadequately provisioned by their government.

For the next ten years, scores of Russian youths were regularly and routinely sent abroad, individually or in groups, for naval apprenticeship. Some were assigned to artisans or wharf masters, while others were placed on ships, '*na praktike*'. The original injunction to study the naval arts was repeated for all subsequent groups, both of commoners and of gentry, and it appeared in the actual progress reports which their overseers sent back from Europe. Most of the groups were comprised largely of commoners, typically the advanced class of the Moscow school. Gradually

[20] *Materialy . . . flota*, iii. 295–300.
[21] 'Diplomaticheskaya perepiska angliyskikh poslannikov pri Russkom dvore', *Sbornik Imp. Russkago istoricheskago Obshchestva*, xxxix (1884), 112–13.
[22] Ibid., pp. 293–4.

their instructions became more specific, ordering a given student to specialize in riggings, another in ship construction, etc. A report from England and Holland in March 1708 stated that 'in winter they study navigation, and in summer they go to sea on military ships and are trained to become naval officers'. Of a group of commoners (*ucheniki prostykh porod*) sent in 1709, seventeen had already served in the fleet in the rank of *podshturman*, while eleven more were taken from the Moscow Mathematical School 'for the completion of instruction in navigation and the knowledge of maps'.[23] Reports from 1713 specified those students abroad who were actually '*na praktike*', that is, serving their apprenticeship on board a merchant or military ship. Later reports actually specified the ships and precise duties of each man assigned to a foreign fleet. The instructions given to the scores of Russian students had nothing to do with the acquisition of a general education, and the aspects of their training which interested the authorities in Russia had nothing to do with their social life or their absorption of European culture.

In addition to the students from the fleet and the Moscow school, there were occasional dispatches of groups of young nobles. The sending of gentry became increasingly frequent after 1715 when the St. Petersburg Naval Academy was established. The new academy was supposed to depart from the Moscow school in its cultivation of arts appropriate for the nobility. Its first director was a French nobleman, the Baron Saint-Hilaire. Its proposed curriculum, known to us from a note in Peter's own hand, was to include the following:[24]

Arithmetic
Geometry
Fencing or the Manual of Arms
Artillery
Navigation
Fortifications
Geography
A knowledge of the parts of a ship's
   structure and rigging

[23] *Materialy . . . flota*, iii. 18, 25–6, 60–1, 74–5, 81–95, and *passim*.
[24] Ibid., iii. 327.

Drafting
Dancing, for 'posture' (optional)

However, these innovations, especially the polite arts, were slow to materialize, largely because the old teachers and texts of the Moscow school were simply transferred to the banks of the Neva. Farquharson's St. Petersburg curriculum in April, 1719, four years after the academy's opening, showed no changes except the addition of 'geodesy', a course in surveying which Magnitsky was teaching also in Moscow. By March 1720 only twenty-five students, less than 10 per cent of the actual enrolment, had received any instruction in fencing. There was, in short, no significant change in the earlier curriculum. Furthermore, the new St. Petersburg Academy was never exclusively a school for the gentry. Four days after its founding, the Admiralty instructed the Moscow school to cease enrolling gentry, but in the same note it ordered the new academy to be kept at its full complement of 300 students, with all vacancies to be filled by commoners (*iz prostykh raznochintsev*). Non-nobles occupied many of the positions at the academy from its founding until it was closed in 1752.

Well-born students of the Naval Academy were soon being dispatched to Europe. Ivan Neplyuev recorded the travels of fifty gentry who were sent to Venice and France in 1716.[25] His father was a small landholder who held eighty souls at his death in 1709. Ivan, born in 1693 near Novgorod, was married in 1711. In 1715, aged twenty-three, he was sent to Novgorod to learn elementary mathematics. Subsequently he was enrolled at the newly opened St. Petersburg Naval Academy, and assigned to the new *Gardes de la Marine* (*Gardemariny*), the élite corps of gentry destined for leadership posts. Neplyuev's group sailed from Revel when the ice broke in the spring of 1716. They travelled to Venice via Copenhagen, Hamburg, and Amsterdam. In his instructions to the Venetian officials, Peter wrote:

According to his speech, the *pospolite* of Venice promised to accept into his naval service our young noblemen, and therefore we are sending to Venice twenty-seven men, whose orders have earlier been

[25] *Zapiski Ivana Ivanovicha Neplyueva (1693–1773)* (St. Petersburg, 1893).

applied for and obtained, so that they may be used in your service on galleys, and not on ships (*korabli*), and that they be divided up, both for the learning of languages and for the better practice of navigation through various trials, and especially [by placing them] one man to a ship, and in order that they at first might be promoted from the lowest rank.[26]

In accord with Peter's instructions, the group was assigned to the Venetian fleet. They participated in naval combat in the war with Turkey in 1718–19, and Russians, as well as Venetians were killed in action. In 1719 Peter ordered the group to Spain. They travelled across northern Italy—Venice to Ferrara, Bologna, Florence, Pisa, Livorno, by sea to Genoa, and along the Riviera. They visited the French Naval School at Toulon where seven Russians and 120 French students were learning navigation, naval engineering, artillery, drafting, ship-rigging, the soldiers' manual of arms, dancing, swordsmanship, and horsemanship. Likewise in Marseilles they encountered another group of thirty Russians similarly engaged in naval studies.[27] All three of these groups were comprised of nobles. Unlike earlier and later groups, these *Gardes de la Marine* attended the European aristocratic naval schools, for they were to be officers as well as seamen.

Eventually Neplyuev's group reached its destination, Malaga, where another naval training school existed. Their stay in Spain was less than fruitful.

Like the Spanish [Neplyuev recorded], we went always to the academy, except that we did not go to Mass. And we studied with those [Spanish] students the Manual of Arms, [and learned] to dance and to fight with swords; when it was time for mathematics, then we sat idly, because we could not study since we did not know the language. . . . And we wrote many times to St. Petersburg to Admiral Fedor Matveevich Apraksin and to Holland to [our supervisor] Prince Boris Ivanovich Kurakin, and requested them to report to his tsarist majesty that we be ordered into [Russian] service, [because] our lives have no use at all, because our fencing and dancing lessons could not be of use to the service of his majesty.[28]

The *Gardes* of 1716 were something of an exception to the

[26] Ibid., p. 15.   [27] Ibid., p. 58.   [28] Ibid., pp. 73–4.

general pattern of Russian seamen abroad in the Petrine period. Assigned to the new formal naval schools, they were to become officers rather than mere artisans. But educationally their orders were as narrowly defined as the others.

The anecdotal material stemming from Peter's navigators in Europe will always amuse students of Russian history. The over-whelming weight of evidence, however, indicates that the prac-tice of sending students abroad was not an unfortunate whim of Peter the Great, not a 'stopgap' measure prior to the creation of schools in Russia, and not a lightly considered attempt to 'en-lighten' Russia. Peter and his lieutenants, like Kurakin and I. B. Lvov in Amsterdam, knew perfectly well how the European nations trained their naval forces, and showed considerable diplo-matic and pedagogical skill in almost effortlessly bringing Russians into that international seafaring apprentice system.

Among Russians studying in Europe, there were exceptions, of course, but they were treated as such, and they prove the general rule. For example, two of Peter's cousins, sons of Lev Naryshkin, were sent to England to be educated, and in fact remained for thirteen years to that purpose. Younger than the great majority of seamen, they were eight and fourteen years of age, and their dis-patch required a special diplomatic effort which specifically referred to their 'education', not to the 'practical part of navigation'.[29] Other individuals were occasionally sent for their education and for specialized training, for example, in medicine, but they should not be confused with Peter's navigators, who were the vast majority of the travellers and who produced the travel accounts which make the episode famous.

Assessing the social impact of any educational institution is never an easy matter. One can find few intellectually rigorous attempts to evaluate the social significance of Petrine schools or of other educational institutions or practices in Russia in the eighteenth century.[30] A limited amount of evidence, however,

---

[29] *Sbornik*, pp. 1, 31–2, 42, 137–8, 166; Peter later intervened and insisted that they too should receive some practical experience at sea; ibid, pp. 173–4.

[30] An exception is, of course, Professor Marc Raeff's *Origins of the Russian In-telligentsia: The Eighteenth-Century Nobility* (New York, 1966). He deals only with a single class, and is far more concerned with the service obligations of the gentry

suggests that Petrine foreign training had real importance in the formation of modern Russia, and that it influenced areas far removed from the Russian navy.

Undoubtedly Peter's navigators acquired more than a knowledge of knots, tides, spars, and black powder in Europe. The contribution of foreign study to Russia's stock of naval officers and technical skills is, however, the most obvious and most easily documented. For example, Privy Councillor, President of the Admiralty College, General-Admiral Count Fedor Matveevich Apraksin had studied shipbuilding in Amsterdam with Peter the Great in 1697.[31] Fedor Ivanovich Soymonov was born a poor *dvoryanin*. He attended the Moscow school between 1708 and 1712, and was then sent to Holland for his naval apprenticeship. Eventually he became a vice-admiral, a vice-president of the Admiralty College, the Governor of Siberia, and a Senator. A commoner, Denis Spiridonovich Kalmykov, studied in Holland and England, and rose to the rank of rear-admiral. Vice-Admiral P. G. Kashkin, Admiral A. I. Polyansky, Admiral I. L. Talyzin, and scores of other high-ranking naval officers all had practical naval training in Europe. Gradually Peter was able to replace the foreign officer corps of his early reign with Russians, and many of them had been trained abroad. Foreign study also contributed to the training of the geodesists, surveyors, mineralogists, and engineers who were to explore Siberia, the Arctic, and East Asia on numerous expeditions in the first half of the century.[32]

In the area of technical training at home, foreign study paid valuable dividends. The success of the St. Petersburg Naval Academy was due to two officers trained in Europe. Grigory Grigorevich Skornyakov-Pisarev joined the academy in 1719 and published the first book on mechanics in Russian. He was joined in 1722 by Aleksandr Lvovich Naryshkin, one of Peter's nephews whose foreign education had been carefully planned in 1708.

than with formal schooling. See the important review of Raeff's book by Michael Confino, 'Histoire et psychologie: à propos de la noblesse russe au xviiie siècle', *Annales: Économies, Sociétés, Civilisations*, xxii, no. 6 (Nov.–Dec. 1967), 1163–1205.

[31] Biographical data from Berkh, op. cit.
[32] Veselago, *Morskoy istorii*, pp. 602–3; Plekhanov, op. cit., p. 13.

Together they were responsible for restructuring the curriculum of the academy to make it a more practical prelude to naval apprenticeship. Together these two men transformed the Naval Academy in the twenties into the kind of school Peter had envisaged.

In addition to a predictable improvement in naval training and staff, the sending of students abroad influenced Russian cultural life in other ways. Remarkably few diaries or memoirs were written in the second half of the seventeenth century or in the Petrine period. This was apparently not a popular literary genre. It was, therefore, surely no accident that three memoirs should have been written by men who had been sent to Europe. It was also no accident that they returned to the West, Tolstoy and Neplyuev becoming ambassadors and Kurakin the overseer of the training of other Russian naval craftsmen.

There were other literary effects of foreign study. Dmitry Mikhaylovich Golitsyn was one of the *stolniki* of 1697. Generally regarded as one of the most erudite figures of the period, he was an active patron of literature, responsible for the translation of many Western works into Russian.[33] In addition, the practice of sending Russians abroad was responsible for the revitalization of the traditional literary genre of travel narratives. 'The Tale of the Seaman Vasily', 'The Tale of Alexander, A Russian Nobleman', 'The Tale of the Russian Merchant Ioann', and 'The Tale of a Russian Nobleman's Son' all deal directly with young men sent abroad for study.[34] Although they followed the literary conventions of seventeenth-century Russian *povesti*, although they were probably written after 1725, topically and lexically they mirrored the Petrine age, and reflected the impact of foreign training on Russian culture.

Finally, foreign study influenced the development of Russian art. In 1716 Peter sent a group of young self-trained Russian artists

---

[33] P. Pekarsky, *Vvedenie v istoriyu prosveshcheniya v Rossii* (St. Petersburg, 1862), pp. 257–63.

[34] On these tales see G. N. Moiseeva (ed.), *Russkie povesti pervoy treti XVIII veka* (Moscow and Leningrad, 1965); see also D. D. Blagoy, *Istoriya russkoy literatury XVIII veka*, 3rd ed. (Moscow, 1955), pp. 34–42. In English, see H. B. Segal, *The Literature of Eighteenth-Century Russia* (N.Y., 1967), i. 41–3, 119–40.

abroad, ostensibly to learn ships' decoration. Ivan Nikitin, the son of a priest, was twenty-eight when sent to Europe. He studied in Italy and France and returned in the early 1720s. Andrey Matveev was fifteen when sent to Holland, where he remained for twelve years. After their return, they quickly established themselves as the best of Russia's portrait-painters in the first half of the century. On the basis of their work, Peter's wife, Catherine I, almost opened an academy of art in Russia. Only Nikitin's untimely and scandalous marriage to a non-Russian delayed and finally prevented its establishment.[35] At any rate, the origins of modern Russian painting are to be found in Peter's programme of foreign naval study.

These kinds of cultural benefits are directly attributable to Peter's sending of students to Europe, but they were unrelated to the purpose of foreign study, which was never conceived by Peter to be a means of enlightening Russia. Because the Petrine students by and large returned to Russia, unlike those dispatched a century earlier by Boris Godunov,[36] their studies have been seen as Russia's first step toward Westernization.[37] Such a broadly cultural interpretation has merit, but it tends to obscure the narrower and more sensible reasons for which Peter sent Russians abroad, and the limited ends he had in mind.

[35] P. N. Petrov, 'Russkie zhivopistsy-pensionery Petra Velikago', *Vestnik izyashchnykh iskusstv*, i, no. 1, 66–97; no. 2, 193–222; N. Kovalenskaya, *Istoriya russkogo iskusstva XVIII veka* (Moscow, 1962), pp. 39–45.

[36] G. Vernadsky, *The Tsardom of Muscovy 1547–1682* (New Haven, Conn., 1969), i. 215–16.

[27] See for example, B. H. Sumner, *Peter the Great and the Emergence of Russia* (London, 1950), p. 205.

Part Three
Aspects of Catherine II's Russia

G. GARETH JONES

Novikov's Naturalized Spectator

CATHERINE THE GREAT decided in 1769 to encourage the writing of moral weeklies in Russia by establishing her own journal *All Sorts* which was launched anonymously with G. V. Kozitsky, her literary secretary, as the executive editor.[1] In a way this was a continuation of Catherine's literary enthusiasms. The Legislative Commission whose deliberations had recently been brought to a close, had not only been summoned to respond to the *Nakaz* or *Instruction*—that compilation from the pages of the European *philosophes* which Catherine viewed as a literary work as much a political document—but had also been used as a training-ground for young Russian writers. An apparatus of secretaries was established to record the proceedings of the general assembly and the sub-committees of the Legislative Commission in daily journals, and the director of the journals, A. P. Shuvalov, was made directly responsible to the Empress, who showed a keen interest in the written record of the proceedings. One of the tasks entrusted to Bibikov, Marshal of the Legislative Commission, was to organize for the *St. Petersburg News*, the official gazette, the writing of a monthly report for which Catherine had a model in mind: 'Mr. Marshal,' she wrote to Bibikov, 'I enclose journals of the English Parliament,[2] in order that you can have them read by the person to whom you will entrust the making of the monthly account of your daily minutes for publication in the *News*. Catherine.'[3] Catherine clearly hoped that the Commission would

[1] P. P. Pekarsky, *Materialy dlya istorii zhurnalnoy i literaturnoy deyatelnosti Ekateriny II* (St. Petersburg, 1863), pp. 1–6.

[2] The House of Commons had decided to print its Journals in 1742, the work being supervised by Samuel Richardson, Printer to the House of Commons, and pioneer of the novel as author of *Pamela; or, Virtue Rewarded*. See J. C. Trewin and E. M. King, *Printer to the House: the Story of Hansard* (London, 1952), p. 12.

[3] *Zapiski o zhizni i sluzhbe Aleksandra Ilicha Bibikova* (St. Petersburg, 1817), p. 108.

produce the equivalent of Parliamentary Debates. The secretaries chosen for this work were not the clerks in state service who seemed not to have been considered suitable for these literary ventures. To keep a well-written record of the Commission's proceedings, a number of highly literate men were needed, and Catherine found them principally among the enthusiastic young *literati* of the Guards Regiments, many of them recent graduates of Moscow University. Accordingly, a signal from Adjutant-General Count Kirill Razumovsky dated 17 August 1767 to Procurator-General Vyazemsky informed him that twenty-two army men from St. Petersburg had been commanded to join the secretariat of the Commission.[4] One of these was Nikolay Novikov, a twenty-four-year-old member of the Izmaylovsky Regiment, who had already tried his hand at publishing a friend's work, and was to become journalist, publisher, historian, and a social figure whose activities in Moscow in the 1780s were so influential that they led Klyuchevsky to label the 1780s in Russia as 'Novikov's decade'.[5]

If Novikov was a tyro publisher, some of his companions had already practised as literary translators and essayists in consciously literary groupings such as those which had crystallized around Mikhail Kheraskov at Moscow University.[6] By summoning these young literary men to act as minute takers at her Legislative Commission, Catherine, whether consciously or not, was developing their sense of being a distinct literary coterie, and also engineering in Russia that significant identification of the parliamentary reporter and magazine essayist—one thinks in particular of Samuel Johnson—which existed in London. Yet, whereas in London a wary Parliament had fought shy of and attempted to curb the dangerous journalist beast, in Moscow and St. Petersburg Catherine, of necessity, seems to have gone out of her way to train her innocent young scribblers as political animals. Novikov, together with the other young men, as they sat at their desks in the Kremlin's Granavitaya Palace, must have honed their political wits and

---

[4] G. Makogonenko, *Nikolay Novikov i russkoe prosveshchenie XVIII veka* (Moscow and Leningrad, 1952), pp. 85–6.
[5] V. O. Klyuchevsky, *Sochineniya* (Moscow, 1959), viii. 249.
[6] See A. V. Zapadov, *Istoriya russkoy zhurnalistiki XVIII—XIX vekov* (Moscow, 1963), pp. 35–6.

developed a keen eye and ear for social observation in an assembly which had summoned together deputies from all corners and classes of the Russian Empire and which in its debates, clumsy as they often were, groped towards the formation of a rudimentary public opinion in Russia.

Although Catherine, impatient with the politics of her Legislative Commission, used the pretext of the war with Turkey to bring its deliberations to an end, her literary interests, after finding a temporary home in that assembly, were directed to another channel. As before, Catherine looked to Western Europe and particularly England for her model, endeavoured to maintain the close collaboration of the young writers with her initiative, and sought to keep them under her wing. And the young writers were content to play the traditional role for which the history of Muscovy had prepared them of serving under the *opeka*, or tutelage, of the autocrat and Russian state. The new model made itself manifest in a weekly miscellany, *All Sorts (Vsyakaya Vsyachina)*, which cast itself in the role of a solicitous Russian *babushka* calling on her 'grandchildren' to follow her journalistic example. The result was that 1769 saw the quick flowering—and in most cases the fading—of a number of weeklies, the most significant of which by far was Novikov's *The Drone (Truten)* which first appeared in May of that year.

The model was Addison and Steele's *Spectator* to which *All Sorts* was heavily indebted, not only in direct translations and paraphrases, as V. F. Solntsev indicated in 1892, but also in its tone, manner, and general purpose.[7] It is reasonable to see the weeklies that sprang up around *All Sorts* as more recruits to that army of imitators of *The Spectator*, the most fashionable literary invention of the eighteenth century in Europe. 'A history of the European *Spectator*-type periodicals could now, I think, be written,' wrote Paul Van Tieghem in 1930, 'a fine subject of general literature whose unity is evident and of very great interest',[8] and Ernest Simmons, at much the same time, looking in at the Russian scene

[7] V. F. Solntsev, 'Vsyakaya Vsyachina i Spektator' in *Zhurnal Ministerstva Narodnago Prosveshcheniya*, 1892, no. 1, sect. II, pp. 125–56.

[8] Paul Van Tieghem, *Revue de synthèse historique*, i (1930), 127 quoted by Donald F. Bond (ed.), *The Spectator* (Oxford, 1965), i, p. xcvi.

from the outside, recognized the essential unity of *All Sorts* and
its collaborators with the other European journals of the *Spectator*
type, declaring that 'it is perhaps no exaggeration to affirm that
the *Spectator* was the most significant factor in the origin and
development of the Russian satirical journals of the eighteenth
century'.[9]

However, the evident unity of this type of essay periodical has
not until very recently been fully acknowledged within Russia itself.
Recent researches by Yury Levin into the acceptance of English
journalism in eighteenth-century Russian literature have, as he
rightly claims, shown that 'the acceptance in eighteenth-century
Russia of the English journalism of the Enlightenment was incom-
parably greater than hitherto thought'. Statistics are eloquent
enough. According to Levin's data, which he does not claim to be
exhaustive, over 300 separate papers or articles drawn from English
periodicals served as material for more than 400 items in over 50
Russian periodicals and other publications. The most popular
periodical in Russia was *The Spectator*, translations from which
formed more than half the examples noted by Levin.[10]

Nevertheless, while demonstrating the extent of the use of
material from the English periodicals, Levin minimizes the importance of the use of the English genre of the *Spectator*-type periodical on the curious grounds that the influence was not direct:

> In the satirical journals 1769–74 which appeared after *All Sorts*,
> articles of English origin are a comparatively rare phenomenon. True,
> many of these journals in their construction are similar to the English
> satirico-didactic 'periodical papers'. But this type of publication had
> long become a general European one, and moreover in Russia it was
> finally confirmed by *All Sorts*. Therefore, there is no foundation for
> referring to an English influence in this context.[11]

Levin seems to have been unable to free himself from the prevailing view that a number of the 'grandsons' called into being by
their *babushka*, *All Sorts*—and in particular Novikov's *The Drone*—

[9] Ernest J. Simmons, *English Literature and Culture in Russia (1553–1840)* (Cambridge, Mass., 1935), p. 111.
[10] Yu. D. Levin, *Angliyskaya prosvetitelskaya zhurnalistika v russkoy literature
XVIII veka* in *Epokha prosveshcheniya*, ed. M. P. Alekseev (Leningrad, 1967), p. 79.
[11] Ibid., p. 61.

rebelled against her prescriptions. Novikov's biographers have in the past contrasted the home-bred, original compositions of *The Drone*, concerned with the realities of Russian life, with the abstract nature of the satire of *All Sorts*, abstract, because, as Solntsev had shown, the latter's material was drawn to a great extent from *The Spectator*. There is an implication in this view that *The Drone* is somehow different in genre from *All Sorts* and other *Spectator*-type journals. Simmons too—although by translating the title of Novikov's journal as *The Idler* he reminds one of the English influence—seems to accept this view of its distinctiveness. 'Only such fearless editors', he writes, 'as N. Novikov in *The Idler*, *The Painter* and *The Purse*, and F. Emin in his *Infernal Post* dared to satirise in a straightforward manner the real social evils of the time, and the zeal of these writers quickly brought to an end the literary movement which the satirical journals represented.'[12] That administrative measures were used to suppress Novikov's early journals is one of the myths surrounding him for which no firm evidence exists.[13] Although he in fact managed to complete a full year's run of *The Drone* and brought it to a decorous close, it has been constantly affirmed that Catherine herself out of personal pique at the success of a rival journal, often blunt in its social criticism, closed it down. This forcible closure is a necessary part of a picture formed a century ago of Novikov as an early representative of Russian populism in heroic and lone literary combat against a hypocritical autocrat, and carefully cultivated since then by populist-minded literary historians. The grandsons, encouraged by their solicitous grandmother, engaged in controversy among themselves, and *The Drone*, it is true, crossed swords with *All Sorts* on the literary question of the decorum of satire, but controversy was willed by the official journal and was waged under her tutelage. In this light, the polemics between *The Drone* and *All Sorts*—sometimes incorrectly personalized as a clash between Novikov and Catherine—may be seen as an act of collaboration rather than defiance.

[12] Ernest J. Simmons, op. cit., p. 111.
[13] See my forthcoming article 'The Closure of Novikov's Truten' in *The Slavonic and East European Review*.

Yet *The Drone* is a distinctive journal. Not, however, by virtue of any wilful deviation from the genius of the *Spectator*-type periodical, but because its author had a clear perception of the purposes and implications of that genre. 'Mr. Spectator', the supposed editor of the magazine bearing his name, had by 1769 wandered far and wide from his little patch of England whose bounds were drawn at the time of the Norman Conquest—to the American colonies on one side of the globe and to Sumatra on the other.[14] He had entered Russia by the early 1720s,[15] but it was only now that he became truly naturalized there. The main distinguishing feature of the *Spectator*-type journal was that it was not the organ of a party or the mouthpiece for its editor's own views; there was to be no definite 'programme'. The paper purported to be the work of a *persona*, obviously created by the real editor who remained concealed and anonymous. It was the *persona*, the fictitious author, who gave tone and unity to the periodical paper: thus Isaac Bickerstaff, a tattler in ladies' assemblies, was to determine the nature of *The Tatler*, and Mr. Spectator, a silent man observing life from its quiet fringes, was to give his name to *The Spectator*; while Steele and Addison retained their anonymity in both cases until the last numbers. Mr. Spectator was not the sole organizer of his papers but was assisted by 'his ordinary Companions', members of a club, who were meant originally, it seems, to represent various points of view in society and to play individualized roles in the journal as it unfolds, although this initial aim is only partly realized. The fictitious personality of the editor surrounds himself with entertaining persons who play their part in the pages of the periodical. These *dramatis personae*[16] are able to show us contemporary ideas, ethical, political, and economic in the concrete situations of real life and in all sorts of ways. The aim of the editorial personality and his companions is to edify but simultaneously to amuse, and the tone of the language of *The Spectator* is conversational, half-jocular, half-serious for the conversational tone is an essential ingredient of the genre. If the

---

[14] *The Spectator*, ed. Bond, i, pp. lxxxv–lxxxvi.
[15] Yu. D. Levin, op. cit., pp. 12–14.
[16] *The Spectator*, ed. Bond, i, p. xxiv.

Spectator-type periodical has its pretended editorial personality, it also has to sustain the pretence of a readership in sympathy with this personality and prepared to accept his unbiased authority. The device of Mr. Spectator's fictional club, 'his ordinary Companions', partly serves to create the illusion that the readers too may become vicarious 'ordinary Companions' and converse with the editor on friendly terms. More important in this respect is the widespread use of correspondents' letters which, whether genuine or feigned, suggest that the periodical is a meeting-ground for readers. In the case of *The Spectator* itself, many of these letters were genuine but Addison in No. 542 admitted to composing some himself and recasting others; his reasons tell us a great deal about the crystallized genre of *The Spectator* as a whole, as well as about the specific importance of the 'letters to the editor':

First, out of the Policy of those who try their Jest upon another, before they own it themselves. Secondly, because I would extort a little Praise from such who will never applaud any thing whose Author is known and certain. Thirdly, because it gave me an Opportunity of introducing a great variety of Characters into my Work, which could not have been done, had I always written in the Person of the *Spectator*. Fourthly, because the Dignity Spectatorial would have suffered, had I published as from my self those several ludicrous Compositions which I have ascribed to fictitious Names and Characters. And lastly, because they often serve to bring in, more naturally, such additional Reflections as have been placed at the End of them.[17]

Novikov marked off his own journal distinctly from the other 1769 magazines by the choice even of his title. The title of *All Sorts* reflected one feature of the *Spectator*-type journal—its wide-ranging social commentary, reaching from philosophical abstractions to the minutiae of day-to-day social behaviour, and its miscellaneous nature was confirmed by the titles of the 'grandchildren', M. D. Chulkov's *Both This And That*, V. G. Ruban's *Neither This Nor That*, L. I. Sichkarev's *Mixture*. *All Sorts* retained a *persona* flanked by companions, it is true, but its projection of the *babushka* did little more than mark an acknowledgement of the convention.[13]

17 Ibid. iv. 438–9.
18 See Yu. D. Levin, op. cit., p. 48, who acknowledges the fact that *All Sorts*,

In his own choice of title, on the other hand, Novikov called attention primarily to his fictitious editor, the Drone.

Just as *The Spectator* began with a characterization of Mr. Spectator, so *The Drone* begins with a presentation to its readers of the person with whom they are expected, in the course of their weekly reading of the magazine, to enter into a special relationship—half pupil, half confidant. Mr. Spectator ingratiated himself to his readers with some subtle self-disparagement as he sketched his own character:

Thus I live in the World, rather as a Spectator of Mankind, than as one of the Species; by which means I have made my self a Speculative Statesman, Soldier, Merchant and Artizan, without ever medling with any Practical Part in Life. I am very well versed in the Theory of an Husband, or a Father, and can discern the Errors in the Oeconomy, Business and Diversion of others better than those who are engaged in them; as Standers-by discover Blots, which are apt to escape those who are in the Game. I never espoused any Party with Violence, and am resolved to observe an exact Neutrality between the Whigs and Tories, unless I shall be forc'd to declare my self by the Hostilities of either side. In short, I have acted in all the parts of my Life as Looker-on, which is the Character I intend to preserve in this Paper.[19]

It is precisely this capacity of the fictitious editor for standing aloof from the world of affairs and service in taciturn idleness which gave the new type of journal its peculiar force. From his distant vantage-point the looker-on could range over the various parts of his society at will; being a mere passive onlooker, although an impediment in the affairs of the world, is paradoxically a positive advantage for the journalist. Despite his aloofness, Mr. Spectator saw himself as 'not altogether unqualified for the Business I have undertaken', and succeeding English journals took the point, calling themselves *The Idler, The Lounger, The Rambler*.

With his sketch of the Drone, Novikov demonstrated that he fully understood the genre of the *Spectator*-type journal, and was able to exploit it it to allow himself the latitude which the assumed

alone of the Russian essay periodicals, attempted to imitate the English original in this respect. He does not concede, however, that Novikov made any significant use of the literary convention.

[19] *The Spectator*, ed. Bond, i. 4–5.

persona of *The Spectator* gave to Addison and Steele. The Drone's fault of laziness makes him as well qualified a journalist as Mr. Spectator. It prevents him from entering the normal avenues of social advancement, but Novikov from the start Russifies his reincarnation of the 'Dignity Spectatorial'—his is no blind imitation of the original—and Mr. Editor of *The Drone* baulks not at the English careers of 'statesman, soldier, merchant, and artizan', but at the normal Russian ones of the military, the bureaucracy, or the Imperial Court. But this introductory sketch is not a personal statement of the true feelings of the young Novikov who had recently retired from the Guards, as has often been maintained:[20] the sketch cannot be understood without one's being aware of the *persona*'s literary parentage. Like Mr. Spectator's, his idleness enables him to cast a benign eye over the foibles of society, and although he cannot hope to write his own useful compositions since 'my upbringing and intellectual gifts have placed some insuperable obstacles in the way', yet like a true Drone he hopes to feed on the works of others and by publishing them achieve the moral journal's aim of bringing 'profit and diversion to his readers'. The readers of these journals are not expected to be passive; in both cases they are drawn into a new relationship by being invited to participate in the journals' activities. Mr. Spectator's direction that contributions should be sent to 'Mr. Buckley's Little Britain',[21] is echoed by *The Drone*'s direction that they should be sent 'to the bookseller at whose shop these papers are sold'.[22] The true nature of the genre of Novikov's *Drone* becomes apparent if one asks the question, 'Who is Mr. Drone?' He is then recognizable as a literary device, the lynchpin of the *Spectator*-type journal, and less a lusty grandson of Catherine's *All Sorts* than a direct descendant of Addison and Steele's Mr. Spectator.

But he is extremely Russian in his reincarnation, and Novikov shows not only the breadth of his literary culture in his understanding of the genre, but the sharpness of his intelligence in

[20] A. V. Zapadov, *Novikov* (Moscow, 1968), pp. 62–3; and G. Makogonenko, op. cit., p. 109.   [21] *The Spectator*, ed. Bond, i. 6.
[22] P. N. Berkov (ed.), *Satiricheskie zhurnaly N. I. Novikova* (Moscow and Leningrad, 1951), p. 47.

exploiting the genre to the demands of Russian society. The Drone is not identical with his creator, Novikov, who, although not a nobleman of first rank, came from a long noble line, was comfortably well off and well connected. The literary device is fleshed out as a Russian person in the second issue of *The Drone* which prints a letter[23] from an uncle telling us that his nephew is from the provinces, from a destitute gentry family, so that he will be obliged to earn a living although he may receive—it is conditional on behaviour pleasing to the irascible uncle—an inheritance of 300 serfs from the latter. The uncle hints at some of the 'insuperable obstacles' mentioned in the first issue, which the Drone's upbringing had placed in the way of a literary career: the uncle reveals himself as an obscurantist, deeply affronted by the unprofitable enlightenment brought to the backwoods by one of Catherine's newly appointed bright young metropolitan procurators. The readers' suspicions are confirmed in the fifteenth issue when, through the medium of another letter from the uncle, they learn that until the age of twenty the young Drone had pleased his late father by shunning secular learning and absorbing nothing but 'the wrath of God'.[24] His sole reading matter was the Bible and the Lives of the Saints; his only educational achievements were vast feats of memorization, particularly the ability at the age of sixteen to know the whole calendar of Church services by heart. But the young man, laments the uncle, has wandered far from the paths of righteousness, no longer observes fasts, has taken to reading secular books, has learnt foreign languages—the key to heretical, schismatic works—and, what is worse, uses that knowledge to translate foreign works in order to corrupt those innocent of the barbarian tongues.

The uncle, treated with disdainful amusement by his nephew, on account of his conservative views which are so superannuated that they have lost their validity, is reminiscent of the most memorable of Mr. Spectator's companions, Sir Roger de Coverley. At this point, too, Novikov seems to be exploiting to the full the resources of the *Spectator*-type journal. Mr. Spectator, intent on establishing, in a society emerging from recent violence and public

---

[23] *Satiricheskie zhurnaly N.I. Novikova*, ed. Berkov, pp. 49–51.   [24] Ibid., pp. 100–3.

disorders, a spirit of urbane moderation, smiles at the quaint old Tory knight, yet at the same time readers were made aware that the latter's quaint ways reflected attitudes which were reprehensible in a well-ordered society. The moderation is given some dramatic highlighting by the shadow of Sir Roger. Seen as a Russian Sir Roger, the uncle too acts as a foil to the editorial *persona* in a similar way. His attitudes—those of the die-hard bigots still opposing the Petrine reforms—are dangerous, yet because they are so old-fashioned, he is at the same time a laughable, and therefore lovable, character. There is no need to attack him violently: obscurantism had been censured a full forty years previously by Antiokh Kantemir in his satires,[25] and in the second half of the eighteenth century, the nephew—conscious of his recently discovered independent individuality—finds his relative's appeal to him as a clansman to further the fortunes of his clan, the *rod*, through an outmoded client system somewhat ridiculous.

The portrayal of the uncle, by setting the editorial *persona* in a historical perspective, makes him more recognizable, and the main attraction of Mr. Editor of *The Drone* was undoubtedly the readers' recognition of the character portrayed, and the identification of themselves with him. This is the man from the poverty-stricken ranks of the gentry who had rejected the surest means of social advancement—through employment in the bureaucracy—and elected instead to make his way in society by embracing those cultural values which gave shape to the new image of nobility. The leap that the uncle's nephew, Ivanushka, had made from the ignorant, xenophobic bigotry of the old Muscovite clans to the new secular Western European culture was a move many of *The Drone*'s readers had possibly made, and most probably witnessed. And already Novikov, through his created *persona*, was considering a choice that later was to become familiar to the lesser gentry: the choice of being a *chinovnik*, a servant in the bureaucratic state apparatus, or a member of the literary intelligentsia.

To the disadvantage of laziness Novikov's Drone added the

[25] Antiokh Kantemir's satires were not published in Russia until 1762. They had, however, already appeared in London in 1749 in a French prose translation by O. Gouasco. See Antiokh Kantemir, *Sobranie Stikhotvoreniy*, ed. Z. I. Gershkovich (Leningrad, 1956), p. 34.

disadvantage of lowly birth, albeit within the gentry caste. Yet if the disadvantage of laziness could be turned to advantage, so could the social placing. It is interesting to contrast Novikov's decision at this point with that of the editors of the German moral weeklies of the first half of the century. Although their editors were generally of the middle class and aiming at a middle-class readership whose values they wished to affirm, yet to gain authoritative stature in the eyes of their readers they had a tendency to ennoble their fictitious editors.[26] Novikov does the reverse, partly perhaps to conform with the middle-class ethos which was characteristic of the *Spectator*-type journal, but also to chime with Catherine's policy of encouraging the growth of an urban middle class in her Empire, which was in accord with the Enlightenment's general high regard for the class. Her attempts to augment the influence of the burgesses at her Legislative Commission had been frustrated by the nobility,[27] but it is significant that Novikov had acted as minute taker for the sub-committee on the 'middling sort of men'. It is not that a middling sort of man was always acceptable to his readers as editor. The conventions of the *Spectator*-type journal were spelt out to a young lady correspondent towards the close of the first part of a successor magazine, *The Painter*, in 1772, since she had objected to the low birth of the 'craftsman' editor. The defensive reply suggests that she was not alone in being affronted: so it had to be explained that the real writer was not 'one of the descendants of Ham' but a nobleman, and a very cultured nobleman at that.[28] In *The Drone*, the social placing is maintained consistently, and even in 1770 it is used as an excuse by a young lady for forgiving the Drone his coarseness since 'you have not frequented society enough, have not had the time to sort out the customs of our contemporaries, and, consequently, following the customs of your forebears, you are unable to please us, viz: young ladies and many illustrious gentlemen.'[29]

The original Spectator had realized that his authority could be

[26] Pamela Currie, 'Moral Weeklies and the Reading Public in Germany, 1711–1750', *Oxford German Studies*, iii (1968), 69–86.

[27] Paul Dukes, *Catherine the Great and the Russian Nobility* (Cambridge, 1967), pp. 55, 81.   [28] *Satiricheskie zhurnaly N. I. Novikova*, ed. Berkov, pp. 368–71.

[29] Ibid., p. 188.

augmented by gathering around him a number of like-minded correspondents, a 'Fraternity of Spectators'. It is interesting that one of the fraternal drones who gives added stature to the editorial *persona* in charge of *The Drone* is a sixty-year-old burgess, a *meshchanin*, from Tver, interested in the laws, commerce, and customs of other nations and also one of the reasonable and knowledgeable supporters of *The Drone*'s attitudes. The approbation of a man, noble in all but rank, is signalled by his name Chistoserdov or Pureheart.[30] Similarly Pravdulyubov, identified as a procurator (Catherine's inspector of justices), has a character as clear as his name of Truthlover: he is a stern moralist, with the firm polemical style of the advocate and adept at legal quibbling as when he helps *The Drone* to wriggle out of a controversy on the decent bounds of satire with *All Sorts* by arguing persuasively that 'satire against a particular person' (*satira na litso*) does not mean that a person is named or even recognizable.[31] Truthlover's role as an inspector of the work of others makes him a suitable fraternal drone. Mr. Spectator had seen the possibility of rallying to his side men who shared his laziness of disposition: 'I would recommend this Paper', he wrote, 'to the daily Perusal of those Gentlemen whom I cannot but consider as my good Brothers and Allies, I mean the Fraternity of Spectators who live in the World without having anything to do in it.'[32] As early as its fifth issue, it is suggested that *The Drone* will have among its correspondents a fraternity of drones when Pravdulyubov announces that he is one: 'Perhaps', he writes, 'messrs critics will say that it is very fitting for me as a Drone to have dealings with the Drone but it is much more reasonable and laudable for me to be a Drone harmful to the evil deeds of others, than the bee who flits everywhere and cannot distinguish or discover anything.'[33] Similarly I. Pryamikov (or I. Straightforward), signing himself 'your well-wisher', reveals himself as one of the fraternity by his introduction to his letter, 'You are lazy and I too am not diligent', and by his conclusion in which he excuses his bad orthography by his 'accursed

[30] Ibid., pp. 72, 74.
[31] Ibid., pp. 137–9.
[32] *The Spectator*, ed. Bond, p. 45.
[33] *Satiricheskie zhurnaly N. I. Novikova*, ed. Berkov, p. 59.

laziness'.[34] One of the most engaging companions is N. N.—it is tempting to think that the Latin initials used may in this case represent not an indefinite person but the real Nikolay Novikov—a garrulous raconteur who makes his presence felt by the number and length of his appearances.[35] He brings the bustle of the Moscow streets into the journal with his rush of words, salty proverbs, the dry joke told by a Russian against himself which has the ring of an authentic current piece of wit about it, 'I do not know why the air here is so very different from that in England. There wise men go mad, while here, those without reason are considered intelligent.'[36] He also has a critical eye, and one of his most entertaining pieces of reporting is the exasperated account of an attempt to get travel documentation from an uncaring bureaucratic machine infected with malicious obstructionism.[37]

N. N. is instantly recognizable as a most clubbable man, and *The Drone*'s supporting characters, briefly sketched and undeveloped though they may be, nevertheless correspond to the members of the Spectator's club. In his pages, Novikov seems to have suggested to his readers the delights of the eighteenth-century English club before such institutions had taken root in Russia. In the next decade the Masonic lodges would provide a home for clubbable men, and it was a frequenter of the Urania Lodge of St. Petersburg, F. Gardner, who founded the influential *Angliysky Klub*, the English Club, in the capital in 1770.[38] Not surprisingly Novikov participated enthusiastically in the life of the lodges, eventually becoming one of the leaders of Russian masonry.[39]

Novikov did not limit his appeal to possible members of his fraternity, and through his editorial *persona* attempted to achieve a personal relationship with a wide range of readers who were presented in all their variety in the final December numbers which bid farewell to the old year of 1769.[40] In their reaction to the per-

34 *Satiricheskie zhurnaly N. I. Novikova*, ed. Berkov, p. 65.

35 Ibid., pp. 76–9, 90–5, 116–18, 222–3.   36 Ibid., p. 90.   37 Ibid., pp. 222–3.

38 G. V. Vernadsky, *Russkoe masonstvo v tsarstvovanie Ekateriny II* (Petrograd, 1917), pp. 21 ff.

39 For examinations of Novikov's role in Russian masonry, see A. N. Pypin, *Russkoe masonstvo XVIII i pervaya chetvert XIX v* (Petrograd, 1916), pp. 169–204, and G. V. Vernadsky, op. cit.

40 *Satiricheskie zhurnaly N. I. Novikova*, ed. Berkov, pp. 172–7.

sonality of the Drone, the 'readers' showed how he had achieved his desired mixture of instructive enlightenment—in his appeal to Slaven (Goodfellow) and Zrelum (Maturemind); diversion—in his appeal to Vertoprakh (Giddyhead) and others; and social liveliness—in his appeal to the intelligent women readers. It is not the cosiness of the club that delights the Drone so much as the breadth of his appeal to a pluralistic society. Despite the often schematic character sketches, there is sufficient differentiation in the character portrayal to suggest the multifarious aspects of the society with which the Drone has dealings. The form of this type of periodical enabled a society to become more conscious of itself, and in particular more conscious of its variegated complexion. The genre seemed to flourish best in a society such as that which gave birth to the original *Spectator*, a society unsettled, shifting yet in search of a coherent self-image. For this reason perhaps, the earlier German versions were much more successful in the changing cities of the North than in the closed, traditional communities of the South.[41] St. Petersburg at the close of the 1760s was certainly a society in which the genre could flourish; Catherine's Legislative Commission had sent its deputies homewards, more conscious of their society and of the need for it to search out a new equilibrium, and Catherine's establishment of her *All Sorts* encouraged this search.

In fostering a self-image for a society, the *Spectator*-type journal did not play a passive role, but the editorial *persona* presented himself as a social arbitrator, and the 'letters to the editor', the most common mode of the journals, are significant since through them the fictional figures and the wider society of readers submit to his patronage and acknowledge his authority as a social arbitrator. That a mentor of social graces should have been welcome in the Russia of the 1760s seems very likely judging from the reminiscences of Andrey Bolotov, an amateur scholar, who recalled his ignorance of 'private' society life on retiring from the army and returning to Moscow in 1762 and his self-conscious learning of polite manners.[42] Men like Bolotov, eager for social poise, would

---

41 Pamela Currie, op. cit., p. 85.
42 Andrey Bolotov, *Zhizn i priklyucheniya Andreya Bolotova opisannye samin im dlya svoikh potomkov* (Moscow and Leningrad, 1931), ii. 223–7.

seem to have been natural readers of the 1769 journals for this reason. Yet this was not the case. When Bolotov was invited by Novikov in 1779, shortly after the latter had been given a ten-year lease on the press of Moscow University, to contribute material for a country-life supplement to a University publication, the *Moscow News*, Bolotov maintained that he had no previous knowledge of Novikov.[43] Novikov, in fact, despite his promotion of the middling sort of man had to rely heavily on the patronage of the Court, led by Catherine's example, for the success of his early ventures.

But the success of *The Drone* was marked. It outsold the official *All Sorts* and the other 'grandchildren', and its popularity must be ascribed to Novikov's evident deep understanding of the purposes of the *Spectator*-type journal which found a ready response in the growing self-consciousness of the Russian cultural élite. Although it is difficult to judge with any certainty the influence of *The Drone* and the other journals of its type on the subsequent development of Russian literature, yet the claim often made for their English equivalents, namely that they prepared the way for the English social novelists by training their readers to appreciate nuances of social behaviour, can also be made for the Russian *Spectator*-type journals. Opinions and ideas were never served up plain in *The Drone*. They were shown as functions of individuals; and they are always individuals set in a society of characters peopling its pages. Inhumanity and the maltreatment of serfs is reported in an intercepted letter;[44] injustice is the bribing of a justice with a gold watch, told as a rambling tale by N. N.;[45] ignorance is revealed in a noble dandy's conversation with Chistoserdov.[46] But the entertaining social portraits are stiffened with a constant moral concern, and this too was to be a common feature of subsequent Russian literature.

For Novikov personally, the year's run of *The Drone* enabled him to devote himself fully to his main passion, the world of books. Although *The Drone*'s successor—its title of *The Tatler*

[43] Andrey Bolotov, op. cit. iii. 275–6.
[44] *Satiricheskie zhurnaly N. I. Novikova*, ed. Berkov, pp. 140–1.
[45] Ibid., p. 91.
[46] Ibid., p. 74.

(*Pustomelya*) acknowledged its parentage openly—was closed after two monthly issues, the subsequent *Painter* of 1772 was very successful and his magazine journalism gave Novikov the experience, the capital, and, most important of all, the patronage at Court which was necessary for his future career as historian, publisher, and animator of Russian literary life. His involvement with the classical type of satirico-moral journal did not continue beyond *The Painter* which was the last periodical of his to proclaim the fictitious editorial *persona* in its title. While following Western European cultural trends and fashions at a distance, on finally adopting a Western influence Russia would tend to strive hurriedly to catch up with lost time and telescope a leisurely development into a few short years. As a Freemason, Novikov was to cram the development of Masonry from its early days as a variation of an English social club to its mystical manifestation of the close of the century into the ten years from 1775; similarly, as a publisher of magazines, he hastened in Russia the slow change of the self-confident editorial *persona* during the eighteenth century to the doubting outsider of the century's end.[47] The idler viewing society from its fringes, and the painter standing back, brush in hand, to view his subject, were in the eighties becoming surprisingly similar to the isolated and superfluous romantic hero; and the magazines published by Novikov—although perhaps not strictly edited by him—reflected more and more the uncertainties of man's inner life. At its close, Novikov's literary career was as subject to the interests of the state as at its beginnings; while the confident Drone was an ally, a mentor of a coalescing society, made more aware of itself by the literary flourishes of Catherine's Legislative Commission, Novikov's private stance as a man apart in the days following the French Revolution and in the inevitable twilight of the Empress's reign was sensed to be a threat to authority. In 1792, after interrogation by Sheshkovsky, he was sentenced to fifteen years' imprisonment in the Schlusselberg fortress, and although released in four years' time on the accession of Paul, he had already become one of the first victims in the lengthy martyrology of Russian literature.

[47] See Ronald Paulson, *The Fictions of Satire* (Baltimore, Md., 1967), pp. 185–210.

7

ARTHUR WILSON

Diderot in Russia, 1773–1774

CATHERINE II profited greatly, both intellectually and in public esteem, from her relationships with the French *philosophes*. Of no one was this truer than of Diderot. And he profited from the relationship too, though more financially than intellectually. From her accession in 1762 until his death in 1784 her shadow fell across his path. Sometimes it felt good to him and sometimes, one suspects, it felt like the shirt of Nessus.

Only a few weeks after the *coup d'état* of 1762 Catherine II offered to have the *Encyclopédie* printed at Riga. This proposal, which Diderot for various reasons refused, came at a time when the licence to publish the work in France had been suspended and when it was uncertain whether the final volumes could be published there.[1] Then, in 1765, Catherine II purchased Diderot's library, which he had put up for sale to provide for the dowry of his daughter Angélique. The Empress bought the library for 15,000 livres, unexpectedly making two stipulations very favourable to Diderot. One was that he should remain in possession of his books; the other was that he should be paid 1,000 livres each year to act as caretaker of the collection. And when this honorarium was overlooked the second year—and Diderot let it be known that it had—Catherine took very effective steps to see that it did not happen again. She paid him in a lump sum fifty years in advance.[2]

This sensational occurrence greatly contributed to making Diderot one of the most conspicuous and celebrated men of his time. In return he was naturally glad to perform various services.

---

[1] Count Ivan Shuvalov to Diderot, 20 Aug. 1762, O.S. (Denis Diderot, *Correspondance*, ed. Georges Roth and Jean Varloot, 16 vols. (Éditions de Minuit, Paris, 1955–70), iv. 173–4; hereafter cited as Diderot, *Corr.*).

[2] Ibid. v. 26, 32; vi. 354, 360.

For example, he strongly recommended Falconet to do the statue of Peter the Great which has become the symbol of St. Petersburg–Leningrad and which was one of the successes of her reign. He effectively urged Falconet to accept the commission once it had been offered. He also recommended Le Mercier de La Rivière, the physiocrat whose trip to Russia in 1767–8 was a notable failure. He tried, unsuccessfully, to persuade Claude-Carloman de Rulhière to destroy the veridical but damaging manuscript of his 'Anecdotes sur la révolution de Russie en l'année 1762'; and he facilitated many of Catherine II's art purchases, especially that of the Crozat collection in 1772.[3]

The question of whether Diderot was morally obliged to visit Russia in order to show his gratitude was not long in arising. Catherine II herself was always tactful about this, but Falconet, writing from St. Petersburg, was quite clamorous in insisting that Diderot owed it to himself as well as to the Empress to undertake the journey. Diderot never refused. But he procrastinated. However, with Angélique married and set up in her own establishment, and with the last volumes of the plates of the *Encyclopédie* in the hands of the subscribers, there was no good reason left why Diderot should not embark upon the journey which Falconet was always telling him he ought to take and which Catherine II plainly desired and expected. In late 1772, apparently, he made up his mind to go, and in early 1773 there were many rumours in Paris of his impending departure.[4] He finally got off on 11 June 1773, going first to The Hague, where he visited his old friend Prince Dmitry Golitsyn.[5]

Diderot was a reluctant traveller. Never in England, although

---

[3] Falconet (Diderot, *Corr.* vi. 180–2, 235, 248, 251, 277–87, 338; *Sbornik*, i (1867), 289; xvii (1876), 375–7). Le Mercier de La Rivière (Diderot, *Corr.* vii. 93–5; viii. 35, 111–12, 129; for a caustic account of the whole episode, see Albert Lortholary, *Le Mirage russe en France au XVIIIe siècle* (Boivin, Paris, 1951), pp. 179–86). Rulhière (Diderot, *Corr.* viii. 32–3, 63–4, 128, 137; cf. Lortholary, *Le Mirage russe*, pp. 186–91). Purchases of pictures (Diderot, *Corr.* viii. 28–9, 72, 222; ix. 36, 56–7; xii. 48–9).

[4] Decision in 1772 (because Falconet received word of it in St. Petersburg 21 Jan./1 Feb. 1773 (ibid. xii. 196)).

[5] 11 June 1773 (Mme d'Épinay to Galiani, 13 June 1773 (Louise de La Live d'Épinay, *Gli ultimi anni della Signora d'Épinay. Lettere inedite all'Abate Galiani 1773–1782*), ed. Fausto Nicolini (Bari, 1934), p. 37)).

he knew English books so well and had many English friends; never in Italy, though sometimes he had talked, not very seriously, of going to see the pictures there. He never in his life saw mountains, except for the rather gentle ones in Germany that he saw later this year; and he saw the ocean for the first time at Scheveningen, making a special trip '[to salute] Neptune and his vast empire' the very day of his arrival at The Hague.[6] His travels were customarily intellectual ones, journeys up and down his study, and it was only rarely that he even made the trip to his birthplace in Langres. In fact, he spoke of travel as something slightly morbid, like an addiction. 'As for me, I do not approve of going far off from one's country except between the ages of eighteen and twenty-two.'[7] Yet here he was, going to St. Petersburg when he was sixty years old.

His departure had evidently been accompanied by a good deal of hurly-burly, with Diderot at his most emotional. Still, he sensibly gave his wife power of attorney, by act of 28 April 1773. As the time of leaving approached, there were farewell visits to pay, such as calling on the scientist La Condamine.[8] There were also farewell calls to be received at the Rue Taranne, notably one by Devaines, who recounted later that Diderot told him that at their last family dinner, just finished, his wife, his daughter, and he had been so upset that they could not eat. At that very moment Mme Diderot appeared before the two men—'a priceless woman, with her little bonnet, her pleated dress, her bourgeois figure, her arms akimbo, her shrill voice'—and rebuked Diderot for having missed the meal at home in spite of his promises.[9]

[6] Diderot, *Corr.* xiii. 15.

[7] To Sophie Volland, 12 Oct. 1760 (ibid. iii. 131). The same sentiments in the *Salon de 1767* (Denis Diderot, *Salons*, ed. Jean Seznec, 4 vols. (Clarendon Press, Oxford, 1957–67), iii. 221).

[8] Power of attorney (Paris. Bibliothèque Nationale, *Diderot, 1713–1784* (Paris, 1963), item 480). Farewell visits (Diderot, *Corr.* xiii. 11). In the month before leaving Paris, Diderot signed contracts on behalf of Catherine II with Pierre-Charles Levesque (7 May 1773) and with Antoine-Nicolas Imbert (13 May 1773) to be governors of the School of Cadets at St. Petersburg (contracts published in *Cahiers Haut-Marnais*, no. 24 [premier trimestre 1951], 13–15). Diderot highly recommended Levesque to Falconet and Mlle Collot (Diderot, *Corr.* xii. 228–9).

[9] Charles Brifaut, *Souvenirs d'un académicien sur la Révolution, le Premier Empire et la Restauration*, 2 vols. (Paris, 1921), i. 33–5, this quotation p. 34.

Diderot certainly seems to have given the impression of being disorganized, for Mme d'Épinay wrote of him two days after he had gone, 'The Philosopher is a singular kind of child, really. He was so astounded the day of his departure to be actually obliged to start out, so frightened at having to go further than Grandval, so woebegone to be having to pack his bags.'[10]

At The Hague Diderot was very comfortably installed (with a servant assigned all to himself) in the Russian embassy at 22 Kneuterdijk. This was a handsome house that had belonged in the previous century to the Grand Pensionary Oldenbarnevelt.[11] Diderot greatly enjoyed his stay in Holland. 'The more I get to know this country, the better I adapt myself to it. The soles, the fresh herrings, the turbots, the perch, and what they call *water-fish* are the finest folk in the world.' Presently, though, he began to fear stomach trouble, but this in turn was averted by judicious internal applications of Rhine wine.[12] Of his hostess, Galitsyn's bride, the Countess Amalie de Schmettau (1746–1806), Diderot wrote appreciatively, 'She has read; she knows several languages; ... She plays the harpsichord, and sings like an angel, ... As she is well informed and is logical, she argues like a little lion.' He also mentioned the splendid walks to be taken and spoke especially of his fondness for the sea. 'Scheveningen was in all seasons my favourite promenade.' Life was quiet at The Hague, almost like life in the country, and he enjoyed it.[13]

Not that he did not have much to accomplish, and was not frequently on the go. While he was in the Netherlands he explored the possibility of having his collected works published by M.-M. Rey of Amsterdam. He visited Haarlem, Amsterdam, Zaandam (where Peter the Great had learned the ship-building trade), and Utrecht. Two days after he arrived in The Hague, he went to Leyden. 'I have seen pictures, engravings, princes, and savants.' Among the princes were the brothers William and Charles

---

[10] Épinay, *Gli ultimi anni*, ed. Nicolini, p. 37.

[11] Diderot, *Corr.* xiii. 15; Denis Diderot, *Œuvres complètes*, ed. Jules Assézat and Maurice Tourneux, 20 vols. (Paris, 1875–7), xvii. 443 (hereafter cited as A.-T.). A. W. De Vink, 'De Huizen aan den Kneuterdijk No. 22', *Die Haghe Jaarboek 1921–1922* ('s-Gravenhage, 1921), pp. 120–92, esp. p. 186.

[12] Diderot, *Corr.* xiii. 31, 34, 38, 47.

[13] A.-T. xvii. 443, 449; Diderot, *Corr.* xiii. 31, 32, 33, 35–6.

Bentinck. Among the savants were the youthful Van Goens, professor of Eloquence, History, and Greek at the University of Utrecht; François Hemsterhuis, the 'Dutch Plato', and Isaac de Pinto, whom Diderot had previously known in Paris.[14] During his stay at The Hague Diderot read Helvétius's posthumous *De l'homme* ['Concerning Man, his Intellectual Faculties, and his Education']. This work, which had just been published, was put through the press by Golitsyn himself, and the French authorities suspected Diderot of having written the introduction to it. Diderot read the work pen in hand, thus beginning the *Réfutation de l'ouvrage d'Helvétius intitulé L'Homme* which is one of Diderot's least-known and most significant books. In addition, he was writing the final version of the *Paradoxe sur le comédien*.[15]

Diderot took notes of his observations in the Netherlands, fortifying himself with suggestions made by Linnaeus in his *Instructio peregrinatoris* (Uppsala, 1759) on the proper ways of preparing oneself to travel profitably. Eventually these notes, depending very heavily for their factual material on two previously published handbooks but still containing a very great deal of Diderot's own observations and style, became his *Voyage de Hollande*. The *Voyage*, embracing as it does numerous social and political observations, is characteristic of its author: 'But throughout Holland one of the continually and deliciously moving things is that one never encounters there the sight of abject poverty or the spectacle of tyranny.'[16]

[14] A.–T. xvii. 450–7; Diderot, *Corr.* xiii. 15, 32–3, 24–7; Épinay, *Gli ultimi anni*, ed. Nicolini, p. 39. Diderot asked Jean-Nicolas Sébastien Allamand, a professor at Leyden, to find a publisher for him (Allamand to M.-M. Rey, 17 June 1773 (Herbert Dieckmann, *Cinq Leçons sur Diderot* (Geneva, 1959), p. 20)). Regarding Van Goens and Hemsterhuis, see the excellent articles by Henri L. Brugmans, 'Autour de Diderot en Hollande', *Diderot Studies*, iii (1961), 55–71, and 'Diderot, Le Voyage de Hollande', in *Connaissance de l'étranger: Mélanges offerts à la mémoire de Jean-Marie Carré* (Paris, 1964), pp. 154–8. Regarding de Pinto, see Alan J. Freer, 'Isaac de Pinto e la sua *Lettre à Mr. D[iderot] sur le jeu des cartes*', *Annali della Scuola Normale Superiore di Pisa*, 2nd Ser. xxxiii (1964), 93–117; and the same, 'Ancora su Isaac de Pinto e Diderot', ibid. xxv (1966), 1–7.

[15] Voltaire to d'Alembert, 16 and 26 June and 14 July 1773 (François-Marie Arouet de Voltaire, *Voltaire's Correspondence*, ed. Theodore Besterman (Geneva, 1953–   ) (listed by serial number), nos. 17342, 17353, 17382 (hereafter cited as 'Besterman, no.   ')). Diderot, *Corr.* xiii. 37, 46, 56.

[16] Ibid. 46. Regarding Linnaeus, see Sergio Moravia, 'Philosophie et géographie à la fin du XVIIIᵉ siècle', *Studies on Voltaire and the Eighteenth Century*,

Through the summer interested persons in Paris and St. Petersburg began to wonder whether Diderot would get further than The Hague after all. He himself did not sound too sure.[17] Then a *deus ex machina* appeared on the stage and resolved all problems. This was a young Russian (born in 1742) from one of the great families, Aleksey Vasilevich Naryshkin, one of the chamberlains of Catherine II. A friend of Beccaria and having previously known Diderot at Paris, Naryshkin was at Aix-la-Chapelle in May 1773 taking the waters. He 'has persuaded me that it would be a great pleasure for him and for me to travel and talk together some hundreds of leagues in the same coach'.[18] In August Naryshkin showed up at The Hague and the two travellers started out on 20 August.

Diderot's correspondence shows that at first he intended to go by way of Berlin. Grimm's letters to his friend, Count Nesselrode, at that time a chamberlain of Frederick the Great, also show that it was expected that Diderot would spend a week at Berlin and at Potsdam. Grimm, who trembled for Diderot's behaviour at a court, begged Nesselrode to be the visitor's guardian: 'I commend Denis to your charity. If you do not outdo yourself, he is capable of doing everything wrong. . . . Make him do what he ought to do and only what he ought. Ask him why he hasn't written me even once.'[19]

In fact, however, Diderot and Naryshkin took a more southerly

lvii (1967), 968–9. The *Voyage de Hollande* is published in A.–T. xvii. 363–471; passage quoted here is p. 378. Gustave Charlier, 'Diderot et la Hollande', *Revue de Littérature Comparée*, xxi (1947), 193–206, pointed out that Diderot borrowed his facts very freely and without acknowledgement from François-Michel Janiçon, *État présent de la République des Provinces-Unies et des Païs qui en dépendent*, 2 vols. (The Hague, 1729–30), and also (Charlier, art. cit., pp. 207–27) from François-Alexandre Aubert de la Chesnaye des Bois, *Lettres hollandoises, ou les mœurs, les usages et les coutumes des Hollandois, comparés avec ceux de leurs voisins*, 2 vols. (Amsterdam, 1750).

[17] Épinay, *Gli ultimi anni*, ed. Nicolini, pp. 39, 46, 52; Étienne-Maurice Falconet, *Correspondance de Falconet avec Catherine II, 1767–1778*, ed. Louis Réau (Paris, 1921), pp. 206, 206–7, 208–9; Diderot, *Corr.* xiii. 41–3, 44–5, 48.

[18] Ibid. xii. 230; xiii. 41, 45, 50. For Naryshkin, see Anne Basanoff, 'La bibliothèque russe de Diderot', Association des bibliothécaires français, *Bulletin d'informations* xxix (June 1959), 72. For a letter from Naryshkin to Beccaria sent from Aix-la-Chapelle, 2 May 1773, see Cesare Beccaria, *Dei delitti e delle pene*, ed. Franco Venturi (Turin, 1965), p. 649.

[19] Diderot, *Corr.* xiii. 46, 49; Grimm to Nesselrode, 11 and 25 Sept. 1773 (*Sbornik*, xvii [1876], 282–3).

route. Perhaps it was because, according to Grimm's theory, Princess Golitsyn had made Diderot fear lest he be poorly received at Berlin.[20] Another explanation is that the travellers had to hurry, especially if they were to arrive in St. Petersburg for a great state event on 9 October, the marriage of the heir apparent to a German princess. As a court chamberlain, Naryshkin probably very much wanted, indeed needed, to be there. When, therefore, they were delayed by Diderot's having a bad attack of colic at Duisburg, in the Ruhr, Naryshkin evidently decided to avoid the additional delays attendant upon a visit to Berlin and Potsdam and they went via Leipzig and Dresden instead.[21]

On his journey through Germany Diderot met the German man of letters Friedrich Heinrich Jacobi, who subsequently wrote of Diderot more in wonder than in admiration.[22] At Dresden he visited the art galleries, and was probably shown through by Christian Ludwig von Hagedorn, the author of the important *Betrachtungen über die Malerei* (1762) [*Observations on Painting*]. At Dresden too Diderot had a conversation with the Spanish ambassador about the clergy in Spain.[23] Just previously, at Leipzig, Diderot's views on religion had displeased his auditors, according to the testimony of two dissenters. But there is no doubt that he made a memorable impression:

His vivacity is extraordinarily great. . . . He speaks with a warmth and vehemence that almost benumbs us colder-blooded souls. Anyone who wants to make an objection or contribute something to the conversation must seize the moment quickly and at the same time speak with confidence. . . . He seizes all occasions to preach atheism, and sometimes he preaches it really with the passion of a fanatic.[24]

[20] Grimm to Nesselrode, 28 Dec. 1773 (Vasiliy Alekseevich Bilbasov, *Didro v Peterburge* (St. Petersburg, 1884), p. 165; *Sbornik*, xvii. 283–4).

[21] Diderot, *Corr.* xiii. 64; Grimm to Nesselrode, 5 Oct. 1773 (*Sbornik*, xvii (1876), 283). Diderot's own notes of his itinerary to and from Russia, giving the distances traversed but not the exact dates, are in Herbert Dieckmann, *Inventaire du Fonds Vandeul et inédits de Diderot* (Geneva, 1951), pp. 267–78.

[22] Roland Mortier, *Diderot en Allemagne (1750–1850)* (Paris, 1954), pp. 32–3.

[23] Paul Vernière, 'Diderot et C. L. de Hagedorn: Une étude d'influence', *Revue de Littérature Comparée*, xxx (1956), 254. The Spanish ambassador at Dresden was Don Joseph Onis (Denis Diderot, *Mémoires pour Catherine II*, ed. Paul Vernière (Paris, 1966), pp. 166–7, 302).

[24] Georg Joachim Zollikofer to Christian Garve, Leipzig, 18 Sept. 1773 (Daniel

It is evident that Diderot, not much caring what the Germans and Russians were accustomed to in religious discussions, was taking with him a reputation for atheism.

The travellers pressed on, several times travelling night and day and going as much as forty-eight hours without stopping. The roads were abominable. Yet Diderot said he felt less tired than he would have been from a walk in the Bois de Boulogne. He concluded that the motion of the coach was a good counteraction to his too sedentary life. Indeed, he felt inspired to write eight occasional poems, about 'The Post from Königsberg to Memel', about gnats in Poland, about Naryshkin's toothache, and, in detail, about the purchasable but dangerous charms of 'The Servant Girl at the Sign of the Cloven Hoof, in Riga'.[25] But at Narva he was attacked by colic again. Not wanting Naryshkin to be delayed, Diderot dissimulated his state, and they went on. They arrived, with Diderot 'more dead than alive', on 8 October 1773, the day before the marriage of Grand Duke Paul to Wilhelmina of Hesse-Darmstadt.[26]

Diderot expected to stay at Falconet's, 'where I counted upon finding some herb tea, a syringe, and a bed'. For months he had been anticipating the delicious pleasure of a reunion: 'What a moment, for you and for me, when I shall be knocking at your door, when I shall enter and rush into your arms....' Instead, sick as he was, he received a very brusque and chilling reception. Although a small chamber had previously been prepared for him, now there was none, for Falconet's artist son, a pupil of Sir Joshua Reynolds, had unexpectedly arrived from London and was now

Jacoby, 'Diderot in Leipzig', *Euphorion*, vi (1899), 646, 647); the whole letter (ibid. 645–9) is of great interest. The second source of information, but perhaps not an eyewitness, was Karl Lessing, who wrote to Gotthold Ephraim Lessing on 21 Oct. 1773, 'Rathe, was er da gethan hat! Oeflentlich vor dem Thore, im Kreise einer Menge Professoren und Kaufleute, den Atheismus gepredigt' (Gotthold Ephraim Lessing, *Sämtliche Schriften*, 23 vols. (Stuttgart, 1886–1924), xx. 287–8).

[25] 'The Servant Girl' was published by Dieckmann, *Inventaire du Fonds Vandeul et inédits de Diderot*, p. 280. For a list of the eight poems, see Brugmans, 'Autour de Diderot en Hollande', *Diderot Studies*, iii. 68, who publishes nos. 7 and 8, previously *inédites* (ibid., pp. 68–71); nos. 3, 4, 5, and 6 published by Dieckmann, op. cit., pp. 279–82; nos. 1 and 2 (A.–T. ix. 20–7, 36–41). It is possible that Diderot wrote some of these in 1774, on his way out of Russia.
[26] Diderot to his wife, 9 Oct. 1773 (Diderot, *Corr.* xiii. 63–5).

occupying it. Meanwhile, no alternative plans had been made for Diderot, so that when he arrived he had no choice save that of going to an inn or of asking the Naryshkins to put him up. This they graciously did, and Diderot remained at the Naryshkin town house throughout his stay at St. Petersburg.[27]

Diderot's reception by Falconet must have been a very disagreeable experience for the newcomer. He was ill, in a strange country, the language of which he did not speak, and yet he was turned away by his old friend upon whom he had counted so implicitly. It is true that Falconet's son had arrived unexpectedly, but that was on 19 August, almost eight weeks before. Falconet subsequently attempted to explain his strange behaviour by claiming that he had heard (though at second hand) that the Naryshkins were preparing an apartment for Diderot and that consequently he had taken for granted that Diderot knew of this and had accepted the Naryshkin offer. At the time Diderot, who was trying to calm down his wife, furious at the news of Falconet's reception, professed to find Falconet's explanation satisfactory. But in the long run Diderot evidently thought the excuses less than convincing, for his daughter, writing in 1787, declared that her father's 'soul was wounded forever'.[28]

Diderot had heard much of the royal marriage, especially as it was Grimm who had really engineered the match. Diderot could have been present at it, too, had it not been that his trunk was at the customs and the only clothes he had were those he was wearing; besides, he had forgotten his wig somewhere *en route*, 'three or four hundred leagues from here'. But perhaps he watched the wedding cortège from the Naryshkin palace, for it is located on one side of the large square fronting on the great Cathedral of St. Isaac, and the route of the procession passed that way. 'The Weather was remarkably fine,' reported Sir Robert Gunning to the Earl of Suffolk, 'which added much to the splendid appearance

[27] Diderot, *Corr.* xiii. 65–7; Diderot to Falconet, 20 May 1773 (A.–T. xviii. 329). Falconet's house and atelier were in the Millionnaya, a street parallel to the Neva and very close to the Hermitage (Diderot, *Mémoires pour Catherine II*, ed. Vernière, p. i).
[28] Diderot, *Corr.* xiii. 145. Diderot's daughter (A.–T. i. pp. lii–liii). Young Falconet's arrival (Falconet *père* to Catherine II, 20 Aug. 1773 (*Correspondance de Falconet avec Catherine II*, ed. Réau, pp. 212–13)).

of the Equipages and Dresses, the Magnificence of which nothing could exceed.'[29]

Diderot's visit to Russia was a widely anticipated event. So much so that presently the British minister reported in code, 'Monsieur Diderot is at length arrived here.' Even Diderot must sometimes have wondered just what experiences might be awaiting him. For Catherine II had recently dealt with D'Alembert very cuttingly and Diderot must have known that she had. It proved how formidable a person—and a crowned head—Catherine II could be. D'Alembert, counting upon her good graces previously expressed at frequent intervals, had asked her as a personal favour to release eight French volunteer officers who, while serving with the Poles, had been captured by the Russians. The Empress refused, but D'Alembert had the temerity to ask again. This time her refusal was peremptory and barely polite, indicating quite clearly that D'Alembert had more than used up his store of goodwill. It is not surprising that Diderot wrote to his wife, who may have been suggesting that he ask Catherine II for some favour, 'Listen, my dear, the greater the sovereign's kindnesses towards me, the more I must use them with discretion.'[30]

Catherine II, being a politically minded woman, was probably very grateful to Diderot for making the effort to come to thank her. There was great publicity value for her in his pilgrimage. People long remembered that Mme Geoffrin had travelled to Warsaw in 1766 to visit Stanislas Poniatowski, the King of Poland. Now an even more celebrated personage was travelling to Russia to see the Empress. It was good for public relations. Consequently she played up to the occasion, gave him a welcome that Grimm described as 'most *distingué*', and certainly accorded Diderot a great share of her time. It is true, though, that she had an unusual

[29] Diderot, *Corr.* xiii. 64, 68. Public Record Office, State Papers Foreign 91 (Russia), vol. xciv, f. 84ʳ (1/12 Oct. 1773). Gunning to Suffolk, 8/19 Oct. 1773 (P.R.O., loc. cit., f. 93ʳ).

[30] D'Alembert to Catherine II, 30 Oct. 1772 (Jean Le Rond d'Alembert, *Œuvres et correspondances inédites de d'Alembert*, ed. Charles Henry (Paris, 1887), pp. 250–5); her reply, 20 Nov. 1772 (ibid., pp. 255–6); his reiterated request, 31 Dec. 1772 (ibid., pp. 256–60); her final refusal (ibid., pp. 260–1). These letters also in *Sbornik*, xiii (1874), 279–84, 288–92. For this incident, see Lortholary, *Le Mirage russe*, pp. 199–204, 366–8. Diderot, *Corr.* xiii. 82 (Oct. 1773).

amount of leisure just then: she had just dismissed Vassilchikov as her lover and had not yet designated Potemkin to that post.[31]

Soon after Diderot's arrival—probably no later than 15 October and certainly by the end of the month—he was seeing the Empress daily, with a standing appointment for a lengthy personal interview beginning at three in the afternoon. Diderot was profoundly impressed by Catherine II. He was especially moved by the sight of her visiting the School for Noble Girls that she had founded and of her letting the little things, 'no taller than cabbages', gather around her, caress her, and throw their arms around her.[32] She, for her part, found Diderot astonishing but claimed that she was enchanted by him. In letters to Nesselrode, to Meister, and to Mme Necker, Grimm (who had been in St. Petersburg since mid September) spread the news of Diderot's success:

> And with her he is just as odd, just as original, just as much Diderot, as when with you. He takes her hand as he takes yours, he shakes her arm as he shakes yours, he sits down by her side as he sits down by yours; but in this last point he obeys sovereign orders, and, as you may imagine, a man does not seat himself opposite to Her Majesty unless he is so obliged.

A Carmontelle drawing of Diderot and Grimm in conversation shows the former with his hand on Grimm's shoulder in just one of these attention-demanding, sleeve-plucking gestures. 'Just as much Diderot', wrote Grimm, 'as if he were in the synagogue of the Rue Royale' (meaning at D'Holbach's). A letter from Catherine II to Mme Geoffrin, the original of which has never been found, is said to have been of the following tenor: 'Your Diderot is a very extraordinary man. I cannot get out of my conversations with him without having my thighs bruised and black and blue. I have been obliged to put a table between him and me to shelter myself and my limbs from his gesticulations.' D'Escherny, the source for this anecdote, quite evidently accepted the story as being a fair

---

[31] 'L'accueil le plus distingué' (Grimm to Mme Geoffrin, 10 Nov. 1773 (Stanislas II, *Correspondance inédite du roi Stanislas-Auguste Poniatowski et de Madame Geoffrin (1764–1777)*, ed. Charles de Mouÿ (Paris, 1875), p. 464 n.)). Vernière, in Diderot, *Mémoires pour Catherine II*, ed. Vernière, p. iv.

[32] Diderot, *Corr.* xiii. 76–7, 79, 81–2; *Correspondance de Falconet avec Catherine II*, ed. Réau, pp. 223–4.

description of Diderot's usual behaviour. It was commonly said, remarked D'Escherny, that Diderot at table was in the habit of pinning the arms of his neighbours on both sides of him, talking ceaselessly, and still managing to eat with the heartiest of appetites.[33] The courtiers must have found Diderot as difficult to deal with as he them, and for opposite reasons. He was not used to people who had trained themselves to be full of dissimulation; they were disconcerted by a person who was so naïve, so easy to mislead, but who had such august backing. One of Diderot's 'two little Germans', who by this time had achieved an important post in Russia as secretary to Grand Duke Paul, put it this way:

He [Diderot] was at all the fêtes, all the galas, all the balls, always wearing a black suit. People's judgement about him is conditioned here by this singularity. Some look upon him with enthusiasm. Others say, 'Why, is that all it is?' . . . I perceive that it is terribly difficult to sustain a big reputation; and that it is very perilous to pass from one's study into a brilliant court . . .[34]

On 23 October/3 November the Russian Academy of Sciences honoured Diderot and Grimm by electing them foreign members.[35] The resident membership at that time seems to have been eleven, of whom by far the most distinguished were the Swiss Leonhard Euler and his son Jean-Albert Euler, both mathematicians. Diderot's letter of thanks to the Academy on 27 October/7 November contains an especially interesting statement: 'Had the

---

[33] Grimm to Mme Necker, 13 Nov. 1773 (Gabriel-Paul-Othenin de Cléron, comte de Haussonville, *Le Salon de Mme Necker, d'après des documents tirés des archives de Coppet*, 2 vols. (Paris, 1882); quotation from the London 1882 ed., i. 143). Grimm to Nesselrode, 2 and 19 Nov. 1773 (Bilbasov, *Didro v Peterburge*, pp. 158, 160). Grimm to J. H. Meister, 8 Nov. 1773 (Clara Adèle Luce Herpin, [pseud. Lucien Percy] and Gaston Maugras, *Une Femme du monde au XVIIIᵉ siècle. Dernières années de Madame d'Épinay*, 2nd ed. (Paris, 1883), p. 480). Grimm's arrival in mid September (Catherine II to Voltaire, 11/22 Sept. 1773 (Besterman, no. 17467)). François-Louis d'Escherny, *Mélanges de littérature, d'histoire, de morale et de philosophie*, 3 vols. (Paris, 1811), iii. 131.

[34] L. H. Nicolay to (?) Ring, 11/22 Oct. 1773 (Jacques Donvez, 'Diderot, Aiguillon et Vergennes', *Revue des Sciences Humaines*, N.S. lxxxvii (July–Sept. 1957), 288–9). See also *Sbornik*, xvii (1876), 282. Diderot attended the masked ball held as part of the wedding festivities, a few days after 9 Oct. (Grimm to Mme Geoffrin, 10 Nov. 1773 (Stanislas II, *Correspondance inédite du roi Stanislas . . .*, ed. de Mouÿ, p. 464 n.)).

[35] *Procès-verbaux des séances de l'Académie impériale des Sciences depuis sa fondation jusqu'à 1803*, ed. K. S. Veselovsky, 3 vols. (1897–1900), iii. 104.

Académie of Paris been free, long ago its choice would have justified yours.'[36] At the session of 1/12 November the new foreign members were inaugurated and Diderot then read to his new confrères an elaborate questionnaire seeking information about Siberia.[37] The questionnaire revealed a great deal of knowledge of Siberia—at least to the extent of asking apposite questions about it—and of interest in it, and perhaps was inspired by Diderot's hope that he might soon be editing a new *Encyclopédie*, Russian style.[38] The answers to his questions were read to the Academy on 2/13 December but it was voted to submit these to the approval of the Director of the Academy, Count Vladimir Orlov, before sending them to Diderot.[39] It rather looks as though this consent was never given. If so, it shows how difficult it was for a person even with Diderot's backing to get any information on conditions in Russia. Strangely enough, the session in which he was inaugurated was the only meeting of the Academy of Sciences that Diderot attended, even though twenty-six of them were held before he left the city in 1774.[40]

Meanwhile, what did Diderot and Catherine II find to talk

[36] Jean-Albert Euler, Perpetual Secretary of the Academy, wrote to Diderot of his election the day it occurred, 23 Oct/3 Nov. 1773 (*Uchenaya Korrespondentsiya Akademii Nauk XVIII Veka, 1766–1782*, ed. Inna Lyubimenko [Trudy Arkhiva, ii, 1937], letter no. 1141, p. 240). Diderot replied to Euler 25 Oct./5 Nov. (facsimile in Denis Diderot, *Le Neveu de Rameau*, ed. Gustave Isambert (Paris, 1883), facing p. 94; text published in Diderot, *Corr.* xiii. 85). Diderot's previous letter of acceptance, addressed by mistake to Academician Staehlin under the impression that he was the Secretary, has never been found (ibid.). Diderot's formal letter of acceptance to the Academy, 27 Oct./7 Nov. 1773 (photograph in *Uchenaya* . . ., p. 439; text published, ibid., p. 441); published in Russian translation by M. V. Krutikova and A. M. Chernikov, 'Didro v Akademii Nauk', *Akademii Nauk SSSR Vestnik*, vi (1947), 69–73. Voltaire had been a member of the Academy since 1746 and D'Alembert since 1764 (*Uchenaya Korrespondentsiya,* p. 442 n.); foreign honorary members received a pension of 200 roubles a year (ibid., p. 39).

[37] *Procès-verbaux des séances de l'Académie impériale des Sciences . . . jusqu'à 1803,* iii. 105. Diderot's letter of acceptance was read to the Academy at its séance of 28 Oct. (ibid., p. 104).

[38] This questionnaire, and the answer prepared by a Professor Erik Laxmann, published by Jacques Proust, 'Diderot, l'Académie de Pétersbourg et le projet d'une *Encyclopédie russe*', *Diderot Studies*, xii (1969), 113–17, 118–25. Regarding Laxmann, see ibid., pp. 117–18, 128.

[39] *Procès-verbaux des séances de l'Académie impériale des Sciences . . . jusqu'à 1803,* iii. 105, 109.

[40] Ibid. iii. 105–18 and *passim*.

about? The answer does not have to depend upon the imagination, for Diderot drew up a series of memoranda and left them with the Empress. These memoranda sometimes treat of literary matters but more often discuss political, economic, social, and legal questions, and are very reformist in tone. The 'Historical Essay on the Police Power in France' reaches from Clovis and Charlemagne and Charles VII to the current judicial changes of Maupeou, of which Diderot strongly disapproved. He had begun the preparation of this elaborate essay in response to Naryshkin's suggestion, perhaps while still *en route* to St. Petersburg, a pretty clear indication that Diderot took the initiative in these conversations of suggesting to Catherine II what the topic of discussion should be. These memoranda, of which there were sixty-five, with titles like 'The Action of the Sovereign and of a Third Estate', 'Of Manufactures and Factories', 'On Tolerance', 'Concerning the Administration of Justice', ranged from short notes to lengthy full-dress articles.[41] Their preparation required research as well as literary skill and in their detail and precise information they strongly illustrate the fact that Diderot was becoming an empiricist in the social sciences as well as in the natural ones.

The title-page of these memoranda, in Diderot's own hand, ran as follows: 'Philosophical and historical, etc. miscellany. . . . In the year 1773, from 15 October until 3 December.'[42] They were published, not too accurately, in 1899, with a misleading rearrangement of Diderot's original sequence. It is only since 1966 that a rigorously edited edition has become available. This now allows it to be seen that Diderot's conversations with the Empress were at a level far above mere chit-chat. As Paul Vernière reconstructs what must have happened:

Before each meeting Diderot drew up some notes on subjects of his own determining or sometimes on those suggested to him by

[41] Diderot, *Mémoires pour Catherine II*, ed. Vernière, pp. 1–36, 45–7, 242–3, 253–4, 97–104.
[42] *Mélanges philosophiques, historiques, etc . . . . dont on trouvera la table page suivante. Année 1773 depuis le 15 oct. jusqu'au 3 décemb. même année.* The manuscript is now no. 728 in the Department of Manuscripts of the Library of the Winter Palace, kept at the Moscow General Historical Archives (Diderot, *Mémoires pour Catherine II*, ed. Vernière, pp. vii–viii).

Naryshkin. At the Winter Palace the reading of these would be followed by a discussion. After the interview, Diderot revised, sometimes corrected, rearranged these memoranda before placing them in the hands of the Empress.[43]

Diderot's ambition was to convert Catherine II to the philosophy of the Enlightenment, or at least to reinforce what there were of her liberal convictions. In order to accomplish this, he presented his views by tactful indirection or adroit analogy or skilful insinuation, rather than by open confrontation. One of his most serious and earnest chapters was entitled 'The Daydream of Denis the Philosopher'. After all, he was dealing with a sovereign whom Voltaire described at that very time as wielding 'the most despotic power on earth'.[44]

These notes and essays—on the desirability of free competition in commerce and in government jobs, on the importance of settling the succession to the Russian throne, on the legislative commission that Catherine II had convened in 1767, on public education, on luxury, usury, divorce, academies, 'On a Way of Drawing Benefit from Religion and Making it Good for Something', etc.—explain why Diderot could write to his wife, 'I worked a great deal while *en route*; I am working a great deal here.'[45]

Catherine II now and again asked him some very searching questions in return, and in answering them Diderot had to call on all his resources of tactfulness, a commodity which his friends thought he had in very slender supply. She pressed him to tell her what was in Rulhière's manuscript about the *coup d'état* of 1762. 'As for what concerns you in it, Madame,' Diderot replied, 'if you

[43] Diderot, *Mémoires pour Catherine II*, ed. Vernière, p. ix. The Diderot memoranda were first published by Maurice Tourneux, *Diderot et Catherine II* (Paris, 1899), pp. 91–457. The deficiencies of this edition were made known by S. Kuzmin, 'Zabytaya rukopis Didro', *Literaturnoe Nasledstvo*, lviii (1952), 927–48. See also Paul Vernière, 'Les Mémoires à l'Impératrice: Autour d'un manuscrit de Diderot perdu et retrouvé', *Annales de l'Université de Paris*, xxxvi (1966), 34–42.

[44] Voltaire to D'Alembert, 26 June 1773 (Besterman, no. 17353). 'Ma rêverie à moi Denis le philosophe' (Diderot, *Mémoires pour Catherine II*, ed. Vernière, pp. 37–44).

[45] Diderot, *Corr.* xiii. 82. Diderot, *Mémoires pour Catherine II*, ed. Vernière, pp. 48–9, 50–1, 59–60, 129–44, 145–60, 192–4, 204–5, 250–1, 269–70.

hold in high esteem the proprieties and the virtues, those outworn rags and tatters of your sex, this work is a satire against you; but if grand designs, if patriotic and manly ideas interest you more, the author depicts you as a great princess, and, taking everything together, does you more honour than harm.' To which she replied, 'You make me want to read it more than ever.'[46] Diderot praised the Empress fulsomely—'the soul of Brutus with the charms of Cleopatra'—to her face, in conversations with others, and in his letters.[47] But he also had the courage to let her guess at his disapproval of the partition of Poland. And he pertinaciously spoke out against despotic government:

A despot, be he the best of men, commits a crime by governing according to his own sweet will. He is a good shepherd who reduces his subjects to the level of animals. . . . One of the great misfortunes that could happen to a free nation would be two or three consecutive reigns of a just and enlightened despotism. Three sovereigns in a row like Elizabeth, and the English would have been imperceptibly led to a condition of servitude of which no one could predict the end.[48]

At St. Petersburg Diderot suddenly found himself caught up in the diplomatic manœuvrings of great powers, perhaps very much against his will. He had left Paris with no official responsibilities or commissions. On the contrary, the Duc D'Aiguillon wrote scornfully and resentfully about Diderot to the French ambassador at St. Petersburg; and it was said around Paris that

[46] Durand to D'Aiguillon, 9 Nov. 1773 (*Sbornik*, xvii [1876], 288).

[47] 'The soul of Brutus with the charms of Cleopatra' (Diderot to Princess Dashkov, 24 Dec. 1773 (Diderot, *Corr.* xiii. 135–6)). Praise to her face (Diderot, *Mémoires pour Catherine II*, ed. Vernière, pp. 42–4); to Falconet about her, 6 Dec. 1773 (Diderot, *Corr.* xiii. 121); to his wife and daughter, 30 Dec. 1773 (ibid., p. 142–4). A quatrain by Diderot appeared in the Stockholm copy of the *Correspondance littéraire* for Jan. 1774 (Vincent E. Bowen, 'Two Unpublished Poems by Diderot', *Modern Language Notes*, lxxiii (1958), 191):

> Ah! qu'ils sont vastes ces palais!
> Ils le seraient bien davantage,
> S'il fallait y placer l'image
> De tous les heureux qu'elle a faits.

[48] Diderot, *Mémoires pour Catherine II*, ed. Vernière, pp. 39–40, 117–18. Cf. Arthur M. Wilson, 'The Development and Scope of Diderot's Political Thought', *Studies on Voltaire and the Eighteenth Century*, xxvii (1963), 1890–1. For much sharper comment by Diderot on the partition of Poland, see A.-T. iii. 264.

when Diderot inquired of the proper minister whether the government had any objection to his going to Russia, the reply was that far from there being any objection to his going, he could remain there if he liked. But once arrived at St. Petersburg, Diderot was made to feel differently by the French ambassador, François-Michel Durand de Distroff. 'I have told M. Diderot what I expect from a Frenchman. He has promised me he will efface, if it be possible, the prejudices that this princess has against us.'[49]

According to Sir Robert Gunning, the British minister at St. Petersburg, who in this instance received his information from Count Panin, the Russian Minister of Foreign Affairs, Diderot vehemently resisted such a departure from his proper sphere.[50] Nevertheless, whether by flattery or by threats, he was persuaded to try to get Catherine II to change her foreign policy—this was the burden of the memorandum that he entitled 'The Daydream of Denis the Philosopher'—so that presently Sir Robert Gunning, reversing his earlier dispatch, was reporting that

Count Panin acquainted me in the utmost Confidence and under the seal of secrecy that Mo͏ͬ Diderot had taken advantage of the constant Access he has had to the Empress to put into her hands a few days ago a paper given him by Mͬ Durand containing proposals for a peace with the Turks; which the Court of France engage to obtain if its good offices were accepted by her. Mo͏ͬ Diderot apologized for acting thus out of his sphere, by the fear he had of being thrown into the Bastille when he returned home, should he have refused complying with the French Minister's request. Her Majesty's answer, as Mo͏ͬ Panin tells me, was that on that account she passed by the impropriety of his conduct, on the condition that he faithfully reported to the Minister the use she made of the paper, which was throwing it into the fire.[51]

If this was the way it happened, it must have been discomfiting

---

[49] D'Aiguillon to Durand de Distroff, 2 Dec. 1773 (Diderot, *Corr.* xiii. 101–2); Durand to D'Aiguillon, 6 Nov. 1773 (Tourneux, *Diderot et Catherine II*, pp. 78–9). Permission to go to Russia (Louis Petit de Bachaumont, *Mémoires secrets pour servir à l'histoire de la république des lettres en France*, 36 vols. (London, 1777–89), xiii. 145 n. [21 Sept. 1773]).

[50] Tourneux, *Diderot et Catherine II*, p. 245.

[51] Sir Robert Gunning to the Earl of Suffolk, 12/23 Nov. 1773 (P.R.O., State Papers Foreign 91 [Russia], vol. xciv, f. 136ͬ; capitalization and punctuation of this quotation modernized).

and humiliating to Diderot. Furthermore, he must also have greatly apprehended lest his standing with the Empress be disastrously undermined. Yet as late as 31 December 1773 the French ambassador was still under the impression that Diderot was continuing to try to influence her policy:

> The conferences of Catherine and Diderot continue without interruption and get longer from day to day. He has told me, and I have reason to believe that he is not untrustworthy, that he has described the danger of the Russian alliance with the King of Prussia and the utility of one with us.[52]

Meanwhile, Diderot's success with the Empress did not preclude his being very homesick. Grimm reported on 25 November that Diderot had 'the Swiss sickness *in gradu heroico*, enough to make me anxious sometimes'. The news from home, however, was reassuring. Angélique's first child, a daughter, was born in September: 'Well, my dear,' Diderot wrote to her, 'here you are, a mother. The Lord only knows what a grave and wise personage you are going to become.' Mme Diderot, who had spent the early weeks of Diderot's absence grumbling to her heart's content, constantly rearranging the furniture, and discharging servants almost as soon as she hired them, was very helpful in her daughter's accouchement and earned Diderot's high praise for thinking to ask the sculptor Pigalle to be the child's godfather.[53]

How did Diderot spend his time when not in conference with the Empress? A good part of it was consumed in being ill. In November and into December he had a stubborn case of the colic and was unable to go with the Empress to Tsarskoe Selo, whither she had invited him. 'The cold and the waters of the Neva deranged his health prodigiously', wrote his daughter later. 'I am convinced that the journey shortened his life.' His health was still uncertain in January, as Catherine II mentioned in a letter to Voltaire, and he was so ill in February that it delayed the start of

---

[52] Durand to D'Aiguillon (*Sbornik*, xvii [1876], 289). D'Aiguillon replied on 29 Jan. 1774, 'On ne peut que savoir gré à M. Diderot de travailler à détruire l'ascendant du Roi de Prusse sur Catherine' (ibid., p. 290).

[53] Grimm to Nesselrode (Bilbasov, *Didro v Peterburge*, p. 163). Diderot, *Corr.* xiii. 73, 78, 80.

his journey home.[54] Another considerable part of his time was spent in the literary work necessary for his preparation of memoranda of conversations with Catherine II, together with (most probably) his critique of the book by Hemsterhuis and, perhaps, his *Réfutation de l'ouvrage d'Helvétius intitulé L'Homme*. 'I am working prodigiously, and with an ease that astonishes me.'[55] During his stay at St. Petersburg he sat for the haunting portrait that Dmitry Levitsky (1735–1822) did of him, a portrait that now hangs in the Museum of Art of the City of Geneva.[56] And he spent part of his time, though perhaps not much of it, in studying Russian, as is proved by the interlineations and marginal notes he made on a Russian grammar and some other Russian books he brought back to Paris.[57]

Sometimes he visited Falconet, though there is no evidence that Falconet ever visited him. Diderot especially wanted to see the statue of Peter the Great. This sculpture was now far advanced in its modelling stage and there had already been transported from a bog in Finland—one of the engineering feats of the century—an enormous granite boulder of 275 tons to serve as the statue's base. Diderot praised the sculpture to the skies. 'I always knew that you are a very able man; but may I die if I thought that you had anything like this in your head. How could I have guessed that

[54] Colic in Nov. and Dec. (Diderot to Alexander Galitsyn, 25 Nov. 1773 (Diderot, *Corr.* xiii. 114); Grimm to Nesselrode, 6 Dec. 1773 (Bilbasov, *Didro v Peterburge*, p. 164)). The 'Neva distemper' (Diderot to his wife and daughter, 30 Dec. 1773 (Diderot, *Corr.* xiii. 141–2, 143); and to Sophie Volland, 29 Dec. 1773 (ibid., p. 141)). Diderot wrote on 9 Apr. 1774, 'J'ai eu deux fois la *néva* à Pétersbourg' (ibid., p. 227). Illness in Jan. and Feb. 1774 (Besterman, no. 17664; Grimm to Nesselrode, 1 Mar. 1774 (Bilbasov, *Didro v Peterburge*, p. 177); Baron de Nolcken to J. F. Beylon, 3 Mar. 1774 (Tourneux, *Diderot et Catherine II*, pp. 467–9)). Regarding Diderot's health in Russia see the testimony of Diderot's daughter (A.-T. i. liii).

[55] Diderot, *Corr.* xiii. 145, 228.

[56] Regarding Levitsky, see Denis Roche, 'Un portraitiste petit-russien au temps de Catherine II: Dmitri-Grigoriévitch Lévitski', *Gazette des Beaux-Arts*, 3e période xxix (1903), 494–507; also Louis Réau, *L'Art russe de Pierre le Grand à nos jours* (Paris, 1922), pp. 125–8.

[57] Jacques Proust, 'La grammaire russe de Diderot', *Revue d'Histoire Littéraire de la France*, liv (1954), 329–31; 'Diderot et le xviiie siècle français en U.R.S.S.', ibid. 324; V. I. Chuchmarev, 'Ob izuchenii Deni Didro russkogo yazyka', *Voprosy Filosofii*, iv (1953), 192–206. (This article also in French translation: 'Diderot et l'étude de la langue russe', *La Pensée*, liii (Jan.–Feb. 1954), 67–74.)

this astounding conception could exist in the same understanding by the side of the dainty image of the statue of Pygmalion?'[58]

A person as sociable as Diderot would want to spend much of his time in a congenial group. This, however, was not easy for him. He could not spend all his time with Catherine II; it was hard to recapture the feelings of intimacy he had once shared with Falconet; nor does he seem to have made the Naryshkin palace the centre of his social life, although he received the visits of Nolcken, the Swedish ambassador, there. Nicolay recalled in his memoirs that Diderot was often invited to the houses of highly placed courtiers, where he constantly played the role of a declared atheist and was abhorred by everybody. And Grimm admitted that Diderot had made 'no conquest here, save that of the Empress'.[59]

Diderot was fully aware of court factions at St. Petersburg, for in 1768 he had reminded Falconet to remember, when he met Nicolay and La Fermière, Diderot's 'two little Germans' of some years before, that they belonged 'to M. Panin and the Grand Duke; while you belong to General Betskoy and the Empress'. So perspicacious a comment may explain why Diderot had not been very eager to come to Russia in the first place. But now, when Nicolay remonstrated with Diderot for being so heedless of courtier opinion, he merely smiled and said, 'I court the favour of the lady of the house only, and scarcely care about the servants'.[60]

The circle at the Court that Diderot found the most congenial

[58] Diderot, *Corr.* xiii. 116–17; see also Diderot's comments in Dieckmann, *Inventaire du Fonds Vandeul et inédits de Diderot*, pp. 230–1. The boulder was got into its present location by Sept. 1770; see the account of moving it in Edmund Hildebrandt, *Leben, Werke und Schriften des Bildhauers E.-M. Falconet, 1716–1791* (Strasbourg, 1908), pp. 46–7; also D. E. Arkin, 'E. M. Falconet', *Istoriya Russkogo Iskusstva*, vi (1961), 382.

[59] Visits of the Swedish ambassador (Tourneux, *Diderot et Catherine II*, pp. 465, 468). L. H. von Nicolay, *L. H. Nicolay (1737–1820) and his Contemporaries*, ed. Edmund Heier (The Hague, 1965), p. 83. Grimm to Nesselrode, 30 Dec. 1773 (Bilbasov, *Didro v Peterburge*, p. 167).

[60] A.-T. xviii. 282; Roland Mortier, 'Diderot et ses "Deux Petits Allemands"', *Revue de Littérature Comparée*, xxxiii (1959), 194. Nicolay, *L. H. Nicolay*, ed. Heier, p. 83. Sir Robert Gunning reported to the Earl of Suffolk on 22 Nov./3 Dec. 1773 (in code) that 'His [Diderot's] Flattery to the Great Duke was full as gross, but, to this Young Prince's Honour, He has shown as much contempt for it as Abhorrence of this boasted Philosopher's pernicious principles' (P.R.O., State Papers Foreign 91 [Russia], vol. xciv, f. 183); similarly, same to the same, 7/18 Jan. 1774 (ibid., vol. xcv, ff. 67ᵛ–68ʳ). Gunning's source of information was probably Panin.

and hospitable was that of which General Betsky was the bell-wether. This included Nicolas-Gabriel Clerc, physician of the Corps of [noble] Cadets at St. Petersburg; Anastasya Sokolov, Betskoy's natural daughter and a favourite maid-in-waiting of Catherine II; and Mme Sophie de La Font and her daughter Wilhelmine, both associated with the School for Noble Girls that Catherine II had established at the Smolny Convent in 1764.[61] This was the circle that was most concerned with Catherine II's art acquisitions and her educational reforms, precisely the areas of two of Diderot's enthusiasms. Diderot, in fact, having been greatly impressed by the amateur theatricals at the Smolny Convent but struck by the number of 'shocking utterances on these innocent lips', had volunteered to clean up Molière and Racine and other classics of the French theatre, 'sixteen or seventeen of them'. Thus would be eliminated anything inimical to the young girls' innocence. Voltaire had previously consented to adapt some of these works but his zeal had flagged. 'What Voltaire has not done and what he could have done better than I, I shall do. I have promised it to Your Imperial Majesty and I shall keep my word.' Over a year later Diderot was still promising 'the comedies for the young ladies'.[62] No actual examples of his bowdlerizing, however, have come to light.

In addition to this promise to the School for Noble Girls, Diderot also became connected with another of Catherine II's educational establishments, this time as honorary curator of the Asylum for Foundlings at Moscow. In gratitude the Council of the Imperial Household of Education, headed by Betskoy and with seven other signatories, awarded Diderot a diploma, though just what duties he undertook are not known.[63]

---

[61] Diderot, *Mémoires pour Catherine II*, ed. Vernière, pp. xii–xiii. Diderot sent greetings to these various persons in a letter to Clerc from The Hague, 8 Apr. 1774 (Diderot, *Corr.* xiii. 213–17).

[62] Diderot, *Mémoires pour Catherine II*, ed. Vernière, pp. 52–3, 258; Diderot to Catherine II, 6 Dec. 1775 (Diderot, *Corr.* xiv. 175). Cf. Diderot's 'Projet d'une pièce de théâtre', modelled after Molière's *Les Femmes savantes* (Diderot, *Mémoires pour Catherine II*, ed. Vernière, pp. 95–6).

[63] Undated; there is a description of this *diplôme* in the catalogue of the Diderot exhibition at the Bibliothèque Nationale in 1963 (*Diderot 1713–1784* [Paris: Bibliothèque Nationale, 1963], item 493). For a photograph of the diploma, see

Diderot made serious efforts to secure information about conditions in Russia. 'I do not neglect any effort to inform myself here.' Though unsuccessful, so far as is known, in getting from the Academy of Sciences information about Siberia, he wrote on Catherine II's recommendation to Count Münnich, the Imperial Director of Customs. 'Pardon this importunity on the part of a foreigner who would very much like not to return home entirely ignorant.' His questions were searching ones: what is the annual amount and value of the production of grain, of hemp and linen, of timber? How much of it is sold abroad? What is the approximate population of the Empire, of Moscow, of Petersburg, of other principal cities? What are the annual exports of pottery and leather goods, fish and caviar? What are the imports of horses, of oil? What is the ratio of a day labourer's wages to the cost of bread? What are maritime freight rates? Does the coastal trade employ many ships? The Empress begs you to try to find for me a tabulation as complete as possible of weights and measures. Also of monies. Are there any banks or insurance companies in the Empire? What is the total revenue of the Empire? What is the public debt?[64]

So far as is known Münich never replied to this inquiry.

Diderot had asked the Empress these questions and many more. There are said to be 7,300 monks and 5,300 nuns in Russia. Is this number diminishing? What is the condition of the Jews in Russia? What are the laws regulating the grain trade? What is the annual distillation of grain alcohol? What are the regulations regarding tobacco? Are you increasing your mulberry culture and your silk farms? What are the legal rights of landowners in Russia? Does not the servitude of the rural workers adversely affect agriculture? To many of these questions Catherine II gave replies to her own satisfaction without referring to Münich. To Diderot's question

Georges Dulac, 'Diderot dans le monde', *Le Français dans le monde*, xxxv (Sept. 1965), 31. Signatories besides Betskoy were Aleksey Durnov, Andrey Lopukhin, Nikolay Saltykov, Aleksandr Pavlov, Bogdan Umskoy, Prince Mikhail Dolgoruky (?), and Petr Nashchokin.

[64] 31 Jan. 1774 (A.–T. xx. 45–6; also in Tourneux, *Diderot et Catherine II*, pp. 558–9). The questionnaire (A.–T. xx. 46–8; Tourneux, *Diderot et Catherine II*, pp. 559–61).

about the serfs she replied 'I know of no country where the worker loves his land and his home more than in Russia.'[65]

Catherine II always found Diderot's play of intellect brilliant and dazzling. But what was her considered opinion of him as the novelty wore off? She always praised him, but a cynic might say that that was to be expected as a part of the public relations game. Besides, the word that she repeatedly took refuge in when describing him to Voltaire, 'extraordinary', can be ambiguous and not very discriminating. 'I find in Diderot an inexhaustible imagination, and I reckon him among the most extraordinary men who have ever existed.' In a letter some time later she wrote, 'Diderot's is a most extraordinary head . . . the hearts of all men should be of his stamp.' And again, 'It's a very extraordinary head. You do not often find any like it.' The more one analyses these judgements, the more ambiguously they can be interpreted. The Empress was reported by the French ambassador at the end of 1773 as saying that in certain respects Diderot was a hundred years old and in others he was not ten.[66]

It may be significant that Diderot's memorandum book of his discussions with Catherine II gives a terminal date of 5 December 1773, three whole months before he left St. Petersburg. Does this not suggest that he himself was aware that after that date their conversations had not been of a nature that could effect policy? Perhaps so, for Diderot's questioning of the Empress and then of Count Münich, though occurring after 5 December, was merely for the purpose of Diderot's receiving information. Moreover, in spite of the French ambassador's reporting that the conferences got longer from day to day, Diderot himself wrote to his family on 30 December that, though he had the privilege of daily access to the Empress's study, he used the privilege only every three days, his reason being that he wanted to avoid exciting envy and enmity.[67] No doubt a good reason, but why had he not felt its

[65] Tourneux, *Diderot et Catherine II*, pp. 532–56; reprinted in Diderot, *Corr.* xiii. 162–91. Catherine's remark about the worker loving his land (Tourneux, *Diderot et Catherine II*, p. 541; Diderot, *Corr.* xiii. 170).

[66] Catherine II to Voltaire, 7/18 Jan. 1774 (Besterman, no. 17664); 19/30 Jan. 1774 (Besterman, no. 17683); 15/26 Mar. 1774 (Besterman, no. 17770). Durand to D'Aiguillon, 31 Dec. 1773 (Diderot, *Corr.* xiii. 146).

[67] Ibid., p. 142; also to Princess Dashkov, 24 Dec. 1773 (ibid., p. 136). For a

cogency sooner? Perhaps sometime in November or December Catherine II had made him feel that she did not value his advice so highly as he had previously supposed. Such was her account of their relations when, years later, she talked about Diderot to the Comte de Ségur:

I frequently had long conversations with him, but with more curiosity than profit. Had I placed faith in him, every institution in my empire would have been overturned; legislation, administration, politics and finances, would all have been changed for the purpose of substituting some impracticable theories.

However, as I listened more than I talked, any one, on being present, would have supposed him to be the commanding pedagogue and myself the humble scholar. Probably he was of that opinion himself, for, after some time, finding that he had not wrought in my government any of those great innovations which he had advised, he exhibited his surprise by a sort of haughty discontent.

Then speaking to him freely, I said: 'Monsieur Diderot, I have listened with the greatest pleasure to all that your brilliant genius has inspired you with; but all your grand principles, which I understand very well, though they will make fine books, would make sad work in actual practice. You forget, in all your plans for reformation, the difference between our two positions: you work only upon paper, which submits to every thing; it is altogether obedient and supple, and opposes no obstacles, either to your imagination or to your pen; whereas I, a poor Empress, I work upon human nature, which is, on the contrary, irritable and easily offended.'

I am satisfied that, from that time, he pitied me, and looked on me as one possessed only of a narrow and ordinary mind. From that moment he spoke to me only on literary subjects, and politics disappeared from our conversations.[68]

It must be remembered that the moment of Diderot's visit became singularly unpropitious for liberal reforms in Russia. Not only was Catherine worried about bringing to an end successfully the war with Turkey then going on, but also this was precisely

---

discussion of this question, see Diderot, *Mémoires pour Catherine II*, ed. Vernière, pp. xxiii–xxiv.

[68] Louis-Philippe, Comte de Ségur, *Memoirs and Recollections*, 3 vols. (London, 1825–7), iii. 34–5.

the time of the Pugachev revolt, perhaps the most serious and dangerous peasant uprising (from the point of view of the existing regime) in the history of the Tsardom. Only some three weeks after Diderot's arrival in St. Petersburg, the British minister reported that 'An extraordinary council was held the other day in consequence, it is said, of accounts being received of a fresh insurrection of the Don Cossacks, as well as of one in the Province of Orenburg . . . .'.[69] In St. Petersburg the revolt was treated as a non-event. 'Everything relative to the insurrection in the Province of Orenburg is kept as secret as possible . . .' On Christmas Day the government did issue a proclamation (in Russian) guardedly acknowledging the rebellion, but as late as February 1774, not long before Diderot left St. Petersburg, the British minister remarked that the reports of the revolt were still 'kept very secret'.[70] So far as can be ascertained, Diderot had no intimation of the revolt at the time, though a year later, it is true, he claimed that Catherine II had told him about it.[71] The revolt intensified through December 1773 and January 1774, causing D'Alembert to wonder in a letter to Voltaire in February whether Catherine II could keep her throne. Of course the worry of it nagged at her: 'The Empress is at present a good deal out of Order', wrote Sir Robert Gunning on 24 January/4 February 1774. 'She has been frequently so of late; and it is possible that the disagreeable Turn affairs have taken has somewhat contributed to her indisposition. The Insurrection in Orenburg, and the Height it has been allowed to get to, has certainly given her great Uneasiness.' Eventually Pugachev was captured and executed and the revolt collapsed, but when Diderot left St. Petersburg this was still months away. In February Gunning wrote,

It does not escape Observation that the Empress's Temper is much altered of late; that there does not appear the same Affability and

[69] Sir Robert Gunning to the Earl of Suffolk, 22 Oct./2 Nov. 1773 (P.R.O. State Papers Foreign 91 [Russia], vol. xciv, f. 106ᵛ).

[70] Richard Oakes to William Fraser, 5/16 Nov. 1773 (P.R.O., loc. cit., vol. xciv, f. 126ʳ); Gunning to Suffolk, 28 Jan./8 Feb. 1774 (P.R.O., loc. cit., vol. xcv, f. 98). For other reports regarding the attempt to keep secrecy (P.R.O., loc. cit., vol. xciv, ff. 118, 181, 193).

[71] Diderot, *Corr.* xiv. 108.

Condescension about Her, that She has hitherto been remarked for. The embarrassed Situation of her Affairs has probably had an Effect upon her Disposition, as well as upon her Health . . .[72]

This was certainly not a propitious time for a liberal *philosophe* to be suggesting change.

While at St. Petersburg Diderot got a bitter taste of the malice of Frederick the Great. A review of the recent unauthorized edition of Diderot's collected works, published at Amsterdam in 1773, appeared in the *Nouvelles Littéraires* of Berlin on 21 December of that year. Within three weeks it was being sedulously circulated at the Russian Court. Grimm thought that Samuel Formey, the Secretary of the Prussian Academy, was the author. Some 'charitable' person, said Grimm, had not only informed Diderot that this attack upon him was going the rounds in St. Petersburg but also had said that it had been written by a 'most illustrious hand'. Heavy with sarcasm, the review was either written by Frederick II or inspired by him. It was up to date, thus conveying all the greater air of authenticity: the author mentioned the Diderot had become a member of the Russian Academy and even knew that he had asked it for information regarding Siberia. The reviewer remarked of Diderot's articles on philosophy reprinted from the *Encyclopédie* that they had not been hard to do; all that had been necessary was to translate them from Brucker, whose work, the reviewer stated, was far superior to what any encyclopaedist was capable of. He called Diderot's *Pensées sur l'interprétation de la nature* 'a sublime tissue of nonsense', the *Bijoux indiscrets* 'a masterpiece of unreason and indecency', and declared that Diderot's plays 'are not written so that they can be acted and are scarcely better suited to be read'. In short, the reviewer hoped

---

[72] D'Alembert to Voltaire, 26 Feb. 1774 (Besterman, no. 17722). Sir Robert Gunning's reports of worsening conditions (P.R.O., loc. cit. 94, ff. 199, 204, 208, 212). Gunning to Suffolk, 24 Jan./4 Feb. 1774, and same to same, 14/25 Feb. 1774 (private and most confidential) (P.R.O., loc. cit. 95, ff. 96, 114). Pugachev was handed over to the authorities on 15 Sept. 1774 and was executed on 10 Jan. 1775. Two excellent studies on the Pugachev revolt have recently been published: John T. Alexander, *Autocratic Politics in a National Crisis: The Imperial Russian Government and Pugachev's Revolt / 1773–1775* (Bloomington, Ind., 1969); and Marc Raeff, 'Pugachev's Rebellion', in *Preconditions of Revolution in Early Modern Europe*, ed. Robert Forster and Jack P. Greene (Baltimore, Md. [1970]), pp. 161–202.

that his comments would help potential buyers to decide 'whether to procure this treasure for themselves or to get along without it. It is probable that the majority of sensible folk will take the latter course.' At St. Petersburg, according to Grimm, this review was being circulated by no less a personage than the Prussian ambassador.[73]

Frederick wanted Diderot to pass through Berlin, and even sent a special emissary, Count Goertz, to St. Petersburg to talk Diderot into it.[74] No doubt it was a matter of general remark that Diderot had not travelled via Berlin on his way to Russia and Frederick II wanted to be sure that this slight would not occur again. As late as 11 March 1774 he expected to be seeing Diderot in Berlin or Potsdam.[75] But at the same time the King was writing very critically of Diderot, as in a letter to D'Alembert:

Diderot is at St. Petersburg, where the Empress has heaped favours upon him. They say, however, that people find him argumentative, boring; he is for ever harping on the same string. I do not know what there is about his works. I cannot abide reading them, intrepid reader though I am. There is a self-satisfied tone and an arrogance about them that revolts my instinct of liberty.

And soon there began to circulate in Europe rumours coming from Berlin that Diderot had been subjected to derision by some of the courtiers in St. Petersburg.[76]

Grimm wanted to return to Paris by way of Berlin for business

[73] For the text of the review, see Tourneux, *Diderot et Catherine II*, pp. 523–31. Either inspired by Frederick II or written by him (ibid., pp. 76–7; Adrienne D. Hytier, 'Le Philosophe et le despote: Histoire d'une inimitié, Diderot et Frédéric II', *Diderot Studies*, vi (1964), 74–5). Written by Formey (Grimm to Nesselrode, 7 Feb. 1774 (Bilbasov, *Didro v Peterburge*, p. 174)); Guy Turbet-Delof, 'A propos d' "Émile et Sophie" ', *Revue d'Histoire Littéraire de la France*, lxiv (1964), 54). Circulated by the Prussian ambassador [Count von Solms] (Grimm to Nesselrode, 14 Jan. 1774 (Bilbasov, *Didro v Peterburge*, pp. 170–1)). Diderot felt injured by this attack, which he referred to quite publicly (Durand to D'Aiguillon, 29 Jan. 1774 (*Sbornik*, xvii. 289–90)).

[74] Grimm to Nesselrode, 28 and 30 Dec. 1773 and 14 Jan. 1774 (Bilbasov, *Didro v Peterburge*, pp. 165, 167, 171; cf. Hytier, art. cit., pp. 74–9); Durand to D'Aiguillon, 29 Jan. 1774 (*Sbornik*, xvii. 289). Diderot led Goertz to believe that he might go by way of Berlin after all (Grimm to Nesselrode, 1 and 11 Mar. 1774 (Bilbasov, *Didro v Peterburge*, pp. 177, 179)).

[75] Mortier, *Diderot en Allemagne*, p. 39.

[76] 7 Jan. 1774 (Diderot, *Corr.* xiii. 147). In reply, 14 Feb. 1774, D'Alembert courteously and tactfully defended Diderot (D'Alembert, *Œuvres complètes*, v

reasons, with perhaps a call upon King Stanislas Poniatowski at Warsaw on the way, and at first it had been presumed that Diderot would go home in his friend's company, probably in February.[77] At this point, in spite of Grimm's efforts, Diderot absolutely refused to go near Berlin.[78] So resolutely did he refuse that the plans for their returning together had to be foregone, a decision made by mid January. As Diderot explained to Mme d'Épinay, how could he tell that Frederick II would not choose to insult or humiliate him, once the King had him there? 'I was thoroughly resolved . . . above all to avoid the King of Prussia, who does not like me, whom I heartily repay in kind, whose welcome would not have afforded me great pleasure and from whom a marked coolness would have mortified me exceedingly.'[79]

During the last few weeks of Diderot's stay in St. Petersburg he seems to have passed into a strange stage of inactivity. He wrote only three letters between the first of the year and his departure on 5 March, one introducing the Comte de Crillon to Princess Dashkov, one of farewell to the Russian Academy of Sciences (in which he asked again for the reply to his questions on Siberia), and one of farewell to the Empress herself.[80] The only other specific event on record during those eight weeks was the presentation to Diderot by the Metropolitan of St. Petersburg and Novgorod of

(1822), 346–7; see also same to same, 25 Apr. and 1 July 1774 (ibid. v. 348–9, 351)). Dieudonné Thiébault, *Mes Souvenirs de vingt ans de séjour à Berlin*, 3rd ed., 4 vols. (Paris, 1813), ii. 305–6. Wilson, *Diderot, The Testing Years*, pp. 90–1. For another example of a rumour originating in Berlin, see Grimm to Nesselrode, 1 Mar. 1774 (Bilbasov, *Didro v Peterburge*, p. 178).

[77] Feb. departure (Catherine II to Voltaire, 7/18 Jan. 1774 (Besterman, no. 17664); Diderot to Sophie Volland, 29 Dec. 1773 (Diderot, *Corr.* xiii. 141)). On 6 Dec. 1773 Grimm had asked Nesselrode whether Diderot would be welcome at Berlin (Bilbasov, *Didro v Peterburge*, p. 164).

[78] Grimm to Nesselrode, 28 and 30 Dec. 1773 (ibid., pp. 165, 167). Letters from Mme Geoffrin to Stanislas Poniatowski, 8 May and 27 June 1774, prove that the King had hoped that Diderot would visit him at Warsaw (Stanislas II, *Correspondance inédite du roi Stanislas . . .*, ed. Mouÿ, pp. 465, 470). In Apr. 1774 Grimm did visit Warsaw on his way to Berlin (Jean Fabre, *Stanislas-Auguste Poniatowski et l'Europe des Lumières* (Paris, 1952), p. 348).

[79] Grimm to Nesselrode, 17 Jan. 1774 (Bilbasov, *Didro v Peterburge*, p. 172). The Hague, 9 Apr. 1774 (Diderot, *Corr.* xiii. 238).

[80] To Princess Dashkov, 25 Jan. 1774 (ibid., pp. 152–5); regarding Crillon, see Tourneux, *Diderot et Catherine II*, p. 466 n. To Jean-Albert Euler, Secretary of the Academy of Sciences, 22 Feb. [? o.s.] 1774 (Diderot, *Corr.* xiii. 196–7). To Catherine II, 11/22 Feb., 1774 (ibid., pp. 198–201).

a magnificent copy of the Bible in Cyrillic characters, published at Kiev in 1758. This treasure is now in the Bibliothèque Nationale at Paris, Diderot having sold it to the Bibliothèque du Roi as soon as he got home.[81] And that is the sum of his activities for two months as far as any evidence remains.

This meagre record, especially the lack of letters to friends and relatives at home, what does it signify? Illness, certainly; but also, most likely, dispiritedness. 'M. Diderot has told me that he writes to nobody', remarked Crillon to D'Alembert in late January. '"I am too far off from my friends to talk with them. I have tried twenty times. After I have said, 'My relatives, my friends, I want to get away, I want to get away', nothing else occurs to me." '[82]

Persons at St. Petersburg friendly to Diderot acknowledged that he had been the victim of intrigues while he was there, so that perhaps the Berlin rumours of a mathematical prank having been played upon him were not wholly fabricated. Grimm wrote to Nesselrode in January, 'You would not be able to believe all the obscure and underhanded persecutions that Denis has experienced here.' Another of Nesselrode's St. Petersburg correspondents spoke vaguely but unmistakably of the courtiers' dislike of Diderot, finally remarking that 'He had the fate that most men have who pay too little attention to envy and jealousy to answer calumnies'. And the Swedish ambassador (who tried hard to get Diderot to return by way of Stockholm) wrote of him at the time of his departure, '. . . during his stay at Petersburg he was exposed to the most envenomed jealousy and to the blackest calumny. Frankness and freedom from self-interest are virtues that slaves are unworthy of feeling and which they detest. The Russians were in despair that a man possessing these qualities should have free access to their sovereign . . .'[83]

---

[81] 'Viro doctissimo atque honoratissimo Dno Dideroto hunc sacrum librum dono mittit Platto Archiepiscopus Twerensis et Caszinensis. Petropoli 1774. Jannuarii 28 die' (Bibliothèque Nationale: Rés. A 461). Sale to the Bibliothèque du Roi (Jean Porcher, 'Russkie knigi Diderota v Parizhe', *Vremennik obshchestva druzey russkoy knigi*, iii (1932), 128–33; Basanov, 'La bibliothèque russe de Diderot', p. 86).

[82] 25 Jan. 1774 (Tourneux, *Diderot et Catherine II*, p. 466).

[83] Regarding a prank alleged to have been played on Diderot, see Thiébault, *Mes Souvenirs de vingt ans de séjour à Berlin*, ii. 305–6; Wilson, *Diderot, The Testing*

Since the two friends were not returning together, the Empress appointed a Greek named Athanasius Bala to accompany Diderot. Little is known of Bala, whom Grimm described as 'likeable and reliable', save that he was a minor official in the Russian diplomatic service, that he had been secretary of the Russian delegation at the Conference of Foksiany in Moldavia in 1772, and that Diderot came to like him very much.[84] By late January plans were settled for Diderot to return to The Hague, perhaps to stay there several months. And on 5 March 1774 he started out.[85]

During his stay in St. Petersburg Diderot had refused gifts that he thought were too sumptuous. The Empress had wanted to give him an expensive muff, but he said he would only lose it; and an elegant pelisse, but he accepted only one of fox, 'such', wrote Nolcken, 'as the lowest class of bourgeois wear in our country'.[86] He did accept 3,000 roubles for his expenses, a sum which came to 12,600 livres when he exchanged it. In addition, he asked for an inexpensive memento of her, a 'bagatelle', the value of which consisted only in her having used it: 'Your cup and saucer'. In response she gave him when he left a cameo ring, the stone of which was cut with her portrait. But the exchange was not all one-sided. Diderot made parting gifts too. He gave Catherine II an enamel plaque and two small pictures. These, added to the cost

Years, pp. 90–1. Grimm to Nesselrode, 14 Jan. 1774 (Bilbasov, *Didro v Peterburge*, p. 171). General-Quartermaster Fedor Vilimovich Bayer [Bauer] to Nesselrode, 10 and 24 Jan. and 27 Feb. 1774 (*Sbornik*, xvii. 282). Nolcken to Beylon, 29 Nov./ 10 Dec. 1773 and 20 Feb./3 Mar. 1774 (Tourneux, *Diderot et Catherine II*, pp. 464–5, 468–9).

[84] Bala (Grimm to Nesselrode, 7 Feb. 1774 (Bilbasov, *Didro v Peterburge*, p. 173; see also ibid., p. 322); 'homme de mérite' [Nolcken to Beylon, 20 Feb./3 Mar. 1774 (Tourneux, *Diderot et Catherine II*, p. 468)]). Diderot's esteem for Bala (Diderot, *Corr.* xiii. 218–20). For the Conference of Foksiany, see the *New Cambridge Modern History*, viii: *The American and French Revolutions* (Cambridge, 1965), p. 263.

[85] First mention of return via The Hague (Grimm to J.-H. Meister, 29 Jan. 1774 [Herpin (Percy) and Maugras, *Dernières Années de Madame d'Épinay*, pp. 480–1]) 5 Mar. 1774 (Diderot, *Corr.* xiii. 226). Diderot had allowed the pertinacious Count Goertz to believe that he might after all decide to go by way of Berlin, but he never did intend to do so (Grimm to Nesselrode, 30 Dec. 1773 and 1 Mar. 1774 (Bilbasov, *Didro v Peterburge*, pp. 167, 177)).

[86] Grimm to Nesselrode, 19 Nov. 1773 (ibid., p. 161); Diderot to his family, 30 Dec. 1773 (Diderot, *Corr.* xiii. 143); Nolcken to Beylon, 20 Feb./3 Mar. 1774 (Tourneux, *Diderot et Catherine II*, p. 468).

of gifts he felt he owed the Naryshkins for their kindnesses to him, added up to a value of about six or seven thousand livres. The Parisian bourgeois, the boy from provident little Langres, was not exactly niggardly.[87] Of course, he could afford these gifts and still not be out of pocket, for the Empress paid for his carriage and travelling expenses back to The Hague.

Diderot took great pains with his farewell letter to Catherine II, and asked the advice of Grimm and other trusted friends before submitting it. It is a courtier's document—no wonder Grimm approved of it. Diderot described the pain that he felt upon leaving and declared that his relatives and friends could not possibly receive a greater proof of his fondness and attachment than his tearing himself away from the Empress to return to them. Catherine II liked that, and quoted it to Voltaire. Diderot liked it too, and used large portions of his letter, unchanged, when he wrote to his mistress, Sophie Volland.[88]

Some months later Diderot confessed that he had not really seen Russia. He had rejected the opportunity to go to Moscow, somewhat to his subsequent regret. As for St. Petersburg, 'Petersburg is just the Court: a confused mass of palaces and hovels, of *grands seigneurs* surrounded by peasants and purveyors.'[89] But he had seen the Russians, and the things he said about them still rang true in the opinion of Gustave Lanson, a famous French professor who for five months in 1886 had taught French literature to the Tsarevich, later Nicholas II. Diderot, in one of his memoranda to the Empress, said things about the Russian people which only a perceptive person sensitive to social realities could have felt.

It seems to me that in general your subjects err on the side of one extreme or the other, either in believing their nation too advanced or in

[87] Reciprocal presents (Diderot, *Corr.* xiii. 229–30). Cup and saucer (ibid., p. 233). Cameo (Grimm to Nesselrode, 1 and 11 Mar. 1774 (Bilbasov, *Didro v Peterburge*, pp. 177, 180)). Gunning reported to Suffolk, 28 Feb./11 Mar. 1774, that Catherine gave Diderot 22,000 roubles (P.R.O., State Papers Foreign 91 [Russia], vol. xcv, f. 149r).

[88] Grimm's approval (Diderot, *Corr.* xiii. 235). The letter of farewell (ibid., pp. 198–201). Warmed over for Sophie Volland (ibid., p. 209). Catherine II to Voltaire, 15/26 Mar. 1774 (Besterman, no. 17770).

[89] To Mme Necker, 6 Sept. 1774 (Diderot, *Corr.* xiv. 72). 'Cinq ans avant que Diderot y vînt, des 3.699 maisons de Pétersbourg 573 étaient en pierre . . .' (Henri Tronchon, *Romantisme et préromantisme* (Paris, 1930), p. 262).

believing it too backward. . . . I seem to have observed quite generally a circumspection, a distrust which seems to me to be the opposite of that attractive and straightforward frankness which characterizes spirits that are lofty, free, and secure . . .

Diderot declared to the Empress that in Russia 'there is a nuance of panic terror in the attitude of people. Apparently it is the result of a long series of revolutions and of a prolonged despotism. They always seem to be existing just before an earthquake or just after it, and they have the appearance of trying to find out if the ground is really firm under their feet.' Lanson said of these remarks, 'Whoever has observed that over there knows how to look.'[90]

The evidence regarding Diderot in Russia leaves one with the feeling that his visit turned out to be a not very joyous one. At some time—we do not know just when or where—Diderot burned the notes on Russia that he had taken.[91] Why? No very cheerful reason suggests itself. Perhaps he himself provided the answer, indirectly, in what he wrote to Mme Necker in 1774:[92]

I will confess to you very much under my breath that we *philosophes*, who give the impression of best having known what despotism is, have seen it only through the neck of a bottle. What a difference there is between a tiger painted by Oudry and a tiger in the forest.

[90] Gustave Lanson, in *Revue d'Histoire Littéraire de la France*, vi (1899), 639; he was reviewing Tourneux, *Diderot et Catherine II*, where the relevant passage is pp. 176–7 (in Diderot, *Mémoires pour Catherine II*, ed. Vernière, pp. 66–7). Private tutor to the Tsarevich (Pierre Leguay, *Universitaires d'aujourd'hui* (Paris, 1912), p. 70).
[91] Dieckmann, *Inventaire du Fonds Vandeul ef inédits de Diderot*, p. 70.
[92] Diderot, *Corr.* xiv. 72–3.

IN-HO L. RYU

Moscow Freemasons and the Rosicrucian Order

A Study in Organization and Control

I

NIKOLAY IVANOVICH NOVIKOV (1744–1818) and Freemasonry under Catherine the Great are topics which have not been suffering from undue neglect by historians. In addition to several full-length monographs and countless shorter studies published before 1917, a steady stream of works has been appearing also in recent years, devoted to some specific aspect of Novikov's activities or Freemasonry, or making a fresh assessment of his place in the history of Russian culture.[1] No one disputes the signal place Novikov occupies as the first major private publisher of journals and books and, indeed, the founder of the book-publishing trade in Russia. Historical consensus disappears, however, when it comes to the question of determining the source of the unprecedented energy and success with which Novikov tackled his publishing, educational, and other public enterprises and earned the name 'Novikov decade' for the 1780s.

Since Novikov and those who supported him during this period by major financial contributions or personal participation were, almost without exception, well-known Freemasons, many historians saw in Freemasonry the source of inspiration which motivated them in their multi-faceted civic activities. One serious difficulty with this view is that the particular organization which Novikov and his collaborators chose to join was the Rosicrucian Order, the most esoteric and reactionary branch of the extremely multifarious spiritual and social phenomenon which went by the

[1] A very clear demonstration of the continuing interest in the subject of Novikov was a special conference on it held in December 1968, jointly at the Pushkinsky Dom and Tartu University.

name of Freemasonry. Rosicrucianism had little in common with the broadly humanitarian and philanthropic ideal generally attributed to the low-degree systems such as the English Freemasonry which had prevailed in Russia in the preceding decade. The only significant public activity of the Rosicrucian Order headquartered in Berlin was the campaign it mounted against the militant rationalist offshoot of Freemasonry, the Bavarian Illuminati, in the mid 1780s. The Order's heavy reliance on occultism, alchemy, and magic as the highest means available towards the attainment of secret knowledge, allegedly preserved among their 'unknown superiors', made it so suspect even in the eyes of the Masonic world that most major Masonic groups refused to recognize any relationship between Freemasons and Rosicrucians. Conversely, the Rosicrucians, claiming to be the sole possessors of the secret the Masonic herd was in vain seeking, looked upon the Masonic systems with condescension and contempt, and pursued a much more secretive and restrictive course in their recruitment and organizational policy, utilizing the Masonic degrees simply as stepping-stones leading to their own system of nine degrees.[2]

Not surprisingly, some students of Novikov's activities, such as Nezelenov, interpreted the influence of Freemasonry as totally negative, and saw the most fruitful period in Novikov's career in the 1770s when he was not yet seriously involved in Freemasonry.[3]

---

[2] According to a table adopted after the reorganization of the Order of Rose Cross in 1777, the Rosicrucian degrees were as follows (N. S. Tikhonravov (ed.), *Letopisi russkoy literatury i drevnosti*, 5 vols. (Moscow, 1859–63), v. ii. 32):

Cabalistic calculation
known only to the
superiors of the order		*Degrees*	*No. of Holders*
1	9	Magi	7
2	8	Magistrates	77
3	7	Adepts	777
4	6	Majors	788
5	5	Minors	779
6	4	Philosophers	822
7	3	Practitioners	833
8	2	Theoretical Brothers	844
9	1	Juniors	909

[3] A. I. Nezelenov, *Nikolay Novikov, izdatel zhurnalov, 1769–1785 gg.* (St. Petersburg, 1875).

Others, especially Soviet specialists on the eighteenth century, take a similarly negative view of Freemasonry, but defend Novikov's reputation by insisting that his involvement with Freemasonry was superficial and had little influence on his 'enlightening' activities.[4] The prevailing opinion among the Western scholars today seems to follow the somewhat awkward conclusions drawn by Pypin and Bogolyubov.[5] In their view, Novikov's involvement in Freemasonry was undeniable and Rosicrucianism did possess most unsavoury characteristics. But the Russian Freemasons, including Novikov, by remaining in the lower degrees in the system, were able to stay clear of the most dubious features of the system such as alchemy and magic used only in the high degrees, and somehow transformed Freemasonry in Russia into a genuine civic movement dedicated to the ideal of moral self-improvement and service to society and fatherland.[6]

Much of the confusion and difficulty in determining the role which Freemasonry played in the development of Russian culture seems to stem from the failure to draw a distinction between the two rather distinct ways in which the term Freemasonry may be understood in historical literature—Freemasonry as a social movement operating through the system of secret lodges, and Freemasonry as a mental attitude. In the second half of the eighteenth century, Freemasonry represented, above all, a state of mind created as a reaction to the militant rationalism of the *philosophes* and the inability of the established Churches to cope with this challenge effectively. Instead of placing the wager totally on the deified human reason, the Masonic mentality sought to preserve room for feeling, intuition, and imagination. While refusing to stay within the confines of the Churches, the Masonic mind missed the solace offered by faith and trust in authority. In this sense, Freemasonry was a very widespread mental attitude permeating

[4] See P. N. Berkov, *Istoriya russkoy zhurnalistiki XVIII veka* (Moscow, 1952); and G. P. Makogonenko, *Nikolay Novikov i russkoe prosveshchenie XVIII veka* (Moscow and Leningrad, 1951).

[5] B. A. Bogolyubov, *N. I. Novikov i ego vremya* (Moscow, 1916). A. N. Pypin, *Russkoe masonstvo, XVIII i pervaya chetvert XIX v.* (Petrograd, 1916).

[6] J. Billington, *The Icon and the Axe, An Interpretive History of Russian Culture* (New York, 1966), pp. 256 ff.; and M. Raeff, *Origins of the Russian Intelligentsia: the Eighteenth Century Nobility* (New York, 1966), 165 ff.

deeply the arts and literature of the day and attracting a wide gamut of persons running from Mozart to Cagliostro, from Nikita Panin to the youthful Karamzin.[7] Freemasonry, at the same time, also referred to secret organizations whose basic units, the lodges, were linked together and subordinated to strict hierarchical chains of command transcending national boundaries. Originally, the lodges were 'secret' only in the sense in which most private clubs or professional fraternal societies are, but as the movement spread from England to the Continent, its esoteric aspect, the claim to possess a special body of knowledge, received increasing stress. As Masonic systems, each professing to be the sole possessor of genuine Masonic wisdom, multiplied, so did the number of Masonic degrees along the hierarchy which the novices were required to climb as the road towards the source of genuine Freemasonry. Each of these degrees was granted only on condition of obedient fulfilment of the instructions from above, coming usually in the form of moral catechism, couched in hieroglyphics, accompanied by elaborate symbolistic ritual, and a promise to keep complete secrecy concerning these transactions. In certain of these high-degree systems or the Strict Observance Freemasonry, of which the Rosicrucian Order was an offshoot, the organizational distance separating the novices from those who actually controlled the hierarchical command-structure from the top became so great that very often the rank-and-file Freemasons remained ignorant of the true identity of their Masonic leaders, let alone their hidden design. As a result, such organizations, carefully structured as secret societies, could be exploited for purposes which were hidden not only from the eyes of the outside world, but remained un-revealed even to those who joined the lodges out of curiosity, craving for high-sounding degrees and glittering costumes, or simply for diversion as often as out of an earnest desire to seek the elusive Masonic wisdom. In this respect Russians who were curious about Freemasonry and wanted to find the system which repre-sented the genuine Masonic source were at a special disadvantage,

[7] For a discussion of the Masonic mentality, see: H. Schneider, *Quest for Mysteries: the Masonic Background for Literature in Eighteenth Century Germany* (Ithaca, N.Y., 1947); and A. Viatte, *Les Sources occultes du romantisme, illuminisme, théosophie, 1770–1820*, 2 vols. (Paris, 1928).

since all well-known Masonic systems, with the notable exception of the Melissino system, had originated outside Russia and were led by foreigners.[8] Because of the great secrecy in which all Masonic systems enveloped themselves, it was difficult to find out the identity of persons heading a particular system, not to speak of its true content, which, by its very nature, was supposed to be impenetrable from outside. In most cases, the initial contact had to be established through foreigners residing in Russia who still possessed connections in their homeland. It was thus a former master of the Brunswick ducal Court, George Reichel (1729–91), who brought the Zinnendorf system with him to Russia in 1770, while an adventurer of international notoriety, George Rosenberg, and his brother in the Russian forèign service, were instrumental in introducing the Russians to Swedish Masonry.[9] The most that these intermediaries could bring in the way of concrete proof of the genuineness of their source were certain catechisms and rituals to be used in the initiation of aspirants into the lower degrees, and the patents of Grandmastership such as the one I. P. Elagin received from the English Grand Lodge in London in 1772. Apart from that, the commitment to work in a particular system, that is, the vows of secrecy and obedience, as a *sine qua non* of the revelation of the Masonic wisdom, had to be made on the words of those who had established the initial contact between the foreign Masonic source and the Russian candidates. Novikov and his Masonic circle in Moscow were to be no exceptions, both in their reliance on a foreigner, Professor I. G. Schwarz of Moscow University, in their search for genuine Freemasonry,

---

[8] P. I. Melissino (1724 or 1726–97), a Greek by origin and a graduate of the Cadet Corps, who later became a general of the artillery and its chief inspector, was an inventor of a high-degree system. The Melissino system was characterized by four higher degrees above the three St. John's, and a secret chapter called the 'Conclave', which presumably contained the hermetic secret of making gold. The secrecy with which he guarded his system even among the Freemasons, and the important attention given to hermetic sciences, etc. bring it very close to the Rosicrucian Order in nature although there was, evidently, no direct relationship between the two (C. Lenning, *Encyclopädie der Freimaurerei*, 3 vols. (Leipzig, 1822–8), ii. 460 ff., and M. D. B. Baron de Corberon, *Un Diplomate français à la cour de Catherine II, 1775–80: Journal intime du chevalier de Corberon*, 2 vols. (Paris, 1901), ii. 3 ff.).

[9] Pypin, op. cit., pp. 153 ff.; *Russkaya Starina* (1882), xxxv. 543; and M. N. Longinov, *Novikov i Moskovskie Martinisty* (Moscow, 1867), p. 175.

and in their acceptance of Rosicrucianism almost solely on his words.

II

I. G. Schwarz (d. 1784) occupies a rather singular place in Russian history. Both as a professor of Moscow University who worked intimately with a number of select student groups and as the man who brought Rosicrucianism to Russia, he left an imprint on Russian culture rivalled by few other foreigners who happened to set foot in that country. Strangely enough, however, little is known of his personal background or of the precise nature of the relationship which had bound him to Novikov and other Russian Freemasons in their countless activities.[10]

According to Novikov, Schwarz was a Transylvanian by origin. He was brought to Russia in 1776 as a tutor for a wealthy, noble family in Mogilev. He then was invited to Moscow three years later by Prince Nikita N. Trubetskoy, who had arranged for him a position as Extraordinary Professor of German at the two gymnasia attached to Moscow University. A Herrnhuter pastor who had been an intimate associate of the professor, both at the University and outside, Ivan Ivanovich Vigand (1744–1808), tells us in his memoirs that when Schwarz arrived in Russia he came already as a secret agent of the Rosicrucian Order in Germany.[11] It seems more than likely that Schwarz had enjoyed a certain reputation among the Masonic circles prior to his arrival in Russia and, in fact, secured his new job in Russia through Masonic connections. For, shortly after his arrival, he not only joined a Lodge, but was

[10] The accounts of Schwarz's activities given by Longinov and later historians are largely based on Tikhonravov's entry in the *Biografichesky Slovar Professorov i Prepodavateley Imperatorskago Moskovskago Universiteta* (Moscow, 1855), which in turn had as its main source Schwarz's own account of his activities given in a memorandum he wrote in 1782 in order to present his grievances against Curator Melissino. This highly biased document, together with the testimonies of his devoted students, created such a halo around the name of the professor that other, more unfavourable testimonies concerning his character and influence have not received much attention from the historians. Schwarz's memorandum was printed in full in the German original in *Letopisi russkoy literatury i drevnosti*, ed. N. S. Tikhonravov, v. 96–110.

[11] Vigand, 'Pastor Vigand. Ego zhizn i deyatelnost v Rossii, 1764–1808', *Russkaya Starina*, lxxiv (1892), 561.

soon entrusted by Mogilev Freemasons to make a trip to Courland on their behalf in search of higher degrees.[12] Upon his return he organized a new lodge in the Strict Observance system and became its master.

Trubetskoy was probably also motivated by a desire to benefit from Schwarz's reputed connections in the Masonic world of Europe when he took the trouble to secure a position at the University for a man whom he had just met through a mutual friend, V. I. Maykov, another Freemason.[13] This was a time when interest in Freemasonry had reached a new height in Russia, and Trubetskoy, a wealthy and prominent Muscovite aristocrat enjoying the reputation of a generous host and patron of arts and entertainment in Moscow society, was among the most passionate seekers after Masonic high degrees. After repeated disappointments encountered in the English, Reichel, and Swedish systems, serious Russian Freemasons such as Trubetskoy were drawing the conclusion that they could find genuine Freemasonry only through a search carried out independently of any irksome guidance provided by foreign Grand Lodges. In order to do so, however, the Russian Freemasons still found themselves in need of assistance from persons who could presumably lead the way to the genuine source, and Schwarz evidently was one such person in Trubetskoy's opinion. Shortly after Schwarz's arrival in Moscow, a so-called 'scientific' lodge, 'Harmony' (*Garmoniya*), was organized by Trubetskoy with the avowed aim of conducting an open-minded search for genuine Freemasonry. Schwarz became a member, along with M. M. Kheraskov, I. P. Turgenev, Prince A. A. Cherkassky, Prince Engalychev, A. M. Kutuzov, and N. I. Novikov. Needless to say, Schwarz, a stranger to Moscow society and a man of totally obscure social origin, offered little reason besides his Masonic credentials, to be included in such a select inner group of Moscow notables, many of whom were personally related to Prince Trubetskoy.

The only other member of the lodge 'Harmony' who did not quite stand in the same social bracket was Novikov, the well-

---

[12] Longinov, op. cit., p. 78. The translations here as elsewhere are my own.
[13] Ibid., p. 79.

known publisher who had moved to Moscow just a few months earlier as the new director of the Moscow University printing press. It was the same Prince Trubetskoy who had been instrumental in arranging a ten-year lease on the university's press for Novikov. Although Novikov seems to have regarded his arrival in Moscow in the same year as Schwarz as a happy coincidence, there are indications that Novikov's good fortune in securing the lease may have been a part of a pre-arranged affair between Trubetskoy and Schwarz. Novikov had originally made Trubetskoy's acquaintance in his capacity as master of a Masonic lodge some time around 1776 and had accepted, upon the Prince's insistence, the seventh degree in the Swedish system in spite of his own misgivings concerning that system. It was during his visit to Trubetskoy in the same year, 1778, that the resident curator of Moscow University and Trubetskoy's half-brother, Kheraskov, first sounded him out on the possibility of taking over the management of the university press.[14] Novikov insisted when being interrogated by Sheshkovsky in 1792 that when he first arrived in Moscow he kept Schwarz at a distance because of his distaste for the Strict Observance Freemasonry to which the German professor adhered, but there is ample evidence that Schwarz, on his part, greatly valued Novikov's work from the beginning and made every effort to draw the enterprising publisher into joint undertakings between them. In a memorandum which he had intended to submit to the senior curator of Moscow University, I. I. Shuvalov, in 1782, Schwarz spoke of his effort to help Novikov by trying, on his part,

1. to spread correct principles of education;
2. to supply Novikov's press with translated and useful materials to be printed; and
3. to attract capable foreigners into the field of Russian education to replace the many ignorant ones currently engaged in teaching and, further, to train native Russians for teaching.[15]

Novikov may indeed have been suspicious of Schwarz at first and kept his interest in Freemasonry only peripheral to his overwhelming desire to make a success out of the university press newly

[14] Ibid., p. 77.   [15] *Letopisi*, v. 103–4.

entrusted to him. But the enormous sympathy and interest with which the German professor viewed his printing enterprise could not but ward off the publisher's initial wariness. They soon became inseparable, in Novikov's own words.[16] Besides, the invitation to join the lodge 'Harmony', composed of such prominent members of Moscow society, must have been most welcome to Novikov at a time when, Masonic interest aside, he, as a newcomer to Moscow without great resources of his own, was knowingly facing an immense uphill struggle in his bid to revitalize the university press, which had fallen into a disgraceful state.[17]

Whatever misgivings Novikov may have had concerning Schwarz's connection with Freemasonry, his reservations about the professor or Freemasonry seem to have disappeared altogether by the early spring of 1783, when he was writing enthusiastic letters to A. A. Rzhevsky, commenting on the great service Schwarz had rendered to the Russian brothers by discovering genuine Freemasonry for them.[18] The intervening event which had such a decisive effect, not only on Novikov's attitude toward Freemasonry, but indeed on the history of the Masonic movement in Russia, was the trip which Schwarz undertook to Courland and Germany from June 1781 to February 1782. He brought back from this trip not only the promise of the Provincial Grandmaster of the Strict Observance Freemasonry in Europe to help recognize Russia as an independent Masonic Province free from arrogant Swedish tutelage, but also Rosicrucianism which Novikov and other members of 'Harmony' accepted as the genuine Freemasonry they had been looking for.

Officially, Schwarz took a leave of absence from the university by pleading ill health and pointing out the valuable services he could render to the university by establishing a communication between the Russian university and the learned world of Europe while recuperating in a warm climate.[19] But the true purpose of the trip was Masonic. As far as Novikov and other members of 'Harmony' knew, Schwarz was going on this Masonic mission on

[16] Longinov, op. cit., p. 78.   [17] Ibid., pp. 65 and 77.
[18] Ya. L. Barskov, *Perepiska moskovskikh masonov 18go veka, 1780–1792 gg.* (Petrograd, 1915), pp. 245 ff.
[19] N. S. Tikhonravov, *Sochineniya*, 3 vols. (Moscow, 1898), iii. 69.

their behalf. Entrusting him with two unaddressed letters to be delivered to whichever source of genuine Freemasonry he might discover, and one thousand roubles for spending and the purchase of books, the Moscow Freemasons vaguely instructed him that 'he should seek and try to obtain the acts of Freemasonry, the principle of which we received from Reichel, but should not accept the Strict Observance, French, or any other system possessing a political character; but if he could not find it there, then he should try to discover where it might be found'.[20]

Since Novikov's group was unprepared to underwrite the cost of the entire trip, as Novikov later testified, they reluctantly accepted Schwarz's suggestion that they combine their effort with P. A. Tatishchev, another wealthy devotee of high-degree Freemasonry. In spite of Tatishchev's reputation as an extremely mistrustful man, miserly and almost misanthropic, Schwarz had succeeded in recommending himself as a tutor to Tatishchev's son, already a young man. Now Tatishchev was willing to finance Schwarz's trip on condition that the German professor accompany the young Tatishchev to the source of genuine Freemasonry.[21]

According to Novikov, Schwarz's first step was Courland, where he had developed some Masonic connections already in his pre-Moscow days. The Courland Freemasons gave him letters of recommendation to the Provincial Grand Master of the Strict Observance Freemasonry in Europe, Duke Ferdinand of Bruns-wick, and to his deputies in the Berlin lodges of 'Three Globes' (Zu den drei Weltkugelen), Wöllner and Theden. From Courland, Schwarz proceeded to Berlin and there he was appointed the Supreme Director of the Theoretical Degree in the Order of Golden Rose Cross, a secret inner circle of Freemasons headed by Wöllner.[22]

Johann Christoph von Wöllner (1732–1800), a gentleman in attendance at the Court of Prince Henry of Prussia, better known later as the favourite of Frederick William II, responsible for the restrictive religious edict of 1788, had been one of the main actors in German Strict Observance Masonry. Around 1779, Wöllner came into relationship with the groups of believers in alchemy and

[20] Longinov, op. cit., p. 80.   [21] Ibid.   [22] Ibid., p. 81.

magic who had been quite active underground in Germany for some time and claimed connection with the mythical society of the Golden Rose Cross.[23] Well aware of the confusion and mood of despondency reigning in the Masonic world, Wöllner and his ally, Johann Christian Anton Theden (1714–97), another adept of hermetic sciences attached to the Prussian Court as a surgeon, conceived the idea of founding a more secretive 'inner circle' by making a direct appeal to the genuinely religious sentiment, as well as the occultist instinct, of men joining the Masonic lodges. According to Wöllner, the Masonic degrees were only the 'threshold' of the Rosicrucian temple into which only the worthiest will gain admittance:

> Every genuine R.K. knows that Freemasonry was founded by the highest superiors of our Order to serve as the nursery in which men are brought up and prepared to be received in the true high Order. Freemasonry is the threshold of the temple, whose hidden entry will be discovered and opened only by the worthiest Freemasons. As for the hieroglyphics themselves, they reveal their true meaning and essence only within our most Holy Order; they remain, by themselves, dead letters and mere playthings with which to pass time.[24]

The 'unknown' superiors of the Rosicrucian Order, according to Wöllner, were the true successors of Jesus Christ, wielding magical powers of clairvoyance. They would reveal themselves to the world in the near future and bring, to the chosen few fortunate enough to have been received by the Order, indescribable bliss to be experienced right in this world. According to a document entitled 'Commentaries on various truths of the Order for the use of qualified brothers of the district of the Ofiron[25] Ober-Haupt Directory, 1781', the Order's exhortation for moral self-cultivation through asceticism and sacrifice of worldly fortune was only a necessary preparation for the receipt of

further delights which belong to the joys of the temporal life, which

---

[23] On Wöllner and the Rosicrucian Order, see: R. Gould, *Gould's History of Freemasonry throughout the World*, rev. by Dudley Wright (New York, 1936), iii. 166 ff.; Barskov *Perepiska*, pp. 219 ff.; Lenning, *Encyclopädie*, iii. 245 ff.

[24] Ibid., p. 261.

[25] Wöllner's Rosicrucian name.

the most temperate brothers of the Order can harvest and enjoy to the fullest degree on this side of the grave. The highest superiors of our Order possess in their keeping the guardianship of a secret key to the great hidden treasure of the entire nature. They will open this rich storeroom of their own will, and obtain from it everything which man needs for steady health, long life, and carefree living. We, out of good will, remain silent about the great higher secrets of the Order. To those who keep them in secrecy, they guarantee indescribable happiness before which no other happiness, no exhilaration, no glitter of the world even deserves to be called a shadow . . .[26]

It is not known how Schwarz first approached the Wöllner group. By a patent dated 1 October 1781, and signed by Theden under his Knights Templar name, Johann Christian Eq. a. Tarda, Schwarz received an important appointment as 'the only Supreme Director' of the Theoretical Degree of the Rosicrucian Order in the 'entire Russian Empire and its territories'. The terms of the appointment were:

1. This degree should be given to no one but the Old Scottish Masters and, even then, only to those who, imbued with true piety, fear of God, and love of mankind, are worthy of recognition.

2. This degree and the instruction attached to it may be read only in the presence of Schwarz. No brother, whatever his calling may be, should be allowed to copy them.

3. He should communicate the instructions in such a fashion that it will be finished in nine meetings.

4. He should try to explain it to the brothers to the best of his intelligence.

5. He should keep this degree completely secret, and therefore be extremely cautious in selecting members.[27]

In addition to submitting to Theden the list of newly admitted Theoretical Brothers each year, the patent continued:

Brother Schwarz is also obliged to send each year ten roubles for each brother admitted, in good notes of exchange, for the benefit of our treasury for the poor. Each brother pays before admission seven

[26] P. P. Pekarsky, 'Dopolneniya k istorii masonstva v Rossii XVIII stoletiya', *Sbornik II otd. Imp. Ak. Nauk*, vii, no. 4 (1870), 68–9.

[27] S. V. Eshevsky, *Sochineniya po russkoy istorii* (Moscow, 1900), p. 216.

Thalers, out of which four remain at the disposal of Supreme Director Schwarz for acquisition of necessary supplies and other things. In this he is responsible to no one but me.[28]

In view of the gravity of the assignment entrusted to Schwarz and, in particular, the insistence on strict secrecy concerning the Theoretical Degree, it seems quite unlikely that Schwarz himself was a completely new recruit to the Rosicrucian inner circle. He must either have been associated with the Rosicrucians in Berlin prior to his immigration to Russia, as Vigand suggests in his memoirs, or, at least, have been in communication with them prior to his arrival in Berlin in the autumn of 1781.[29] It is most probable that the new mission assigned to him by Theden came in recognition of the successful preparatory work he had already carried out in Russia, namely, winning the confidence of Novikov, Prince Trubetskoy, and other prominent and wealthy Russian aristocrats such as Tatishchev, and planting himself in a strategic position as a professor of the university.[30]

The suspicion that Schwarz's activities in Moscow even before his trip to Germany, and especially his eagerness to cultivate the friendship and confidence of Novikov, were all parts of a carefully premeditated plan is further confirmed by certain peculiarities noticeable in Schwarz's conduct both during and after this trip. While Novikov made it clear in his later testimony that he remained, until Schwarz's return from his foreign trip, suspicious of Schwarz in regard to Freemasonry even while appreciating the professor's profound devotion to the cause of educating the young, Schwarz, on his part, had been clearly determined to include Novikov in the new Masonic network he was planning to organize in Russia. The short patent signed by Theden contained no reference to specific Russian Freemasons, but it pointedly singled out Novikov by name: 'And since brother Supreme Director reported that brother Nikolay Ivanovich Novikov, director of the Imperial University Press, possesses true virtues and has

---

[28] Eshevsky, op. cit.
[29] See note 11, above.
[30] Six months after he had arrived in Moscow, Schwarz was promoted to Ordinary Professor of Philosophy at the university.

performed many services, we, therefore, wish to give him permission to supervise this degree.'[31] Obviously Schwarz was already confident that Novikov would accept Rosicrucianism on his word as the genuine Freemasonry they had been seeking, and agree to become its active propagator. This apparently unsolicited honour was conditional, as was to be expected. The patent continued: 'Brother Nikolay Ivanovich Novikov in the presence of these brothers gives a pledge that he recognizes Schwarz as the Supreme Director, will render him loyalty and obedience, will not admit anyone without his permission, and in general will fulfil everything mentioned above with the greatest care.'[32]

The main purpose of Schwarz's journey was undoubtedly achieved with the acquisition of this Rosicrucian patent which granted him a dictatorial power over his Russian subordinates on condition of his obedience to Theden, and, in fact, became the corner-stone of the organizational reform of Moscow Freemasonry following Schwarz's return. There was, however, another important task which Schwarz had to accomplish before he headed back to Russia. In 1781 the Rosicrucian group of Wöllner and Theden had not yet formally renounced their allegiance to the Provincial Grandmaster of Strict Observance Masonry, Duke Ferdinand of Brunswick, and continued to maintain an official relationship with the Masonic lodges as a convenient cover under which recruiting for their secret inner order could continue.[33] In keeping with this policy, Schwarz proceeded to Brunswick to present a formal request to Ferdinand to take the Moscow lodge 'Harmony' under his protection and help Russian Masons in their bid for recognition as a separate Masonic province independent of the Swedish Grand Lodge, under whose jurisdiction Russia had until then been placed. Characteristically enough, in his memorandum to Ferdinand, dated 22 October 1781, almost a month after he had received his Rosicrucian appointment, Schwarz presented himslf as a mere

---

[31] Eshevsky, op. cit., p. 216.   [32] Ibid., pp. 216–17.

[33] Wöllner's own lodge in Berlin, the 'Three Globes', did not openly terminate its adherence to the Grandmaster of European Freemasonry, Duke Ferdinand of Brunswick, until November 1783. Wöllner's circular declaring his independence from all existing Masonic systems, above all, from the decisions reached at the Wilhelmsbad Congress, was received in Russia in the Spring of the following year, and was published in Eshevsky, op. cit., p. 227.

envoy of Peter Tatishchev and Nikolay Novikov, whom he
called the Chief Masters of 'Harmony'.[34] He told Ferdinand about
his visit to the Old Scottish lodges in Mittau, but not a hint was
given of the arrangement he had entered into with the Wöllner–
Theden group in Berlin. Ferdinand, who had been displeased with
the rebellious attitude of the IXth Masonic Province, the Swedish
Grand Lodge, warmly responded to the Russian request for independence and promised his support at the forthcoming Masonic
congress scheduled to meet in Wilhelmsbad in the following year.

According to Novikov, the Moscow Masons felt disappointed
when Schwarz told them of the relationship he had entered into
with Duke Ferdinand. Only Tatishchev, an ardent follower of
high-degree Masonry, felt triumphant. Schwarz, however, told
Novikov and Trubetskoy, in the absence of Tatishchev, that his
promise to Ferdinand to reorganize the lodges along the Strict
Observance line was only a temporary, formal concession necessary to secure Russia's right of representation at the forthcoming
Masonic congress, where the issue of Russia's Masonic independence would be discussed. For the brothers of the inner group,
Schwarz reassured them, he indeed brought the genuine Freemasonry, which had nothing in common with the high degrees
and other paraphernalia of the Strict Observance Masonry which
Novikov so detested. This true Freemasonry, Rosicrucianism,
instead, offered the shortest path to the knowledge of self, nature,
and God, in accordance with Christian precepts.[35]

The actual outcome of the Wilhelmsbad Congress at which
Russia was formally recognized as the VIIIth Independent Masonic
Province seemed to justify the position Schwarz took in deciding
to affiliate the Russian lodges with the Strict Observance System.
The Moscow Masons, greatly elated by the assurance of their
independence from the arrogant tutelage of the Swedes, eagerly
undertook the task of organizing the VIIIth Province, and by
February 1783 Novikov was able to inform Rzhevsky of the
officers of the newly instituted Provincial Chapter as follows:

1. Provincial Grandmaster: Vacant.
2. Prior: P. A. Tatishchev, Peter, *eq. ab. cygno triumphant.*

34 Eshevsky, op. cit., p. 207.   35 Longinov, op. cit., pp. 81–4.

3. Deacon: Pr. Yu. N. Trubetskoy, Georgy, *eq. ab. fortitudine.*
4. General Inspector: Pr. N. N. Trubetskoy, Nikolay, *eq. ab. aquila boreali.*
5. Treasurer: N. I. Novikov, Nikolay, *eq. ab. ancora.*
6. Chancellor: I. G. Schwarz, Georgy, *eq. ab. aquila crescente.*
7. General Procurator: Pr. A. A. Cherkassky, Aleksey, *eq. ab. aquitate.*[36]

M. M. Kheraskov, P. P. Tatishchev, and V. A. Vsevolozhsky were also included in the Provincial Chapter as members at large. The post of Provincial Grandmaster was left vacant, Novikov and Trubetskoy later confessed, in the hope of persuading Grand Duke Paul to become their titular head, as many other European princes had done in their countries.[37] The Directory of the Province, the standing executive body responsible for day-to-day business, was headed by Novikov as president.

Working under the Provincial Grand Chapter was a network of Masonic lodges which were grouped into prefectures headed by mother lodges. These mother lodges, led by Tatishchev, Prince Nikita Trubetskoy, Novikov, Prince G. G. Gagarin, the former head of Swedish Freemasonry in Russia, and Rzhevsky as respective masters, alone had the right to confer the degree of Scottish Knight, the first high degree above the three regular Masonic degrees, which the Rosicrucians regarded as prerequisite to admission into their own Theoretical degree.

Impressive as it might appear, the newly organized Provincial Chapter of the independent VIIIth Masonic Province was a shadow organization, outlined only on paper. It would have had a reality only in so far as the Freemasons constituting the Chapter recognized the authority of Duke Ferdinand, who had again been elected the titular head of European Freemasonry at the Wilhelmsbad Congress, the very same Congress which recognized Russia's independence. But, as Novikov testified, the relationship between the Moscow Masons and Ferdinand was only nominal and even the exchange of formalities stopped altogether shortly afterwards

---

[36] Barskov, op. cit., p. 245.
[37] Longinov, op. cit., p. 118; *Sbornik Imperatorskago Russkago Istoricheskago Obshchestva*, ii (St. Petersburg, 1868), 119.

because from the beginning they knew that the system by which the brothers of their inner group was going to work was Rosicrucianism, not the Strict Observance Masonry.[38] The façade of the independent Masonic province was carefully upheld, however, because it served the important function of appeasing the national pride of Russian Freemasons such as Trubetskoy and Novikov and, in addition, gave them prestige and an aura of authority in dealing with other Freemasons who still took the Strict Observance system, such as the Swedish, seriously. An even more important point which Schwarz himself must have seen clearly in promoting the fiction of Russia's Masonic independence was the fact that once this independence was recognized, no one presumably would have the right to interfere with the internal operations of Russian Freemasonry and challenge the authority of the Provincial Chapter. Now, Schwarz's name was included in the Chapter in the modest capacity of Chancellor, but other officers were all men who would be his subordinates in the Rosicrucian hierarchy, the only one which they recognized as meaningful. In other words, the façade of the independent provincial Chapter would enable him to rule over the Masonic lodges in Russia via his Rosicrucian charges, without revealing his identity. Schwarz could hardly have devised a more effective means of warding off the challenge and competition coming from many other foreign Masonic adepts in Russia, each of whom sought to capture the bewildered Russian Freemasons by claiming to represent the only true Freemasony and eagerly unmasked each other.

The response of the Moscow Freemasons to Schwarz's announcement that he did in fact succeed in establishing contact with the genuine source of Freemasonry could only be called ecstatic. Prince N. Trubetskoy wrote to Rzhevsky, whom he was cultivating as the potential Rosicrucian contact in St. Petersburg:

Beloved and respected brother! We are fortunate because God has blessed our work. He is the only source of wisdom and knowledge; he alone can lead those who strive toward Him with pure heart to the untainted source and knowledge of His chosen ones, who can lead us

---

[38] Barskov, op. cit., pp. 251–2, 255.

to the perception and knowledge of Him through the knowledge of nature and knowledge of self. I may, as a Christian, assure you that by a miraculous manner incomprehensible to me, the hand of God led our deputies seeking the inner order to the cleanest source, absolutely uncontaminated. This source is our guide; we know the brothers in Europe who are guided by this unique source. Be assured that Sweden herself cannot give anything except the hieroglyphics; she herself knows that this source exists somewhere, is looking for it, but has not found it.[39]

Novikov was no less sanguine in his expectation of the great blessings to flow from this newly discovered source, Rosicrucianism, and expressed unreserved appreciation of Schwarz:

... All these circumstances, and above all the counsels, explanations, instruction, frankness and candour, devotion and a burning desire to secure the well-being of our fatherland, and brotherly love foreign to all selfishness, of our beloved brother in the Order, Ivan Gregorevich Schwarz, and the genuine papers of the Order in his hand, allowed the Moscow Masons to see the Order in its superbly beautiful form and, finally, to their undeserved fortune, they obtained the greatest reward of the embrace and blessing of the Order. They already smell the heavenly and wholesome fragrance of the Order enlivening human nature. They have already been allowed to quench their thirst for knowledge from the source of Eden, abundantly and incessantly flowing from the beginning of the ages into all four corners of the universe. In such happiness would they envy the poor and dark knowledge of the Swedes?[40]

The gullibility and naïvety which Novikov and Trubetskoy exhibited in accepting Schwarz's word that Rosicrucianism was the very source of wisdom they had been looking for is all the more ironic in view of the fact that both of them were vehemently critical of all other prominent foreign Masonic intermediaries active in Russia, such as Ribas and the Rosenbergs, and proudly proclaimed that no other foreigner, with the single exception of Schwarz, was trustworthy enough to be included in the administration of the new Masonic regime they were establishing.[41] The

[39] Ibid., p. 239.   [40] Ibid., pp. 243–4.
[41] Ibid., p. 255.

incongruity of choosing to subordinate themelves to some unknown superiors in a foreign land, after having rejected the Swedish tutelage as injurious to national pride and honour, seems to have utterly escaped them.[42]

Given this mood of jubilation and gratitude into which Schwarz's introduction of Rosicrucianism put the Moscow Masons, there seemed little that stood in the way of Schwarz's plan to reorganize Moscow Freemasonry under his control with a view to an eventual extension of his domination over the Masonic movement in the entire Russian Empire. Within a year of his return from Germany, a vast and intricately intertwined organizational network was in operation under his direction as the only Supreme Director of Rosicrucianism in Russia. Furthermore, this secret network was so cleverly constituted that no one but he and his superiors in Berlin was in a position to see the total structure.

On the most superficial level was the Friendly Society of Learning (*Druzheskoe uchënoe obshchestvo*), which was publicly opened in November 1782 with the funds Schwarz had obtained from Tatishchev and other Masonic patrons. The avowed purpose of the society was promotion of learning, moral self-cultivation, and public and private well-being through profitable employment of leisure and fraternal contact.[43] All persons interested were invited to join it and the Society even received the blessing of the Governor-General of Moscow, Zakhar Chernyshev, and Archbishop Platon. This Friendly Society of Learning, together with the various student groups it supported, was the point of contact between the secret Rosicrucian Society and the Moscow public. On this public level, the positions held by Schwarz, Novikov, Kheraskov, and other Freemasons at the university and in various branches of the provincial government, were of great strategic value in obtaining the support for their cause of persons not formally associated with Freemasonry. In addition to Schwarz's public lectures given at the University and at home, and various student

---

[42] Novikov told Sheshkovsky, speaking of his initiation into the Rosicrucian Order: 'It was still unrevealed and unknown to us by whom and when this society was founded. This is clear from all our papers. It, however, was called the true and ancient order . . .' (Longinov, op. cit., p. 100).

[43] Ibid., pp. 6–7.

seminars which the professor personally supervised, the books and journals published by Novikov at the university press served as the media through which the Rosicrucian philosophy could be disseminated in an indirect manner so as not to incur suspicion. All that the Moscow public was able to see, presumably, was an energetic display of concern for education and philanthropy on the part of some idealistically motivated Moscovite aristocrats, the enterprising publisher of books, Novikov, and his German friend, Professor Schwarz. Many of these men were rumoured to be Freemasons, but it was only later with the intensification of their activities that the initially friendly curiosity gave way to open hostility of the official circles and that the confused Moscow society began to call them by the mistaken name 'Martinists'.[44]

Underneath this level of public activities lay the second, Masonic level proper, already hidden from public view. Here, Novikov, Trubetskoy, Tatishchev, and others functioned in their capacity as officers of the Provincial Chapter and Masters of mother lodges or prefectures to which several individual lodges were subordinated. The rank-and-file Freemasons paid dues and contributions for charity in anticipation of the promised Masonic wisdom which they believed would come with their advance along the hierarchy of high degrees in the Strict Observance system.

The third, ultimately the only truly effective, level in the organization of Moscow Freemasonry was the Rosicrucian structure which lay hidden under these two public and semi-public levels of activity. At the top of this secret hierarchy of command stood Schwarz as the only Supreme Director appointed by Berlin. His Rosicrucian identity was known in Russia only to those who

---

[44] The term 'Martinists' was originally popularized by Le Mercier de la Rivière in the *Tableau de Paris* and referred to the followers of the mystical doctrine of Louis Claude de Saint-Martin, whose book, *Des Erreurs et de la vérité*, published in 1775, caused quite a sensation. The Russians who called the Novikov group 'Martinists' apparently also associated them with Saint-Martin whose book appeared in a Russian translation in 1785. Many people in Europe, however, used this term in reference to the disciples of Saint-Martin's early mentor, Martines de Pasqually, now led by Jean-Baptist Willermoz. Saint-Martin's teachings did not constitute a significant part of the Rosicrucian teaching and the Berlin Rosicrucians emphatically denied any association with the Martinists when their Russian charges were beginning to be called by that name (Lenning, *Encyclopädie*, ii. 398 ff.; Schneider, op. cit., p. 54; Pekarsky, op. cit., p. 74).

were appointed Chief Directors of the Theoretical degree on condition of obedience to him and absolute secrecy concerning their work or relationship. As had been arranged between Schwarz and Theden, Novikov was promptly admitted into the Theoretical degree and appointed a Chief Director. Some of Novikov's Masonic associates, such as I. P. Turgenev, A. M. Kutuzov, S. Gamaleya, V. V. Chulkov, I. Lopukhin, and his own brother Aleksey, were in turn also admitted into the same Theoretical degree and placed under Novikov's direction.[45] A few months later, Schwarz told Novikov to draw up a petition for his formal admission into the Rosicrucian Order and also to collect similar petitions from his charges. Only then, Novikov, who had been admitted into the Theoretical degree 'without any rites', expressed some hesitation since he still lacked a clear conception of the nature of commitment he was about to make.

On this occasion, I asked him to give me a true conception of the Order and what its objective was; he answered that its objective was knowledge of God, nature, and self, by the shortest and truest path. I asked if there was anything in the Order against Christian teaching. He answered, No! The Order in its teaching proceeds in accordance with the guidelines of Christian teaching and demands from its members that they be better Christians, better subjects, better citizens, fathers, etc. . . . than they had been before entering the Order.[46]

When Novikov further questioned Schwarz concerning the admission of others into the Order, the Supreme Director told him that 'he would take the petitions from the others and I should not speak with anyone except him and those from whom I collected the petition, since this was strictly forbidden'.[47] Indeed, the vows of secrecy with which Schwarz bound each recruit into the Rosicrucian organization were so effectively enforced that it was only after Schwarz's death that Novikov found out that his associates in 'Harmony', such as Prince Nikita Trubetskoy and his brother Yury, Prince Cherkassky, Prince Engalychev, and Kheraskov had also been admitted formally into the Rosicrucian Order by sending petitions to Berlin through Schwarz, and some of them had

[45] Longinov, op. cit., p. 84.   [46] Ibid.   [47] Ibid.

been appointed Chief Directors, like Novikov himself, with groups of Theoretical Brothers in their care.[48]

Those who were initiated into the Theoretical degree, such as Gamaleya, Turgenev, and Lopukhin, were holders of Masonic degrees above the Scottish Master and known on the Masonic level as masters of individual lodges working under the jurisdiction of the VIIIth Province. Their Rosicrucian affiliation was known only to the Chief Director immediately in charge. Likewise, they were informed of the identity only of their immediate Chief Director and those Theoretical Brothers who were working together under him, but not of the Supreme Director or other Chief Directors. At the initiation the candidate took the oath:

I, N. N., freely and after serious consideration, promise: (1) for all my life to worship the eternal, omnipotent Jehovah in spirit and truth; (2) to try as much as possible to know His power and wisdom through nature; (3) to abstain from the vanity of the world; (4) in so far as my ability permits, to strive to promote the well-being of my brothers, to love them and help them, both by advice and action, in all their needs; and finally, (5) to observe unbreakable silence as truthfully as God is immortal.[49]

The newly initiated also paid an admission fee as well as making more sizeable contributions in support of the various public and secret enterprises sponsored by the Rosicrucians. These, and additional funds at the disposal of the Theoretical Brothers as masters of individual Masonic lodges, were then entrusted to Schwarz, who sent part of them to his Rosicrucian superiors in Berlin in accordance with the terms of his appointment as the only Supreme Director in the Russian Empire and her territories.[50]

The work of the Theoretical Brothers consisted mainly of studying the 'Instruction of the Theoretical Brother', brought by

[48] Ibid., p. 85.   [49] Eshevsky, op. cit., pp. 239–40.

[50] Far greater sums of money besides the admission fees were collected on the pretexts of building a central treasury for alms-giving in Berlin and of supporting various Masonic enterprises in Russia. These contributions were compulsory, and only certain persons could be exempted in accordance with specific regulations. Pekarsky, op. cit., p. 71.

Schwarz from his trip, under the supervision of the Chief Director. The private presses of Novikov and Lopukhin, established in
1783 after the edict permitting private printing presses, and a third,
secret press under Schwarz's personal direction, printed books
such as Hutchinson's *Spirit of Freemasonry*, *Simple Instruction on
Prayers*, or *On Seven Days of Creation*, to aid the Chief Directors
in explaining the content of the 'Instruction'. It was, however,
strictly forbidden for them to disclose these sources to their
charges or, on being obliged to speak about these books with out-
siders by chance, to give any indication that they represented part
of the Rosicrucian teaching.[51] The 'Instruction' itself did not
contain much beyond certain basic theosophical notions drawn
from various sources such as Jakob Boehme, Johann Arndt,
and Johannes Scheffler, better known as Angelus Silesius. The
Theoretical Brothers, however, were assured that these teachings
represented only the very first step toward the attainment of
untold bliss such as Wöllner promised in the 'Commentaries'
cited earlier.[52]

When the Theoretical Brothers completed the study of their
instruction, the most reliable and desirable among them, from
the point of view of the Rosicrucian superiors, were instructed to
submit petitions for their formal admission into the Rosicrucian
Order. When a Theoretical Brother became a *bona fide* Rosicrucian a new Rosicrucian name was given in place of the Knights
Templar name he used in the Masonic lodges. Novikov thus
became Colovion in place of *eq. ab. ancora*; Trubetskoy, Pinnatus;
and Schwarz, Garganus. On this level the group character altogether disappeared and each Rosicrucian worked individually
with his Director. When distance separated them, they communi-
cated in writing, using their Rosicrucian name and in accordance
with a prearranged format. The instruction on secret written
communications between the Rosicrucians read:

The letter received by the superior is called the '*Otpusk*' and the one
addressed to persons below, '*Uvedomlenie*'. They should be written
by point: 1, 2, 3, and so forth. In answering, no mention should be

[51] Barskov, op. cit., pp. 260 and 263.
[52] See pages 208, above.

made of the content of the points. One should simply answer, for instance, to the first point . . ., to the second point, to the third point, etc.[53]

One of the most important obligations of the Rosicrucians was to hold the so-called quarterly convention, a special meeting at which all their papers, except a few to be preserved in the secret archives, were brought together to be burnt by the Director. Still, the format of the secret correspondence was so designed as not to reveal either the identity of the correspondents or the full substance of their correspondence in case these papers fell into foreign hands. The emphasis on secrecy had no limit. When Schwarz lay sick Wöllner told Schröder, who was to succeed Schwarz as the Rosicrucian liaison between Berlin and Moscow, that

When a Rosicrucian is dying, his coat of arms should be sent back to Berlin and every Rosicrucian should, during every minute of his life, take extreme care of his secret papers so that not a single piece of them may fall into a foreign hand in case of his sudden death. If they are not completely disposed of, they can disturb even the peace of his soul. Even a Junior[54] should be told of this, and Garganus should send over his coat of arms.[55]

That the Moscow Rosicrucians dutifully fulfilled these instructions is borne out by the fact that in spite of government seizure of their papers in 1792, the Novikov group revealed hardly any material incriminating them in the secret Rosicrucian network. None of Schwarz's own papers has ever come to light except the Rosicrucian patent of 1781 signed by Theden, his correspondence with Duke Ferdinand and his assistants, and a memorandum addressed to the senior curator of Moscow University, I. I. Shuvalov.[56] The Rosicrucian patent clearly was a document which had to be preserved in their archives while the other papers had nothing to do with Rosicrucianism. Even the content of Schwarz's lectures, through which he spread the Rosicrucian ideas, has been reconstructed by later historians out of the notes taken by his students

---

[53] Pypin, op. cit., p. 341.
[54] The lowest Rosicrucian degree below the Theoretical.
[55] Barskov, op. cit., p. 227.
[56] Printed in *Letopisi russkoy literatury i drevnosti*, ed. Tikhonravov, v. 96–110.

and descriptions of them contained in the tributes paid by his former students.[57]

The number of Russians who actually joined the Rosicrucian network by being initiated into the Theoretical degree did not seem to have greatly exceeded sixty, according to an estimate based on the testimonies of Novikov and Prince Trubetskoy,[58] but their dominion was spread widely over the Russian Empire through the scattered Masonic lodges of which most of them were masters. The man who built and controlled this secret network of enormous spiritual and financial potential, Schwarz, died in the spring of 1784, just when the organizational task seemed to have reached the first round of completion. Judging by the influence he had exerted on the education of young students at Moscow University, by popularizing a philosophical position capable of providing a point of support to those who felt bewildered and confounded by the unprepared confrontation with militant rationalism, his legacy and contribution to the development of Russian culture seems to have been positive enough. In the testimonies of those who knew him personally, he appears either as a saint and sage, dedicated to the spiritual well-being of his adopted fatherland with total selflessness, or as a religious fanatic with a tyrannical temperament and great cunning. In the end, however, Schwarz's ultimate intention and design in taking great pains in order to establish such an ingeniously structured secret organization, in subordination to the Wöllner group in Berlin, still remains a mystery. The full effect of Rosicrucianism on the life of those Russians whom he had won over to his cause would be seen only after his death. In the meantime, according to his friends who were with him during his last days, Schwarz himself seems to have experienced a spiritual crisis, lying on his death-bed. Vigand reported in his memoirs:

The leader of this society, Professor Schwarz, showed me full confidence and revealed to me the hidden purpose of the society, which

[57] Some excerpts from Schwarz's lectures appear in the journals published later by his disciples such as the *Drug Yunoshestva* and *Sionsky Vestnik*, in addition to those found in the *Slovar Mosk. prof.*

[58] For a full list of Russian Freemasons named by Novikov, see *Sbornik Imperatorskago Russkago Istoricheskogo Obshchestra*, ii (1868), 145–51.

was nothing but the subversion of the Orthodox faith in Russia; I advised him to act more cautiously, to abandon mysticism, and not to mix his own aims with the aim of the community,[59] so that they would not do each other harm. In regard to the religious reform, Schwarz had already progressed very far and his plan was near accomplishment, but his extraordinary labours soon brought him the ordeal of sickness; I visited him every day and he always asked me to talk about the Saviour to him. But we could not speak freely, since the Freemasons were always eavesdropping on us, fearing lest under the influence of a spiritual mood so new to him, he might give away their secret. I also tried to avoid this in every way, but once he spoke out that this was a diabolical order and that if the Lord granted him the cure, then he would join the community. When Schwarz passed away the Freemasons asked me to give a funeral oration in the Russian language.[60]

Another story comes from Princess V. A. Trubetskoy, wife of Nikolay, at whose estate Schwarz died. When she and her husband entered the sick room after Schwarz had suffered a prolonged coma, the dying Rosicrucian director exclaimed: 'Be happy, my friend, I just faced the judgement and was acquitted. Now I can die in peace.'[61] Perhaps Schwarz, in spite of his intelligence and knowledge of the European Masonic world, had been as much deceived as Novikov and other Russian Masons in his acceptance and promotion of Rosicrucianism.

III

It is difficult to think of many secret societies designed with greater ingenuity and thoroughness of attention to details, yet the mere possession of a secret organization was what which distinguished Rosicrucianism from other schools of Freemasonry. The oath of secrecy and obedience to masters required of the novices was a customary practice both in the low-degree and high-degree systems. The Rosicrucian command system, like other Masonic organizations, but unlike some other underground societies, also lacked a positive sanction which could be used in case of default.

[59] The Herrnhuter community.   [60] Vigand, op. cit., p. 562.
[61] Longinov, op. cit., pp. 210–11.

As a quasi-religious organization, it had to rely on voluntary submission of the members acting out of faith in the system. The uniqueness of the Rosicrucian episode in Russian history, however, lay precisely in the serious and comprehensive manner in which the oath of secrecy and obedience to the Rosicrucian superiors operating from Berlin affected the lives of men who had voluntarily taken it.

Among the Freemasons who adhered to other Masonic systems, their Masonic obligation usually did not go much beyond regular attendance of the lodge, observation of secrecy concerning rites, and occasional donations to fraternal and charitable causes. Their Masonic activities could be rather neatly compartmentalized so as not to affect their relationship with, and conduct in, the outside world except through the moral self-consciousness and humanitarian concern which the attendance of the lodges presumably awakened in some of them. The more mystically inclined of them conducted their own pursuit of Freemasonry by delving into the enormous store of theosophical and hermetic writings. When the Swedish Masonry in Russia gave some indication that the price to be paid for the high Masonic degrees offered by the system was a political involvement in support of the Swedish ruling house, the movement was nipped in the bud by the watchful Catherine. In the case of the Rosicrucians, however, Schwarz's success in keeping the organization in complete secrecy delayed the decisively hostile reaction of the government, and the induction into the Rosicrucian establishment became, for the most seriously involved of the Russians, a commitment to dedicate practically their entire life and fortune in pursuit of the Rosicrucian panacea in compliance with the dictates of their foreign superiors.

The most interesting and revealing case was that of Novikov. The famous publisher had shown some hesitation before sending in a petition for his formal admission into the Rosicrucian Order and, apparently, tried to preserve a certain independence from Schwarz in regard to his publishing activities, but his independence did not last long. A series of *otpuski* he had written to his Rosicrucian director shortly after Schwarz's death have survived, most probably through the neglect of the addressee, and reveal that by

the summer of 1784, he had become a genuine convert to Rosicrucianism.[62] In the first of these confessional reports, Novikov
said, after acknowledging his great debt to the decea ed Schwarz:

I sincerely and frankly confess before you, highly worthy Superior,
that I did not understand, or rather poorly and incorrectly understood,
the precious pillars on which the Holy Order is built. I thought that a
man may by himself love God and his fellow men, and even mistakenly
believed that I fulfilled these. I thank my Saviour with tears in my
eyes; he allowed me to feel and recognize my stupidity, and understand
and realize that love is the gift of God, the perception and enjoyment
of which he permits only to his holy ones. . . . I write these lines in
tears; I thank my Saviour and will thank and glorify his mercy for
ever for, during my sickness, about which you know, and after that,
he allowed me perception and feelings which had been foreign to me.
How sweet, joyful, and elating it is to experience momentarily the
humility, after which follows love. Often pride, often stupid obstinacy,
often wilfulness hid such realization from me. I am convinced, highly
worthy Superior, that the clean and uncorrupt prayers of our merciful
and wise fathers and highly glorious superiors intercede for us and
draw to our fatherland the mercy and the blessing of the Almighty.[63]

The significance of such confessional reports as this lies not, as
Novikov's apologists were quick to point out, in the fact that he
had previously shown a certain wilfulness and independence, but
that now he was repenting and felt himself body and soul bound
to his Rosicrucian superiors, whom he called 'the true priests of
the only true and invisible Church of our Saviour Christ, to whom
he promised by his mercy to stay with them to the end of the
world, and gave keys both to lock and unlock'.[64] Repeated reference to his recent illness appearing in these reports, and the marked
interest the Moscow Rosicrucians showed in the Rosicrucian
universal medication later, all indicate that Novikov probably
felt himself particularly indebted to the Rosicrucian superiors for
his restored health, and that his actual conversion to Rosicrucianism, as distinct from his formal admission into their secret organization, had taken place sometime in the autumn or winter of
1783-4 when Novikov lay seriously sick, as Schwarz was at the

---

[62] These *otpuski* have been published in Pypin, op. cit., pp. 343 ff.
[63] Ibid., pp. 343-4.　　　　　　　　　[64] Ibid., pp. 344-5.

same time, for about four months.[65] In another *otpusk* belonging
to the same series, he says:

> In general, h.w.s. [highly worthy Superior], since the time of my
> illness, about which you know, I experience in myself, thanks to the
> mercy of our Saviour, a great change. From that time, I count a new
> epoch in my life; during that time, and since then, I very vividly feel
> the merciful right hand of the Saviour tearing me away from the jaws
> of hell and the claws of Satan. When I think about my duties and how
> I ought to be, I despise and am disgusted with myself, but when I look
> at what I had been before, then tears of repentance and gratitude flow.
> And now I have already bathed this report of mine in tears. Be eternally
> praised, glorified, and extolled, merciful Saviour of the sinners, the
> holy order, our wise and merciful fathers and highly glorious
> superiors![66]

The main concern of the Wöllner group in eagerly awaiting
Novikov's *otpuski*, written in answer to their questions, lay not
simply with the state of Novikov's soul or the benefit to be granted
to his beloved fatherland, as the enterprising but naïve Russian
publisher sincerely believed. The Berlin Rosicrucians were most
anxious to hear about the financial state of the new printing
company being established in Moscow. This was the famous
Typographic Company, the new public enterprise of the Moscow
Rosicrucians launched in the autumn of 1784, which replaced the
Friendly Society of Learning and became the centre of Rosicrucian
activities. A substantial portion of Novikov's *otpuski* is concerned

---

[65] The Russian Rosicrucians were seriously interested in the Rosicrucian 'practical work', i.e. alchemy. In addition to Kutuzov, who was sent to Berlin to be
initiated into the Rosicrucian 'science', some young students such as Nevzorov
and Kolokolnikov were also sent to Europe on Rosicrucian stipends to study
chemistry as a step leading to the Rosicrucian chemistry. For Trubetskoy's correspondence with Kutuzov concerning certain chemicals with healing power,
see Barskov, op. cit., pp. 92, 105, 135. Lenning's *Encyclopädie* also has a curious
reference in this connection. Under its entry on Schröder, it says: 'Als Professor
Schwarz . . . 1784 starb, wurde S-r (Sacerdos) specialler Oberer derselben in
Russland und war derjenige, welcher die Rosenkreizer in Berlin angriff und das
Silanun (Stillstand der Arbeiten) hervorrief. Man erzählt von diesem S., dass
er um den erkrankten Schwarz zu retten, mit Courierpferden von Moskau nach
Berlin geritten sei, um von Wöllner (Ophiron) die verheissene Universalmedicin
zu holen, welche er auch erhielt, die aber glücklicherweise für Schwarz zu spät
kam, denn die chemische Untersuchung erwiess, dass die Dosis tödlich gewesen
wäre' (quoted in Barskov, op. cit., pp. 286–7).

[66] Pypin, op. cit., p. 345.

with this subject, indicating that at least a partial control over his famous publishing activities was the price he had to pay in return for the physical and spiritual health for which he believed himself indebted to the Rosicrucian Order. Furthermore, the information contained in these *otpuski* is fully corroborated by a diary kept by Baron Schröder, the Rosicrucian successor of Schwarz, as liaison between Moscow and Berlin.[67] A consideration of a more practical nature which seems to have persuaded Novikov to surrender even a small part of the control over what clearly was his life project was the thought that, with the Rosicrucians' help, he could perhaps disentangle himself from the enormous financial difficulties he was encountering after having ambitiously expanded the business of the university press on borrowed credits. The new capital investments made by the founding members of the Typographic Company could provide Novikov, who also became a shareholder and business manager by investing printed books in place of money, with the ready cash he so badly needed in order to placate his creditors.[68] Novikov wrote to his superior:

Highly worthy Superior, I and brother Schwarz started executing your order to compile a detailed report on the state of typographic affairs. . . . I will complete it as quickly as I can and send it to you with my dispatches. I testify on my conscience that this burden weighs on me; I impatiently wait for the day when I could be merely your agent and execute your orders, which can be fulfilled after the actual establishment of the company. I most sincerely admit that I deserve this suffering as a punishment because, at the beginning of these affairs, I did many things following my own judgement and expanded the business very widely; partly also, some unexpected circumstances have led it to such great expansion that one man alone is incapable of coping with it. But however heavy this burden may be, I will fulfil your command and the will of our highest, greatest superiors in sincerest obedience.[69]

It is clear, from these reports and Schröder's diary recording his talks with the Wöllner group concerning the Rosicrucian work in Russia, that Berlin provided the list or the originals of many of the

[67] This diary is found in Barskov, op. cit., pp. 215–34.
[68] See n. 71, below.   [69] Pypin, op. cit., pp. 342–3.

books printed by the Typographic Company and supervised its business transactions to the minutest detail. Not satisfied with the control they exercised indirectly through Novikov, Wöllner apparently instructed Novikov to hand over the business altogether to Baron Schröder. Novikov obediently handed over the management, the *otpuski* reveal, reserving only the actual handling of printing for his own brother, Aleksey.[70]

Together with these *otpuski*, Novikov entrusted Baron Schröder, who was leaving for Germany, with business accounts, lists of books he was planning to print, had already printed, and was in the process of printing in both the secret and public presses under his direction, and Masonic acts in his possession, with indications of sources and translators. Novikov's testimony to Prozorovsky in 1792 was to reveal that he did not keep the business accounts of the university press and the private Typographic Company separate.[71] Thus, by placing himself at the service of the Rosicrucian superiors in Berlin in connection with the affairs of the Typographic Company, he had also put the university printing press indirectly within the reach of their influence.

Another important aim which the Rosicrucians set out to achieve, besides controlling the printing establishments in Moscow, was the induction of Grand Duke Paul into their Order. They tried to do this by first approaching the persons close to the 'small court' such as Prince G. P. Gagarin, A. B. Kurakin, and Prince Nikolay Repnin. The architect Bazhenov, who had been admitted to the Rosicrucian Order through Novikov, paid special visits to the Grand Duke, Novikov and Trubetskoy later confessed, as their envoy, for this purpose.[72] In spite of the widely rumoured sympathy of Paul for mysticism and his personal intimacy with

---

[70] Pypin, op. cit., p. 343.

[71] When Prozorovsky pointed out that the expenditures of the Typographic Company had exceeded the total amount of the capital invested by the various members, Novikov replied that ready cash had been obtained from advance subscriptions to various journals printed at the university press and other subsidies the university press had received from various sources including the Imperial Cabinet (Longinov, op. cit., p. 67).

[72] Novikov's testimony concerning this was not included in Longinov's version, but was later printed in *Sbornik*, ii. 117–23.

some of the Freemasons, the attempt proved to be abortive, and only became one of the immediate causes behind Catherine's decision to deal a final blow to Novikov and his fellow Rosicrucians in 1792.

When Catherine's attention became riveted on Novikov, starting around 1785, and the Typographic Company began to show signs of financial trouble, Berlin's eagerness to keep Novikov in close relationship with them seems to have diminished. Baron Schröder, who never fully inherited Schwarz's mantle of authority among the Russian followers and dedication to the Rosicrucian cause, abruptly demanded the reimbursement of the capital which he had invested in the Rosicrucian enterprises in Moscow, to the utter stupefaction and fury of Novikov. In 1786 Novikov was already experiencing enormous financial strain as a result of Catherine's decrees impounding many of the books printed by him, pending the outcome of an investigation of their content by Archbishop Platon. When the difficulties for Novikov redoubled in 1787 as a result of the edict forbidding the printing and sale of all books touching on religion, the Rosicrucian superiors in Berlin sent notes of consolation, praising the humility and forbearance with which Russian Rosicrucians suffered persecution, but disclaimed any responsibility for the printing of mystical books, reprimanding the Russian followers for having been over-zealous and hasty in expanding their network.[73] Finally, a *silanum* was proclaimed, calling for temporary cessation of all activities. Wöllner had in the meantime become a minister of the Prussian state with the accession of his Rosicrucian protégé, Frederick William II. Now he had at his disposal more direct means of achieving his aims than by incurring the suspicion of the Russian government. The Russian Rosicrucian with whom Berlin chose to communicate directly was no longer Novikov but Prince Trubetskoy. In 1788 the Rosicrucian organization in Russia was restructured into a 'Haupt-directory' and Trubetskoy was appointed its head. Novikov's former Rosicrucian charges, such as Lopukhin and Turgenev, were taken away from him, leaving him only his brother and his faithful friend Gamaleya. Although

---

[73] Pekarsky, op. cit., pp. 72 ff.

Novikov himself never seems to have become disenchanted with Rosicrucianism, he had shown some resistance to spending much money on students who were sent to Germany to study the Rosicrucian chemistry. His relationship with the wealthier and more aristocratic of the Russian Rosicrucians, such as Trubetskoy and Lopukhin, became so strained on account of the dwindling Typographic Company that they even began to talk about bringing a lawsuit against Novikov.[74]

The Rosicrucian hold on Russians did not completely stop even after the arrest and punishment of Novikov and his fellow Rosicrucians in 1792. The most tragic fate was that of A. M. Kutuzov, probably the most gifted and sensitive of all Russian Rosicrucians. In August 1782 he wrote a letter to his friend Turgenev, protesting that the cure suggested to him, Rosicrucianism, was in fact the cause of his extreme melancholy and depression.

The second cause is that very one which you prescribed to me as the means to my cure, I mean knowledge of self. Will you believe me, my friend, that so long as I remained ignorant in the discussion of this matter, I was in peace. I regarded myself as one of the foremost men in the world, everything cheered me, and I thought myself capable of everything. But now, having begun to practise assiduously in this holy science, I notice in myself baseness concerning which no thought had ever entered into my mind before.[75]

Commenting on the incessant command to pray, he also wrote:

I also tell you something about prayer. If you think I do not want to pray at all, such a thought is very unjust, and you do not know me at all. No, dear friend, I am not yet so abominable. But I insist that in my situation it is meaningless to pray, and that prayer without action cannot be effective. What good is it to me to say, 'Lord have mercy' and at the very same time think something for which I myself know that I should be punished. To someone who is steeped in sorrow, can there be free thought?[76]

In 1787, against his own wishes, Kutuzov was transferred to Berlin

[74] Barskov, op. cit., pp. 189–90.
[75] Yu. M. Lotman, 'Sochuvstvennik A. N. Radishcheva A. M. Kutuzov i ego pisma I. P. Turgenevu', *Uchenye Zapiski Tartuskogo Universiteta: Trudy po russkoy slwyanskoy filologii*, cxxxix, no. 6 (Tartu, 1963), 300.
[76] Ibid.

for apprenticeship in the Rosicrucian science, since he seemed best qualified to meet the specifications sent by Berlin.[77] At first he was torn between his desire to return to his friends in Moscow as quickly as possible and a developing interest in the Rosicrucian chemistry. Exhorted to stay by his Rosicrucian friends and after undergoing a great deal of torment and suffering, the same man eventually became the most helpless convert to Rosicrucianism. In July 1791 he wrote: 'They opened to me something about which I dare not write; I think that you yourselves can already guess. One condition is that I remain here with them at least three years in order to bring our common intention to fruition by unified efforts.'[78] He implored Trubetskoy to sell even the last bit of property left to them jointly in order to enable him to wait out this crucial last moment before the long-promised Rosicrucian harvest would be reaped:

For God's sake, pay attention to my words and apply that ardour which produces great works and almost anything out of nothing. One of the brothers has returned from a trip, during which he had the good fortune to meet very important persons. From them he heard that N. is now in Persia, and that in a year surely everything will be decided. Many districts will be struck off, among others, Regensburg, Augsburg, and Nuremberg. They say that tribulations up to now have been sent deliberately for the test of the brothers, but at the end [of the *Silanum*] the remaining [brothers] will receive something substantial. Pray to God that we remain, and pray with me and for me. Please free me from worldly cares.[79]

Abandoned by his Rosicrucian brothers, many of whom had by then been rehabilitated to important worldly positions after the accession of Paul, Kutuzov died in Berlin in 1797, utterly destitute and broken-hearted.

From the surviving evidence, it is not clear what the ultimate design of the Wöllner group was in making such a great effort to entice the Russians. Greed for the money of the wealthy Russian aristocrats was certainly one motive, if one is to judge by the number of wealthy Russians who suffered near bankruptcy on

[77] Barskov, op. cit., p. 134.   [78] Ibid., p. 137.
[79] Ibid., p. 163.

account of their involvement in Rosicrucianism.[80] But the elaborate scheme which Wöllner used in order to ensnare the sincerely religious and patriotic publisher, Novikov, and control his publishing activities, the effort to win over Paul, and Wöllner's subsequent activities as Prussian Minister of Education and Public Instruction, all indicate that money was only a small part of the deal, most probably the means to an end. In spite of all the dabblings in the more dubious forms of religiosity such as theosophy, alchemy, and other hermetic sciences, Rosicrucianism undoubtedly possessed many characteristics of a religious order. Perhaps Vigand, the Herrnhuter friend of Schwarz, came closest to the truth when he described Schwarz as a religious fanatic bent on subversion of the Orthodox faith in Russia.[81] Even if the fight against the *philosophes* and re-establishment of the Christian religion were the final, hidden goal, as apologists such as Lopukhin insisted,[82] it is hardly likely that the cause which Wöllner and his associates wanted to promote in so determined a fashion was Russian Orthodoxy.

Catherine's charge of sectarianism against Novikov was completely justifiable even if the man involved was himself not conscious of his deviation from the Orthodox Church of which he remained at heart the truest son. The involvement of the Grand Duke's name, and the many complaints she received concerning the financial ruin of many prominent families, gave her not only a sufficient excuse but also an obligation as a sovereign to strike at the root of the Rosicrucian movement. At any rate, the spirit which Rosicrucianism promoted was anything but critical social consciousness or independent civic initiative with which Freemasonry under Catherine has often been credited and Catherine's severe punishment of Novikov explained. That indeed such an awakening was noticeable in Russia around the time of the Rosicrucian activities was a mere coincidence, for which an explanation has to be sought elsewhere.

    [80] I. V. Lopukhin, 'Zapiski Moskovskago Martinista Senatora I. V. Lopukhina', *Russky Arkhiv*, i (1884), 11.   [81] See pages 222–3, and note 60 above.
    [82] V. N. Tukalevsky, 'Iz istorii filosofskikh napravleniy v russkom obshchestve XVIII veka', *Zhurnal ministerstva narodnogo prosveshcheniya*, v (1911), 44.

ANTHONY G. CROSS

The British in Catherine's Russia: A Preliminary Survey

In his sketch entitled 'Angliyskaya progulka' ('A Walk in the English Style') and published in 1772 in the third of his famous satirical journals, Nikolay Novikov suggested that 'The English have replaced the French: nowadays women and men are falling over themselves to imitate anything English; everything English now seems to us good and admirable and fills us full of enthusiasm. But we, unfortunately, are so addicted to things foreign that we frequently consider even their vices virtues.'[1] It is a view which would seem to lend credence to the formula by which the reigns of the three empresses Anna, Elizabeth, and Catherine reflect in turn the dominance of things German, French, and English; yet it is important to point out that it was Gallomania—which Count Francesco Algarotti had noted already at the end of Anna's reign in 1739[2] and which was rampant at Elizabeth's Court, abetted by 'une nuée de Français de toutes couleurs'[3]—that spread throughout Russia among the upper classes under Catherine and was to exercise the wit of Russian journalists, dramatists, and poets at least until the end of Alexander I's reign. Only with Pushkin did the Anglomaniac emerge as a fully developed figure;[4] earlier, certain aspects of Anglomania were used only in the characterization of the more generalized figure of the cosmopolitan or

---

[1] *Satiricheskie zhurnaly N. I. Novikova*, ed. P. N. Berkov (Moscow and Leningrad, 1951), pp. 328–9.

[2] *Letters from Count Algarotti to Lord Hervey and the Marquis Scipio Maffei, containing the state of the trade, marine, revenues, and forces of the Russian Empire* (London, 1769), i. 81.

[3] M. de la Messelière, *Voyage à Pétersbourg, ou nouveaux mémoires sur la Russie* (Paris, 1803), p. 124.

[4] Cf. Grigory Ivanovich Muromsky in 'Baryshnya-krestyanka'.

xenomaniac.[5] There is nothing surprising in this, for somewhat ironically Anglomania was itself a by-product of French influence, a reflection of that admiration for England fostered in the writings of such as Voltaire and the abbé Prévost; its initial impact was thus of an intellectual character and it may be argued that even after the enthusiasm spread to the more superficial aspects of social life, Anglomania, certainly under Catherine, was free of many of the excesses and frivolities which characterized its French counterpart. The reception of English literature, predominantly via French versions, and the dissemination of works touching on English life and institutions have been reviewed in some detail by E. J. Simmons[6] and the extent of Russian translations from English literary journals and poetry may be accurately gauged from the excellent contributions of Yu. D. Levin,[7] but these are subjects which are not central to the present study. They are, none the less, an important part of the background against which the activities of the British in Catherine's Russia may be discussed.

In a number of articles and a book entitled *Britain's Discovery of Russia 1553–1815*, M. S. Anderson has contributed greatly to what he has called 'the study of a subject which has hitherto attracted comparatively little attention from scholars in Great Britain'.[8] Welcoming the book, the Soviet scholar P. N. Berkov pointed to the lack of works which were devoted to a balanced assessment of both general and specific aspects of Anglo–Russian cultural interchange and to the absence of information about English communities in Russia.[9] The German and French communities in

---

[5] Cf. N. I. Strakhov's Bezmozglov in his *Satirichesky vestnik* (1790); *Russkaya proza XVIII veka*, eds. A. V. Zapadov and G. P. Makogonenko (Moscow and Leningrad, 1950), ii. 611 ff.

[6] *English Literature and Culture in Russia (1553–1840)*, Harvard Studies in Comparative Literature, xii (Cambridge, Mass., 1935), pp. 73–203.

[7] 'Angliyskaya prosvetitelskaya zhurnalistika v russkoy literature XVIII veka', *Epokha Prosveshcheniya: Iz istorii mezhdunarodnykh svyazey russkoy literatury*, ed. M. P. Alekseev (Leningrad, 1967), pp. 3–109; 'Angliyskaya poeziya i literatura russkogo sentimentalizma', *Ot klassitsizma k romantizmu: Iz istorii mezdunarodnykh svyazey russkoy literatury*. ed. M. P. Alekseev (Leningrad, 1970), pp. 195–297.

[8] (London, 1958), p. vii.

[9] 'Tomas Konsett, kapellan angliyskoy faktorii v Rossii (K istorii russko-angliyskikh literaturnykh svyazey v 1720e gody)', *Problemy mezhdunarodnykh literaturnykh svyazey*, ed. B. G. Reizov (Leningrad, 1962), pp. 3–4, 7.

Moscow found their historians,[10] but the only English work which promised similar treatment for the British contributes almost nothing of substance.[11] Nevertheless, the materials for such a work exist; something of their wealth may be gauged from Anderson's work and there remain numerous untapped manuscript sources in English and Russian archives. The present study is a preliminary survey of aspects of British activity in Russia in one particular reign. It does not primarily seek to stress British influence on Russian life and thought; it is concerned with providing an informational framework without which certain questions of influence cannot properly be raised.

I

By the time Catherine came to the throne the British had been in Russia for over two hundred years and had enjoyed great influence and power, particularly in the spheres of commerce and diplomacy. There had naturally been times when their fortunes fluctuated and their authority was challenged by other nations, and this pattern was to be continued in the eighteenth century. Nevertheless, in many respects, under Catherine they enjoyed the halcyon days of their influence, partaking of benefits which only a widespread enthusiasm for their country, its life, institutions, and literature could bring. The number of British in Russia in various capacities certainly increased throughout Catherine's reign and although this fact is generally recognized, there is considerable vagueness about the total involved. The vast majority was to be found in the capital St. Petersburg and it is on the basis of statistics available for that city that an estimate for the country as a whole may be hazarded.

The Reverend William Tooke, Chaplain to the British Factory in St. Petersburg, compiled in the church register a list of 482 British who were resident in the capital and Cronstadt in 1782–3,

---

[10] A. W. Fechner, *Chronik der evangelischen Gemeinden in Moscau*, 2 vols. (Moscow, 1876); F. Tasteven, *Histoire de la colonie française de Moscou* (Moscow and St. Petersburg, 1908).

[11] C. L. Johnstone, *The British Colony in Russia* (Westminster, [1898]).

although there are numerous obvious omissions.[12] Certainly within a decade the figure was over a thousand. Heinrich Storch on the basis of some dubious calculations arrives at a total of 930 in 1789,[13] and John Parkinson, an Oxford don who visited Russia in 1792–3, gives 1,500.[14] The accelerating growth of the British community may be gauged from the estimate of 2,500 for the end of Alexander I's reign.[15] These totals may be judged in the context of the general population growth of the city: 95,000 in 1750, 192,000 in 1784, 220,000 in 1800, 336,000 in 1811.[16] At no time, however, were the British among the best-represented foreign groups. Storch's breakdown of the 32,000 foreigners representing one seventh of the city's population in 1789 might serve as a very approximate guide: 17,660 Germans, 3,700 Finns, 2,290 French, 1,860 Swedes, 930 British, and 50 Dutch.[17] The French total in particular fluctuated greatly in the early 1790s and Parkinson believed that there were only 1,000 there in 1792. The number of British in other parts of Russia is comparatively insignificant. Dr. Robert Lyall estimates on the basis of the Moscow church register that there were only 200 British there in 1823; in a further table he gives a total of 126 for the year 1805 out of an over-all number of 3,811 foreigners (of whom over a quarter were Germans and over a fifth French).[18] A figure not in excess of 100 would seem probable for the end of Catherine's reign. If one were to add another 200 to represent those British who were scattered throughout the towns and estates of provincial Russia and serving in the Baltic and Black Sea fleets, and allowance were made for a considerable migrant British population—tourists and craftsmen of all varieties—an over-all total not exceeding 2,000 would seem appropriate for the last years of Catherine's reign.

[12] British Factory in Russia Register 1706–1815, Guildhall Library, London, MS. 11, 192B, f. 72.　　[13] *The Picture of Petersburg* (London, 1801), p. 88.
[14] 'A Northern Tour', unpublished MSS., 6 vols., iv, unfoliated. Parkinson wrote in fact 15,000, which I have taken as an obvious slip of the pen. I am grateful to Mr. William Collier for permission to quote from the manuscript.
[15] A. B. Granville, *St. Petersburg* (London, 1828), ii. 203.
[16] *Leningrad: Entsiklopedichesky spravochnik* (Moscow and Leningrad, 1957), p. 33; W. H. Parker, *An Historical Geography of Russia* (London, 1968), p. 204.
[17] *The Picture of Petersburg*, p. 88.
[18] *The Character of the Russians and a Detailed History of Moscow* (London, 1823), pp. 379, 532.

Although the activities of the British in places far removed from the capital are part of the general picture of English penetration into Russia, few of these seemingly attractive episodes can be satisfactorily documented: exceptional and individual cases are those of Michael Maddox, the Moscow theatrical impresario,[19] and of Samuel Bentham in the Ukraine and Siberia.[20] It is the British community in St. Petersburg, 'in its social composition a sort of transplanted City of London in miniature',[21] which is the inevitable focal point.

At the heart of this community were the merchants of the British Factory, as the Russia Company was known in St. Petersburg. As the capital grew in majesty and splendour throughout the century, the British merchants acquired some of the finest locations in the city, including what became known by the end of Catherine's reign as the English Quay or Line. Now called Quay of the Red Fleet, its original name was Galley Quay and in the early days of St. Petersburg it had been an unattractive collection of workers' huts, together with a lodging-house built by Prince Menshikov for visiting foreign craftsmen and a tavern frequented by workmen from the shipyards. The turning point in its development came with the establishment in 1762 of a Commission for the Stone Construction of St. Petersburg and Moscow (Kommissiya o kamennom stroenii Sankt-Peterburga i Moskvy, 1762–96). In the next decade or so was built that impressive row of three-storied stone houses on the left bank of the Neva, some with 'balconies large enough to drink Tea',[22] and most with a house at the back giving on to Isaac Street which belonged in the

[19] Cf. Olga Chayanova, *Teatr Maddoksa v Moskve 1776–1805* (Moscow, 1927).

[20] Matthew S. Anderson, 'Samuel Bentham in Russia, 1779–1791', *American Slavic and East European Review*, xv, no. 2 (1956), 157–72; Walther Kirchner, 'Samuel Bentham and Siberia', *Slavonic and East European Review*, xxxvi no. 87 (1958), 471–80; K. A. Papmehl, 'The Regimental School Established in Siberia by Samuel Bentham', *Canadian Slavonic Papers*, viii (1966), 153–68; Ian R. Christie, 'Samuel Bentham and the Western Colony at Krichev, 1784–1787', *SEER* xlviii, no. 3 (1970), 232–47.

[21] James Cracraft, 'James Brogden in Russia, 1787–1788', *SEER* xlvii, no. 1 (1969), 223.

[22] 'The Journal of Elizabeth 3rd Wife of the 1st Baron Dimsdale on a Journey to Russia in the Year 1781', unpublished manuscript in possession of the present Baron Dimsdale, to whom I am grateful for permission to consult a typescript of the manuscript.

main to members of the English community. The whole complex was known as Galley Yard, and was flanked to the west by the Kryukov Canal which was crossed by an elegant raisable bridge. This region's importance as the heart of the British community was emphasized by the presence of the English Church in a house acquired by the Factory in 1754,[23] as well as by a tavern and a coffee-house.

Some impression of the way of life of the community may be gleaned from the accounts and correspondence of travellers visiting Catherine's capital: comparatively little was written by the residents themselves, with the notable exception of Tooke. In one of several passages on the British which he added to his translation of Heinrich Storch's *Gemälde von Peterburg*, he writes:

The English stationary at St. Petersburg are mostly merchants, acquire and expend a great deal of money, live like their countrymen at home [. . .] In the houses of the Britons settled here a competent idea may be formed of the english manner of living. Furniture, meals, establishment; everything is english—even to the chimney-fire. Here where wood is in such plenty, the Englishman fetches his coals from home.[24]

Lady Elizabeth Craven's letters of 1786 offer a very similar picture.

[. . .] I find English grates, English coats, English coal, and English hospitality, to make me welcome, and the fire-side chearful—I have never yet been fortunate enough to make any acquaintance in the world of commerce; but if all English merchants and their families are as well informed and civil as those I find here—I should be very glad to be admitted into the city of London as a visitor, to enjoy a little rational conversation, which at the court-end is seldom to be found.[25]

According to James Brogden (1765–1842), the son of a prominent member of the Russia Company in London, who also noted the 'English fire Place where they burn new Castle and Scotch coal': 'the houses of the English and the other civilized

---

[23] Granville, *St. Petersburg*, ii. 202. For details of the church and its chaplains, see my 'Chaplains to the British Factory in St. Petersburg, 1723–1813', *European Studies Review*, ii, no. 2 (1972), 125–42.

[24] Storch, *The Picture of Petersburg*, p. 574.

[25] *A Journey through the Crimea to Constantinople* (London, 1789), pp. 125–6.

Europeans are fitted up with every convenience, even at the expence of appearance, by which as in all other things we are so peculiarly distinguished from the Russians, whose prevailing passion seems to be the desire of shew.'[26] In most published sources a positive interpretation is given to aspects of life in the British colony which frequently hardly merit it and attention is drawn to the harmony and mutual support which existed among the British merchants not only by such as Tooke but by such perceptive observers as the French ambassador, the Comte de Ségur.[27] Nevertheless, as the unpublished letters of Richard Sutherland (b. 1772), the son of Catherine's Court Banker, Baron Richard Sutherland, reveal, dissension and ill will often split the community.[28]

The British enjoyed a distinctive relationship with families of the Russian nobility, who were 'remarkably affable to Strangers, especially the English'.[29] Although the British were said to live with 'that cautious reserve which every where distinguishes them'[30] which was not necessarily an engaging quality, as one of their visiting fellow-countrymen observed,[31] they had powerful admirers and supporters at Court. Memoirs of the period make frequent reference to the Anglophilia of such as Catherine herself, Counts I. G. Chernyshev and A. R. Vorontsov, Princess E. R. Dashkova, N. A. Zagryazhsky, and others, more and more of whom had first-hand knowledge of England. Important forms of social intercourse were the series of balls organized during the winter season by the British merchants and the activities of the English Club. In the winter of 1787–8 there were seven balls 'held at the English Inn, which is one of the best houses in the Line & belongs to a Russian nobleman'.[32] Brogden has left a

---

[26] Cracraft, 'James Brogden in Russia', p. 231.

[27] *Mémoires ou souvenirs et anecdotes*, ii (Paris, 1826), 299.

[28] Extracts from these letters (covering the period 1792–1800) have appeared in my article, 'The Sutherland Affair and its Aftermath', *SEER*, 1, no. 117 (1972), 257–75.

[29] Cracraft, 'James Brogden in Russia', p. 230.

[30] Granville, *St. Petersburg*, ii. 482.

[31] [Lionel Colmore], *Letters from the Continent; describing the manners and customs of Germany, Poland, Russia, and Switzerland, in the years 1790, 1791, and 1792* (London, 1812), pp. 113–14.

[32] Cracraft, 'James Brogden in Russia', p. 232.

graphic description of the first of the series, attended by Prince
G. A. Potemkin, Count A. A. Bezborodko, the foreign ambassadors, many Russian nobles, and most of the British merchants:

Country Boamkin, as they call Country Bumkin, is a very favorite
dance, tho' they make it quite different from the dance so called in England. The supper is very elegant, but so much in fashion is everything
English that Beefstakes, Welsh Rabits & Porter is the most fashionable meal. I myself saw the Duke of Capriola, the Neapolitan Embassador, in his red heeled shoes, very busy at a great Beef Stake, a dish
I dare say he had never tasted in Italy. These dishes are as fashionable
among the ladies as the Gentlemen; the former, tho' they do not eat
many sweetmeats at Supper, pocket them & apples without Scruple.[33]

In 1770 the English Club, described by the historian of Catherine's
St. Petersburg, I. G. Georgy, as not only the oldest but also 'the
most exclusive and most respectable' of the capital's clubs, was
founded and meetings held in hired rooms in Galley Street.[34] It
was to become an important meeting-place for members of the
British community and Russian nobility; by the beginning of the
1790s it had moved to permanent quarters by the Moyka and had
a membership of 300, with a waiting-list of over 100 'candidates'.
Many of its members, including its founder, the merchant Francis
Gardner (1745–1813), were also members of a much more broadly
based but at that period in some of its activities a not dissimilar
organization—Freemasonry.

On 1 June 1771 the Lodge of Perfect Union in St. Petersburg
was granted its warrant or constitution by the British Grand
Master, Henry Somerset, Duke of Beaufort, and entered as Lodge
no. 414 on the Engraved Lists of the Grand Lodge of England.[35]
It seems to have begun its activities in 1770, at approximately the
same time as the English Club, and its first master was Joseph
Brigonzi, who resigned in June 1771 and was succeeded by the
merchant banker William Gomm, Jr.[36] Primarily on account of

[33] Cracraft, 'James Brogden in Russia', p. 233.
[34] *Opisanie rossiysko-imperatorskogo stolichnogo goroda Sankt-Peterburga i dostopamyatnostey v okrestnostyakh onogo* (St. Petersburg, 1794), pp. 629–30; M. I. Pylyaev, *Stary Peterburg* (St. Petersburg, 1887), pp. 216–17.
[35] John Lane, *Masonic Records 1717–1894*, 2nd ed. (London, 1895), p. 176; Robert Freke Gould, *The History of Freemasonry* (London, n.d.), iii. 215–16.
[36] 'Journal of the Lodge of Perfect Union from the 13th June 1771 to the 30th

the smallness of the rooms in which the Lodge gathered, it was decided to limit membership to twenty-four (later to thirty) and to invite no more than six visitors to any meeting. A predominance of British Masons is to be expected, but from the beginning the Lodge presents a markedly cosmopolitan composition in its officers, members, and visitors. In 1771–2 five of its officers, including the Master, were British (one was Samuel Swallow, the British Consul-General); the senior steward was Russian—Count Ivan Golovkin; the secretary, Dutch—François van Zanten; the orator, French—Sébastien de Villiers. Prominent Russian visitors included: Count A. P. Shuvalov, Count A. K. Razumovsky, V. I. Bibikov, L. A. Naryshkin, and I. P. Elagin, who was appointed Provincial Grand Master by the Grand Lodge of England in 1772. When further lodges under the English system were founded by Elagin, British Masons began to visit them. Besides the normal Lodge meetings, other functions were organized of a wider social nature. An important date in the Masonic calendar, the Feast of St. John, was celebrated in 1771 with 'a Concert Supper and Ball', attended by some eighty guests.[37]

II

In accordance with Peter the Great's edict which made St. Petersburg the trading centre of the Russian Empire, the British Factory was obliged in 1723 to move from Moscow to the capital. Twenty-five years earlier, the Russia Company, its parent body in London, had entered upon a new and distinctive phase of its history with the passing of an Act by Parliament which broadened its membership and reorganized its structure and practices.[38] Early in the reign of Catherine Britain's trading privileges which had been guaranteed by the commercial treaty of 1734 were

May 1772', f. 1. I am grateful to the United Grand Lodge of England for permission to consult this manuscript.

[37] Ibid., f. 2. See my 'British Freemasons in Russia during the Reign of Catherine the Great', *Oxford Slavonic Papers*, N.S. iv (1971), 43–72.

[38] Rudolph Robert, *Chartered Companies and their Role in the Development of Overseas Trade* (London, 1969), pp. 63–4.

successfully renegotiated by Sir George Macartney for another twenty-year period up to 1786. However, crises in the late 1770s and 1780s, such as the Armed Neutrality of 1780, created a difficult climate for the next re-signing of the treaty, which was effected only in 1793, when events in France were a deciding factor in the general climb of British fortunes in Russia. Nevertheless, throughout Catherine's reign, trade between Russia and England increased enormously and the port of Cronstadt was dominated by English merchant ships. Vast quantities of hemp, iron, linen, tallow, and other raw materials made their way to Britain, but it is rather the nature of the often far less substantial imports from Britain into Russia which is of more immediate interest.

In 1790 there were some twenty-eight merchant houses, usually consisting of two, three, or more partners, which were part of the British Factory;[39] the sale of imported goods was conducted at their warehouses and at the Customs House, but also at an increasing number of private shops and establishments. Up to 1782 foreign goods were usually sold at the Gostinyi dvor, the capital's official trading centre, but a relaxing of the regulations saw shops mushrooming throughout the city, frequently in parts of houses owned by the Russian nobility. In 1791 there seem to have been four establishments known as 'The English Shop', run by Messrs. Hoy and Bellis at 74, Malaya Millionnaya, by Samuel Hawkesford on the corner of Nevsky Prospekt near the Admiralty, by a Benjamin Hudson in the house of Countess Matyushkina, and by a Mr. Hubbard (later by Mrs. Sarah Snow), in Pervaya Liniya on Vasily Island.[40] There were numerous shops, yards, and houses where English saddlers, stonemasons, shoemakers, and watchmakers conducted their business.

In 1800 the Cambridge don, Edward Daniel Clarke, noted that 'whatever they [the Russians] possess useful or estimable comes to them from England. Books, maps, prints, furniture, clothing, hard-ware of all kinds, horses, carriages, hats, leather, medicine, almost every article of convenience, comfort, or luxury, must be

[39] Georgy, *Opisanie Sankt-Peterburga*, p. 219.
[40] *Sanktpeterburgskie vedomosti*, no. 26 (1 Apr. 1791), 463.

derived from England, or it is of no estimation.'[41] Although exaggerated, Clarke's indications of spreading British dominance over what might be called the Russian consumer market may be substantiated from the pages of the twice-weekly *Sanktpeterburgskie vedomosti* (*St. Petersburg News*), a particularly rich source of information on many aspects of British activity in the Russian capital. Almost all the items Clarke enumerates are offered for sale, with a deliberate emphasis on the adjective *angliysky* (in its three variant spellings); it was a campaign to 'buy British' that received critical support from Catherine's *ukaz* of May 1793, which, following the rupture in Franco-Russian relations, prohibited the import of French goods. There followed long lists of items, 'the greater part of which merely encourage excess and ruinous luxury and the others can be replaced by Russian products and articles or be obtained from places with which our subjects may carry on permitted and profitable trade'.[42] Not surprisingly, the newspaper was dominated thereafter until the end of Catherine's reign by advertisements of British goods and of the services offered by British tradesmen.

Georgy listed beer, cloth, horses, coal, and pottery as particularly prominent imports from Britain,[43] and all of them, with the exception of coal, became the necessities rather than the luxuries of the way of life of the fashionable Russian upper classes. Beer, fabrics, and pottery were not simply imported; they were produced also in Russia at manufactories established and run by the British. Archdeacon William Coxe opined that he had 'never tasted English beer and porter in greater perfection and abundance' than in St. Petersburg[44] and the demand was so great that three Englishmen set up their own breweries. The last of them was soon advertising in 1790 'for sale at the new English brewery in Nevskaya sloboda near the Small Okhta ferry locally brewed, English-type strong beer without added colouring, at 60 copecks a gallon'.[45] From about 1770, the year in which Josiah Wedgwood

[41] *Travels in Various Countries of Europe Asia and Africa*, i (London, 1810), 90.
[42] *Sanktpeterburgskie vedomosti*, no. 40 (20 May 1793), 893.
[43] Georgy, *Opisanie Sankt-Peterburga*, pp. 213–14.
[44] *Travels into Poland, Russia, Sweden and Denmark*, i (London, 1784), 433.
[45] *Sanktpeterburgskie vedomosti*, no. 12 (8 Feb. 1790), 180.

received his first order from Catherine, English pottery was much sought after;[46] some five years earlier the Gardner porcelain factory had been established at Verbilki near Moscow and was producing fine dinner services, china figures, etc.[47] In 1753 Richard Cozens (b. 1726), the son of Peter the Great's shipbuilder, set up a printed-cloth factory at Krasnoe Selo on the old Riga road and enjoyed a virtual monopoly in this field at the beginning of Catherine's reign.[48] Other factories and works were set up by Englishmen in St. Petersburg and its environs with varying degrees of success. Among the most enduring were the two sugar factories started in 1752 by John Cavanaugh (d. 1783) and controlled after his death by his son John,[49] and amongst the most short-lived, the vodka distillery set up around 1780 on her estate near Narva by one of the most colourful of British residents, the notorious Elizabeth Chudleigh, Duchess of Kingston (1720–88).[50] A flourishing factory in the heart of the city by the Moyka was the starch and indigo works of Gressen and Parland, launched in 1791 with an impressive advertising campaign which emphasized that their indigo was superior to the imported variety because of the quality of Russian materials and possessed the twofold advantage of being twice as effective and twice as cheap.[51] An official

[46] On Wedgwood's relations with Russia see: Eliza Meteyard, *The Life and Works of Josiah Wedgwood*, ii (London, 1865), 273–306; *The Selected Letters of Josiah Wedgwood*, eds. Ann Finer and George Savage (London, 1965), pp. 105–6, 144–6, 151–2, 161, 195, 299–300.

[47] The Francis Gardner who established the porcelain factory is not to be confused with the Francis Gardner who was the founder of the English Club and a St. Petersburg merchant. See Yury Arbat, *Farforovy gorodok* (Moscow, 1957), pp. 6–10. (Arbat does not completely unravel the complexities of the respective family trees.)

[48] William Richardson, *Anecdotes of the Russian Empire* (London, 1784), p. 68; Georgy, *Opisanie Sankt-Peterburga*, pp. 706–7; M. Tugan-Baranovsky, *Russkaya fabrika*, 7th ed. (Moscow, 1938), i. 53; P. G. Lyubomirov, *Ocherki po istorii russkoy promyshlennosti XVII, XVIII i nachala XIX veka* (Moscow, 1947), pp. 143, 255, 630.

[49] *Arkhiv knyazya Vorontsova*, xiii (Moscow, 1879), 475–6; Georgy, *Opisanie Sankt-Peterburga*, pp. 140, 162, 228. The Cavanaughs also seem to have had a linen mill: Cracraft, 'James Brogden in Russia', p. 240.

[50] *Dostopamyatnaya zhizn i osobennye priklyucheniya Gertsogini Kingston* (Moscow, 1793), pp. 228–9; Charles E. Pearce, *The Amazing Duchess* (London, n.d.), ii. 326; Elizabeth Mavor, *The Virgin Mistress* (London, 1964), pp. 186–7.

[51] *Sanktpeterburgskie vedomosti*, no. 4 (14 Jan. 1791), 56–7; Georgy, *Opisanie Sankt-Peterburga*, p. 230.

document of 1794 which listed the factories and works then operating in the city, attributed eleven out of a total of 162 to British owners: four out of the six existing rope factories belonged to British merchants (Elizabeth Vernon, John Claxton, David Gilmore, and Francis Gardner), but perhaps the most notable entry is of the iron works run by Francis Morgan and the brothers James and Charles Baird.[52] Charles Baird (d. 1843), who created a vast empire in nineteenth-century St. Petersburg, was one of the most famous of foreign industrial entrepreneurs in Russia; his major iron foundry began to operate in 1800, but already in the last years of Catherine's reign his enterprise and skill were much in evidence. He had come to Russia in 1786, one of the skilled Scottish technicians who accompanied Sir Charles Gascoigne, the director of the Carron iron works near Falkirk, and in 1792 joined forces with Morgan (whose daughter, Sophia, he married two years later).[53]

Francis Morgan himself was an outstanding representative of master craftsmen whom the Russians termed artists (*khudozhniki*) and one of the few Englishmen in this general category whom Georgy singled out. Characterized as 'a maker of optical, physical, mathematical and other instruments', he and James Jackson, 'an artist making musical instruments',[54] figure alongside the architect Charles Cameron and the engraver James Walker. Before entering into partnership with Baird, Morgan ran what was essentially a workshop in his own home facing the Kamenny Theatre, as well as having a room provided for him in the Academy of Arts, where he had taught since 1772. He was held in great esteem by members of the Academy of Sciences, particularly by Wolfgang Ludwig Krafft, the Professor of Experimental

[52] 'Vedomost sostoyashchim v S.-Peterburge fabrikam, manifakturam i zavodam 1794 goda sentyabrya — dnya', *Sbornik Imperatorskogo Russkogo Istoricheskogo Obshchestva*, i (St. Petersburg, 1867), 352–61. This does not record the factories, often far removed from the capital, which were owned or rented by British merchants stationed in St. Petersburg.

[53] *Russky biografichesky slovar* (Kraus rpt., New York, 1962), ii. 728; William L. Blackwell, *The Beginnings of Russian Industrialization 1800–1860* (Princeton, N. J., 1968), pp. 251–3.

[54] William Tooke, *The Life of Catherine II Empress of Russia*, 5th ed. (Dublin, 1800), iii. 331; Georgy, *Opisanie Sankt-Peterburga*, p. 572.

Physics, who recommended the purchase of his work as well as his employment in delicate repair work.[55] His most famous 'line' was thermometers—he was the supplier to the Academy of Sciences and seemingly to Catherine herself. Clarke visiting Tula, Russia's would-be Sheffield, comments on the general but poor imitation of English hardware and adds that

the best work we saw was in a manufactory of barometers, thermometers, and mathematical instruments; but the artificer was a German, who had been instructed under English masters in Petersburg. The late Empress bought up almost all the work which her English workmen completed. To encourage them, she ordered spectacles by the gross, and afterwards distributed them in presents. In her palaces she had thermometers in every window; and as the servants continually broke them, her workmen had sufficient demands to keep them in constant labour by providing a supply.[56]

The *St. Petersburg News* carries notices of numerous other English craftsmen offering their wares and skills; prominent are watchmakers, stonemasons, shoemakers—and saddlers. The Russian nobility's wish to imitate the life and habits of the English gentry was particularly noticeable in its cult of English horses and dogs. As early as 1740 the Empress Elizabeth purchased sixty-three pairs of dogs of different breeds from the Prime Minister, Robert Walpole, and put aside the house which had formerly belonged to Volynsky for her hunting hounds and their handlers, who included two highly paid Englishmen.[57] In Catherine's time it was considered as fashionable for the lady to own an English dog as it was for a gentleman to own an English horse. Horses, as Georgy noted, were a major import item and with them came considerable numbers of British grooms, ostlers, blacksmiths, and dealers. British saddlers provided and repaired the saddles and bridles; British blacksmiths repaired the imported English carriages and British coachmen drove them. Horse-racing in its turn became a fashionable sport and again the British were involved in its organization. A typical announcement in the *St.*

Petersburg News in 1792 gives details of a race organized by a certain Hughes and of the silver cup to be awarded to the winner.[58] British grooms and coachmen were frequently in the employ of noble Russian families;[59] so too were British valets, tutors, governesses, occupying positions usually associated with the French. Some advertised their ability 'to dress hair and shave beards', as well as their knowledge of languages other than English, although many offered instruction in the English language.[60] Some were undoubtedly of the quality of the Englishman who told Sir John Carr that 'in summer I be clerk to a butcher at Cronstadt, and in winter I teaches English to the Russian nobility's children',[61] but there is evidence that knowledge of English was slowly increasing. At the end of 1793 a certain John Elmore established a school 'where children of both sexes are taught in English reading, writing and arithmetic'.[62] However, French was obviously the language that the British were generally obliged to speak when foreigners were present, as Brogden notes,[63] and this applied to such institutions as the English Club and the Masonic Lodge.

III

The merchants, entrepreneurs, and craftsmen whose activities have been mentioned represent what might be termed the more independent sections of the British community. The grooms, valets, and governesses, however, are representative at the lower levels of the considerable number of British subjects in Russian

[58] *Sanktpeterburgskie vedomosti*, no. 53 (2 July 1792), 1032.

[59] The Grand Duke Paul had an English coachman named Clark, who 'had driven three kings': 'The Journal of Elizabeth 3rd Wife of the Ist Baron Dimsdale'. Cf. Clarke's amusing remarks on the fashion among the Moscow gentry in 1800: *Travels*, i. 143. Also M. S. Anderson, 'Some British Influences on Russian Intellectual Life and Society in the 18th Century', *SEER* xxxix, no. 92 (1960), 160–1.

[60] *Sanktpeterburgskie vedomosti*, no. 69 (27 Apr. 1790), 1122; no. 73 (10 Sept. 1790), 1186; no. 68 (26 Aug. 1791), 1378–9; no. 69 (27 Aug. 1792), 1340; no. 14 (18 Feb. 1793), 294.

[61] *A Northern Summer; or Travels round the Baltic, through Denmark, Sweden, Russia, Prussia, and part of Germany, in the year 1804* (London, 1805), p. 293.

[62] *Sanktpeterburgskie vedomosti*, no. 90 (11 Nov. 1793), 2058.

[63] Cracraft, 'James Brogden in Russia', p. 228.

service. It is precisely those men who were enlisted directly into
the service of the Empress at the higher levels whose names and
achievements are often, but not always, better known. It is sometimes admittedly difficult to draw a sharp distinction between
what may be termed the 'independent' and 'dependent' British.
Masters such as Morgan or the watchmaker Robert Hynam
(d. 1817)[64] had private workshops, although they were in a sense
also 'by appointment to her majesty'; Catherine's banker, Baron
Sutherland (1739–91), was also the head of a large merchant
house. Nevertheless, there are others who may be properly discussed in the 'dependent' category. Georgy indicated three groups
of Englishmen as particularly prominent in the capital: merchants,
sailors, and gardeners.[65] Merchants and naval officers would figure
in any list, but gardeners might be replaced or preceded by
architects, painters, doctors, or technical advisers.

The temptation to suppose that English gardeners were
numerous in St. Petersburg arises most probably from the obvious
vogue for 'the English garden' as well as from the fame of John
Bush, Catherine's head gardener and the only Englishman of this
profession named by Georgy. Many of the great houses of the
nobility had gardens similar to that belonging to Count Bezborodko on the Vyborg Side, 'completely in the English style,
with clumps of bushes, winding paths, streams, small islands,
arbours and suchlike'.[66] Although Bush (or Busch) is frequently
cited, only Gladys Scott Thomson seems to recognize that there
were two Bushes.[67] John Bush was the head of a noted nursery
garden at Hackney, the tenant of Jeremiah Bentham, Samuel's
and Jeremy's father, and went out with his family to serve
Catherine in the late 1770s.[68] It seems likely that he returned to

---

[64] Hynam was a talented mechanic who invented a machine for measuring the
speed of sound and made precise weighing scales. He was elected to a corresponding membership of the Russian Academy of Sciences in 1800. See *Protokoly zase-
daniy Konferentsii Imp. Akademii Nauk*, iii. 542, 693; B. L. Modzalevsky, *Spisok
chlenov Imp. Akademii Nauk 1725–1907* (St. Petersburg, 1908), p. 163; *Arkhiv
knyazya Vorontsova*, xxx (1881), 197; Herbert Swan, *Home on the Neva* (London,
1968), 47–59.

[65] Georgy, *Opisanie Sankt-Peterburga*, p. 165.

[66] Ibid., p. 159. See also ibid., pp. 162, 680, 698, 702, 710, 714, 722.

[67] *Catherine the Great and the Expansion of Russia* (London, 1947), p. 228.

[68] *Correspondence of Jeremy Bentham*, ii (London, 1968), 349–50.

England sometime after the death of his wife, Ann, in July 1785. His son Joseph remained in Russia at least until 1813, and it was he who produced the magnificent plan of the gardens and palace of Tsarskoe Selo in 1789.[69] The other outstanding English gardener of the period was William Gould, who was responsible for supervising the gardens at Peterhoff and laying out those of the Taurida Palace. He was Potemkin's head gardener and was acclaimed by Robert Ker Porter as 'the Repton of Russia'.[70] Bush and Gould apart, the other noteworthy if generally unnoted gardener was Mowat, summoned by the Duchess of Kingston in 1778 from Thoresby to supervise her Narva estates. She acquired for him the title of Imperial gardener, of whom there were eleven in the 1790s.[71] Commercial gardeners flourished in St. Petersburg particularly in the 1780s and 1790s, but they were in the main Germans, although there are indications of other English gardeners on noble estates around the capital.[72]

It was entirely in keeping with Catherine's own early predilection for the English style of gardening that John Bush was the first British artist in the more generally accepted sense of the word whom she persuaded to enter Russian service.[73] He was followed in 1779 by the Scot Charles Cameron (1746–1812), the first British architect in a field traditionally dominated by the Italians and the French. Cameron was given a studio in John Bush's apartments above the orangery at Tsarskoe Selo and in May 1784 married one of Bush's four daughters, Catherine (d. 1817).[74] Characterized by Catherine II in 1779 as 'écossais de

[69] According to the Register of the British Church, Joseph Bush married (i) Sarah Gordon in 1793 and (ii) Mary Ann Pitt in 1809. The last entry is of the birth of a son (his eighth child by the two marriages) in December 1812: MS. 11192B, ff. 136, 243, 268. His *Plan du jardin et vues de différens bâtimens de sa majesté impériale à Zarsko Zelo* was engraved by Tobias Miller.

[70] *Travelling Sketches in Russia and Sweden during the years 1805, 1806, 1807, 1808* (London, 1809), i. 58.

[71] *Correspondence of Jeremy Bentham*, ii. 207; Mavor, *The Virgin Mistress*, pp. 174–6.

[72] Georgy, *Opisanie Sankt-Peterburga*, p. 239; Coxe, *Travels into Poland, Russia, Sweden and Denmark*, i. 287.

[73] In 1772 Catherine had written to Voltaire: 'J'aime à la folie présentement les jardins à l'anglaise . . .' (quoted by Anderson, 'Some British Influences', p. 159).

[74] There is a considerable literature on Cameron as well as considerable controversy about details of his biography. See V. N. Taleporovsky, *Charlz Kameron*

nation, jacobite de profession, grand dessinateur nourri d'anti-
quité, connu par un livre sur les bains anciens',[75] he was to achieve
lasting fame for his work on the palaces at Tsarskoe Selo and
Pavlovsk; the height of his influence and authority came under
Catherine, although he was to remain and work in Russia over
thirty years. He was responsible for bringing to Russia a large
contingent of Scottish craftsmen and masons, who were housed in
Sophia, the administrative centre of Tsarskoe Selo which he had
designed and built, and instrumental in securing for Catherine the
services of the only other two British architects known to be
active during her reign.[76] Adam Menelaws (1756–1835) and
William Hastie, also both Scots, worked with Cameron at
Tsarskoe Selo and in the Crimea on the palace at Bakhchisaray.
Menelaws, whose activity is known to posterity primarily from
the account of Granville who met him over thirty years after
Catherine's death,[77] seems not to have been mentioned by
Catherine, although she praises Hastie to Baron Grimm in 1794
as 'un sujet très recommandable: il a fait des choses charmantes'.[78]
    It has been suggested that Cameron's good standing with
Catherine encouraged her to engage other British artists—sculptors, painters, engravers—and certainly the early 1780s saw a
number of them working in St. Petersburg. Her invitation to
Richard Brompton (1734–83) secured his release from debtor's
prison in London, but in Russia 'his silly vanity led him into a
pompous style of living, which entirely precluded any improvement in his circumstances',[79] and after his death on 1 January 1783

(Moscow, 1939); G. Lukomsky, *Charles Cameron* (London, 1943); Tamara Talbot
Rice, 'Charles Cameron, Architect to the Imperial Russian Court', *Charles Cam-
eron c. 1740–1812*, Catalogue of the Arts Council Exhibition ([London, 1967]), pp.
7–24; Isobel Rae, *Charles Cameron Architect to the Court of Russia* (London, 1971).
My dates for Cameron's birth and marriage are based on the Register of the British
Church: MS. 11192B, ff. 79, 261.

    [75] *SRIO* xxiii (St. Petersburg, 1878), 157–8.
    [76] For details about the Scottish workers, see Talbot Rice, art. cit., pp. 17–22.
Many of them returned to Scotland in the summer of 1790, as is evident from the
lists of departures in *Sanktpeterburgskie vedomosti.*
    [77] Granville, *St. Petersburgh*, ii. 90, 93–5, 487, 489, 507, 509, 511, 517.
    [78] *SRIO* xxii. 611–12. On Menelaws and Hastie, see A. A. Tait, 'British Archi-
tects in the Service of Catherine II', *Charles Cameron c. 1740–1812*, pp. 25–6.
    [79] Edward Edwards, *Anecdotes of Painters who have resided or been born in England*
(London, 1808), pp. 174–5. Edwards says that Brompton had no children, but he

his widow was obliged to call a meeting of his St. Petersburg creditors in an attempt to settle the considerable debts he had incurred.[80] Although his fellow-countrymen seem to have had little respect for him—Samuel Benthan called him 'a Great scoundrel'[81]—Catherine was delighted with the portraits he produced, particularly of the Grand Dukes Alexander and Constantine. Of some sixteen paintings by British painters said by Georgy to be in Catherine's collection in the Hermitage in 1792 three were by Brompton.[82] Brompton seems to have arrived in Russia early in 1780; in 1781 he was followed by the sculptor Thomas Banks (1735–1815), who like Cameron and Brompton had spent several years studying in Italy. He managed to sell Catherine a marble statue of Cupid which he had exhibited in London earlier in 1781 and although he remained in St. Petersburg for only one year he received further commissions, including one which reveals Catherine's sense of humour on the subject of the Armed Neutrality.[83]

In 1784 perhaps the most famous pair of British artists to work under Catherine, the mezzotint engraver James Walker (1748–1819?) and his young nephew, the painter John Atkinson (1775–1831), arrived in St. Petersburg. Walker had earned a considerable reputation for his portrait plates, especially for those after Romney, and his work in Russia fully justified his imperial appointment. Tooke lists 'among his excellent performances [. . .] the Empress in her travelling dress, Prince Potemkin, General Lanskoy, Admiral Greig';[84] unfortunately many of his plates were lost at sea off Great Yarmouth, when he retired from Russian service in 1802.[85] Atkinson, who had returned to England the

had three in Russia, and the names he gave them afford a further insight into his character: Alexandra, Katherina, Alexander Constantine (MS. 11192B, ff. 67, 70, 74).

[80] A. P. Myuller, *Byt inostrannykh khudozhnikov v Rossii* (Leningrad, 1927), p. 83.   [81] *Correspondence of Jeremy Bentham*, ii. 512.

[82] *SRIO* xxiii. 176, 206; Georgy, *Opisanie Sankt-Peterburga*, pp. 480–1. Catherine owned canvases by Sir Joshua Reynolds. See the interesting article by Frederick W. Hilles, 'Sir Joshua and the Empress Catherine', *Eighteenth-Century Studies in Honor of Donald F. Hyde* (New York, 1970), pp. 267–77.

[83] *Dictionary of National Biography*, i (London, 1908), 1053–4.

[84] Tooke, *The Life of Catherine II*, iii. 329.

[85] *Bryan's Biographical Dictionary of Painters and Engravers*, v (London, 1905),

previous year, had had as his pupil Aleksandr Pavlovich and was noted for two huge historical canvases which were hung in Paul's Mikhaylovsky Palace.[86] In England Atkinson and Walker began work in 1803 on their *Picturesque Representation of the Manners, Customs and Amusements of the Russians*, which was eventually published in three large volumes in 1812.

IV

An English traveller in Russia in 1775, John Richard, suggested that doctors 'were scarce and generally Scotch',[87] although in fact what he meant was that of the few doctors he had encountered one or two were Scots. Nineteenth-century historians of Russian medicine, despite their arbitrary omission of many of the graduates of Russian medical schools and preoccupation with the presence and achievements of foreign doctors, nevertheless provide statistics which reveal the degree of distortion in Richard's statement. Yakov Chistovich lists 511 doctors who were granted 'the right to practise' by the Medical College in the eighteenth century and of these only 19 are British. Fourteen of Chistovich's British doctors practised under Catherine, although only one appears in Aleksandr Nikitin's listing of the 69 most eminent physicians working during this same period.[88] Nikitin does include three more British doctors, but only one may be properly considered an addition to Chistovich's list. It is none the less true that twelve of Chistovich's doctors were either Scots or were trained at Edinburgh University, although only four (if we add the name of Matthew Halliday who is overlooked by both Nikitin and Chistovich) were in Russia when Richard was there.

Two of the four, John Rogerson (1741–1823) and Matthew

330; *DNB* xx. 523–4; D. A. Rovinsky, *Podrobny slovar russkikh graverov XVI–XIX vv.*, i (St. Petersburg, 1895), 129–45.

[86] N. P. Sobko, *Slovar russkikh khudozhnikov*, i, no. 1 (St. Petersburg, 1893), 254–6; *DNB* i. 695–6; *Russky biografichesky slovar*, ii. 353.

[87] *A Tour from London to Petersburgh, from thence to Moscow, and Return to London by way of Courland, Poland, Germany and Holland* (London, 1780), p. 35.

[88] Chistovich, *Istoriya pervykh meditsinskikh shkol v Rossii* (St. Petersburg, 1883), appendix X, pp. lxvi–ccclxvi; Nikitin, *Kratky obzor sostoyaniya meditsiny v Rossii v tsarstvovanie Imperatrisy Ekateriny II* (St. Petersburg, 1855), pp. 35–71.

Guthrie (1743–1807), are perhaps the best known of all the British doctors serving in Catherine's Russia.[89] Their careers in many respects run parallel courses, although Guthrie's was always overshadowed by Rogerson's and their fame is sealed not only by the numerous references to them which are found in the memoirs of the period but also by the anecdotes associated with their names. Rogerson after his appointment as Catherine's first physician in 1776 became the Empress's trusted friend during the last twenty years of her life and received from her numerous marks of favour, including an estate in White Russia; Guthrie served more humbly as physician to the Noble Cadet Corps from 1778, but achieved wider recognition for his work in scientific and cultural fields.

Nevertheless, the one British doctor whose name is invariably mentioned in histories of Catherine's reign, Thomas Dimsdale (1712–1800), did not practice in Russia, but paid two visits there, in 1768 to inoculate the Empress and Grand Duke Paul against smallpox and in 1781 the Grand Dukes Alexander and Constantine. Not only was Dimsdale created a Baron of the Russian Empire and Councillor of State but Britain received an accolade from the Metropolitan at the thanksgiving service for the Empress's recovery as 'that island of wisdom, courage, and virtue'.[90] Certainly thereafter Catherine, for all her general mistrust of doctors, was inclined to be less sceptical about the competence and methods of British practitioners, whose careers prospered accordingly.

Before Dimsdale left St. Petersburg in 1768, an inoculation hospital was set up under the supervision of Matthew Halliday (1732–1809) who had arrived in Russia in the reign of Elizabeth

---

[89] On Rogerson, see my 'John Rogerson—Physician to Catherine the Great', *Canadian Slavic Studies*, iv, no. 3 (1970), 586–93. On Guthrie, see my 'Arcticus and The Bee (1790–4): An Episode in Anglo-Russian Cultural Relations', *Oxford Slavonic Papers*, N.S. ii (1969), 62–76; and K. A. Papmehl, 'Matthew Guthrie— The Forgotten Student of 18th Century Russia', *Canadian Slavonic Papers*, xi (1969), 167–81.

[90] Richardson, *Anecdotes of the Russian Empire*, p. 36. Dimsdale's own account of his first visit to Russia is found in his *Tracts on Inocculation* (London, 1781). See also Tooke, *The History of Catherine II*, i. 363–72; V. A. Bilbasov, *Istoriya Ekateriny Vtoroy*, i (Berlin, 1900), 265–8; Frank G. Clemow, 'Medical Men and Matters in Russia in the XVIIIth Century', *Proceedings of the Anglo-Russian Literary Society*, xxviii (1900), 15–19.

and whose career is invariably confused with that of his son, William.[91] In 1771 Halliday was sent to Moscow to assist in containing an outbreak of the plague and was rewarded with a life's pension for his services. He continued to administer free inoculation to the poor at his hospital in St. Petersburg into the 1790s and inherited Dimsdale's mantle by inoculating Paul's other children, Grand Duke Nicholas and Grand Duchess Anna, for which he was promoted by an Imperial decree of 14/25 May 1799.[92] He apparently also established a merchant firm in the capital and bought the large island separated from Vasily Island by the River Smolenka, which was known up to the Revolution by a garbled version of his name: Goloday, and is now called The Island of the Decembrists.[93]

The eldest of Halliday's children, William, was born in St. Petersburg soon after 1766 and trained at Edinburgh, London, and Tübingen before entering Russian service in 1785. He spent many years in Rylsk in Kursk province before settling in Moscow in 1792, practising there before a disagreement over a new appointment led to his dismissal in 1797.[94] The example of a son following in his father's footsteps was also true of John Grieve (1753–1805), whose father, James Grieve, served almost thirty years in Russia under Anna and Elizabeth. Grieve, whose elder sister, Johanna, had married another famous Scots doctor, James Mounsey, who had retired in 1772 as the last holder of the post of *arkhiater* or head of the medical chancery created originally by Peter the Great, became in the mid 1780s first physician to Paul, who lavished honours on him during his own reign.[95] Grieve was one of the doctors who examined Paul's body after his murder; another was James Wylie (1765–1854), the Scottish surgeon whose fame belongs essentially to the reigns of Paul and

[91] Cf. Anderson, 'Some British Influences', p. 153.

[92] *Sanktpeterburgskie vedomosti*, no. 19 (7 Mar. 1791), 323; George Lefevre, 'Sketch of the Origin and Present State of Medicine, and of Medical Institutions in Russia', *British and Foreign Medical Review*, i (1836), 605; *Azbuchny ukazatel imen russkikh deyateley dlya russkogo biograficheskogo slovarya* (Kraus rpt. Vaduz, 1963), pt. 2, p. 619.

[93] Ibid., pt. 1, p. 129.

[94] Chistovich, op. cit., p. cxxxii.

[95] Ibid., pp. clii.

Alexander, but who served for six years under Catherine as under-surgeon in the Eletsky infantry regiment.[96] Wylie was only one of a number of British doctors attached to the Russian army and navy. Henry Holloway, an Englishman, served with the army in Finland from 1788 and in the following year George Cayley was appointed to the Vyborg field hospital; Robert Simpson was attracted into Russian service by Admiral Greig in 1774 and was on his flagship, the *Rostislav*, when the admiral died in 1788.[97] Simpson subsequently became chief physician at the naval hospital at Cronstadt. A further British doctor who came to Russia in the same year as Simpson, and whose activities are closely connected with the Russian navy, was Jonathan Rogers (1739–1811), author of *Pharmocopaea navalis Rossicae* (1806) and chief physician to the Admiralty under Alexander.[98]

V

The connections of Simpson and Rogers with the Russian navy are one aspect of the important role played by British naval officers during Catherine's reign. The tradition of British doctors in Russia stretched back to the days of Ivan the Terrible and was to continue almost unbroken up to the Crimean War; the naval tradition, by the very absence earlier of a Russian fleet, began in the time of Peter the Great. In the latter part of Peter's reign British masters replaced the Dutch as the principal builders of Russia's warships, in which an increasing number of British officers sailed; in the reigns of Anna and Elizabeth the British still loom large, particularly as shipbuilders.[99] When Catherine came to the throne, the Russian navy was nevertheless in bad order: the descendants of the great shipbuilders, Richard Cozens and Alexander Sutherland, had become merchants, although the venerable Lambe Yeames (1707–87), 'the great Shipbuilder at Peterburgh

[96] Ibid., p. cxxv; A. Francis Steuart, *Scottish Influences in Russian History* (Glasgow, 1913), pp. 131–2; W. Horsley Grant, *Russian Medicine* (New York, 1837), pp. 90–1.
[97] Chistovich, op. cit., pp. cxxxii–cxxxiii, clxxiv, ccxciv–ccxcv.
[98] *Russky biograficheskiy slovar*, xvi. 334; Nikitin, op. cit., p. 59.
[99] M. S. Anderson, 'Great Britain and the Growth of the Russian Navy in the Eighteenth Century', *Mariner's Mirror*, xlii (1956), 132–5.

an englishman but a thick skull',[100] was still at work; there were few officers left to command. Catherine followed the pattern set by Peter the Great of sending young cadets to England to receive training on British ships and of attracting large numbers of British officers into her own navy. (It is a pattern repeated with varying degrees of success during her reign in many fields, particularly the agricultural and technological.) Catherine was so successful in recruiting, with the blessing of the British government, competent and experienced officers, markedly different from 'the attained Jacobites and officers dismissed by court-martial of Peter the Great's day',[101] that in 1791 her ambassador in London could write: 'Notre service, depuis le chevalier Knowles et surtout par les soins de l'amiral Greigh, était sur le pied anglais.'[102]

Catherine's reign saw two important naval campaigns—against the Turks in 1769–73 and against the Swedes in 1787–90: the first is renowned in Russian naval history for the defeat of the Turkish fleet at Chesme in July 1770; the second for a number of actions, the most important of which was the battle of Hogland in July 1788. In both campaigns, British officers commanded a high percentage of the Russian ships involved and performed with heroism and skill, but from the beginning mutual recriminations between the British and Russian officers and considerations of national pride distorted assessments of their respective contributions. It is understandably difficult for any nation to attribute responsibility for its victories, if not for its defeats, to the actions of foreigners, yet there seems little doubt that British expertise and discipline in particular were essential to the ultimate success of both the Chesme and Hogland engagements. Of the nineteen ships engaged at Chesme, six, including two of the four fireships, were commanded by British officers (Samuel Greig, William Roxburgh, George Arnold, James Body, Robert Dugdale, and Thomas Mackenzie); five of the seventeen ships in the Russian line at Hogland were under British commanders (Francis Denison,

[100] *Correspondence of Jeremy Bentham*, ii. 209.
[101] Fred T. Jane, *The Imperial Russian Navy: Its Past, Present, and Future* (London, 1899), p. 728.
[102] *Arkhiv knyazya Vorontsova*, ix (Moscow, 1876), 198.

Samuel Elphinston, Stephen Scott, George Tate, and James Trevenen). There were many more English officers involved, particularly in later actions against the Swedes, and in 1788 the over-all commander of the Russian fleet was Greig, whilst in the earlier campaign, under the supreme command of Count Aleksey Orlov, Admiral Grigory Spiridov's seniority among the flag officers was disputed by Captain John Elphinston (1722–85). Both in the Mediterranean and in the Baltic British officers complained about the incompetence and insubordination of the Russians and their side of the story is preserved in contemporary written accounts. In 1772 an unashamed eulogy of Elphinston, written by an unknown fellow officer, was published in London and accepted predictably by the British press as 'a just representaation of facts'.[103] Greig's more balanced account of the same campaign was published much later,[104] and James Trevenen's papers about the Swedish actions only recently.[105]

This is not the place to examine all aspects of the British contribution to the Russian navy, which has received much attention in recent years from scholars.[106] One figure who necessarily appears in any such discussion but who has not received satisfactory treatment, is Admiral Sir Samuel Greig (1735–88). Although the main details of his biography are well known and oft repeated— he appears in both the *Dictionary of National Biography* and the *Biographical Dictionary of Eminent Scotsmen*, although unfortunately their corresponding Russian volume was never published[107]—the importance and breadth of his activities in Russia make him

[103] Review of *An Authentic Narrative of the Russian Expedition against the Turks by Sea and Land*, *Critical Review*, xxxiii (1772), 138.

[104] 'Sobstvennoruchny zhurnal kapitan-komandora (vposledstvii admirala) S. K. Greyga v Chesmensky pokhod', *Morskoy sbornik*, ii, no. 10 (1849), 645–60; no. 11, 715–30; no. 12, 785–827.

[105] *A Memoir of James Trevenen*, eds. Christopher Hill and R. C. Anderson, Publications of the Navy Records Society, ci (London, 1959).

[106] In addition to his already cited 'Great Britain and the Growth of the Russian Navy in the Eighteenth Century', see M. S. Anderson, 'Great Britain and the Russian Fleet, 1769–70', *SEER* xxxi, no. 77 (1952), 148–63; R. C. Anderson, 'British and American Officers in the Russian Navy', *Mariner's Mirror*, xxxiii (1947), 17–27; William C. Chapman, 'Prelude to Chesme', ibid., lii (1966), 61–76.

[107] *DNB* viii. 549–50; Thomas Thomson, *Biographical Dictionary of Eminent Scotsmen* (London, 1878), ii. 181.

much more than an outstanding naval commander. If Admiral
Sir Charles Knowles (1704?–77) represents Catherine's greatest
capture in terms of rank from the British navy,[108] Greig is an
example of a humble master's mate, whose talents blossomed
extraordinarily during twenty-five years in Russian service. He
was truly loved by Catherine, who heaped countless honours on
him, and when he died, his death occasioned national mourning
on an unprecedented scale.[109] The comte de Ségur, an impartial
observer, remarked: 'l'impératrice fit une perte qui lui coûta de
justes larmes; l'amiral Greig mourut. Chef actif, administrateur
éclairé, habile amiral, guerrier intrépide et modeste, il emporta au
tombeau l'estime de ses ennemis, et les regrets de tous ceux qui
l'avaient connu.'[110] Almost alone among British naval officers, he
enjoyed the respect of both his British and Russian comrades,
particularly of Count Aleksey Orlov. For Trevenan, he was 'my
third tutelar genius, my household god, my successor to Cook
and King'.[111]

He was invariably sought out by British tourists who visited
Cronstadt, where he was Governor and did much to reorganize
the port and plan, among other things, the new prison, which
brought the praise of John Howard.[112] Another important aspect
of his activity there which is frequently overlooked was his
founding of a Masonic Lodge, Neptune, in 1779.[113] Originally

---

[108] On Knowles, see 'Biographical Memoir of the Late Admiral Sir Charles
Knowles's Services in Russia, during the years 1770, 1771, 1772, 1773, and 1774',
Navy Chronicle, ii (1799), 265–82; Al. Sk., 'Admiral Nouls', *Morskoy sbornik*, ii
(1849), 509–27; *DNB* xi. 292–4.

[109] Greig's kinsman, Andrew Swinton, travelling to Russia to see him, arrived
in Revel shortly after the admiral's death. His book contains much information on
Greig in general and the funeral in particular: *Travels into Norway, Denmark, and
Russia, in the Years 1788, 1789, 1790, and 1791* (London, 1792), pp. 123, 135–6, 152–
88, 213–14. See also: *Opisanie pogrebeniya admirala Greyga* (n.p., n.d.); Nikolay
Struysky, *Elegiya v pamyat rossiyskogo imperatorskogo flota admirala Samoyla Karlo-
vicha Greyga* (Moscow, 1788).

[110] *Mémoires ou souvenirs et anecdotes*, iii. 350–1.

[111] *A Memoir of James Trevenen*, p. 156.

[112] *The State of the Prisons in England and Wales, with Preliminary Observations,
and an Account of some Foreign Prisons*, 3rd ed. (Warrington, 1784), p. 91. Other
British visitors to leave accounts of visits to Greig include William Coxe, Sir
John Sinclair, Samuel Bentham, Sir Gilbert Elliot, and Sir Richard Worsley.

[113] Tira Sokolovskaya, 'O masonstve v prezhnem russkom flote', *More*, viii
(1907), 216–52.

occupying the post of Senior Steward, he was Master from 1781 until his death, which brought special memorial services in at least two Lodges in the capital.[114] The Neptune Lodge was unique in that almost 90 per cent of its members were sailors, some British (Greig, Denison, Robert Wilson, Charles Newman, James Nasse) and the remainder Russian.[115]

Greig's interest in the improvement of the facilities of Cronstadt is linked with the activity of British technical advisers and workmen under contract to the Russian government. In July 1782 Catherine described to Grimm how during her recent visit to Cronstadt 'nous avons été voir la machine à feu qui vide le canal.'[116] This was the scientific wonder of the age, the fire-engine which was given honourable mention in Georgy's description of the sights of the capital and built in the period 1775–7 with British materials and by British experts.[117] Soon after their arrival in St. Petersburg in 1770, Admiral Knowles, whose brief was to supervise ship-building and naval administration, and his secretary, John Robison (1739–1805),[118] had turned their attention to Cronstadt and conceived the idea of replacing the antique windmills used to empty the dry docks by fire-machines imported from Britain. An order was eventually placed with the Carron factory, where Gascoigne with the help of John Smeaton had produced a 'Grand Plan for converting the Mill N into a Fire Engine for draining docks of Cronstadt',[119] but only after Robison had made unsuccessful attempts to bring his friend John Watt to Russia.[120] By the time the group of fourteen workmen under the chief engineer, Adam Smith, had arrived from Scotland late in 1774, Knowles and

---

[114] Two orations were delivered: *Am Grabe Greghs. B. F. v. D.* (St. Petersburg, 1788) and *Slovo na smert V. D. B. Greykha* (St. Petersburg, 1788). See A. N. Pypin, *Russkoe masonstvo XVIII i pervaya chetvert XIX v.* (Petrograd, 1916), pp. 162–6.

[115] Another British member was John Stranack, the master of a merchant ship frequently visiting Cronstadt; Russian members included two instructors in English from the Naval Academy.

[116] *SRIO* xxiii. 246.

[117] Georgy, *Opisanie Sankt-Peterburga*, p. 730.

[118] Robison was made inspector of the Naval Academy at Cronstadt in 1772 and returned to Scotland in 1773 to become Professor of Natural Philosophy. See *Biographical Dictionary of Eminent Scotsmen*, iii. 296–9; *DNB* xvii. 57–9.

[119] P. P. Zabarinsky, *Pervye 'ognevye' mashiny v Kronshtadtskom portu* (Moscow and Leningrad, 1936), pp. 47–50.

[120] Ibid., pp. 150–1.

Robison had left Russia and Greig, who had returned with Orlov from the Mediterranean in the middle of 1773, was now in command at Cronstadt. The first tests of the fire-engine were run in June 1777, five years before Catherine's official visit. The majority of the workmen then returned to Scotland, but Adam Smith remained to supervise the working of the machine and was joined in 1783 by his son, Alexander, who was himself a highly skilled engineer and produced an engine of his own design in 1792.[121]

Greig, who was most impressed by the original fire-engine, ordered another from the Carron works shortly before his death but this never became operational;[122] he was also instrumental in securing for Catherine the services of Gascoigne, the inventor of the gasconade or carronade, who arrived in Russia in May 1786. The Russians had been ordering large quantities of guns from the Carron Company in the 1780s as well as requesting machinery to cast the guns themselves and the engaging of Gascoigne to 'établir une fonderie d'artillerie ici en Russie' was a logical outcome.[123] Gascoigne's willingness to trade with the Russians had brought opposition from his associates, but approaches to Pitt and the British government and a ruling by the courts cleared the way both for continued exports to Russia and for Gascoigne's own departure.[124] As the historian of the Carron Company, R. H. Campbell, has observed, Gascoigne's Russian adventure has been attended by many, largely unfounded legends; but certainly the British community in Russia ostracized for a time both Gascoigne and his sponsor, Greig,[125] and Clarke, who met him in 1800, was voicing the opinion of many of his countrymen in calling him an 'outlaw'.[126]

Gascoigne prospered in Russia, 'where he has a good income,

[121] Zabarinsky, op. cit., pp. 76–7, 124–30. Three of the Scots apparently went to work at Taganrog on the Black Sea, but 'when they came there, there was no work for them to do': *Correspondence of Jeremy Bentham*, ii. 228–9.

[122] Zabarinsky, op. cit., p. 75.

[123] Letter of Greig to Count S. R. Vorontsov, 26 Feb. 1786; *Arkhiv knyazya Vorontsova*, xix. 339.

[124] Ibid., pp. 340–2.

[125] *Carron Company* (Edinburgh and London, 1961), p. 151.

[126] *Travels in Various Countries of Europe Asia and Africa*, i. 256.

lives in more splendour, and has greater connections than he can ever have in this country'.[127] By 1787 he was engaged in reorganizing after the Carron system the Aleksandrovsky cannon works at Petrozavodsk on Lake Onega and the nearby Konchezersky foundry; in 1789 he set up a branch of the Petrozavodsk works at Cronstadt on Kotlin Island, which was designed to make use of the old cannon there and to supply the immediate needs of the fleet.[128] Both at Cronstadt and Petrozavodsk Gascoigne was aided by teams of skilled Scottish workmen.[129]

The impressive achievements of Gascoigne obviously induced Catherine to engage other British specialists, although she was not always so fortunate with the results. In 1794 a certain Thomas English signed a four-year contract to reorganize the casting of guns at the Arsenal in St. Petersburg and at Bryansk and to make the Russian artillery comparable with the best in Europe. English failed dismally to live up to the reputation as 'one of the leading and most skilled masters in his field' and his contract was not renewed.[130]

Inevitably, some of the British engaged in Russian service were unable to justify the high hopes placed upon them. If Catherine's reign was 'a time when almost everyman of Genius in Europe is offering at the Shrine of this most Illustrious of Sovereigns',[131] it is understandable that the less endowed were also eager to make their fortunes there. What is more surprising is that so many of them were able to bluff their way into positions of responsibility and influence. A particularly colourful British example was Major Semple, about whom Jeremy Bentham wrote in 1786: 'Major

---

[127] Letter of Matthew Boulton to Samuel Garbett, 1803, quoted in Campbell, *Carron Company*, p. 153. See also the description by Mary Kynnersley, Baroness de Bode, of the life led by the Gascoignes in Petrozavodsk: William S. Childe-Pemberton, *The Baroness de Bode 1775–1803* (London, 1900), pp. 269–70.

[128] M. Mitelman, B. Glebov, and A. Ulyansky, *Istoriya Putilovskogo zavoda (1801–1917)* (Moscow, 1961), pp. 11–12.

[129] Ivan German, *Opisanie petrozavodskogo i konchezerskogo zavodov, i proizvodimogo pri onykh litya pushek i snaryadov* (St. Petersburg, 1803).

[130] V. Rodzevich, *Istoricheskoe opisanie S-Peterburgskogo Arsenala za 200 let ego sushchestvovaniya 1712–1912 gg.* (St. Petersburg, 1914), pp. 138–41. (Rodzevich, incidentally, is a Russian Colonel Blimp of the first water.)

[131] Letter from Carron Company to John Smeaton in 1773: Campbell, *Carron Company*, p. 74.

Semple took in every body at Petersburg except Sam [Samuel Bentham] who suspected him from the first and cautioned Sir J. H. [Sir James Harris, the British Ambassador] against him but in vain.'[132] Semple, a Scottish soldier-of-fortune, had met the Duchess of Kingston at Calais prior to her departure for St. Petersburg in 1779 and preceded her to Russia, where an impressed Harris introduced him to Potemkin. Potemkin appointed Semple a captain in the Russian army and took him first to Warsaw and then to the Crimea; he is even said to have followed Semple's suggestions for changes both in Russian uniforms and forms of manœuvre. In Russia Semple plagued the Duchess of Kingston, whose god-daughter he married, with demands for money and with threats of violence. He ran up enormous debts before vanishing from Russia to write his autobiography. In the year Bentham mentioned him, his exploits were immortalized in an exposé entitled *Memoirs of Major Semple, the Northern Imposter and Prince of Swindlers*, and it has been suggested that much later Thackeray was to use him as a partial model in the creation of Barry Lyndon.[133] The Benthams were personally involved with yet another charlatan, called Logan Henderson, whom Jeremy Bentham brought with him from Paris to become manager of the botanical garden Potemkin wished to set up in the Crimea. Henderson was accompanied by the Misses Kirkland, said to be his nieces, although the elder was his mistress. Henderson signed a thirteen-year contract and the elder Miss Kirkland was engaged as director of Potemkin's model dairy, but within months of their appointment they were being denounced as 'shameless imposters' to Potemkin.[134]

Semple, Henderson, even the Duchess of Kingston, in her search not for fortune but for attention in her years of decline, are essential but minor figures in the general picture of British activity in Russia, which remains impressive in its variety and quality. Outside the capital the British impact was still minimal,

---

[132] *Correspondence of Jeremy Bentham*, ed. Ian R. Christie, iii (1971), 513.

[133] Pearce, *The Amazing Duchess*, ii. 301–16; Mavor, *The Virgin Mistress*, p. 184; Steuart, *Scottish Influences*, p. 129.

[134] *Correspondence of Jeremy Bentham*, iii. 413–14.; E. I. Druzhinina, *Severnoe Prichernomore v 1775–1800 gg.* (Moscow, 1959), p. 136.

and limited to what might be termed small spheres of influence in Moscow, the Ukraine, and Crimea, but in St. Petersburg itself the British had established themselves as an influential minority, enjoying considerable privileges and occupying certain positions of prominence and influence, which they used in the main to their own and Russia's mutual advantage. The Petersburg British remained predictably very much a community within a community but in no sense isolated from any aspect of the social and business life of the capital. As merchants, bankers, entrepreneurs, craftsmen, artists, architects, doctors, officers, administrators, and technical experts, they made a significant and enduring contribution to Catherine's Russia.[135]

[135] It has not been possible within the limits of this study to deal with the activities of British diplomats at Catherine's Court or to characterize the ever-growing number of British visitors and tourists, who were responsible for many of the contemporary published and unpublished accounts. It is hoped that these subjects, together with more detailed treatment of the aspects of British activity already outlined, will form the basis of a future book.

Part Four
The Arts

1. *Captain Marko Martinović teaching Russian 'boyars' navigation* (oil painting)

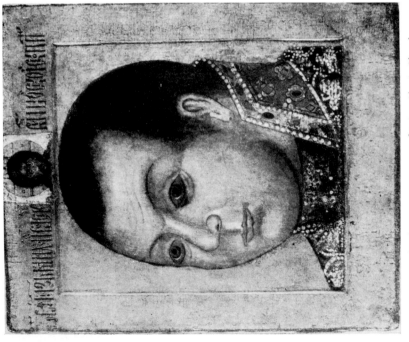

3. A detail of the silver effigy of *The Tsarevich Dimitry* by Gavriil Ovdokimov

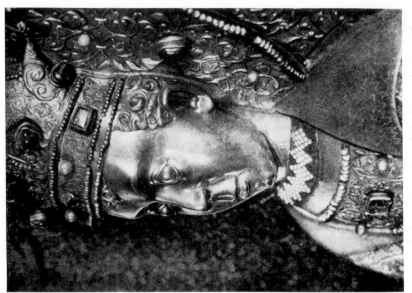

2. Commemorative icon—a *parsunya*—of *Prince Skopin Shuysky*

4 and 5. Architectural details appearing in the background of an icon of *The Metropolitan Aleksey* tentatively attributed to Georgy Zinovev

6. Peter the Great's cottage in Leningrad, close to the fortress of Sts. Peter and Paul

7. Peter the Great's summer palace in Leningrad, as seen from the Fontanka Canal

8. The west front of Peter the
   Great's pavilion of Marli at
   Peterhof

9. Peter the Great's Cabinet of Curios, now the U.S.S.R. Academy of Sciences, Leningrad

10. Icon of *The Virgin in the Heavenly Garden* by Nikita Pavlovets

11. Peter the Great's sketch for the palace, canal, and grounds at Peterhof

12. The central block of Rastrelli's Catherine Palace at Tsarskoe Selo

13. Detail of Rastrelli's Catherine
Palace at Tsarskoe Selo

14. Rastrelli's model for the Convent of Smolny, 1749

15. The Pavlovsk Palace by Charles Cameron

16. The Arabesque Room by Charles Cameron in the Catherine Palace at Tsarskoe Selo

17. The Hermitage Theatre, Leningrad, by Quarenghi

18. A sofa designed by Rastrelli for the Empress Elizabeth's apartments at the Catherine Palace at Tsarskoe Selo, and executed by Russian craftsmen

19 (above right). *A View of St. Petersburg* by Aleksey Zubov, 1727

20 (below right). *Captured Swedish Frigates at St. Petersburg* by Aleksey Zubov, 1722

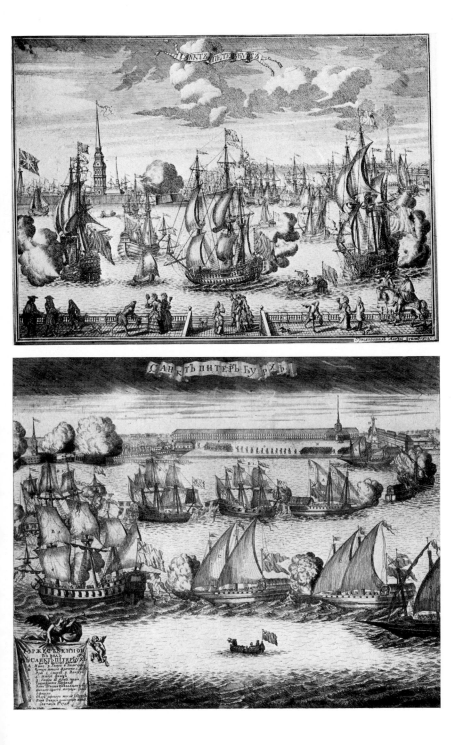

22. Frontispiece to the first Russian edition of Fontenelle's *Entretiens sur la pluralité des mondes*

21. Broadsheet of a Dandy and a Lady, mid-eighteenth century

24. Detail of Rastrelli's bust of *Peter the Great*, 1723

23. *A Peasant Girl Wearing National Dress* by I. Argunov, 1784

25. *The Empress Anna Ivanova and her Blackamoor* by Rastrelli, State Russian Museum, Leningrad

26. *The Princess Elizabeth* by Ivan Nikitin

27 (right). Icon of *The Virgin and the Tree of Russia's Sovereigns* by Simeon Ushakov, 1668

28. *Sarah Fermor* by Vishnyakov

29. *Two pupils of the Smolny Institute* by D. G. Levitsky

31. *The Empress Catherine walking in the Park at Tsarskoe Selo* by Borovikovsky

30. *A pupil of the Smolny Institute* by D. G. Levitsky

32. A decorative panel by A. Belsky, 1754

33. A decorative panel by Firsov

34. *The Empress Elizabeth* by Groot

36. *Count A. Orlov* by Shubin, 1771

35. *Diderot* by D. G. Levitsky

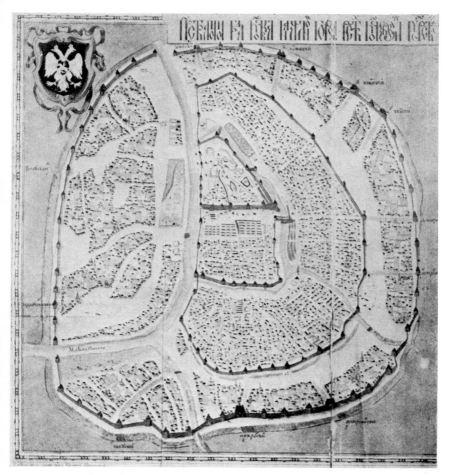

37. Moscow in the mid-seventeenth century

38. Moscow in the mid-eighteenth
century

39 (below). St. Petersburg in the
mid-eighteenth century

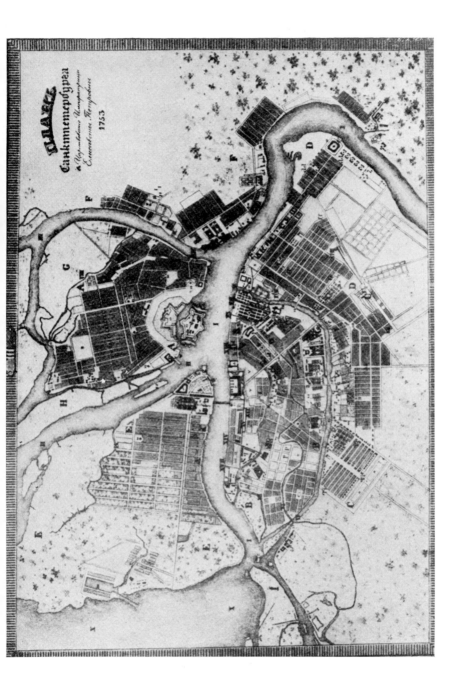

40. Plan of the City Tver

41. Plan of Ostashkov showing the eighteenth-century street plan superimposed on a diagram of the existing street plan (dotted line)

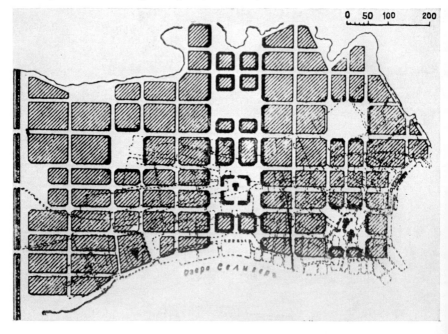

TAMARA TALBOT RICE

10 The Conflux of Influences in Eighteenth-Century Russian Art and Architecture: a Journey from the Spiritual to the Realistic

W HILST few would contest that the arts express all that is noblest in mankind, fewer still will underestimate the part played by society in the moulding of style. Broadly speaking, apart from the prosperous inhabitants of the independent, republican city-state of Novgorod, prior to the sixteenth century very few boyars or merchants could afford to commission works of art. The Church and Crown were virtually alone in being able to do so, the importance of each of these patrons varying according to the economic and political conditions prevailing at any given period. Partly as a result of this, but chiefly owing to its devotion to its religion, the nation was content unquestioningly to subscribe during five centuries or so to the aesthetic standards sponsored by its rulers and prelates. As the sixteenth century drew to its close that attitude showed signs of changing. The break coincided with the need to rebuild a large section of Moscow following the devastations caused there by the Swedish and Polish invaders and the great fire of 1612. By that time the architectural styles in vogue in Western Europe were beginning to make themselves known to Moscow, the great expansion of the country's foreign trade was contributing to the rise of a prosperous merchant class, and the suffering endured during the Time of Troubles combined in spurring the Muscovites to take an interest in politics and to turn their thoughts in new directions. These developments produced a dramatic change of outlook in the capital at the very time when builders and artists were at last finding employment among a cross-section of the town's more prosperous inhabitants.

Among the new ideas attracting the attention of Moscow's

intellectuals at the end of the sixteenth century the concept of man as a terrestrial being led them also to become interested in man's earthly setting. In that climate domestic architecture prospered as it had not done since the Mongol invasion whilst, from as early as the second quarter of the seventeenth century, the more experimentally minded of the religious artists were beginning to produce paintings in which they attempted to blend the canons of Western naturalism with the old iconic tradition. This could best be done by means of portraiture and the works being created in this new manner came to be called 'parsunyas'. The style is well represented by the portrait of Prince Skopin-Shuysky,[1] painted around 1630, some twenty years after his death (Pl. 2). In that year the Court artist Gavriil Ovdokimov combined artistry with remarkable psychological understanding when fashioning the silver effigy of the young Tsarevich Dmitry[2] (Pl. 3). In the course of a couple of decades these iconic portraits evolved in accordance with Ovdokimov's views and developed into the primitive yet naturalistic representations displaying considerable psychological understanding to which the term *parsunya* should rightly apply.[3]

The naturalistic art of the West was making itself increasingly widely known in Moscow by means of the books illustrated by woodcuts which were being imported from abroad, expecially from Germany and the Low Countries. The Russians who were able to visit the West, although few in number, encouraged the trend, stimulating the demand for paintings of a naturalistic kind and directing the attention of many artists to problems of a technical nature, to the role of aesthetics in art,[4] and to the need to justify naturalism in religious art. At much the same time the Baroque style in architecture was reaching Moscow, also at

---

[1] V. I. Antonova and N. B. Mneva, *Gosudarstvennaya Tretyakovskaya Gallereya; Katalog drevnerusskoy zhivopisi* (Moscow, 1963), vol. ii, no. 854, pl. 128; also the late seventeenth-century Muscovite icon of Maxim the Greek, no. 775, pl. 101.

[2] I. E. Grabar (ed.) and others, *Istoriya russkogo iskusstva*, U.S.S.R. Academy of Sciences, iv (Moscow, 1958), 337.

[3] Ibid. iv. 455, for the *parsunya* of Patriarch Nikon.

[4] Semeon Ushakov, *Slova k lyubotshchatelyam ikonogo pisanya* (1667); and G. Filimonov, *Semeon Ushakov i sovremennaya emu epokha russkoy ikonopisi* (Sbornik na, 1873).

second hand, this time by means of the master builders who had encountered it in the border lands of Poland, Belorussia, and the Ukraine. The successful construction of such buildings naturally depended upon exact calculations, careful planning, and precise delineation; in fact it required the presence of architects using architectural drawings as their guides, yet neither such trained men nor such drawings were to be found in Moscow before the closing decades of the seventeenth century. Only then did some men emerge able to work in the new manner. In architecture their presence led to the substitution of rooms of various shapes in place of the traditional square and rectangular ones, and to the adoption of more elaborate ground-plans and elevations for the buildings which contained them; in painting their presence was responsible for the introduction into the background of some icons (Pls. 4 and 5) of carefully delineated contemporary structures. In the final decades of the seventeenth century this attitude culminated in the erection of statues of foreign origins on a building's roof, encouraging the secularization of religious architecture, as in the case of the Church of the Virgin of the Sign at Dubrovitsy,[5] built between 1690 and 1709.

Although the innovators were few in number and their ideas were sternly resisted by the Church and a vast body of traditionalists, yet, in the 1670s, they included no less a person than Tsar Aleksey. Unfortunately, however, the modernists lacked unity, a sense of direction, a clearly defined goal. Instead of banding together in an attempt to evolve a specific style by blending native traditions with Western naturalism, each patron expected the artist of his choice to comply with his own reactions to the two contradictory trends. The results were often so confused that the experiments carried out by the Westernizers created little more than a ripple and the innovations never expanded into a swell.

When Peter cut the furrow which his architects and artists were to tread he put an end to the existing anomalies but he also prevented any of the existing trends from developing into independent styles. Since the Tsar depended upon his builders for the

<hr />

[5] Tamara Talbot Rice, *A Concise History of Russian Art* (London, 1965), ill. 114.

precise, visible form of his new capital, the town of his dreams, he concerned himself first with architecture. During the five years which elapsed between his return to Russia from his first foreign tour and the laying in 1703 of St. Petersburg's foundation stone, Peter had thoroughly assimilated the impressions which had come to him as a result of all that he had seen when abroad. As a result, although he never succeeded in completely dissociating himself from his Muscovite background, his ideas were so definite that he had no difficulty in imposing them on all the architects and artists whom he employed, whether foreign or Russian. Proceeding without a plan to guide him in the task of building his new capital he never faltered, his discernment enabling him both to establish its outlines and to provide the country with the basis of a new, Westernized style which he invested with the forcefulness and vitality essential to any truly national and creative school of art.

Peter's first foreign tour had taken him to Prussia, Holland, and England, and thence to Vienna by way of Dresden and Prague, followed by a stop at Cracow, on his return journey. Although unrest among his Streltsy had obliged him to cancel his proposed visit to Venice, he was able to see many fine buildings when passing through the towns lying on his route. In Berlin he may well have seen the plans for the Schloss which Andreas Schlüter was to build there between 1698 and 1706. In the Hague stood Pieter Post and Jacob van Campen's exquisite Mauritzhuis (1633), in Amsterdam van Campen's town hall (begun 1648), but both were probably by then being eclipsed in Dutch eyes by Justus Vingboon's Trippenhuis (1662) and by the splendid houses being built in serried ranks along Amsterdam's three major canals, the Heerengracht, Kiesergracht, and Prinzengracht. Similarly in London admiration for Inigo Jones's splendid Banqueting Hall (completed 1622) must have been veering towards the numerous new buildings which Christopher Wren was erecting in the City. There is no record to tell us whether the Tsar inspected St. Paul's Cathedral or any of the smaller City churches such as St. Vedast with its spirelike tower, but he did visit the King at Kensington Palace, recently enlarged by Wren to take the place of the unfinished Palace of Whitehall. Peter must also have seen Inigo Jones's Queen's House at Greenwich (1616) since he went there several times to inspect the Naval Hospital. In Dresden, where the Zwinger and Frauenkirch had still to be built, the Tsar appears to have had time only to visit the museum, which had to be specially unlocked at midnight and kept open till dawn to enable him to do so. In Vienna Fischer von Erlach had scarcely begun work on any of his vast structures and few of the buildings which Peter could have seen were of recent date, whilst in Cracow the majority dated from medieval times. Of all that he had seen on his travels it was the Dutch school that pleased Peter most; yet even in Holland he had been oppressed by the height of the rooms and had suffered from sleeplessness in beds lacking a canopy.

Peter's love of Holland never wavered and he missed few opportunities of stressing the similarities linking St. Petersburg's climate and environment to those of Holland. Nevertheless he did not employ a Dutch architect until 1720 and never used a Dutch gable. The three foreign architects Peter made most use of in and around his new capital were in turn an Italian, a German, and a Frenchman. The Italian Domenico Tressini (1670–1734) was to remain the longest in his service and it was on him that the Tsar came to depend most. Tressini was born in the province of Lugano, but before coming to Russia in 1705 he had learnt the technique of building on boggy subsoils in Copenhagen. The German, Andreas Schlüter, came to St. Petersburg in 1714, disgraced in the West by the collapse of his adventurously designed Berlin Münzturm, but died there within a year. The third eminent architect, the Frenchman Leblond, was the one on whom Peter must have based his highest hopes, yet he too was to die in Russia after only three years, in his case of smallpox. Thus it fell to Tressini, although perhaps the least talented of the three, to prove the most useful to the Tsar. From the first Tressini showed himself both willing and able to understand Peter's wishes, to grasp his ideas, and to express them in a manner which conformed to the Tsar's taste. Working harmoniously together the Tsar and Tressini quickly established the plans to be adopted for the three distinct types of houses to be built for Petersburg's first inhabitants, those prescribed for the nobility, the well-to-do, and the poor. Even when the Tsar was fully occupied in waging wars and administering affairs he found time personally to examine every constructional enterprise of importance undertaken in or near St. Petersburg. Each major building therefore clearly displays his imprint and countless documents survive to testify to the degree of his involvement. Even the idea of housing the country's Twelve Administrative Colleges under a single roof in what seemed, when seen from the outside, to consist of twelve separate terraced houses of identical appearance, originated with the Tsar, although it fell to Tressini to solve the problem of doing so.

Peter spent his first years in St. Petersburg living in a cottage, the wooden and clay walls of which were painted on the outside to resemble masonry (Pl. 6), but in 1710 Tressini began to build his first real residence, the Summer Palace (Pl. 7). Its lines closely conformed to those of the standard nobleman's house, scarcely exceeding it in size, but Schlüter adorned it with low-relief sculptures. He did not live to execute his designs but they were inserted as planned at its entrance and between the two rows of windows along its façades. Schlüter chose mythological scenes for the purpose, some of which are clearly allegorical in content. The building's ground-plan, like those of Tressini's model houses, adhered to the rectangular shape which had been followed in Russia during many centuries, but the stressing of the centre of each front was an innovation which was to become a characteristic of the Petrine style. In the Summer Palace it was achieved both by the placing of its entrance door and by the siting of a dormer window above it, and also by slightly increasing the space dividing the two centre windows of each front. In 1711, when building St. Petersburg's first Winter Palace,[6] Tressini achieved a similar effect by slightly projecting the building's central block; this he balanced by similar projections at each end so that the building's shape became less that of an E than of a rectangle lacking a side. Four years later a similar ground-plan was used by Braunstein for the first Palace of Peterhof,[7] one which probably

[6] I. E. Grabar, op. cit. v. 73.   [7] Ibid., p. 107.

followed a design of Schlüter's. Later still Braunstein was also to stress the centres of Peterhof's pavilions of Marli (1720–4) (Pl. 8) and the Hermitage,[8] using balconies and roof projections for the purpose.

The style which Peter evolved for St. Petersburg, largely by means of Tressini's help, is often described as the Dutch Baroque yet both these features appear in it so much transformed that it would be better to define it as the Petrine. The main entrance to the Fortress of SS. Peter and Paul which Tressini built in 1717/18 ranks as St. Petersburg's first Baroque monument. Baroque elements are also in evidence in the tower of the fortress's cathedral,[9] which was begun by Tressini in 1712, but not completed till 1733. Certain details in the tower resemble some incorporated by Zarudny in the church which he built in Moscow between 1704 and 1707 for Prince Menshikov, and which is therefore known as the Menshikov Tower.[10] The roots of both are surely to be sought in Moscow for, as in the bell tower of Ivan Veliky in the Kremlin,[11] each of their storeys is slightly set back. The resemblance linking the decorations of the tower of the SS. Peter and Paul Cathedral to those on Zarudny's church may be fortuitous, yet it is wise to bear in mind that Zarudny employed Italian masons when building his church and Italian plasterers when decorating its interior. He flanked its main front at ground level with buttresses resembling half an S in shape; a similar buttress, although it is plain instead of decorated and curls inwards instead of outwards, is to be found on either side of the front of the second and third tiers of the SS. Peter and Paul tower. There the second tier contains in addition a French window which is rounded at the top and surmounted by a pediment, the latter being replaced by a lintel in the tower's third tier. The structure is surmounted by a spire which dominates the city; its height and slenderness are a reflection of Peter's genius and indomitable energy. Measuring a third of the tower's total height the spire seems to pierce the sky.

Until his return to Russia in 1717 from his second visit to the

---

[8] Ibid., p. 109.   [9] Ibid., p. 87.
[10] Ibid., p. 36.   [11] Ibid., p. 311.

West Peter's domestic and private buildings remained small, their character burgherlike, their appearance sober and unostentatious. They differed in these respects alike from the flamboyant mid-seventeenth-century Muscovite style and also from the ornate characteristics in the West's contemporary architecture. However, whilst staying in Paris the Tsar must surely have seen Jules Hardouin Mansart's recently completed Place Vendôme (1696–1708), Delamair's Hôtel Soubise (1705–9), and even if he was unable to inspect Vau's masterpiece, the Chateau of Vaux le Vicomte (1657–61), he must surely have seen pictures of it since certain of its features seem to reappear in some of Peter's later buildings.[12] The Tsar had ample opportunity to examine Versailles for he went there more than once to visit the Regent in order to discuss the question of the marriage of his youngest daughter, Elizabeth, to a French royal prince, even to the young King of France, and also that of a political alliance. He had by then already secured the services of the French architect Leblond. The latter in fact reached St. Petersburg shortly before the Tsar returned to his capital. They met there in 1717, the year marking a new phase in Petersburgian architecture.

Peter's preference for small buildings was still able to make itself felt in the relatively modest dimensions of his Kunstkamera or Cabinet of Curios (Pl. 9). It was designed for him by Mattarnovi in 1718 but completed well after the Tsar's death by Zemtsov, Herbel, and Chiavery to become Russia's first museum. But Peter's visit to France had nevertheless convinced him of the advantages to be derived from impressing foreigners and from now onwards he showed an acute awareness of the importance of making a display. His ideas of what he considered fitting for Russia changed, leaving him determined to adorn St. Petersburg and its neighbourhood with buildings which would hold their own with the West's not only in beauty, but also in size.

Since its foundation in 1703 St. Petersburg had developed in a haphazard manner, centring on its two focal points, the Fortress of SS. Peter and Paul on the Neva's north bank and the Admiralty on its southern, with its main residential quarter situated on the

---

[12] I. E. Grabar, op. cit. v, facing p. 36.

Island of St. Basil. Although Tressini had begun to dig some of
the canals which were to serve as the district's thoroughfares
(they were later converted to streets), no plans had been drawn up
to establish the town's layout or to determine its future form. In
accordance with custom the homes of the working classes had
been grouped according to the trades and callings of their owners.
Leblond commented unfavourably on the absence of a town
plan and on the Tsar's habit of employing numerous architects
without entrusting one with over-all control.[13] Peter accepted
his criticisms and appointed him his architect in chief, assigning
the making of a plan for St. Petersburg priority over other tasks.
It is difficult to imagine Peter's feelings when that ardent rationalist found the distinguished Frenchman's coldly logical, symmetrical proposals too impersonal to be accepted in their entirety.
Leblond's plan was pedantic and so rigid that it made no provisions for future growth, and was therefore also impracticable.
The Tsar must have displayed unusual tact when dealing with his
architect in chief for there is nothing to suggest that Leblond felt
slighted by Peter's reactions to his plan. Although the Tsar let it
fall into abeyance he was able to retain Leblond's services and
goodwill till the latter's death in 1720. He employed Leblond and
the French craftsmen, the majority of them decorators,[14] who
had been brought to Russia by Leblond, chiefly at Peterhof, yet
even there the Tsar often preferred to adopt Mattarnovi's suggestions rather than Leblond's, as he was also to do in the case of
the Summer Gardens in St. Petersburg.

St. Petersburg's main artery, the Nevsky Prospekt or Perspective, had been made in 1712 in order to connect the capital to the
road leading to Novgorod, and work on the Voznesensky Prospekt was put in hand in 1715. Little else was undertaken in the
capital in Leblond's lifetime. At his death the Tsar decided to
adopt Eropkin's suggestion that the town's main centre be transferred from the Island of St. Basil to the Neva's southern bank
and he also decided upon the siting of the last of the three major
roads radiating from the Admiralty, the Gorokhovaya. It was
not, however, completed till 1740. These radiating perspectives—

[13] Ibid., p. 104. [14] Ibid., p. 104.

France's *pattes d'oie* layout—are as characteristic of early St. Petersburg as vistas are of eighteenth-century Western Europe. Although the *pattes d'oie* disposition seems to have been thought of by Louis XIII's gardener, Jean Boyceau,[15] it was not unknown to seventeenth-century Moscow, at any rate at its Court, for Tsar Aleksey had three walks cut on that principle in the large garden which he made at his country house of Izmaylovo, using its main entrance as its axis. Rectangular gardens with symmetrical layouts such as were to be found in Holland must, to judge from Nikita Pavlovets's icon of The Virgin in the Heavenly Garden (Pl. 10)[16], have been better known to contemporary Muscovites for the icon is dated to 1670. The symmetrical gardens laid out at Versailles in 1671 struck a new note by merging with the landscaped grounds in which they were set instead of dissociating themselves from nature, as had been the case in earlier times.

In 1704, when travelling from Petersburg to Cronstadt, Peter found a half-way resting site which enchanted him. He took to using it regularly, dreaming of eventually building a house on it. As early as 1705 he began making rough sketches of it. Five of these survive, one already showing a house, the future Palace of Peterhof, set on the summit of the hill with a broad canal—the future Great Cascade—connecting it with the waters of the Gulf of Finland (Pls. 11 and 12). The building of this dream retreat was delayed till 1713, when it fell to Schlüter to implement the Tsar's ideas. Schlüter started by designing the pavilion of Monplaisir[17] and lived to lay its foundations, although Braunstein was to build it after his death. When Leblond became responsible for all work at Peterhof he found that the shell both of the palace on the hill and of the pavilion of Monplaisir had been erected, the main canal had been dug, work had started on the grotto, and the lower garden had been planted. Leblond produced a new design for the palace and the grotto, but the Tsar preferred Michetti's grotto. Michetti had laid the park's water works in 1710; he was also to complete the Great Cascade and constructed its foun-

15 I thank Mr. Alastair Rowan of Edinburgh University for this information.
16 Antonova–Mneva, op. cit. ii, no. 892, pl. 138.
17 I.E. Grabar, op. cit. v. 19, 82; also N. P. Vyatkin, *Ocherki istorii Leningrada*, U.S.S.R. Historical Institute (Moscow and Leningrad, 1951), i. 136–7.

using wood encased in lead for the purpose. Later Zemtsov, Usov, Mordvinov, and Bank were to replace these by stone ones.

Leblond's death left the Tsar without a French architect but the impact which France had made on him endured. Its influence was responsible for Peter's passionate desire that his daughter Elizabeth should marry a French prince and also for his choice of the French names of Monplaisir, Marli, and Hermitage for his retreats.

The nation's cultural and artistic life marked time under Peter's immediate successors. Although much work which had been started before his death required completing, most of the foreign technicians were discharged in 1728. Many returned to their homes, but others, including the now thoroughly Russianized Tressini, stayed on, Tressini dying there in 1734. Russians automatically took the places of the departed foreigners and carried out most of the small amount of work undertaken in the years following Catherine I's death till the accession of Anna Ivanovna. Although Peter's 'fledglings' had begun returning to Russia from 1724 onwards esteem continued to centre on the older men, notably on Tressini, Eropkin, now secretary to the Building Commission, Usov, the designer of Strelna, and Zemtsov, who had acted in his youth as Tressini's senior assistant. Korobov, assisted by the reliable though somewhat pedestrian Tressini the Younger, was also forging ahead. Yet even the finest of the architects often found themselves to be out of work for Anna Ivanovna's decision to remain in Moscow following her coronation brought St. Petersburg to the verge of decay. Many of its wealthier inhabitants were quietly abandoning it and Peter's young capital was rapidly acquiring a deserted and dejected appearance. Many of its remaining inhabitants, and especially its artists and architects, faced ruin.

In Moscow conditions were equally difficult. Peter's ban on all stone and brick construction outside St. Petersburg had had so disastrous an effect there that even when much of Moscow had fallen into a ruinous condition workmen capable of carrying out essential repairs were sadly lacking. Fortunately the city still possessed several experienced builders and, in the person of Michurin, at least one outstanding architect. Even so, the Empress's decision to reside in Moscow threatened to overwhelm Michurin with work needing to be done urgently if Anna Ivanovna and her courtiers were to be adequately housed. Yet Michurin had at his disposal a mere handful of workmen capable of repairing the finer buildings requiring very thorough restoration. The Empress's decision two years later to transfer the Court back to St. Petersburg gave Michurin and other highly qualified Muscovite architects such as Evlashev and Korobov a chance to tidy the old city, and it also provided employment in St. Petersburg for a new generation of architects, many of them former 'fledglings' of Peter the Great.

It was fortunate for the new capital that an architect of genius was at hand to take up Peter's unfinished tasks. By birth an Italian, by upbringing a Frenchman, Bartolomeo Francesco Rastrelli (1700–71) had come to Russia with his parents in 1716. Although he was still a mere youth at the time, Petersburgians were quick to perceive and appreciate his genius. Even so, Prince Kantemir Hospodar of Moldavia displayed considerable faith and perspicacity when, in 1721, he entrusted so young and untried an architect with the task of designing and building his Petersburgian mansion for him. To judge from surviving illustrations,[18] the Kantemir mansion can have borne little resemblance to the buildings Rastrelli was to design in his maturity. Yet although it is a precocious work in which the Western elements seem to stem from Holland rather than from France, it already clearly discloses the extent of the impact which Russia, her Tsar, and St. Petersburg had made on the young man. The mansion took the form of a two-storeyed rectangle flanked by single-storeyed wings set at right angles to it, their narrow ends topped by pediments which contrasted rather disconcertingly with the traditionally Russian roofing of the main block. The house was lit by high, rather narrow windows which were grouped in pairs in the wings and in threes in the main block. As was customary in Petrine buildings the centre of the main front was marked at ground level by a

[18] I. E. Grabar, op. cit. v. 177.

high, rather narrow entrance arch whilst a niche of similar shape was set above it in line with the windows of the second floor.

Many scholars think that soon after his parents had settled in Russia young Rastrelli went abroad twice, but others maintain that he did so only once, travelling to the West in 1725, shortly after the Tsar's death. Nothing is known about his travels, not even their length or destinations, but Soviet scholars maintain that he could not have gone abroad for more than one year.[19] All agree that he had returned to Russia, never again to leave it, some time before 1730, the year in which Anna Ivanovna announced her intention of moving back to St. Petersburg in 1732. As soon as she had made her wishes known, General Münnich, acting in his capacity of Governor-General of the new capital, hastened to instruct Rastrelli to build in St. Petersburg a large Summer Palace of wood and a public opera house. Both were to be completed in time for the Empress's arrival. Münnich probably followed the advice of the Empress's favourite, Count Biron, Duke of Courland, when choosing Rastrelli for these tasks, for Biron greatly admired the young architect; he must also have played some part in the Empress's decision to employ the young man in Moscow and to appoint him her architect in chief at a salary of 800 roubles a year. Biron was himself to employ him to build two palaces for him in his Duchy of Courland.

During the third decade of the eighteenth century Peter the Great's daughter, the Tsarevna Elizaveta Petrovna, was kept so short of funds that she was seldom able to satisfy her longing to build. Since her passion for doing so was as keen as her father's she must surely have followed the careers of Michurin and Rastrelli with close attention. Whilst Rastrelli's abilities were developing, her taste was also maturing. By 1741, when she made her successful bid for the throne, she and Rastrelli were simultaneously entering upon the most productive and creative periods in their artistic careers. Their tastes were to complement each other to a singular degree and to combine in the course of twenty years in producing a style which, while superficially flamboyant and ornate, was fundamentally so classical and severe that it has

[19] Ibid., p. 176.

the purity and unity essential to all truly great architecture. The gifted and highly intelligent, though singularly ill-educated Empress had received so little schooling that, throughout her life, she continued firmly to believe that reading was injurious to health and she remained unable to comprehend that Britain is an island. As she was never able to travel outside Russia her stock of knowledge failed to increase. Her love of finery encouraged her to delight in exquisitely fashioned, amusing, if ephemeral, trifles rather than in major works of art. Nevertheless, her innate taste triumphed over these handicaps. Although greatly drawn to France her devotion to her own country proved permanent and remained the supreme passion of her life. Aided by Rastrelli, Elizabeth was in due course to provide Russia with a distinctive style and with three counterparts to the Versailles which she had never seen. Rastrelli's reactions to the Russian scale, to the Muscovite love of the flamboyant and of the light and shade effects which contribute to it, the compelling rhythm and vigour of his country's traditional forms of defensive and monastic architecture, all contributed in enabling him to express their jointly shaped visions in an essentially Russian manner. The partnership was a singularly happy and fruitful one, for Rastrelli was able to give tangible expression to all that was finest in Elizaveta Petrovna's taste whilst the Empress provided him with the opportunity of expressing his genius to the full and, by doing so, of revealing himself as one of Europe's truly great architects.

Although Rastrelli created some of Europe's finest architectural structures, like Peter the Great he was to some extent behind his time. His most productive period embraces the years between 1740 and 1760. France had by then already completely abandoned the Baroque style and had begun moving from the rococo to the neo-classical. Britain, whilst retaining some of the elements popular in France and Italy a generation earlier, was wholly absorbed in Palladianism. Rastrelli, however, disregarded the asymmetry that formed the basis of French rococo, avoided the histrionics of Austria's Baroque style, and seemed completely unconscious of Britain's Palladianism. Instead he reverted to Italy's earlier conception of classicism with its stress on symmetry, clarity, and lightness. In this single respect he was attuned to the young neo-classicists, but at the same time he retained the theatrical touch which had been popular in both Italy and France at an earlier date. Although such flamboyance had ceased to be admired in either of these countries, it must have retained some measure of popularity in Spain, for the palace which Zachetti built in Madrid in 1738 is imbued with it.

When Elizabeth ascended the Russian throne she announced her intention of starting where her father had left off, of acting in accordance with his views, and of reviving his policies. It is to her credit that, in artistic matters, she neither intended this to apply nor was expected to do so. Like her father she was fascinated by everything new, but in contrast to him, she was deeply attached to everything traditionally Russian. Her taste was formed by both these attitudes and she expressed both in her creations. Thus the secularization of religious architecture, begun in Peter's childhood and typified by the church at Dubrovitsy, persisted, but at the same time she expressed her desire for a reversion to the five-domed—in Rastrelli's hands often the five-turreted—cruciform type of church of Byzantine origin. The statues which adorned the roof of the Dubrovitsy church tended to disappear from her churches to reappear instead in serried ranks upon the rooves of her palaces. There they were accompanied by flamboyant high-relief sculptures (Pl. 13), the prototypes for which were to be found in the low-relief ones used in Peter's day by Tressini and Schlüter. Michetti's decision to make use of the glass factories which Peter had transferred to the Petersburgian district in order to light the Tsar's interiors by means of large windows was followed by Rastrelli, who also made use of Peter's mechanical dining-room table to produce a more advanced version for the Empress. The assured sweep of Peter's street perspectives, garden paths, and cascades was echoed in Rastrelli's interiors, where room opened into room in a rhythmical succession and on a scale never outmatched in the West. The size of Rastrelli's buildings contrasts sharply with that adopted by Peter the Great, but it was attuned to the Muscovite. It was Rastrelli who kindled the Russian passion for marbles and semi-precious stones by panelling a room in the palace of Tsarskoe Selo with the carved amber slabs which Peter had exchanged with the King of Prussia for fifty of his tallest Grenadiers. But for the Amber Room (completely destroyed in the last war), the Winter Palace might not have acquired its famous Malachite Hall nor the Catherine Palace at Tsarskoe its opaque glass panelled rooms. Similarly, although Russia had maintained regular relations with the Orient from as early as the sixteenth century and although Peter had panelled a room at Monplaisir, and possibly also one in his Summer Palace, with red Chinese lacquer, Rastrelli was the first to experiment with the Chinoiserie style in Russia. Elizabeth was amused by his versions of it. Later in the century Rinaldi was to persuade Catherine II to allow him to decorate several rooms in the Palace of Oranienbaum in the Chinese style, to design a Chinese theatre for the park at Tsarskoe Selo, and to start building the Chinese village there which the Scot, Charles Cameron, was to complete. Yet the style never caught on in Russia, and Elizabeth and Rastrelli remain the only exponents who succeeded in investing it with as much gaiety and exuberance as it acquired in Western Europe.

Although Elizabeth began planning extensions to the Palace of Peterhof within a year of her accession, affairs of state prevented her from embarking on any large scale building activities before 1747. Nevertheless, much of her mature taste is already reflected in the marvellously decorative triumphal arches which Ukhtomsky[20] designed for her coronation in Moscow in 1742. Rastrelli was also working for the Empress at that time, but in accordance with her wishes he was chiefly engaged in studying Moscow's religious architecture since the Empress admired it above all other styles and therefore wished him to regard it as a source of future inspiration. His finest version of the traditional style is to be seen in his model for the Smolny Convent (Pl. 14).

In the final years of Elizabeth's reign tastes had begun to change and Rastrelli's popularity started to decline. The designs he had

[20] I. E. Grabar, op. cit. v. 245, and G. Kachalov's engravings in Ukhtomsky's *Coronation Album*. 1744, *TsGADA* f. Koskovskoy senatskoy kontory, b. 7864, ff. 359–60.

made in 1757 for St. Petersburg's Gostiny Dvor or Merchants' Row were set aside, the commission going a couple of years later to a recent arrival, a young French architect Vallin de la Mothe working in the neo-classical style. The Italian Antonio Rinaldi (1710–94), Catherine II's first architect, worked for her at the time when the French Encyclopaedists, and more especially their strongly Francophile colleague, Melchior Grimm, were influencing the new Empress's taste. The French painter Charles-Louis Clérisseau fanned her admiration for things Roman into a passion and it fell to de la Mothe, who worked in Russia from 1759 to 1775, to express it for her in its most poetic form in his New Holland archway. The Scot, Charles Cameron (Pl. 15), was, from about 1775 onwards, to temper her Roman severity with an admixture of Palladianism by adorning the surfaces of his essentially classical buildings with a lavish yet strictly controlled symmetrical type of decoration as ornate in its own way, if more regular and flat, as Rastrelli's Baroque embellishments. Cameron's pleasure in the use of precious marbles and stones, so brilliantly transposed to opaque glass in the private apartments which he built for the Empress at Tsarskoe Selo, helped to enhance the richness of his painted and plaster designs (Pl. 16). These followed the style which the brothers Adam had made fashionable in Britain.

Catherine greatly admired many features in England's culture. Capability Brown's theories on landscaping nature especially appealed to her. She preferred his park layouts to the regular ones of French origin, and she expressed her admiration for his achievements[21] by naming the palace which her north-Italian architect Quarenghi (1744–1817) built for her at Peterhof between 1781 and 1789 the English Palace because its grounds had been cut in accordance with Capability Brown's principles. Her preference for the Roman style in architecture reached its fullest expression in the Hermitage Theatre (Pl. 17) which Quarenghi built for her in St. Petersburg towards the end of her reign. Although he used the Teatro Olympico at Vicenza as a source of inspiration, the

[21] *Sbornik Imperatorskogo Russkogo Istoricheskogo Obshchestva*, xiii (1874), 256, letter to Voltaire.

building bears a far greater affinity to the West's neo-Roman revivalist style than to the Palladian buildings of northern Italy. Indeed, by the latter part of Catherine II's reign Russian architecture had caught up with that of Western Europe and was henceforth to keep in step with it. Now, however, the Russians intentionally set out to express contemporary architecture in an essentially Russian manner, a result which had until then been achieved unconsciously. Bazhenov is one of the most interesting of the Russian Romantic classicists working in Moscow in the latter part of the eighteenth century. A keen admirer of Italian architecture, he made great use of pillars and pilasters, yet both he and Felten were sufficiently familiar with and attracted by England's neo-Gothic style to experiment with it, Bazhenov when designing the Tsaritsyn Palace (1784/5),[22] Felten the Chesme Palace—a half-way house which he built for Catherine on the St. Petersburg–Tsarskoe Selo road. She named it in honour of the recently won Russian victory and wished the building to resemble a medieval fortress. Felten gave the house a triangular ground-plan, setting a circular hall at its centre, lighting it with tall, narrow windows, and topping its roof with battlements; he designed its church in the same style. These two experiments with the neo-Gothic were not unique. They testify to the closeness of the attention with which Russia's foremost architects followed the work of their Western colleagues and serve also to illustrate Russia's manner of interpreting such alien styles. The difference in handling is equally evident in less eccentric buildings, where porticos, V-shaped pediments, and colonnades epitomize the country's taste. These features therefore came to figure prominently on buildings of a utilitarian nature such as hospitals, barracks, schools, poor houses, and so on with the result that even in the current sumptuous ones they acquired a greater sobriety than is to be found in their Western counterparts. The larger-scale and more impetuous sweep of the Russian buildings also helped in making Russian classicism something altogether distinct from the West's.

The architectural changes which were imposed on Russia in the

[22] I. E. Grabar, op. cit. vi. 110, 111.

eighteenth century were assimilated by the better-off inhabitants with astonishing speed both because they appealed to their aesthetic sense and also because they corresponded so well to the new way of life. The need for a new setting had first been felt at the end of the seventeenth century, when the abolition of the order of seniority made it unnecessary for the dining table and its seats to be permanently fixed to the floor. But although new furniture would have been welcomed by many families, most were obliged to content themselves with that which had remained in use throughout the country since medieval times. In Peter the Great's day, however, single pieces of furniture began reaching both capitals from the West, chiefly from Germany and the Low Countries. Their number was so small that many people arranged for the imported articles to be copied by native carpenters. The increased supply of such novel pieces of furniture encouraged many householders to seek new ways of arranging their interiors. Peter's decision to oblige his courtiers to hold and attend assemblies made further changes necessary and by the 1730s or so the new way of life was taking root in a new setting resulting from an increase in the amount of contemporary furniture being imported from the West and copied at home. Even so, the demand continued greatly to exceed the supply. Even the Empress Elizabeth suffered from the scarcity. Whenever she moved from town to town or palace to palace she was obliged, in the manner of a medieval monarch, to take all her possessions with her. Catherine II has left astonishing accounts of these peregrinations, of the breakages which occurred, and of the discomforts which she no less than the Empress and their ladies had to endure.[23] Rastrelli was obliged to design and supervise the making in the palace workshops of most of the furniture needed to furnish the royal residences he was engaged in building (Pl. 18), and gifts of furniture were warmly welcomed by the Empress and such high-ranking courtiers as the Chancellor Mikhail Vorontsov or her favourite, Ivan Shuvalov. As late as 1744 the Grand Chancellor Aleksey Bestuzhev-Ryumin maintained that he could not afford

[23] Zoé Oldenbourg (trans. Anne Carter), *Catherine the Great* (London, 1965), pp. 96, 97.

to furnish the house which the Empress had built for him on the Neva's embankment. When the Empress failed to provide him with some furniture or with the money with which to buy what he needed, the Grand Chancellor raised a mortgage on the house in England, thereby giving rise to much gossip and speculation both in and outside Russia.

By freeing noblemen from military service the Empress made it possible for those who had served the state in a military capacity to live where they wished. Some took advantage of this concession to settle on their estates, others to live in the rapidly expanding provincial towns. Many more proceeded to employ their serfs on building houses of contemporary form, either by copying a design from a Western engraving or by following the Rastrelli style, but most of these continued to furnish these residences with the carved and painted types of wooden furniture which their forbears had used. The situation underwent a rapid change following Peter III's decision to exempt the nobility from all forms of public service. Many regarded this as an opportunity for travelling in the West. Conditions there impressed and appealed to most of them and some attempted to increase the speed of their own country's Westernization. The effect that had on furniture can best be appreciated by recalling a passage in Andrey Bolotov's Memoirs.[24] Writing for the benefit of his descendants during the closing years of the century, Bolotov compared existing conditions with those that prevailed in his youth when 'our present-day sofas, canapés, armchairs, tambours, card tables, chests and the like, rondeaux, fancy little tables, and similar pieces of furniture were not to be found in middle- and lower-middle-class homes'.[25]

Interiors of Western style naturally required not only furniture but also interior fittings, decorations, and adornments of the Western type. Peter was keenly conscious of this and did his

[24] Andrey Bolotov, *Zhizn i priklyucheniya Andreya Bolotova opisannyya samim im dlya svoikh potomkov* (1789 and Leningrad, 1931), p. 136; also Z. P. Popova, *Russkaya mebel kontsa 18-ogo veka* (Moscow, 1957).
[25] 'Nyneshnikh sof, kanape, kresel, tambur, komodov lomberdnykh i drugikh, rondo, manernykh stolikov i prochee tomu podobnoe ne bylo togda sredi srednego i melkogo meshchanstva.'

utmost to deal with the situation, but the change which he demanded from his artists was far more fundamental in character than that which he required from his architects for he wished his artists to substitute a secular art in place of one which had until then been almost wholly religious in aim and content. Perhaps this ought not to have proved as difficult as it did since the interest which some seventeenth-century Muscovites had begun to feel for man as an individual had acquired fresh impetus from the importance which the Tsar attached to merit, and which he expressed by the introduction of his Table of Ranks. In the artistic field this attitude tended to strengthen the popularity enjoyed by portraiture, but in addition to the depiction of specific people it was now extended to that of localities. In the process the attempts of seventeenth-century painters to produce landscapes, that is to say evocations of nature,[26] were set aside in favour of topographical works, that is to say of portraits of specific towns and architectural complexes (Pl. 19). Battle pieces and depictions of triumphs (Pl. 20) were treated in the same manner and many decades were to elapse before they evolved into true historical paintings. However, they helped in opening a way to allegorical compositions of the type chosen by Schlüter for the decorations of the exterior of Peter's Summer Palace,[27] and these in their turn aroused interest in mythology.

The great esteem in which portraiture was held may well account for the fact that most of the foreign artists who worked for Peter were professional portrait-painters. It was unfortunate that, with the notable exception of the sculptor Carlo Bartolomeo Rastrelli, few were of the first rank, for the changes demanded by Peter were so sweeping in character that, in the absence of superb leaders, Russian artists were to require several decades in which to gain the assurance and sense of independence that enable men of talent to use their abilities to the fullest advantage. Although none of Moscow's late seventeenth-century artists had been able successfully to accomplish the transition from the iconic to the naturalistic style, the *parsunya* served to provide a

---

[26] See e.g. Antonova–Mneva, op. cit. ii, pls. 158–9.
[27] I. E. Grabar, op. cit. v. 445.

stepping-stone linking the two. The issue was, however, complicated by the Tsar's insistence that his nobility and gentry should adopt Western customs, dress, uniforms, and equipment, that they should shave their beards, cut their hair, and wear wigs (Pl. 21). These symbols of the dawn of a new era created a new, instantly obvious distinction between the well-to-do and the poor, and provided the framework for the new, secular school of art. The sudden division of the country's art into the religious and secular led to a further bifurcation—that of the emergence of folk art as distinct from fine art, where only a national art had until then existed. These distinctions were not dependent only on style, but also on the difference in outlook between the rich and poor, the educated and uneducated, fine arts coming to be associated with the sophisticated and prosperous, folk and iconic art with the working classes. In the process the experiments which had been attempted in Moscow at the turn of the seventeenth century in the fields of nude, genre, and landscape painting were forgotten.

Peter was unable to help his artists as much as he had done his builders for his understanding of the fine arts was less acute than that of architecture. The paintings he was best able to appreciate were works of the Dutch school; his response to them was sufficiently perceptive to enable him, when setting them in panelling, to space them according to contemporary taste rather than to compress them as if in an iconostasis. Yet precisely because he was able to turn his hand to many different tasks, becoming something of a Jack of all trades as well as a master of several, Peter firmly believed in the universality of the intelligent man. Where ability was accompanied by industry, as it often was in Renaissance Italy, Peter always expected the happiest results. Although he set great store on learning the Tsar attached singularly little importance to culture—a commodity which was all too seldom to be met with in the Moscow of his youth. As Efros has noted,[28] that attitude led Peter to select the youths whom he wished to train as artists from quite humble homes. This would not have proved a serious drawback had the artistic traditions to which the youths were accustomed in their homes not come suddenly to differ

[28] A. Efros, *Dva veka russkogo iskusstva* (Moscow, 1969), p. 38.

sharply from those which the Tsar wished them to adopt. Some scholars go so far as to maintain that speedier mastery of the new idiom would have been attained had the Tsar been able to attract foreign artists of the highest quality to Russia. Yet on noting how little effect the statues which the Tsar had imported from Venice in 1710 for the Summer Gardens and those that arrived from Italy, Holland, and England between 1716 and 1720[29] had had, or how little the work of a sculptor as outstanding as Rastrelli the Elder had influenced Russia's highly skilled traditional wood carvers, it seems doubtful that a shorter period of readjustment could have sufficed. At the start of Peter's reign public opinion was so opposed to sculpture in the round that even the widely travelled P. A. Tolstoy regarded Greek and Roman statues of pagan gods as no better than idols. Russia's wood carvers therefore continued to produce traditional examples of religious and folk art, and Russia had to wait till the later decades of the century for Fedot Shubin, her first and still today her finest sculptor.

Although the Tsar's envoys combed Western Europe, no truly successful painters could be persuaded to come to St. Petersburg. Nattier and Oudry were among those who refused his invitations; the Marseillais Caravaque (in St. Petersburg from 1716 to his death in 1754), Gottfried Tannhauer or Danhauer (in St. Petersburg from 1710 to his death in 1739) and George Gsell (1673-1740) with his artist wife Dorothea, were among the more accomplished of those who accepted. Although they came primarily as portraitists the Tsar expected them to undertake any tasks on hand, whether these consisted in drawing the exhibits in his anatomical and zoological collections, furnishing designs for set pieces of fire works, or devising decorations for state banquets, festivities, and parades, or even for the costumes to be worn at Court masquerades. Acting on this principle the Tsar required the young Russians who were training as artists in St. Petersburg to study sculpture and painting, which included life drawing, the art of engraving, and also subjects such as cartography, carpentry, the principles of architecture, optics, watchmaking, the production of

<hr>

[29] 'Zapiski polyaka ochevidtsa', *Russkaya Starina* (St. Petersburg, 1879), 26.

mathematical instruments, the technicalities of hydraulics, and those of the building of mills, sluices, and the like.

From the start the Russians showed themselves able to excel in the graphic arts, their centuries-old familiarity with book illuminating and their subsequent experience in the use of wood blocks and printing having developed their innate talent for work of this kind. The books published by the printing presses which Peter had established were adorned with ornate chapter headings and tail pieces formed of groups of trophies, ornate scrolls, delicate naturalistic motifs and full page illustrations (Pl. 22). Their illustrations featured battles, pictures of the country's newest buildings and parks, records of state festivities, firework displays, and triumphs. The Tsar had a number of fine engravers at his disposal, men such as I. Bunin, the illustrator of Istomin's *ABC* (1692–4), Ivan Zubov (1677–c. 1744), and especially the latter's brother Aleksey (1683–c. 1744), who became the best of them all. Efros[30] rightly refers to Aleksey as St. Petersburg's first poet for, in his own sphere, Aleksey's pictures of the new capital are as poetic and evocative as Pushkin's poems. Aleksey Zubov's engravings set a standard which artists such as Ivan Sokolov (1717–57), Grigory Kachalov (1711–59), L. Bunin (dates unknown, but 1714 figures as the latest known date on one of his engravings) or Aleksey Grekov (1723 to after 1770) did not dishonour and which B. Korovin (studied in Paris in 1719 and died in 1741) was able to match. But whilst Aleksey Zubov's engravings show a real feeling for and an understanding of nature, those of his younger colleagues, although possessing the attributes of really fine illustrations, remain essentially topographical works.

The achievements of the engravers were complemented by those of the medallists. In the absence of notable sculptors in the round they became the real followers of Rastrelli the Elder, and it was to them that the Tsar turned for the records he wanted of his triumphs and achievements. Andrey Nartos (1693–1756) worked under Rastrelli for many years and became a fine master of his craft. He inherited from his great Italian teacher something of the grand flamboyance of the Renaissance, and more particularly of

[30] A. Efros, op. cit., p. 44.

Bernini. The heroic style—one so characteristic of the Petrine age—is to be seen at its best in the low-relief sculptures produced as decorations for the column which the Tsar commissioned from Rastrelli the Elder and Nartos in 1721 as a memorial to the Great Northern War. When in London Peter had admired the column known as the Monument which Wren had set up to commemorate the Great Fire. Peter may have had it in mind when commissioning his own column, but Rastrelli's thoughts may well have turned to a Roman example such as Trajan's, whilst many Russians would probably have sought a precedent for the proposed column in that which stood in the sixth century near the Cathedral of Hagia Sophia in Constantinople and bore on its summit a gold statue of the Byzantine Emperor Justinian the Great.[31] The four-foot-high model which Nartos made of Rastrelli's design is also surmounted by an equestrian statue, this time of Peter the Great. It is adorned with low-relief sculptured scenes depicting events such as the founding of St. Petersburg, the Battle of Poltava, and so on. Caravaque supplied Rastrelli with some of the sketches and portraits used for these scenes.

Conditions were less promising in the fields of easel and mural painting. There portraiture held pride of place, as it was to continue doing throughout the century. Caravaque set the standard for Russian portraitists, but he took no account of the Tsar's preference for Dutch art and his rococo style, like that of most of the other foreigners, continued to conform to that in force at most of Western Europe's Court circles. It was to lose its rococo veneer in Anna Ivanovna's reign without, however, acquiring anything Russian in its place. No foreign or native artist thought of reviving the attempts made by some of Tsar Aleksey's painters and the latters' provincial colleagues[32] to establish a school either of genre or of nude painting. The *poteshnye listy*, forerunners of the *lubki* and the equivalents of England's broadsheets, were almost alone in featuring such themes, in part perhaps because the

---

[31] The column appears in the background of an icon of Our Lady's Stole, a work of the Novgorodian school, illustrated in N. Kondakov–E. Minns, *The Russian Icon* (Oxford, 1927), pp. 115–16, pl. 36.

[32] V. G. Brusova, *Yaroslavl Frescoes* (Moscow, 1969), pls. 46–7 and 67; also I. E. Grabar, op. cit. iv. 421 and 437.

depiction in them of religious subjects was forbidden by the Church. Jouvain the Younger's painting of 1727 of *A Peasant with a Beagle*[33] stands out as a well nigh unique example of genre painting, but on arriving in Russia in 1756 the portraitist Pietro Rotari was to create an interest in it by painting for his own satisfaction a series of portraits of peasant women. Their beauty had charmed him and he revealed it to their countrymen. In 1767 Argunov (1727–1802) followed Rotari's lead by painting a portrait of *The Kalmyk Girl, Annushka,*[34] with, in 1784, one of *A Peasant Girl in National Dress* (Pl. 23). Meanwhile, in 1774, Shibanov had produced one entitled *A Peasant's Repast,* following it three years later by one of *Peasants Celebrating an Engagement.*[35] It was these works which opened the road to Venetsianov (1780–1847), the first true exponent of Russian genre painting. Nude painting had, however, to wait for A. A. Ivanov (1806–58) in order to become established, and even then his experiments figure only as details in his religious works, such as in his painting of *Christ Before the People,* or in his allegorical and historical compositions.

From the start the foreign portraitists found it advisable to take account of the Russian desire for physical fidelity and psychological content. Rastrelli the Elder had therefore modified the ornateness he had acquired from Bernini in order to give full expression to the personalities of his sitters. He was brilliantly successful in doing his works, notably his busts of Peter (Pl. 24) and Menshikov and his statue of Anna Ivanovna with her Blackamoor page in attendance (Pl. 25)[36] standing out as extremely revealing human documents. Later in the century a similar striving for veracity was to lead Falconet and Marthe Collot to make use of Peter the Great's death mask when modelling the face of the Tsar's great equestrian statue, the *Bronze Horseman.* It is this striving for psychological content that compensates for the technical shortcomings of the young Russian painters of the Petrine age. It is expressed with particular insight and delicacy by Matveev

[33] M. V. Alpatov, *Vseobshchaya istoriya iskusstv* (Moscow, 1955), ii. pl. 232.
[34] E. Nekrasova, *Russkoe izobrazitelnoe iskusstvo 18-ogo veka* (Moscow, 1967), pl. 29.
[35] Ibid., pls. 57 and 58.
[36] I. E. Grabar, op. cit. v. 462–3, 465–7.

(1701–39)[37] and the brothers Nikitin, but especially by the younger brother, Ivan (Pl. 26) (1688–1741).[38] If any painters of the early eighteenth century can be regarded as sympathizing with Ushakov's support of naturalism[39] it must surely be Ivan Nikitin. His handling of his sitters is, naturally enough, far freer, more sophisticated and accomplished than that achieved by Ushakov (Pl. 27) in his religious works, yet the training which Nikitin received in Florence seems hardly to have affected his very Russian interpretation of the West's naturalistic style. It is only necessary to compare his portrait of Peter the Great on his death-bed with works such as Caravaque's portraits of the Tsar's two young daughters to see how true he remained to himself and to his native traditions.[40]

In 1750 Vishnyakov (1699 to after 1761) was to follow in Ivan Nikitin's footsteps when painting portraits such as those of James and Sarah Fermor (Pl. 28), the children of Count Fermor, director of the Office of Works. Levitsky (1735–1822) was, however, to be the first of the painters to be able wholly successfully to combine psychological veracity with the eighteenth century's love of sophisticated yet muted elegance and refinement. The nature of his achievement can be assessed by comparing his portraits of the Smolny Institute schoolgirls (Pl. 29 and 30), painted around 1773, with Vishnyakov's of the Fermor children. The influence of English artists such as Reynolds and Gainsborough is surely discernible in Levitsky as that of Hoppner, even of Lawrence, is in the work of many rather younger Russians having doubtless in each case reached them by means of mezzotints and engravings. Indeed Borovikovsky (1757–1825) was to go even further, at any rate in his earlier works, in his striving to achieve a Jane Austenish blend of gentle elegance and personality. Later Borovikovsky's romanticism was all too often attained at the expense of psychological depth. Even so, in what other contemporary European Court would it have occurred to an artist to portray his sovereign exercising her favourite greyhound Tom, the gift of her English physician, the first Baron Dimsdale, in the park at Tsarskoe

---

[37] E. Nekrasova, op. cit., pl. 8.
[38] I. E. Grabar, op. cit. v. 324.
[39] Ushakov, op. cit.
[40] E. Nekrasova, op. cit., pl. 4.

wearing old and comfortable clothes, her age clearly indicated, although not satirized (Pl. 31). Goya's cruel portrayal of the King and Queen of Spain is unique in its contempt even for the nineteenth century, but the tradition of forthrightness devoid of sarcasm persisted in Russia and Serov's portrait of Nicholas[41] provides a fine twentieth-century parallel to Borovikovsky's portrait of Catherine II. Borovikovsky's achievement is nevertheless perhaps the more remarkable of the two since he was painting at a time when the Russian Court was at its most regal and extravagant, and its sovereign and courtiers at the height of their magnificence.

Anna Ivanovna was pleasure-loving, vain, selfish, and frivolous. She treated the arts as adjuncts to the Court's furnishings, and employed her artists chiefly to provide her with ballroom, stage, and street decorations. The Empress Elizabeth, too, relied on artists for transitory works of a decorative sort but she also turned to them for more permanent ones taking the form of over-door, ceiling, and wall decorations. She was wise enough to commission work of this type from artists specializing in the decorative arts. Among the foreigners who did so, Peresinotti (who reached Russia in 1742) and A. Valeriani (who arrived there in 1743) were both skilled and sensitive artists. Among the Russians, the brothers Belsky (Pl. 32), together with Firsov (Pl. 33), produced most of the finest painted decorations of their day. Elizabeth also encouraged engravers and illustrators, retaining in book production the scrolls and trophies loved by Peter, though encouraging more flamboyant versions of both these forms. Topographical engravings lost none of their popularity and it was in the latter part of her reign (1753) that the fine draughtsman Matveev produced, though with the aid of a camera obscura, his splendid panorama of St. Petersburg.[42]

At the start of her reign Elizabeth was too preoccupied with political and administrative matters actively to sponsor the arts and at first her courtiers and noblemen were also for the most

[41] T. Talbot Rice, op. cit., ill. 222, p. 241.
[42] G. N. Komelova, *Vidy Peterburga i ego okrestnostey serediny 18-ogo veka* (Leningrad, 1968).

part not sufficiently secure financially to be able to do so on an extensive scale. By the 1750s the situation had altered radically. In consequence painting acquired a new assurance, wider ambitions, and a greatly extended range. Nevertheless, portraiture retained its pre-eminence with the Empress's need on coming to the throne for a series of portraits of herself for use in her government departments and embassies helping perhaps in maintaining its popularity. The nobility and gentry followed her example, those in a position to do so having their portraits painted by leading artists, the others employing their largely self-taught serfs. Three Russians—Argunov, Antropov (1716–95), and Vishnyakov—were especially admired and proved able to compete with foreigners such as the brothers Grooth, Rotari, and Louis Tocqué.

George Grooth came to Russia with his brother in 1743. Although not a painter of the first rank, it fell to him to execute many of the earlier portraits of the Empress, of her nephew the Grand Duke Peter, and of the latter's bride, Catherine. George Grooth must have learnt the intricacies of the courtly style from his father, who was Court painter at Stuttgart. The extent to which he was prepared to flatter his sitters can be assessed by comparing his equestrian portrait of the Empress Elizabeth wearing the uniform of the Preobrazhensky Guards and holding a marshal's baton, her Negro groom standing by her spirited charger (Pl. 34), with Rastrelli the Elder's sculpture of Anna Ivanovna and her blackamoor page. In each case the artist was at pains to emphasize the high rank of his imperial sitter, but Rastrelli's sculpture reveals the essential elements in Anna Ivanovna's character whilst Grooth's painting is almost wholly lacking in psychological content.

Count Pietro Rotari had studied in his youth in Rome and Naples and developed into a great exponent of the courtly rococo style. On arriving in Russia in 1756 he found himself vying with Louis Tocqué (1696–1771), a pupil of Bertin and Nattier. Indeed, Tocqué's reputation stood so high in France that Louis XV's representatives at the Russian Court were convinced that Franco-Russian diplomatic relations would benefit if the painter could be persuaded to visit St. Petersburg for a time. Tocqué was prevailed upon to do so. He arrived in Russia in 1754 and stayed there for two years. By then Petersburgians had not only fully assimilated the Western way of life and fitted it to their own needs, but many had come to share Lomonosov's conviction that Russia would in the ripeness of time acquire her own Platos and Newtons. This belief encouraged many of them to assert their own views and to give rein to their personal inclinations. Although Tocqué's work aroused much genuine admiration, none of the leading Russian artists felt at all inclined to try to emulate him. Elizabeth's policy of employing Russians in preference to foreigners whenever this proved possible fostered self-expression and choice of style. Some artists, as for example the creator of the interesting painting entitled *The Young Artist at Work*,[43] often ascribed to Firsov and dated to about the year 1760, were influenced by Chardin but others, notably Firsov in the works that are undoubtedly by his hand, were more in tune with artists such as N. B. Lepissier, Peron, even Greuze.

By the end of Elizabeth's reign the arts were flourishing throughout much of the country. In architecture Russians such as Bazhenov, Ukhtomsky, Kazakov, and Kokorinov led the field, in painting Levitsky (Pl. 35), Borovikovsky, and Rokotov (1735/6–1808/9), and in sculpture Fedot Shubin's genius had fully matured (Pl. 36). Like the vast majority of Russian artists Shubin was formed in the French school, having first trained under Nicholas Gillet, for twenty years the director of Russia's newly founded Academy of Fine Arts. He then completed his training in Paris and Italy. Like Rastrelli the Elder he learnt to combine flamboyant magnificence with psychological and physical veracity. Although Catherine II's admiration for the French Encyclopaedists enabled French influence to retain its hold during the greater part of her reign the magnificent collection of old masters which she assembled furnished Petersburgians with new, more profound, and far wider standards of comparison than had previously existed. Whilst the young Academy of Fine Arts which Elizabeth had founded in 1758 continued to uphold the

43 E. Nekrasova, op. cit., pl. 62.

French tradition, the works of the old masters tended to weaken its hold by broadening the interests and critical faculties of Russian patrons of the arts. It was in no small measure due to Levitsky's genius that portraiture retained its popularity. The extent of the influence which he exercised over his contemporaries becomes clear if the earlier of Rokotov's works are compared with his later ones.[44] The former tend to conform to the note struck by such foreigners as Rotari, Tocqué, or Torelli, all of whom worked for Catherine II during the earlier part of her reign, but the later ones follow Levitsky in their striving for directness, for the portrayal of character, and for a more sophisticated use of colour. Even Shubin appears to have been influenced by Levitsky and it was a sad loss when, towards the end of Catherine's reign, Levitsky's keen powers of observation began to fail and Rokotov's work also began to show signs of deterioration. The decline of these two great masters enabled Borovikovsky to rise to the position of the third important Russian portrait-painter of the day. By that date the Pugachev rising, the criticisms being expressed by such social reformers as Novikov and Radishchev, and later the outbreak of the French Revolution, combined in radically altering Catherine's attitude towards scholarship and the arts. The definitive change can be said to have coincided with the accession of Tsar Paul—an event which may well have contributed to Levitsky's decline.

Although it was hardly possible for any significant advances to be achieved during Paul's short reign, the arrival in St. Petersburg of certain French refugees did not pass unnoticed by the rising generation of artists, men such as Kiprensky (1782–1836), Tropinin (1776–1867), even the older Borovikovsky. He was among the first to sense the dawn of the Romantic Movement and to respond to it, having perhaps been to some extent prepared for it by Madame Vigée Lebrun, who came to Russia in 1795 and stayed there till 1801. Although her work was widely admired it did not make a very profound impression on Russian painters and, in the long run, J. Morie was to exercise greater influence. He arrived in St. Petersburg in 1795 by way of England, as did

---

[44] I. E. Grabar, op. cit. vii, compare pp. 8 and 11 with pp. 27, 33, or 35.

Patterson, the first in a line of British topographical artists to visit Russia. Morie remained in Russia till his death in 1808 and probably acquainted the Russians with the type of brushwork characterising the late eighteenth-century English school of painting. However, the Italian theatrical artist Gonzago was perhaps the most popular foreigner then in St. Petersburg, yet more time was to elapse before he made his influence felt. Although he arrived in St. Petersburg in 1792 and stayed there till his death in 1831, fifty odd years were to elapse before Alexander Benois's interest in Gonzago's works enabled them to influence some of the theatrical artists belonging to the Society of the World of Art. Of all the trends being tried out at the end of the eighteenth century the Romantic proved the most important, yet its vogue was of short duration in Russia. Then as now its sentimentality failed to make a real appeal; today it is so alien to our outlook that it tends to obscure the very real merits of painters such as Borovikovsky or Kiprensky. In the nineteenth century Russian painters pursuing veracity reacted against it by stripping their work of much of the elegance regarded in the eighteenth century as an essential adjunct to portraiture; the twentieth century was to carry the process of denudation further, divesting both portraiture and genre of its perceptive elements in order to achieve social realism.

The debt owed by Russia's eighteenth-century art to Western Europe can be compared to that which medieval Russia owed to Byzantium. In each case the Russians showed themselves to be highly selective in dealing with these alien styles, quick at adjusting themselves to the new idioms, and capable of transforming them into something distinctive and truly national. In the eighteenth century France, Italy, Holland, and to a lesser extent also England and Germany helped to fashion the Russian mould. They made their influences felt both by means of direct contacts but even more by means of illustrations. Their engravings, mezzotints, and lithographs reached many parts of the country and were often used as guides by serf architects, artists, and peasant craftsmen as well as by highly qualified and experienced urban ones. Kokorinov was but one among many of the latter who did not hesitate to cull ideas for his interior decorations from contemporary

French and Italian illustrations. The Russians derived especial delight from the sight of columns, pilasters, pillars, and pediments and used them so widely that the country's appearance was transformed. By the end of the eighteenth century few districts lacked houses built in the so-called Rastrelli style; still fewer of these houses failed to contain some works of art adhering to the naturalistic idiom. But if architecture often tended unwittingly to re-create the tiered effects found in such seventeenth-century Muscovite buildings as the Terem Palace or the old Printing House, attaining them by means of high-relief sculptured decorations and a clever disposition of windows, in art the change was essentially radical in character, expressing itself clearly in style, presentation, and subject-matter. The road stretching from the *parsunya* to the works of a Levitsky or Borovikovsky had proved long and difficult, at times almost tortuous, yet those who travelled along it succeeded in the course of a century in endowing their country with a truly national form of naturalistic art and a fine school of portraiture.

ALFRED AND JANE SWAN

11 (a) *The Survival of Russian Music in the Eighteenth Century*

THE eighteenth century in Russian history appears to us as a period when in every field of human endeavour the currents and ideas that streamed in from the west, via Poland, so completely overwhelmed Russian life that to search for remnants of the old order seems, on the face of it, a useless task. Music was likewise caught in this wave of importations, for though the sovereigns of Russia were not greatly attached to this art, they favoured the sweep of Italian opera and ways of music-making. First introduced under the Empress Anne, they took root and stayed, topped by the cream of Italian composers, singers, producers, and all that went in the trail of operatic performance.

To find, underneath layers of fashion and adulation, some adherence to ancient Russian traditions, one has to go into regions where modish taste played little or no part. A slavish imitation of foreign examples in the new forms of secular music, such as opera and cantata, met with little resistance, but in the domain of church singing things were different. Here certain time-honoured models were still upheld, especially in monastic circles. The daily order of services, in itself, required a massive musical accompaniment, and it is around such men as Tikhon of Zadonsk,[1] removed from the main arteries of life, that Russian music continued, at least in part, to draw on its own resources.

Up to the early seventeenth century the old, unruffled isolation continued without much disturbance. The century-old chant— the znamenny—was in universal use and only local variants of it were indulged in, as occasion demanded. Some old masters,

---

[1] Bishop Tikhon (1724–83) spent the last twenty years of his life in Voronezh at the Monastery of Zadonsk. He was canonized in 1860.

having become famous, were permitted to change its contours somewhat and introduce patterns borrowed from the folk-song. One of these masters, Fedor the Christian, to distinguish his version of the znamenny melodies from those in current usage, called his chant the Greater Chant, and when listening to it, we seem to hear distant echoes of the folk-song.[2] Fedor was in the entourage of Ivan IV. His art was *hors concours* and unassailable, but woe betide any lesser men who took liberties! We are told that Login, a precentor of the Troitsko-Sergievsky monastery, once dared to elaborate on a note that was to be held firm, only to be promptly called down by the ruling bishop.[3] The church knew how to guard its treasures.

But then the seventeenth century set in with its increasing love of novelty and the curious instruments brought in by the Dutch and the Germans. The znamenny chant gradually lost its hold, and when Nikon became patriarch (1652), the dam was broken wide and new chants resounded in the churches in Moscow. They arrived written on the stave and were often accompanied by some sort of harmony. While the conservative churchmen still clung to the neume notation, the innovators now had free sway and a bitter struggle ensued. A group of learned monks gathered around the elder (*starets*) Aleksandr Mezenets, and in a last desperate effort tried to show the superiority of the znamenny chant, by now supplied with the red explanatory marks of Shaydurov (*Shaydurovskie pomety*). In his 'Alphabet of Znamenny Singing'[4] Mezenets argued against the easy ways of the reformers. This epoch-making work finally saw the light of day in 1668. But it was too late. Nikon, who was not a musician, introduced, along with corrections in the service books, all the 'new music'.

Among the new chants the principal one was from Kiev. It was the time when the whole of the Ukraine passed under Russian rule, and the Kiev singers (*vspevaki*) were welcomed to

[2] Maksim Brazhnikov, 'Russkoe tserkovnoe penie XVI–XVIII v.', *Musica Antiqua Europae Orientalis* (Bydgoszcz, 1966).
[3] N. Kostomarov, *Russkaya istoriya v zhizneopisaniyakh* (St. Petersburg, 1896), i. 701.
[4] St. Smolensky, *Azbuka znamennago penya, startsa Aleksandra Mezentsa* (*1668*) *izdanie* (Kazan, 1888).

Moscow with all their trimmings. The Kiev chant is not unlike the znamenny, only the severity and long flowing lines of the latter are gone. All the strict modal cadences and formulae of the znamenny have assumed a mellower turn and invariably flow into the minor key, so greatly beloved in Ukrainian folklore. When harmonized, they produce a marked impression and this is what the newcomers played on while they enjoyed the patriarch's patronage. Even if viewed as the Ukrainian version of the znamenny chant,[5] the Kiev chant is too replete with intonations, alien to the Russian ear, too reminiscent of Poland to be fully acceptable. But, being more in keeping with the times, it came to stay and played its part in counteracting the Italians when the time came in the eighteenth century.

It was in melodies like the following exaposteilarion of the Kiev Chant that the Russian soul continued to glimmer in adverse times. (The return of the znamenny was not to come for another century.) The exaposteilarion is an early morning canticle, sung in the monasteries at daybreak and symbolizing the appearance of the first ray of light after darkness. The one below is reserved for Monday in Holy Week.

The note of expectation and hope persists in the opening bars, though steadily veiled over by a shadow of doubt. And then, suddenly, in the last bar, the surprising cadence moves into the minor key, as if shutting the door on the beholder: an amazingly subtle touch.

5 S. Skrebkov, *Russkaya kultovaya muzyka XVII—nachala XVIII veka* (Moscow, 1969).

Equally moving are some of the canticles in the other chants introduced to the Moscow of the seventeenth century by the Kiev 'intoners': the Bulgarian and the Greek. This puzzling designation of them has still not been solved, for neither the Bulgarian nor the Greek (Byzantine) singing of the seventeenth century has anything in common with them. Their names—eastern—are rather an open challenge to anything that savoured of Gregorianism—meaning western—when a large part of eastern Orthodoxy had fallen a prey to the Pope (the Uniats).

The Russian 'Bulgarian' has survived in but a few canticles, one of them in honour of Joseph of Arimathea, for his part in the burial of Christ:

The Russian 'Greek' chant is devoid of the ingratiating qualities of the other two, and is a further testimony to the oblivion into which the znamenny had fallen. It starts with an up-beat and then becomes a mere recitative until it reaches the cadence. It thus becomes a mere adaptation of the syllables of the text to the requirements of chanting, but its popularity was considerable and it is still used today.

It must be remembered that all these chants were introduced with appropriate harmonies of the simplest type, pleasing to the

ordinary person's ear, and in this way embedded themselves all the more firmly in the popular mind.

But with all this faint resistance, away from the centres of music, the Russian composers of the seventeenth and eighteenth centuries were, to all intents and purposes, Italians. The western movement began with the arrival in Moscow (*c.* 1681) of Nicholas Diletsky—a kind of Russian Caccini[6]—who came from the University of Vilna with a published *Musical Grammar*, in which he expounded the rules of the 'New Music'. In Moscow he acquired weight and authority at the court of young Tsar Fedor, was widely sought as a teacher, and eventually led Russian music to the limit of conformance. Not all was lost immediately, for among his pupils there was the deacon Vasily Titov, an uncommonly gifted individual, who, with true instinct, tried to save some of the old, by infusing patterns of the znamenny chant into such models as the fashionable 'psalms', and showed much technical ingenuity. But he cannot be viewed even as a transitional figure, for the transition led directly into the lap of the Italians.

An indescribable pandemonium reigned in the fashionable city churches. The church-music historian, Antonin Preobrazhensky, describing the age of Catherine the Great, says:

---

[6] Giulio Caccini (Romano), *c.* 1548–1618, whose 'Nuove Musiche' set the style for one vocal line with accompaniment.

the conviction was that for Russian Church singing the same style was needed as that of the western Catholic Church in Italy. At the invitation of the Empress . . . the members of the Synod visited the Italian opera at Court, and to the great delight of the Empress, nothing showed in the slightest degree their protest either against the invitation itself, or against what they saw and heard. On the contrary, as she once remarked: 'the Holy Synod was present at yesterday's performance and they roared with laughter together with US!' The church composers followed firmly the demands of the time and the spheres, and without a word wrote their pieces, as Concerts for Maundy Thursday or Holy Saturday. And the Empress expressed a characteristic regret about the fact that vocal works with orchestra could not be sung in Church.[7]

These so-called 'Concerts Spirituels' (*Dukhovnye kontserty*) were typical of the eighteenth century. At the moment when the priest withdraws into the sanctum to prepare for the Communion of the people, there occurs an awed halt in the service of the liturgy. This hallowed minute, when everyone present expects the appearance of the host, the reckless Italians chose for the most rampant demonstration of their musical tricks. Elaborate virtuoso show-pieces were sung to the bewildered congregation. Sacred, or semi-sacred, words were added without any scruple to purely secular compositions, the Maestro di Cappella conducted as if he were in a concert hall, and in some private chapels there have even been cases when loud 'bravos' were shouted at the conclusion.[8]

Under these circumstances—and the court at St. Petersburg did only what was usual in the whole of Europe, from Naples to London—all the leading Russian composers of the eighteenth and early nineteenth century grew up. Their training was in the hands of the Imperial Chapel whose gaze was directed to Italy only. Boys were selected in the Ukraine—the cradle of good voices— brought to St. Petersburg, and in time dispatched to the Italian academies for study with famous Italian masters. On their return the lucky ones rose to high positions, while the unlucky ones

[7] A. Preobrazhensky, *Kultovaya muzyka* (Petrograd, 1924), p. 73.
[8] Ibid., p. 71.

perished. The former is personified in Dmitry Bortnyansky, the latter in Maksim Berezovsky.

Bortnyansky was born in Glukhov, in the Ukraine, the residence of the hetman, in 1752. At eight he was already in the Chapel—at eighteen in Italy, with Galuppi. On his return he was long employed at the court of the Grand Duke Paul and in 1793 entered the Chapel. There he rose to the position of Director, was overwhelmed with titles and honours, and died in 1825. Glukhov was also the birthplace of Maksim Berezovsky. In sheer talent he even surpassed Bortnyansky, being awarded the highest distinction and the title of 'maestro' in Bologna. But on his return to Russia in 1775, under very strange circumstances, he was barely noticed and died by his own hand two years later.

The tendency amongst Russian musicologists is now to extol all these westernizers and find in their work traces of originality. Historically this is perhaps right. But musically nothing can be sadder than these attempts to read independent Russian notes into their completely imitative efforts. Glebov (Asafev) has thus expressed himself apropos of two operas of Bortnyansky (*Le Faucon* and *Le Fils rival*) performed at the court of Paul:

> The clever and observant Bortnyansky who was possessed of great gifts and had acquired abroad the necessary technical skill, and who was, moreover, guided by considerable taste, could, without much effort, plan in an artistic fashion, such seemingly hybrid elements. The sense of measure is in this case especially characteristic for him: it helps him to find an attractive way between the exaggerations of Italian sentiment, the dry, though brilliant humour of French comic opera, and the uncouth experiments of Russian realistic simplicity.[9]

The generous Glebov hands it to him in full measure, and it must be admitted that Bortnyansky never set aside all thought of the ancient treasures. At the time of his tutelage in Italy he experimented with a 'German Liturgy' into which he had introduced an 'imitation d'un cantique de Kiovia', obviously a version of the Kiev chant. Later he repeatedly mentioned the znamenny chant, and got as far as a written project, advocating not only its use, but its publication in the original kryuk notation. But none of this

9 B. V. Asafev, *Izbrannye trudy* (Moscow, 1952–7), iv. 32.

ever approached realization, and for decades to come Russian music hovered on the verge of extinction.

But if the eighteenth century failed to bring forth any figures that could by any standard be called Russian or national, it will still rank high in the preservation of national art, because of two remarkable events: the publication of a substantial bulk of church music and the equally substantial collections of folk-music made by the court guslist[10] Vasily Trutovsky.

The project of printing books containing music originated in Moscow with the Superintendent of the Synodal typography, Stepan Byshkovsky. An ardent lover of antiquity, Byshkovsky spared no effort to get the job done thoroughly. From the deacons of the Synod he managed to obtain the oldest extant manuscripts, some of them dating back to the days of Mezenets and the first transcriber on to the stave, Tikhon of Makarevsk.[11] Having arranged them in four separate collections he set them in print in the following order:

(*a*) The Obikhod, the Liber Usualis where the material is presented in the sequence of the daily services:

Vespers, Matins, Liturgy

Here we have the greatest variety of chants. By the side of the znamenny, the Kiev, Greek, and various abbreviated versions are given, so that a comparison becomes possible.

(*b*) The Heirmologion, a vast collection of over one thousand heirmoi. The heirmos was originally the sung part of the Odes of the Great Kanon. At the beginning of each of the nine odes a short connecting link was inserted. These heirmoi are among the oldest examples of the znamenny chant.

(*c*) The Octoechos. When the Byzantine apparatus was brought into Russia, under Vladimir in A.D. 989, the Octoechos, or arrangement of all service canticles into eight echoi (Russian *glasy*), a Byzantine institution, was adhered to. The *glas* is a domain of sound, possessing its own patterns. In the znamenny chant, which may

---

[10] Player on the *gusli*—a Russian stringed instrument.
[11] Tikhon of Makarevsk, a monk and the treasurer of the Patriarchal House in Moscow in the reign of Fedor (1676–82).

have been older than the Byzantine importations, the patterns are sometimes redundant, but this does [not prevent each *glas* from having its own character. It is in accordance with this principle that the canticles are listed in this book (Russian *osmoglasnik*).

(*d*) The order of services for the Nine Great Immovable Feasts of the year:

Nativity of the Virgin, Elevation of the Cross, Presentation of the Virgin at the Temple, Christmas, Epiphany, Purification, Annunciation, Transfiguration, and Assumption of the Virgin.

The task was tremendous. The Holy Synod, which had to sanction the publication, was in St. Petersburg, inert and immovable. Byshkovsky was in Moscow and one wonders how many times he had to pack and travel, so as to get a hearing. Even with all his energy one doubts if he would have achieved his goal, if he had not unexpectedly found an ally from the opposite camp: the Italian-trained bass singer of the Imperial Chapel, Gavriil Golovnya. Golovnya saw in the printing of the books a field of action for himself: the last of the four books—the *Immovable Holidays* (*prazdniki*)—is liberally studded with amplifications, in the form of Italian embellishments, on the body of the chant. Evidently Golovnya wanted to display his voice in the performance of the canticles and since he resided in St. Petersburg and had valuable connections, he played a part in the Byshkovsky venture.

The books appeared in 1772—the result of an unholy alliance of the dedicated Byshkovsky and the vain Golovnya. It is thanks to these transcriptions on to the stave that we can form an idea of the actual sound of the znamenny chant; for neume reading was in abeyance in the eighteenth century, and untold material would have been lost if one were to wait for people like Stepan Smolensky, the nineteenth-century advocate of neume-reading.

Soon after this, another event occurred in the sphere of folk-music. In 1776 the first printed book of folk-songs appeared in St. Petersburg under the title: *Collection of Russian Ordinary Songs with music. Part One*. The name of the collector was not given

(It appeared in full only under the last song of the fourth volume in 1796.) The musical notation was artless in the extreme:[12]

Yet Trutovsky's four volumes (in all eighty songs) became the foundation of an almost uninterrupted flow of folk-music, or what was known as folk-music in the eighteenth century. It took nearly the whole of the succeeding century to arrive at an accurate recording of the way in which folk songs are actually sung. Nowhere did the passion for collecting folk-music assume such proportions as

[12] Quoted from N. Findeyzen, *Ocherki* (Moscow, 1929), vol. ii, p. cxlii.

in Russia. And while in ecclesiastical music we can speak only of holding back the influx of foreign goods, in folk-music we must give the eighteenth century full credit for having unleashed a regular torrent of superbly beautiful melodies that were to become the very backbone of all Russian music over the expanse of nearly two hundred years. But since the main impact of this did not come until well into the nineteenth century, we shall leave it to a subsequent volume.

(b) *Style Formation in Early Russian Keyboard Music*

RUSSIA'S greatest musical resource has been its folk tradition. It has put its stamp on centuries of her music. With this strong asset, she fascinated the outside world as much as she enjoyed the influence of others. Musical styles imported from abroad rarely escaped being coloured with Russian national feeling and 'modality'.

While music historians generally agree that Glinka was the first significant figure of Russian classical music, one must not overlook the fact that the foundations of the nineteenth century were laid in the eighteenth by a group of composers, some native, some foreign, who with the exception of Dmitry Bortnyansky (1752–1825) are largely forgotten.

Whenever one contemplates the history of music in Russia, it is always striking to realize that before the eighteenth century no musical traditions—in the western sense—existed. There was no evolutionary development of forms or styles; no polyphony, no court music of an advanced nature; no development of non-folk-type musical instruments. What did exist was music of the Church and folk-music. How incredible that this great nation lived in such isolation from the rest of Europe and that the music from those periods commonly known as the Middle Ages, the Renaissance, and the Baroque never penetrated east of Poland. From A.D. 900 to 1750 the cornerstone of most European music, be it sacred, be it secular, instrumental or vocal, was the contrapuntal texture of part writing.

During the Middle Ages, roving bands of Russian peasant minstrels were chased from the cities by the clergy, who frowned upon the profane influence of these musical vagabonds. Travelling from village to village throughout the vast steppe, probably along the banks of the great rivers, they kept alive and developed the rich musical folklore of the country. Playing the gusli and the gudok,[1] they were usually accompanied by singers, dancers, and jugglers. Although these minstrels were not the respected artists that their western counterparts were, and their art probably never reached a high degree of refinement, they were responsible for spreading and passing down the many varieties of Russian musical folk culture.

While before the eighteenth century Russia and the West did not enjoy musical cultures that were in any way analogous, the eighteenth century brought the importation of western music and musicians on a grand scale and a movement was created that was to affect permanently the course of music history. Aside from the introduction of Italian opera and French ballet, a long list of musical personages that included such names as Galuppi, Sarti, Traetta, and Paisiello resided in Russia for often considerable periods of time under the patronage of the Russian nobility. Johann Gerstenberg, a Leipzig music publisher, immigrated to St. Petersburg and in 1793 established a printing house there. He not only brought out the works of the Viennese masters, but encouraged the development of a new emerging national style that had a profound effect upon the future course of Russian music. His Russian Series, which will be discussed later in this essay, was a prominent contributor to the marriage of the Russian folk-song to European classical styles.

The earliest body of music to evolve out of this union was that which was written often in variation form for the harpsichord and piano. In its beginning stages this newly born Russian keyboard culture seems to stem largely from idioms intended for the gusli. It is fascinating to note that the birth of Russian keyboard music coincides with that period when the gusli was enjoying its greatest popularity.[2]

[1] *Gusli*—a plucked stringed instrument similar in shape and stringing to the psaltery. Probably one of the earliest folk instruments used in accompaniment, it had a cardinal role in the development of folk-music.

Gudok—an early Russian three-stringed, onion-shaped instrument. Played with a bow, two of its strings were tuned in unison, and the third a fifth higher. It is held in a vertical position.

[2] Flavy Vasilevich Sokolov, 'Narodnye istoki russkoy fortepiannoy muzyk

The Soviet musicologist N. Findeyzen refers us to illustrations from a Novgorod manuscript of the fourteenth century showing several figures each playing a different type of gusli.[3] Another excellent illustration appears in a miniature from the Godunovsky Psalter of 1584.[4]

The instrument and its literature interests us not only because of its antiquity or its role as the direct historical predecessor to Russian piano music, but because it occupied a position of great importance in the whole evolution of Russian national musical culture.[5] During the second half of the eighteenth century gusli scores were sometimes indistinguishable from those written for keyboard. What appears most striking is the number of supportive accompaniment figures typically classical in nature that found their way into gusli literature and then back to the keyboard.

The music of V. F. Trutovsky is one of the earliest and best examples of this.[6] As one studies this repertory it becomes evident how well the variation form lent itself to these folk tunes.

The collection by T. Polezhaev, *Novy rossiysky pesennik* of 1792 (new Russian songbook or collection of various songs with the application of notes, which may be sung by voices, played on guslis, clavichords, violins, and wind instruments), is a fine example of Russian *Gebrauchmusik* of the period. The late Soviet scholar, V. I. Muzalevsky, writes of them: 'It is not difficult to see in these variations the healthy growth of a national piano art. This is the first stage of Russian music in the variation form; the first examples of an everyday keyboard music.'[7]

Dramatic as this statement seems, it does not entirely represent the actual situation.[8] The works of Karaulov, Bortnyansky, Prach, and Trutovsky, which pre-date Polezhaev, demand far

kontsa XVIII veka' (Leningrad, 1956), p. 4 (unpub. dissertation Leningrad Conservatory of Music Library, 1956).

[3] N. Findeyzen, *Ocherki po istorii muzyki v Rossii* (Moscow, 1928), i. 121.

[4] Ibid, p. 172.

[5] Sokolov, p. 42.

[6] V. F. Trutovsky, 174?–1810, born the son of a priest, served under Elizavata Petrovna, Peter III, and Catherine II as a court singer and guslist.

[7] V. I. Muzalevsky, *Russkaya fortepiannaya muzyka* (Moscow and Leningrad, 1949), p. 41.

[8] Sokolov, p. 64.

more from the performer in regard to technical requirements. They also represent a 'higher state of the art'.

The Polezhaev collection was important because it was easy *Hausmusik* that owed its popularity to the fact that it made music accessible to many. Part two, the most interesting section for our purposes, finds the pieces laid out in an indiscriminate order. It is possible to find music for the hunt taken from the repertory of the *Rogovoy* orchestra[9] next to a folk song[10] followed by an aria out of early Russian comic opera.[11]

A whole series of method books for the gusli began to appear. Maksim Pomerantsev's *Azbuka*[12] was one of the first and also the most influential. It had a considerable effect on early Russian piano music. Another book by Kushenob-Dmitrevsky[13] contains many examples that vary from Russian songs to contradances and waltzes. The music here has been characterized as representing techniques that share much in common with piano technique.[14] In fact, even the notation is identical with that of keyboard music.

With the numerous gusli books and song collections pointing the way, it is no surprise that much of the same material reappeared later in the first collections of Russian keyboard music. For example, one of the better-known tunes of the day, *Vo lesochke komarochkov mnogo urodilos* ('Many mosquitoes came alive in the woods'), initially used as set of gusli variations, was reset for harpsichord by Khandoshkin.[15]

---

[9] Polezhaev Collection, part 2, no. 1. The *Rogovoy* orchestra consisted entirely of horns capable of producing only one note. These orchestras were staffed by serfs and sometimes numbered up to 300 players.

[10] Ibid., pt. 2, no. 2.

[11] Ibid., pt. 2, no. 9.

[12] A copy of Maksim Pomerantsev's *Azbuka* is housed in the music section of the Leningrad State Public Library (no. 15, XXII. 290). According to Sokolov, the title-page is lost but the first page shows a schematic diagram of the distribution of strings for the stolovoi gusli. He advertised his method as: 'sposob samy legchayshy uchitsya igrat na guslyakh po notam bez pomoshchi uchitelya'.

[13] This example is in good condition and is presently housed in the Leningrad State Public Library (no. 15.5.2.75) and in the Library of the Soviet Academy of Sciences (no. XVIII Vek, 1808/128).

[14] A. S. Famintsyn, *Gusli*, pp. 110–14.

[15] Source for Khandoshkin's Variations on *Vydu ya na rechenku* is from the *Karmannaya kniga dlya lyubiteley muzyki* published by J. Gerstenberg (St. Petersburg, 1795).

A close examination of the aforementioned sources shows that during the late eighteenth century and early nineteenth century there was an astonishing closeness between music for gusli, harpsichord, and piano. Of course, for reasons of technical accommodation, certain small changes had to be made. Not only was there a concomitance of compositional techniques, but also a sharing of piece-types, e.g. folk-song and variations, aria, and various dance forms. The lighter nature of these forms might give us a clue as to the function of music in Russian courtly society of the time. For obvious historical reasons, Russian musical culture had not evolved to the level of Western Europe. Granted that the West had a 1,000-year lead in both secular and sacred forms (exclusive of liturgical chant), it was for the Russians to absorb certain of the eighteenth-century styles (and not the more complex ones at that) and adapt to them the mood of the Russian nation.

The years 1770–98 produced a large output of published folk-music.[16] Russian folk-songs not only were an integral part of the musical life and culture of the times but found their way into early Russian opera and instrumental music of the first Russian composers. This influence was particularly pronounced on keyboard music. The blossoming of this new keyboard culture also had an effect on instrument production in Russia. By the 1770s, it seems that there was so great an interest in harpsichord and piano music that the imported foreign instruments already in evidence did not suffice. During the 1780s domestic production of keyboard instruments began in St. Petersburg.[17] Piano and harpsichord music thus became all the more accessible to the upper levels of Russian society who were outside the immediate domination of courtly culture.

Late eighteenth-century keyboard music, although intended for either piano or harpsichord, was often stylistically better suited to

---

[16] The following collections appeared: (a) *Sobranie raznykh pesen*, M. D. Chulkov, 1770–4; (b) *Sobranie russkikh prostykh pesen*, V. F. Trutovsky, 1776–95; (c) *Russkie Skazki*, V. A. Levshin, 1780–4; (d) *Sobranie narodnykh russkikh pesen*, N. A. Lvov–I. Pratch, 1790; (e) *Pesennik*, J. D. Gerstenberg i F. A. Dittmar, 1797–8.

[17] P. N. Stolpyansky, *Stary Peterburg. Muzyka i muzytsirovanie v starom Peterburge* (Leningrad, 1926), p. 164.

the piano. Because plucked stringed instruments are so closely associated with Russian folk-music, it might have seemed natural for the harpsichord to step in and assume the role of the gusli. Actually, it was the piano that little by little came to replace the gusli as the instrument for household music making. It soon became the basic accompanying instrument for popular and folk-song, the romance, and almost all forms of instrumental music.

The first known composers to deal directly with Russian folk material were V. F. Trutovsky, V. S. Karaulov, I. E. Khandosh-kin, and V. Palshau. Trutovsky (1740–1810), the virtuoso court guslist, made his mark on Russian music with the first printed collection of Russian songs. The son of a priest, he is considered the father of Russian keyboard music because of his publication, *Variations on Russian Songs for Clavicymbalum or Fortepiano* (1780). Only two of these variation sets have been preserved.[18] They show a marked influence of gusli technique and while in a certain sense they utilize the variation technique with some skill, they both lack the contrapuntal and harmonic enrichment that is evident in the settings of later composers.

It is incredible to look at this incipient Russian music which appeared at the end of the eighteenth century and think back to the centuries of tradition emanating from the West. The ex-haustive keyboard repertories, each with highly individualistic characteristics, and the eventual cross-breedings that took place in Italy, France, England, the Netherlands, Spain, and Germany between the sixteenth and eighteenth centuries, were totally bypassed by Russia. This fact perhaps freed her composers, through lack of knowledge and tradition, to seek their roots elsewhere. While western polyphony developed between the twelfth and eighteenth centuries, Russia produced no musical traditions or composers in any way analogous to this. Its only musical traditions were liturgical monophony and folk-music—the latter feeding the almost sudden appearance of western musical forms with rich thematic content. As in many other

---

[18] Based on the tunes *U dorodnogo dobrogo molodtsa* and *Vo lesochke komarochkov mnogo urodilos.*

spheres, borrowed techniques were used to up-date an ancient cultural heritage. Western music shows us techniques and forms arising out of specific musical needs. The history of Russian music to this day demonstrates the implantation of foreign ideas into native roots.

Although the contribution of Trutovsky was extremely important, the composer V. S. Karaulov, whose variation sets appeared seven years after the publication of Trutovsky's, shows a significant evolution of both style and technique. The Leningrad musicologist V. I. Muzalevsky first uncovered these variations at the end of the 1930s in the archives of the Lenin Library in Moscow. They were found in a single edition together with a Sonata by Ivan Prach.[19] Karaulov is the first Russian to show a high degree of professionalism and talent. His sophisticated use of folk-song material lifted the Russian song variation to a point which set the stage for the further development of this form. They rest on a much higher artistic level than anything that came before them and much that was written after them. These pieces make excellent use of contrapuntal modes often associated with J. S. Bach, and it seems likely that Karaulov might have been acquainted with some of his works.

Little is known about Karaulov, but on the 1787 publication he is referred to as *Gospodin*, or Master, which leads us to believe that he most certainly was not of royal family. Another reference to him is found in the preface of Prach's *Collection of Popular Russian Songs*. It was written by his contemporary N. A. Lvov, and ranks him together with Sarti, Martini, Paskevich, Palshau, and others. Lvov also states that the collection of songs should serve as a 'rich source for musical talents and for the composers of operas, who should employ not only various motifs but also some of the entire songs which in their own strange way should directly give the ears of music lovers new delights and expectations'.

An examination of the *Three Russian Airs* set by Karaulov bears out the contention of Lvov. The attempts of Trutovsky and the anonymous examples that came before him generally represent

[19] *Trois airs russes variés pour le clavecin ou forte piano* par Mr. M. de Karaulov suivis d'une sonate composée par J. Pratsch (1787).

a rather unevolved treatment of the song material with little harmonic and literally no contrapuntal invention. Karaulov presents us for the first time with a creative transformation of the Russian folk-song. The three cycles are based on the following tunes:

1. *Akh, kak toshno mne toshnenko* ('Ah, how sick I feel')
   10 var. in F minor.[20]

2. *Ty detinushka sirotinushka* ('You poor little girl')
   7 var. in C minor.[21]

3. *Vo lesochke komarochkov mnogo urodilos* ('Many mosquitoes came alive in the woods')
   10 var. in E major.[22]

The first two sets are melodies characteristic of the *protyazhny* or slow Russian drawling type, while the last is best described as a *plyasovaya pesnya* (folk-dance song). It is interesting to note that three years after the publication of Karaulov's versions of these songs they appeared in Prach's *Collection of Popular Russian Songs* in almost the exact same harmonizations. This leads one to speculate whether there might have been any creative contact between the two composers. One possibility is that Karaulov in some way directly participated in the selection and harmonization of these songs, and it is likewise possible that Prach used the already made harmonizations of Karaulov, making a few changes.

During the years 1795 and 1796 the publishing firm of Johann Gerstenberg in St. Petersburg issued his *Pocket Book for Music Lovers.* Towards the end of each book appears a set of keyboard variations on a Russian song. The set contained in the 1795 edition is the only remaining harpsichord composition by I. E. Khandoshkin (1747–1804),[23] who was generally known as the first Russian violin virtuoso. He was born a serf but was liberated and achieved fame as a performer-composer both in Russia and

---

[20] Pub. three years later (1790) in Pratch's *Sbornik* (no. 27).
[21] Ibid., no. 31.   [22] Ibid., no. 4.
[23] The authorship of Khandoshkin's Variations was uncovered by N. Findeyzen on the basis of newspaper publications. They have been reprinted in Findeyzen's *Ocherki po istorii muzyki v Rossii,* vol. ii of musical examples, no. 147, and in the anthology, *Russkaya starinnaya fortepiannaya muzyka* (Moscow and Leningrad, 1946), p. 9.

abroad. One might say that Khandoshkin is to the early Russian violin repertory what Trutovsky is to the keyboard literature. It should be added that the surviving example of his work, a variation set based on the song *Many Mosquitoes Came Alive in the Woods*, shows a greater degree of musical sophistication than Trutovsky.

With the possible exception of Karaulov, the music of the Petersburg composer-harpsichordist Wilhelm Palshau (1741–1815) is for reasons of musical culture far more advanced than any so far discussed. Little is known about him, but he was said to have studied in Riga with one of J. S. Bach's last students, most likely Muttel.[24] His known music most clearly shows a greater compositional skill and variety of harmonic and contrapuntal language than that of his Russian counterparts.

Newspaper accounts of the time indicate that he gained wide popularity with concerts of organ, piano, and harpsichord music. These concerts were responsible for introducing to the Petersburg public not only works by pre-Bach composers, but those of Bach and his sons. He became one of the first professional musicians to advance the music of J. S. Bach in Russia. For that alone Russia owes him a great debt. It is paradoxical that Bach was almost a completely forgotten composer in Western Europe and at the same time a latter-day disciple was propagating his works in Russia. His interpretation of Bach's music lingered in the memories of those who heard him perform until the middle of the nineteenth century.[25]

Arriving in St. Petersburg in 1770 from Riga, he seemed to be immediately absorbed into the life of the city. It is known that in 1771 he published two piano concerti (begun in Riga). Unfortunately, only one of his works has been preserved from his Petersburg period with the rest remaining lost or 'undiscovered'. Again it is a set of variations on a Russian air, and is called *Kak u nashego shirokogo dvora* ('Our friendly homestead').

[24] From the columns of the *Peterburgsky nekropol* (T. Sh., stv. 353) it says: 'Palshau, Gotfrid-Vilgelm, imperatorsky kamer muzykant. R. v Gilshteyne 21 dek. 1741, + 23 iunya 1815 g., Smolenskoe evangelicheskoe kladbishche.'

[25] I. K. Cherlitsky, *Muzykalnoe rukovodstvo dlya artistov, i lyubiteley muzyki* (St. Petersburg, 1852).

Written for Gerstenberg's Russian Series, the very first autograph edition contains only five variations and was published anonymously in the 1795 edition of the *Pocket Book for Music Lovers*. The latter editions (2, 3, and 4) came out in the Russian Series proper which was called *Suite des airs russes variés pour le clavecin ou le pianoforte par divers auteurs*. It appeared no earlier than 1797.

The song 'Our Friendly Homestead' is actually a stylization of a popular melody. It is a composed tune by an unknown author who was able to combine the unusual intonation of the peasant 'drawling' song with elements of the late eighteenth-century city song-romance—a form quite popular at the time—complete with exaggerated sentimentalism. The first appearance of this tune was in the Trutovsky collection and it continued to show up in song books right through the nineteenth century.

It is interesting to note that the variation cycles written by native Russians present us with no examples of either the romance or a stylization. It seemed more common for the foreign composer to exploit the latter. The variations of Palshau thus represent an important stepping-stone in the formation of the Russian national school of nineteenth-century piano music. What resulted in an authentic national style emerged out of the interaction of both country and city folk-song with imported styles and forms.

The study of these late eighteenth-century founders of the Russian keyboard school causes us to draw certain lines of evolutionary continuity stemming from the last ten years of the eighteenth century: one is the line from Trutovsky the guslist to Khandoshkin the violinist, where both composers translated elements indigenous to their instruments to the keyboard. We must also note the stream that runs from Karaulov to Glinka and Dargomyzhsky; and finally Palshau who joined the polyphonic traditions of Central Europe to the folk traditions of Russia.

ROBERT E. JONES

12 Urban Planning and the Development of Provincial Towns in Russia, 1762–1796

URBAN planning, the creation of prescribed standards for the construction of cities and towns, was introduced into Russia by Peter the Great in the first quarter of the eighteenth century and became a universal policy of the Russian government during the reign of Catherine II (1762–96). By 1796 the Russian government had directed the planning of more than four hundred cities and towns and had produced a conscious uniformity of urban design throughout the Empire.[1] Because it established the appearance and the character of the modern Russian city, the urban planning of Catherine the Great constitutes one of the important legacies of the eighteenth century in Russia.

Catherine's towns were distinctively European, in imitation of St. Petersburg and in contrast to Moscow, which, despite the reconstruction carried out in the eighteenth century, retained many of the characteristics of an old Russian town. The difference between those two cities symbolized the break between Old Russia and the New Russia that the state was attempting to create. As Catherine explained it:

Moscow is the seat of sloth, partly due to its immensity: one wastes a whole day trying to visit someone or get a message across to them. The nobles are excessively fond of the place and no wonder: they live in idleness and luxury and become effeminate; it is not houses they own there but regular estates. Apart from that the town is full of symbols of fanaticism, churches, miraculous icons, priests, and convents, side by side with thieves and brigands. Nor must one overlook the number

    [1] The official plans were published as a supplement to the first collection of the *Polnoe Sobranie Zakonov Rossiyskoy Imperii* (hereafter *PSZ*) in a separate volume entitled *Kniga chertezhey i risunkov* (St. Petersburg, 1939).

of large factories which create an excessive accumulation of working-men.

Yes, it is true that the construction of St. Petersburg cost much money and many lives; it is a costly city to live in, but in forty years it has given more circulation to money and commerce than Moscow in the five hundred years she has existed; the inhabitants are more docile and polite, less superstitious, more accustomed to foreigners, from whom they always acquire something valuable.[2]

However, Catherine's instructions to rebuild Russian towns so as to give them 'a more European appearance'[3] must be understood in the light of her Instruction to the Legislative Commission of 1767, which began with the assertion that Russia was a European state. For Catherine the contrast was not between Europe and Russia but between that which was internationally European and that which was peculiarly or parochially Russian. The eighteenth-century style in city planning and architecture was an international standard that contrasted as sharply with the style of medieval towns in Western Europe as it did with that of medieval towns in Russia. The Western counterpart of 'Old Russian' or 'Slavic' was 'Gothic', a term coined to designate the style of the 'Middle Ages' (another term of opprobrium) in contrast to that which was modern and rational or 'enlightened'. While 'European' and 'Russian' were not opposites in Catherine's mind, 'European' and 'Old Russian' or 'Slavic' were. They were opposites in the same sense that 'Modern Russian' and 'Old Russian', referring to Russia before Peter the Great, were opposites.

The traditional Russian town, like its Western counterpart, was the product, not of rational planning, but of unplanned, organic growth. An Old Russian or Slavic town was originally a small settlement defended by a wall or palisade. As the town grew, new settlements would spring up outside the original enclosure, and a new wall would then be raised to include and protect the expanded territory. Eventually a series of concentric walls would

    [2] *The Memoirs of Catherine the Great*, ed. D. Maroger, trans. M. Budberg (New York, 1955), p. 365.
    [3] V. A. Shkvarikov, *Ocherki istorii planirovki i zastroyki russkikh gorodov* (Moscow, 1954), p. 83. Catherine used these exact words in ordering the creation of a plan for the city of Voronezh in 1772.

surround the nucleus of the city, the citadel or kremlin, and would divide the larger settlement into distinct rings or segments.[4] The houses in these towns were not built along the streets but were located instead in the middle of courtyards and were surrounded by vegetable gardens, animal pens, and storage sheds. The outbuildings that surrounded a house frequently intruded into the street, which was regarded as an unwelcome restraint on the size of the courtyard or *dvor*, the real focus of urban life. The streets themselves were narrow, twisting, and often impeded with stalls, refuse heaps, and other obstacles.[5] Dirt roads were common although the important thoroughfares would be covered with log planking. Save for the larger churches and a few palaces or government buildings, the entire town would be built of wood, usually pine or spruce, and thus fire was an ever present danger. Once a fire broke out it could seldom be stopped until it had destroyed an entire segment or perhaps the entire city. The Moscow fire of 1712, for example, destroyed more than 3,000 houses and 500 shops, killed approximately 2,700 people, and left one fourth of the city in ruins.[6]

St. Petersburg, on the other hand, was both a planned city and the first city in Russia to resemble the modern cities of Western Europe (see Pl. 39). It was a city created by decree. Having personally selected its site, Peter the Great had prescribed and regulated the building of St. Petersburg in the same authoritarian way that he had ordered the shaving off of beards and the wearing of 'German', i.e. Western, clothes. By imperial decree the streets of the new city were to be broad, straight, and paved with stone.[7] Houses were to be built flush with the streets, along lines specifically drawn for the purpose, and were to form a straight and

---

[4] M. W. Thompson, *Novgorod the Great* (London, 1967), p. x. P. Francastel (ed.), *Les Origines des villes polonaises* (Paris, 1960), pp. 30–6. The traditional pattern of urban development is clearly visible in the map of seventeenth-century Moscow. See Pl. 37. The persistence of this pattern in eighteenth-century Moscow can be seen in Pl. 38.

[5] P. V. Sytin, *Istoriya planirovki i zastroyki Moskvy*, 3 vols. (Moscow, 1950), i. 222.

[6] V. I. Lebedev, 'Blagoustroystvo', *Istoriya Moskvy*, ii: *Period Feodalizma XVIII v.*, pp. 135–6.

[7] S. P. Luppov, *Istoriya stroitelstva Peterburga v pervoy chetverti XVIII v.* (Moscow, 1957), pp. 50–1.

continuous façade.[8] Stone, brick, and other non-flammable materials were to be used in construction in order to reduce the danger of fire.[9] Even the appearance of the houses had to conform to the Emperor's wishes: in 1711 Peter erected a model cottage and ordered the residents to follow its example in building their own houses; in 1714 he ordered the inhabitants to purchase their building plans from his chief architect; and in 1715 he prohibited all construction that did not follow a blueprint approved by the government.[10] Finally, after the creation of several partial plans, an over-all plan for the future development of St. Petersburg was confirmed in 1727, two years after Peter's death.

Influential though the creation of St. Petersburg was, the building of one city could not modernize Russia unless that city became a model for others. Peter obviously had intended that it should, since in 1709 he had created a Chancellery of Construction for the planning of St. Petersburg and had attached to it a school for the training of young architects and planners. The creation of St. Petersburg, however, was such an undertaking in itself that it absorbed nearly all resources available for construction, and Peter was obliged at one point to prohibit stone building in other cities in order to concentrate men and materials in St. Petersburg. Nevertheless, fires continued to necessitate the rebuilding of Russia's cities and towns, and since some building in other towns was necessary, Peter ordered that it be carried out in the new way. Thus the great Moscow fire of 1712 brought forth a spate of decrees ordering that houses in the centre of the city be built of non-flammable materials, roofed with tiles, and erected in straight lines flush with the streets.[11] Those measures were reinforced by subsequent decrees and by the sending to Moscow of a trained architect from St. Petersburg in 1718.[12] After Novgorod was partially destroyed by fire in 1723, Peter ordered that '. . . in the burned-out areas of Novgorod the timber mansions of the well-to-do are to be arranged regularly as in St. Petersburg with a

---

[8] *PSZ* nos. 2855, 3799. The 'lines' of Peter the Great have given their name to the north–south streets of the Vasilevsky Island.

[9] *PSZ* no. 12792. [10] Luppov, *Istoriya*, pp. 47–8.

[11] *PSZ* nos. 2531, 2534, 2548.

[12] *PSZ* no. 3147.

continuous façade and with the streets on a strict plan'.[13] After Peter's death the Russian government repealed most of his building regulations, but persistent fires, especially in Moscow, forced the reinstitution of most of them in 1730 and 1736, and led to the creation in 1739 of the first general plan for the future development of Moscow. More fires there were answered by more decrees specifying the width of the streets and charging the police with the supervision of all construction.[14]

Catherine's major innovation was to generalize the practice of urban planning. When a fire destroyed the centre of Tver in May 1763, leaving much of the town in ashes with no plan of reconstruction, her response was to order the planning not just of Tver but of all cities and towns.[15] From an administrative standpoint Catherine's decree was an intelligent advance over the practice of her predecessors: since frequent fires made the eventual planning of every town a virtual certainty, the preparation of plans before rather than after the fire would eliminate delay and confusion and expedite the rebuilding. In the broader context of Catherine's urban legislation, however, the decree on planning was typical of her policy of dealing with towns on a general rather than an individual basis. Although the cities and towns of Russia differed greatly in age, size, economic development, and other circumstances, they were all to be subject to the same laws and regulations, which spoke simply of *goroda*, a word which can be translated either as 'cities' or 'towns' and meant, in strictly legal terms, that the settlement had no owner.[16] Catherine was conscious of her approach and believed that legislating for all towns in general was both necessary and proper, as she explained in her Instruction to the Legislative Commission:

Though there are many different Situations of the Cities, yet they all in general agree in this, that one particular Law is necessary for them

---

[13] M. K. Karger, *Novgorod Veliky* (Leningrad, 1961), p. 55.

[14] *PSZ* nos. 8556, 9510.

[15] *PSZ* no. 11883.

[16] The legal distinction between a *gorod* and a *selo* or *sloboda* goes back at least as far as the *Ulozhenie* of 1649, which forbade the ownership of a *gorod*. A *selo* or *sloboda*, an agricultural or commercial settlement, on the other hand, could be and usually was the property of a private lord, the Church, the Crown, a factory owner, or the state.

all, *viz.* to determine what a City is, who is to be termed an Inhabitant in it, and who are to compose the Community of that City, and who are to enjoy the Benefit of the Advantages arising from the natural Situation of the Place, and how a Person may be admitted a Citizen.[17]

Indeed generalization characterized Catherine's approach to most subjects and can be seen clearly in writings such as her *Instruction to the Legislative Commission* of 1767, with its chapters entitled 'On Education', 'On the Nobility', 'On the Cities', 'On Inheritances', etc. Although they were unrealistic in the sense that they did not describe existing conditions in Russia, Catherine's generalizations did not ignore the reality of existing conditions that were contrary to her general ideal so much as they established standards towards which existing conditions were to evolve. She was less concerned, for example, with what the towns of Russia were than with what they were to become. Her method not only presupposed growth and progress; it implied that explicit knowledge of the ideal enables humans to direct growth and progress toward the realization of the ideal. In other words, development should proceed with a preconceived idea of the results of that progress—it should be planned. To illustrate the value of planning in advance Catherine could think of no better example than that of urban growth, and in the section of her *Instruction* that dealt with the organization of the police department she wrote:

Exactly the same confusion has happened in the Regulation of this Department, as with the Number of Houses, which compose a City, where the Plan of the Ground was not regularly marked out before the People began to build. When the People begin to build in a City so circumstanced, every one fixes upon a Spot which he thinks most convenient, without the least Regard either to the Symmetry or Extent of the Place he had selected: Whence a Heap of Edifices are huddled together, which can hardly ever be brought into a regular Form by the Efforts and careful Attention of whole Ages.[18]

Since urban planning under Catherine the Great attempted to

17 'The Instruction to the Legislative Commission', Chapter XVII, article 393. *Documents of Catherine the Great*, ed. W. F. Reddaway (Cambridge, 1931), p. 276.
18 Ibid., Chapter XXI, article 545, pp. 296–7.

make towns conform to a preconceived idea of what a town ought to be, it is important to determine what Catherine's idea of a town was. Her legislation and other writings indicate that Catherine thought of towns functionally, in terms of the various roles that they played in the life of the nation. First and foremost towns were administrative centres, focal points of governmental activity in a nation that was sparsely populated and overwhelmingly rural. Some towns were nothing more than administrative centres; all were that at the very least. After the provincial reform of 1775 the shape and size of administrative units were determined by their relationship to a town, and, as before, provinces and counties were named for the town on which they depended. Whereas Moscow and St. Petersburg were the home of the imperial government, the other towns of Russia were really extensions of the state into the countryside, the points at which the imperial government and the scattered population came into contact. Taxes and military recruits were collected there, the troops that preserved order were quartered there, and there also were the courts, the surveying office, and the other government agencies whose activities concerned the residents of the area. Already inseparable from their role as administrative centres at the time of Catherine's accession, provincial towns became even more important in that capacity after 1775 when, as part of the general reform of provincial administration, Catherine decentralized such operations as the administration of justice and the settlement of property questions by increasing the role of local and provincial agencies and decreasing that of the central departments. The reform of 1775 was designed to strengthen the control of the imperial government over the vast territory of the empire, and the provincial towns were the centres from which that control was exercised.

Believing that order and government were but two of the benefits of civilization with which the state should provide its citizens, Catherine also envisaged the towns as centres of health care, education, and public welfare. The intention to develop towns in such a way can be seen in her memorandum of 10 June 1768 to the president of the College of Medicine expressing the desirability of having a chemist in every town[19] or her authorization of a loan of 1,200 roubles without interest to the four new towns founded in Novgorod province in 1772 to be used for the building and maintenance of a school in each town.[20] The first attempt to create such facilities on a national level came with the provincial reform of 1775, which included a doctor, a pharmacist, and two pharmacist's assistants among the public officials to be employed by the government of each county.[21] These were to be hired and paid by the government. The reform also called for the building of schools, hospitals, lazar-houses, lunatic asylums, homes for the aged, orphanages, jails, and workhouses in provincial towns but did not offer to finance their construction out of state funds. Instead, Catherine devised an ingenious scheme to finance the building of such facilities at no extra expense to the state, while satisfying at the same time the demand of the provincial nobles for the creation of local credit institutions. Responsibility for providing social services was vested in a semi-official foundation, known as the Board of Public Welfare, which was to consist of two representatives of each of the major classes of free citizens—nobles, townsmen, and free peasants—under the chairmanship of the provincial governor. The Board was to raise revenue in two ways, through the receipt of charitable donations from private individuals and through its lending operations, which were funded by the government. Each Board was to be given a capital grant of 15,000 roubles to lend to local landowners at interest with the profits going to finance the social work of the Board.[22] Progress was certain to be slow, considering the immensity of the task and the immediate lack of money and other resources, but as the capital of the Board of Public Welfare grew, the social services that Catherine desired would eventually come into being. One day, ideally, the citizens of Russia would be able to find such services in the nearest town.

In Catherine's thinking, towns were also linked with industry

---

[19] *PSZ* no. 13045.   [20] *PSZ* no. 13780.
[21] *PSZ* no. 14392, Chapter I, article 24.
[22] *PSZ* no. 14392, Chapter XXV. The scheme devised in 1775 is clearly the fulfilment of the idea expressed in Chapter XII, article 329, of the 'Instruction'. *Documents*, p. 266.

and commerce; they were in her words 'safe havens for trade and handicrafts' in contrast to the agricultural countryside.[23] As such they were needed to balance the provincial economy by selling manufactured goods and buying surplus agricultural produce.[24] Trade, Catherine believed, increased the wealth of the nation and was therefore highly desirable, hence her approval of St. Petersburg and her belief that it had been a good investment for the nation in spite of the original expense involved in creating it. Manufacturing also increased the wealth of the nation, but it was not an unqualified blessing as the experience of Moscow, with its many factories and its large congregation of working men, had shown. The best arrangement, she thought, was to have a few factories in each town but not too many in any one place.[25]

As centres of trade and commerce, towns were also the home of the middle class, which Catherine defined as those people who were neither nobles nor peasants but who were engaged in 'arts, sciences, navigation, commerce, or handicraft trades' or else were graduates of a secondary school.[26] At the time Catherine made that statement, the three elements of her definition—not being a noble or a peasant, being engaged in trade, industry, or intellectual pursuits, and living in a city or town—were not always found in conjunction with each other, but the policy of her government was to associate them as closely as possible. Thus in the founding of new towns the government tried to avoid designating agricultural villages as the sites of future towns and to select instead settlements where the peasants made their living by trade and handicrafts. Other considerations caused the government to pass over some manufacturing villages, especially if they were in private hands, and to select some agricultural villages for conversion into towns,[27] but such cases were generally the result of necessity rather than policy. According to the procedure first carried out in Novgorod in 1772 and then extended to the new

[23] Introduction to 'The Charter to the Towns', *PSZ* no. 16188.
[24] 'Instruction', Chapter XVII, article 398. *Documents*, p. 277.
[25] Memoirs, p. 381.
[26] 'Instruction', Chapter XVI, articles 380 and 381. *Documents*, p. 275.
[27] See Yu. P. Klokman, *Sotsialno-ekonomicheskaya istoriya russkogo goroda. Vtoraya polovina XVIII v.* (Moscow, 1967), p. 126.

towns founded after 1775, all the residents of a settlement designated as a town automatically became townsmen (*gorodskie
zhiteli*) without having to go through the normal procedure for
such a change in status.[28] The definition of townsmen was further
clarified by the decrees of 17 March and 25 May 1775, which
divided the urban dwellers into two broad categories: merchants
and *meshchanstvo*.[29] Merchants were organized into classes or
'guilds' according to the amount of capital they possessed, while
townsmen who did not have enough capital for membership in
even the lowest guild were enrolled in the *meshchanstvo*. Movement from guild to guild or between the merchant class and the
meshchanstvo was automatic, according to the rise or fall of one's
fortunes. Whereas the status of nobles depended upon aristocratic and service criteria, i.e. birth or service rank, that of townsmen was determined by the bourgeois standard of wealth.

Government policy also tried to foster an identification between towns and merchants or tradesmen who were wealthy or at
least substantial. Active participation in town affairs was restricted
to citizens who had an amount of capital equal to that of a second
guild merchant. Merchants paid a tax on their capital, but were
exempted from the poll-tax that applied to the lower classes, and
they were able to avoid conscription by making a cash payment
in lieu of service. Members of the *meshchanstvo*, on the other hand,
were subject to the poll-tax and conscription just like the peasants.
New enrolments in the merchant class were welcomed: any free
peasant with enough capital to enrol in one of the merchant
guilds was allowed to do so provided he paid both his merchant's
tax and his poll-tax until the next revision of the census rolls, but
entry into the *meshchanstvo* was restricted in 1780 and forbidden
altogether two years later.[30] The reason for restriction and then
prohibition was explained by the Senate, which stated that the
entry of peasants into the *meshchanstvo* '. . . does the towns no
good, considering the poverty of the newly enrolled . . .' and

----

28 *PSZ* no. 13780. See also Klokman, *Sotsialno-ekonomicheskaya istoriya*, p. 101.
29 *PSZ* nos. 14275 and 14327. This definition of townsmen was later broadened
by the 'Charter to the Towns', which included some other groups, especially
raznochintsy among the legal residents of towns.
30 *PSZ* nos. 15459 and 15570.

'does not in the least correspond to the interests of the treasury and increases the number of poor in the towns'.[31] Governor-General Krechetnikov of Kaluga province told the Empress that in his opinion an influx of poor peasants was a danger to the social stability of the towns and that a large *meshchanstvo* possessing no economic skills would only be a burden to society.[32] Examples such as these show that the policy of Catherine and her government was to fill the towns with as many substantial citizens as possible while admitting no more poor ones than necessary.

While the town was the 'haven' of the middle class, the surrounding countryside was the territory of the nobles. Nobles had no corporate or class rights in the towns other than that of maintaining an assembly hall for the meetings of their order. Individual nobles might own a house in the town and could use town law if they so desired, but they did so as citizens of the town, not as nobles. The Charter to the Cities issued in 1785 included nobles who owned houses in a town among its citizens under the category of '*de facto* residents'. As 'havens' of the bourgeoisie in the midst of a countryside and a national society dominated by the nobility, towns did not fit neatly into the legal relationships that governed society as a whole. The state wanted the towns to be the separate dominion of the middle class, and it exempted them from control by the nobles, but it could not exclude the nobles and their influence from them altogether. In some cases the authorities even encouraged the local nobles to settle in the towns because their buying power stimulated the local economy and increased the state's revenue.[33] Towns were in the contradictory position of serving simultaneously as the home of the middle class and as centres for the surrounding countryside that was dominated by the nobility. There was some contradiction as well between the town's role as the haven of the middle class and its role as a centre of administration. Although Catherine tried repeatedly to give the burghers some control over the affairs of the towns, that control was minimal and never included matters of real importance such

[31] *PSZ* nos. 15459 anq 15570.
[32] Klokman, *Sotsialno-ekonomicheskaya istoriya*, pp. 97 and 115.
[33] K. Blum, *Ein Russischer Staatsman. Des Grafen Johann Jacob Sievers Denkwurddigkeiten zur Geschichte Russland*, 4 vols. (Leipzig and Heidelberg, 1857), i. 387.

as the assessment of taxes, control over the police, or planning.[34] Self-government for the towns was inconsistent with the autocratic and bureaucratic nature of the Russian state, especially since the towns served as the headquarters of the state's own administrators.

In particular, Russian towns had virtually no say in the planning of their own development. Local residents could only complain about the government's plan and petition for a redress of their grievances.[35] Responsibility for creating the plans called for by the law of 25 June 1763 was placed in the hands of the provincial governors.[36] After 1785 no plan could be adopted unless it had been examined and confirmed by the Empress herself.[37] Town planning was to embody the policy of the state, not the wishes of the townspeople, and strict centralization of the planning process was one way, perhaps the only way, in which Catherine could make certain that towns would be planned properly, i.e. in accordance with her policies. However, while Catherine and her governors could formulate policy and insist on its implementation, they could not, for a number of reasons, do the actual planning. The translation of policy into blueprints required a planning agency staffed by professionals and subordinate to the state.

The role of a central planning agency for the Russian Empire was filled by the Commission on the Building of St. Petersburg and Moscow, established by Catherine's decree of 11 December 1762. The Commission was composed of three statesmen, General Z. G. Chernyshev, General I. I. Betskoy, and Prince M. I. Dashkov, who were to hire the necessary staff of architects, surveyors,

---

[34] I. I. Dityatin, *Ustroystvo i upravlenie gorodov Rossii*, vol. i: *Goroda Rossii v XVIII stoletii* (St. Petersburg, 1875), pp. 434–48.

[35] For example, Governor-General R. I. Vorontsov wrote that the inhabitants of Kostroma '. . . are to be found in extreme agitation. The town has received a plan in which the town square would occupy a great expanse, such that many houses, including stone ones, would have to be razed. On top of that six other squares are prescribed which ought to take up half of the town. Convinced by the pleas of the residents, I reduced the size of the square somewhat, by which means all of the stone houses could remain unrazed.' Report of R. I. Vorontsov to Catherine II, Sept. 1781, The Central State Archive of Ancient Acts (TsGADA) Moscow, *fond* XVI, *delo* 638, part 1, p. 9.

[36] *PSZ* no. 11883.

[37] Introduction to 'The Charter to the Towns', *PSZ* no. 16188.

clerks, and whatever other help might be needed and direct and oversee the planning of all construction.[38] Although the decree mentioned only the planning and future construction of Moscow and St. Petersburg, the commission actually carried out all of the town planning done in Russia between 1763 and 1796. In 1763, only a few months after its creation, the commission dispatched a staff of four architects to Tver, the first town to be reconstructed under Catherine's law on planning. In conjunction with Governor General Sievers, who was legally responsible for the operation, the four men drew up a general city plan that was finally confirmed in 1767. That plan, the first created by the commission and the first drawn up under Catherine's rule, became a model for the planning of other towns in the succeeding years and decades (Pl. 40).[39]

In addition to the rebuilding of old towns, the Commission on the Building of St. Petersburg and Moscow directed the planning of the hundreds of new towns created during Catherine's reign. Vast areas of eighteenth-century Russia were remote from any town and were therefore equally remote from the operations of the government. One such area lay in the centre of the province of Novgorod, along the chief highway from St. Petersburg to Moscow, where a sizeable population depended for administration on towns that were three or four hundred miles away. To remedy the lack of administration in that region, Governor-General Sievers, who was also Catherine's chief advisor on provincial affairs, proposed the creation of four new towns to serve as centres of administration for no more than 30,000 people each.[40] In 1772 the settlements of Valday, Vyshny Volochek, Borovichi, and Ostashkov were officially designated as towns, their inhabitants were enrolled in the merchantry or *meshchanstvo*, and orders were given to create plans for their future development.[41] From Sievers's reports it is clear that once again the actual

[38] *PSZ* no. 11723. [39] Shkvarikov, *Ocherki istorii*, pp. 156, 160.
[40] In a memorandum to the Senate dated 29 Apr. 1769 Sievers argued '. . . that in so far as it was possible a new town located in the midst of an *uezd* should have approximately 30,000 [inhabitants], and the people should be so divided both for the payment of taxes and for the receipt of courts and administration'. TsGADA, *fond* 248, *kniga* 369/3940, p. 3.
[41] *PSZ* no. 13780. For the plan of Ostashkov see Figure 5.

planning was carried out by agents of the Commission on the Building of St. Petersburg and Moscow, and that he personally examined and confirmed each plan before sending it to St. Petersburg for final confirmation.[42] Again, as with the rebuilding of Tver, Sievers's work, in conjunction with that of the professional planners of the Commission on the Building of St. Petersburg and Moscow, set a precedent for the entire nation. Whenever new towns were created in the future, the decree would state that they were to be 'established on the same basis as the towns of [the province of] Novgorod'.[43] The provincial reform of 1775 extended Sievers's reform throughout the Empire, dividing Russia into provinces (*gubernii*) of 300,000 to 400,000 inhabitants subdivided into counties (*uezdy*) of 20,000 to 30,000 inhabitants each and requiring the existence of a town in every province and county to serve as the seat of administration. To satisfy the provisions of the provincial reform the Russian government founded 216 new towns in the ten years between 1775 and 1785.[44]

No aspect of Catherine's urban programme has been criticized more harshly than the effort to create hundreds of new towns. Critics have emphasized both the artificiality of Catherine's effort to create towns from above, by decree of the state and its agents, and the failure of the towns so founded to take root and develop as real towns.[45] Upon closer examination, however, neither the intentions nor the results of Catherine's attempt to create new provincial towns would appear to merit the condemnation they have received. In the first place, the *primary* goal of the provincial reform of 1775 was the establishment of administrative centres, not towns. The development of those centres into actual towns

---

[42] Blum, *Ein Russischer Staatsman*, i. 363–4, 366, 390. See also Shkvarikov, *Ocherki istorii*, p. 160.

[43] For examples see *PSZ* nos. 14792, 14973, 15060, and 15061.

[44] *PSZ* no. 14392, Chapter I, articles 1 and 17; no. 16188, introduction.

[45] For examples of the criticisms levelled against Catherine's efforts to create new towns see D. I. Ilovaysky, 'Novgorodskaya Guberniya sto let tomu nazad', *Russky Vestnik*, xii (1863), 479–502; I. I. Dityatin, *Ustroystvo*, i. 379; I. I. Dityatin, 'Russky doreformenny gorod', *Stati po istorii russkago prava* (St. Petersburg, 1895), pp. 13–21; V. Gitermann, *Geschichte Russlands*, 3 vols. (Zürich and Hamburg, 1944–9), ii. 220; P. Milyukov, *Ocherki po istorii russkoy kultury*, i (St. Petersburg, 1909), 241.

was a secondary goal adopted in the hope of making them centres of commerce and civilization as well as administration. The presence of the provincial administrators and their staffs would naturally stimulate economic and cultural activity, and therefore the hope of turning the administrative centres into actual towns was not an unreasonable one. Moreover, the designation of the sites of the future towns was for the most part neither arbitrary nor artificial. New towns were established not in empty fields or forests but on the site of existing settlements, whose selection for designation as towns depended on three criteria: administrative convenience, ease of acquisition, and prospects for future growth and development.

To serve its purpose as a centre of administration a provincial town had to be located in an area where there were 20,000 to 30,000 male inhabitants who could be governed from it better than they could be governed from some other town. Preferably the town should be near the centre of such an area in order to be in relatively close contact with all who depended upon it for administration and also, if possible, be near to a main road or navigable waterway in order to facilitate communication with other administrative centres. In those respects Catherine's provincial reform closely resembles the Northwest Ordinance passed by the American Confederation in 1787 and the division of France into districts by the National Assembly in 1790. All three measures were the product of an eighteenth-century, rationalistic approach to administration.

The ease with which a settlement could be acquired by the provincial authorities also counted in the selection of sites for towns. Those already belonging to the government were given preference over those in private hands. Whenever a privately owned village was chosen as the site of a town, the owner was entitled to compensation for both land and serfs, which meant additional expenses and legal complications for the government.[46] Most of the settlements chosen, therefore, belonged either to the

---

[46] A. T. Bolotov, *Zhizn i priklyucheniya Andreya Bolotova*, 3 vols. (St. Petersburg, 1870–3), iii. 663–5. See also Shkvarikov, *Ocherki istorii*, pp. 81–2, and Klokman, *Sotsialno-ekonomicheskaya istoriya*, p. 139.

Crown or to some agency of the state. Most often selected were villages belonging to the College of Economy, which controlled the lands taken from the Church after the secularization of 1764. Thus serfdom and limited resources restricted the government's choice of sites somewhat and caused it to pass up some promising sites that were not already in its possession.[47]

Within the limits set by administrative, legal, and fiscal considerations, the Russian government and its officials tried to select sites that showed promise of developing into true towns. In proposing his new towns to the Senate in 1769 Sievers had stressed the economic and commercial advantages of the proposed sites.[48] Before selecting the sites for the establishment of new towns, the governor-general in charge would inspect each site personally and collect data on its population, commerce, resources, and access to communication. The facts collected would then be forwarded to the Senate to explain and justify his selections.[49]

Because the locations of the new towns were chosen for different reasons, the towns themselves were not all of one type, nor did they share a common future. Some were chosen purely for administrative reasons, failed to develop into true towns, and finally reverted to their former status. A few were already towns in all but name at the time of their designation and merited the new status they received. Still others had the potential to become towns and did in fact grow and develop as Catherine had hoped they would.[50] While some failed and none became large cities, most of the towns founded as a consequence of the provincial reform measured up in time to the role of small provincial towns

[47] Ibid., p. 126.

[48] TsGADA, *fond* 248, *kniga* 3940, p. 5, and *kniga* 3823, p. 4.

[49] The Senate ordered Governor-General Melgunov to make such a personal inspection in Yaroslavl. *PSZ* no. 14590. Melgunov made a similar inspection of Kostroma. *Materialy dlya istorii Kostromy* (Kostroma, 1913), p. 51. R. L. Vorontsov made a similar inspection of the province of Vladimir. TsGADA, *fond* XVI, *delo* 637, p. 11.

[50] See Klokman, *Sotsialno-ekonomicheskaya istoriya*, p. 15, and F. Ya. Polyansky, *Gorodskoe remeslo i manufaktura v Rossii XVIII v.* (Moscow, 1960), p. 17. I. A. Bulygin, 'Ob osobennostyakh srednego povolzhya vo vtoroy polovine XVIII v.', in *Goroda feodalnoy Rossii, Sbornik statey pamyati N. V. Ustyugova* (Moscow, 1966), pp. 488–9, presents detailed statistics on the remarkable growth of the towns in Penza province between 1762 and 1795.

serving as administrative, economic, and social centres for the surrounding countryside.[51]

Different from the towns founded as provincial centres were the new towns established in the territories annexed from Turkey. Founded originally as forts, but planned and developed as towns on the same basis as other new towns, several of the new towns of southern Russia developed into important cities and centres of commerce. Among them were Nikolaev, Ekaterinoslav, Maryupol, Aleksandrovsk, Stevastopol, and Odessa, the most successful of all Catherine's new towns.[52]

Different though the towns of Russia were in age, size, and origin, the legislation of Catherine the Great and the planning of the Commission on the building of St. Petersburg created or at least tried to create uniformity and standardization among them. Thus, with the necessary exceptions of St. Petersburg and Moscow, all towns were to be of a uniform size, 4 versts (2·6 miles) in diameter according to the surveying instructions of 1766.[53] Some towns, especially among those founded after the completion of the general survey, contained less than the prescribed area, however, and had to petition the government to bring them up to standard size.[54] In 1783 town governments—but not individual townsmen—were given permission to buy additional land from the local nobles and incorporate it into the town so long as the town did not exceed the prescribed norm.[55] Despite the complaints of town representatives at the Legislative Commission of 1767,[56] towns were forbidden to spread beyond the appointed boundaries without special permission.[57]

[51] For a detailed discussion of the fate of Catherine's new towns see P. G. Ryndzyunsky, 'Novye goroda Rossii kontsa XVIII v.', in *Problemy obshchestvenno-politicheskoy istorii Rossii i slavyanskikh stran. Sbornik statey k 70-letiyu akademika M. N. Tikhomirova* (Moscow, 1963), pp. 359–70. See also Klokman, *Sotsialno-ekonomicheskaya istoriya*, p. 28.

[52] On the development of cities and towns in southern Russia see E. I. Druzhinin, *Severnoe Prichernomore v 1775–1800 gg.* (Moscow, 1959), especially pp. 79–83 and 247–59.

[53] *PSZ* no. 12659.

[54] Klokman, *Sotsialno-ekonomicheskaya istoriya*, p. 60.

[55] *PSZ* no. 15848.

[56] *Sbornik Imperatorskogo Russkogo Istoricheskogo Obshchestva*, cvii. 92–3, 138, 350.

[57] *PSZ* no. 13780.

Within the geographical limits set by law, each town was planned as a unified whole unless it was naturally divided into districts by a river, in which case each section would have its own general plan. Except for Moscow, the concentric pattern of old Russian cities was completely abandoned. Walls between sections were pulled down, the streets were laid out so as to unite rather than separate the various parts of the town, and often settlements on the edges of the old towns were incorporated and integrated into the new one. In the case of Kostroma, for example, three suburbs were legally incorporated into the old town by the decree of the Senate, and subsequently the old sections and the new additions were physically unified and integrated by the plan created by the Commission on the Building of St. Petersburg and Moscow.

The street plans drawn up in the second half of the eighteenth century were invariably of a radial or a gridlike design, resembling the radial plan of the Admiralty District of St. Petersburg or the gridlike plan of the Vasilevsky Island District (see Pl. 39). In towns that were divided by water like St. Petersburg itself, the most important areas were usually laid out on a radial plan and the others on a grid, an excellent example being Tver (see Pl. 40). In the case of a radial plan, the focal point was usually the old kremlin, a monastery, or the largest church, and consequently those monuments of old Russian architecture were in many cases made even more prominent than they had previously been. With their characteristic domes and towers visible sometimes for miles down the broad, straight avenues, the old buildings gave the eighteenth-century 'European' towns a distinctively national identification. Also present in the plans of almost all towns but featured more prominently in those with radial plans were several squares around which the major public buildings would be grouped. A common arrangement was to have two major squares, one containing the government and administrative buildings and the other the stores and stalls of the merchants, located at either end of the main thoroughfare. The streets themselves were generally quite wide, usually more than seventy-five feet across, both for aesthetic reasons and for limiting the spread of fires. In some cases, especially when the town was to serve as the capital of an entire province, the new streets and squares would be laid out at once, and the older buildings that were in the way would be razed.[58] In less important towns the officials were instructed to leave the existing houses stand until decrepitude or fire made their rebuilding necessary, at which time the streets would be aligned according to the plan.[59]

Street design was but one of the ways in which the state tried to direct the development of towns towards the fulfilment of its policies. Another was zoning. Regulations created three distinct areas for different types of construction: the centre, the area contiguous to the centre, and the outskirts. Construction in the centre was to be compact, expensive, and as magnificent as possible. Public buildings, administrative offices, churches, the nobles' meeting hall, and the homes of the officials formed the nucleus of the town, and the remaining plots were to be filled with private residences of comparable size and quality. Known as 'dwellings of the first class', houses in the centre were to be two storeys in height and built of stone or brick. Anyone who agreed to build such a house would have to pay no taxes on it for five years and in some instances could obtain an interest-free loan from the state to defray the costs of construction.[60] Merchants were given priority in the purchase of building lots in the centre, but any lots not taken by the merchants after one year were made available to the local nobles for the building of their townhouses. If the taker of a lot in the centre did not build a stone house within five years, the property was to be reclaimed by the state.[61] The streets adjacent to the centre were reserved for 'dwellings of the second class', one-storey wooden houses built on stone foundations and often but not always covered with stucco. Because of their greater inflammability, houses of the second class were to be spaced further apart than those of the first, and consequently settlement in the second zone was less dense than in the centre. The out-

[58] Klokman, *Sotsialno-ekonomicheskaya istoriya*, pp. 59–60.
[59] *PSZ* no. 13780.
[60] Ibid. Also William Coxe, *Travels into Poland, Russia, Sweden, and Denmark,* 2 vols. (London, 1784), i. 421.
[61] *PSZ* no. 13780.

skirts of the towns, which were often much bigger than the other two zones combined, were to be filled with the poorest and least desirable housing. Houses there could be built entirely of wood and, except for being built flush with the street and at a considerable interval from each other, were indistinguishable from the houses in a rural village. Zoning regulations produced a residential pattern based on wealth. The richer a townsman was the closer to the centre of town he was likely to live and vice versa. Residents who would not or could not give up agriculture were sometimes removed from the towns altogether and settled in villages beyond the town line.[62] Thus the zoning regulations embodied Catherine's ideas of identifying the towns with commerce and with the middle class and of distinguishing between urban residents on the basis of wealth.

The planners also tried to improve the cleanliness, hygiene, and sanitation of the towns. The plans and the building codes tried in every possible way to reduce the danger of fire, and the zoning laws attempted to eliminate conditions that were obviously dirty, unpleasant, or unhealthy. Efforts were made to move factories that polluted the drinking-water downstream from the towns and to locate other factories in the outskirts and suburbs.[63] The stables of the government coach and postal service were also located at the edges of the towns, and Catherine gave strict orders that 'there shall not be one cemetery within the new towns, but the governor shall locate them in convenient places outside the town away from any habitation'.[64] Fountains, water pipes, drainage ditches, and canals were regularly provided for in the plans of the late eighteenth century, and the government passed strict laws against unsanitary practices such as dumping garbage and waste in the streets.[65] In sanitation as in so many areas the standards of the government were far in advance of the practices of the people, and the government had little alternative but to try to replace the latter with the former any way that it could, knowing that the process would not be easy or of short duration.

[62] Ryndzyunsky in *Problemy obshchestvenno-politicheskoy istorii*, p. 365.
[63] See for example the decree confirming the plan of Cheboksar, *PSZ* no. 14027.
[64] *PSZ* no. 13780.
[65] Shkvarikov, *Ocherki istorii*, p. 120.

The cultural gap between the government and those that it governed accounts for Catherine's reliance on state officials, professional planners, and the police to carry out her urban programme. Although the elected town governments were called upon to improve the towns and to co-operate in meeting the standards set by the government and although certain expenses such as the installation of street lanterns were to be met by the towns themselves,[66] Catherine had little faith in the civic responsibility of her subjects. Instead, compliance was demanded from above through the police, who became the agents and guardians of Catherine's urban programme. In the first supplement to her *Instruction*, Catherine defined the role of the police as being, broadly speaking, the preservation of good order. In specific terms that meant, in addition to the simple maintenance of tranquillity and the suppression of crime, the control of pollution and contagion, the prevention of fires and accidents, the inspection of construction, the preservation of pavements, and the decoration and ornamentation of the town.[67] The reform of 1775 made the police chief responsible for the upkeep of buildings and for sanitation, and the police statute of 8 April 1782 ordered the police to maintain the streets, pavements, water pipes, drainage ditches, and street lights, to enforce existing regulations on cleanliness, sanitation, and pollution, and to regulate and supervise all construction.[68] In all towns the police were appointed by and took their orders from the state officials rather than the town council and thus were part of the chain of command that originated with the Empress herself.

Because the results of Catherine's urban programme differed so widely from locality to locality, its accomplishments are difficult to appraise. It had both failures and triumphs, and in large measure a judgement on the programme as a whole depends upon which one chooses to emphasize; it also depends upon the standard that is used to measure accomplishment—whether one measures

---

[66] See for example the decree of 1783 ordering the town council of Novgorod to pay for the installation and the maintenance of street lanterns, *PSZ* no. 15640.

[67] 'The Instruction to the Legislative Commission', Chapter XXI. *Documents*, pp. 295–9.

[68] *PSZ* no. 14392, article 254, and no. 15379, articles 31–6.

Catherine's programme against the previous condition of Russian towns or against a later awareness that her towns were far from ideal. If Catherine and her contemporaries took exaggerated pride in her programme, later historians more than compensated for it by treating the programme with exaggerated scorn. In Western scholarship Catherine's towns still have not outlived the denunciations heaped upon them by liberal historians of the late nineteenth and early twentieth centuries, many of them members of the Cadet Party, e.g. Ilovaysky, Milyukov, Kizevetter, Dityatin.[69] By emphasizing its most ridiculous failures and by presenting outlandish incidents like Potemkin's project for Ekaterinoslav as typical, the Cadet historians sought to discredit the role of enlightened absolutism in urban development. They emphasized Ekaterinoslav but forgot Odessa, cited the new towns that failed to grow and develop but forgot those that succeeded, pointed to the fact that Paul disestablished many of Catherine's towns but neglected to mention the fact that Alexander re-established most of them again.[70] Nor is it fair to mock Catherine by comparing her ideal of what a town ought to be with the reality of what the towns of Russia were in her own time, for implicit in the entire programme was the notion of planning for the future: the plans and laws created by Catherine's government were considerably in advance of the existing society, and their success or failure depended on the pace of the nation's development. Where development came quickly, as in Odessa, the plans served to organize and direct rapid growth: founded in 1795, Odessa had 15,000 residents and 506 stone houses by 1804.[71] Where development failed to occur, especially in new towns that failed to take root,

[69] In addition to the works of Ilovaysky, Dityatin, Gitermann, and Milyukov cited in footnote 45 on page 334, see A. Korsak, *O formakh promyshlennosti voobshche i o znachenii domashnego proizvodstva v Zapadnoy Evrope i Rossii* (Moscow, 1861), especially pp. 104–10, and A. A. Kizevetter, *Posadskaya obshchina v Rossii XVIII st.* (Moscow, 1903), *Gorodovoe polozhenie Ekateriny II 1785 g. Opyt istoricheskogo komentariya* (Moscow, 1909), and 'Russky gorod v XVIII st.' in the collection of his works entitled *Istoricheskie ocherki* (Moscow, 1912).

[70] Ryndyunsky, in *Problemy obshchestvenno-politicheskoy istorii*, p. 359. The great majority of the towns planned by Catherine's government were not 'Potemkin Villages' but then neither were most of Potemkin's villages. See James A. Duran, 'Catherine, Potemkin, and Colonization Policy in Southern Russia', *The Russian Review*, xxviii, no. 1 (Jan. 1969), 23–36.

[71] S. H. Parker, *An Historical Geography of Russia* (London, 1968), p. 207.

the plans were useless: sometimes even the government buildings were not built, and some towns like Ekaterinodar and Aleksandriya were disestablished soon after their founding.[72] In most towns progress was somewhere between the extremes: provincial capitals, most of which were old towns that were replanned in the eighteenth century, benefited from Catherine's programme and provided one of its greatest justifications. Progress in the county seats was slower, but it was not insignificant: by 1797 Mogola had 202 new houses built since its founding, 8 of them stone or brick; Ostashkov in the same period had 293 new houses, 83 of them stone or brick, plus an orphanage, a school, and 132 shops. Similar development took place in Petrozavodsk, Vesegonsk, Kovrov, Aleksandrov, Borovichi, Gzhatsk, Bogorodsk, Podolsk, Volsk, Dubovka, Egorevsk, and elsewhere.[73] The actual accomplishments of Catherine's programme were not so magnificent as Catherine and her contemporaries imagined they might be, but neither were they illusory and artificial as her later critics have presented them.

The basic problem, of course, was the lack of resources with which to implement the plans immediately. The government recognized the problem when it included no first-class zoning in many small provincial towns, when it ignored the regulations to compromise with reality, and when it devised schemes like the Board of Public Welfare to finance public works for which no other funds were available, but the government refused to accept the existing *status quo* as permanent. Rather than wait patiently for events to take their own course, the government promoted and stimulated progress. A case in point is the effort that was made to improve sanitation and health: the government's plans often included facilities that could not be provided immediately or in the near future, but the alternative would have been to ignore such considerations and allow the towns to grow in the old unplanned fashion, congested, highly inflammable, and lacking all provision for sanitation and hygiene.

[72] Ryndyunsky, in *Problemy obshchestvenno-politicheskoy istorii*, p. 365. *PSZ* nos. 16899 and 17361.
[73] Ryndyunsky, in op. cit., pp. 359–64.

In being ahead of its time Catherine's urban programme was also typical of its time, for in the eighteenth century the thinking of the government ran far ahead of that of the nation as a whole. The Cadet historians who had to deal with Nicholas II did not appreciate that essential difference between the Russia of Catherine's time and the Russia of their own. Besides being generally more advanced and progressive in its thinking, the Russian government of the eighteenth century had a near monopoly on educated talent. Under such circumstances the state inevitably became the agent of modernization, and just as St. Petersburg had been a part of Peter's efforts to modernize the Court, the government, and the upper levels of society, Catherine's towns were part of her effort to extend that modernization into the provinces. Her methods were dictated both by the nature of eighteenth-century thought and by the existing structure of Russian society, and they, no less than the towns themselves, were the distinctive product of the age.

Notes on the Contributors

JOHN G. GARRARD
Is Professor and Chairman of the Department of Slavic Languages and Literatures at the University of Virginia.

MARC RAEFF
Is Professor of History at Columbia University, New York.

HAROLD B. SEGEL
Is Professor of Slavic Literatures at Columbia University, New York.

JAMES CRACRAFT
Is Associate Professor of History at the University of Illinois, Chicago.

MAX J. OKENFUSS
Is Assistant Professor of History at Washington University, St. Louis.

W. GARETH JONES
Is Lecturer in Russian at the University College of North Wales, Bangor.

ARTHUR M. WILSON
Is Professor Emeritus, Dartmouth College.

IN-HO L. RYU
Is Associate Professor of History at Korea University, South Korea.

A. G. CROSS
Is Reader in Russian at the University of East Anglia.

TAMARA TALBOT RICE

Is the widow of the late Professor James Talbot Rice, Professor of History of Art at Edinburgh, and is author of numerous books on Russian art.

ALFRED SWAN

Was Professor of Music at Temple University, Philadelphia, until 1969. He died in 1970.

JANE SWAN

Is Professor of Russian History at West Chester State College.

J. SPIEGELMAN

Is Professor of Music at Sarah Lawrence College.

ROBERT E. JONES

Is Assistant Professor of History at the University of Massachusetts.

Index